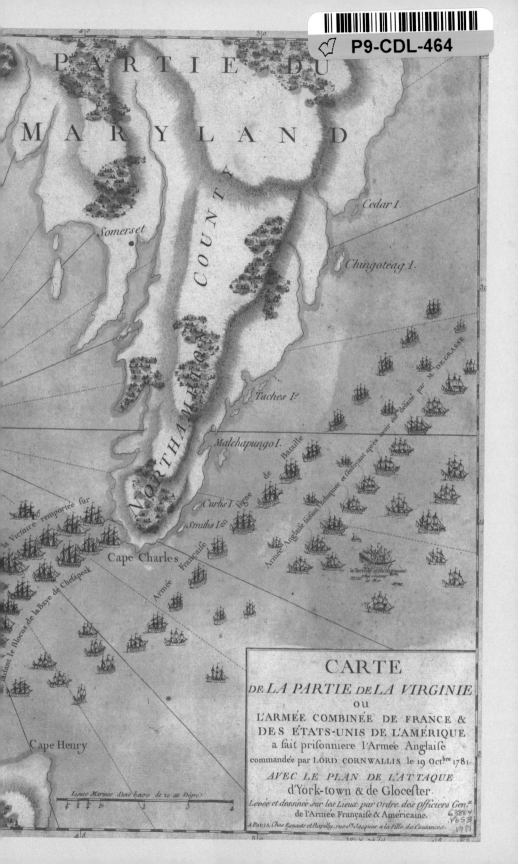

PARTIE DU

MARYLAND

Cedar I.

Somerset

Chingoteag. I.

NORTHAMPTON COUNTY

Taches I.

Malchapungo I.

M. DE GRASSE

Bataille de

Curtis I.

Armée Anglaise faisant Echiquier et l'attaquant après avoir été déeinté par M. DE GRASSE

Smiths Is.

Cape Charles

Armée Française

la Victoire remportée sur

le Terrible qu'à été gagnant plus avancé la Mer

faisant le Blocus de la Baye de Chesapeak

Cape Henry

Lieues Marines d'une heure de 20 au Dégré

1   2   3   4

CARTE

DE *LA PARTIE* DE *LA VIRGINIE*

ou

L'ARMÉE COMBINÉE DE FRANCE &

DES ÉTATS-UNIS DE L'AMÉRIQUE

a fait prisonniere l'Armée Anglaise

commandée par LORD CORNWALLIS le 19 Oct.bre 1781.

AVEC LE PLAN DE L'ATTAQUE

d'York-town & de Glocester.

Levée et dessinée sur les Lieux par Ordre des officiers Gen.x
de l'Armée Française & Américaine.

A PARIS, Chez Esnauts et Rapilly, rue St. Jacques a la Ville de Coutances.

In the Hurricane's Eye

IN THE
HURRICANE'S
EYE

THE GENIUS
of
GEORGE WASHINGTON
and the
VICTORY at YORKTOWN

NATHANIEL PHILBRICK

VIKING

VIKING

An imprint of Penguin Random House LLC

375 Hudson Street

New York, New York 10014

penguinrandomhouse.com

Map illustrations by Jeffrey L. Ward

Credits for other illustrations appear on pages 347–349.

ISBN 9780525426769 (hardcover)

ISBN 9780698153226 (ebook)

Printed in the United States of America

1 3 5 7 9 10 8 6 4 2

Set in Adobe Caslon Pro

Designed by Marysarah Quinn

TO MELISSA

CONTENTS

PREFACE

The Land and the Sea

For five years, two armies had clashed along the edge of a vast continent. One side, the Rebels, had the advantage of the land. Even when they lost a battle, which happened more often than not, they could retire into the countryside and wait for the next chance to attack.

The other side, the Empire, had the advantage of the sea. With its fleet of powerful warships (just one of which mounted more cannons than the entire Rebel army possessed in the early years of the war), it could attack the Rebels' seaside cities at will.

But no matter how many coastal towns the Empire might take, it did not have enough soldiers to occupy all of the Rebels' territory. And without a significant navy of their own, the Rebels could never inflict the blow that would win them their independence. The war had devolved into a stalemate, with the Empire hoping the Rebels' rickety government would soon collapse, and with the Rebels hoping for the miraculous intervention of a powerful ally.

Two years before, one of the Empire's perennial enemies, the Rival Nation, had joined the war on the Rebels' behalf. Almost immediately the Rival had sent out its own fleet of warships. But then the sea had intervened.

. . .

WHEN FRANCE ENTERED the American Revolutionary War in the spring of 1778, George Washington dared to hope his new ally had put victory within reach. Finally, the British navy's hold on the Atlantic Seaboard was about to be broken. If the French succeeded in establishing what Washington called "naval superiority," the enemy's army would be left open to attack from not only the land but also the sea. But after two and a half years of trying, the French had been unable to contain the British navy.

First, an inexplicably protracted Atlantic crossing prevented French admiral Comte d'Estaing from trapping the enemy's fleet in Philadelphia. Shortly after that, d'Estaing turned his attention to British-occupied New York, only to call off the attack for fear his ships would run aground at the bar across the harbor mouth. A few weeks after that, a storm off the coast of southern New England prevented d'Estaing from engaging the British in a naval battle that promised to be a glorious victory for France. Since then, a botched amphibious assault at Savannah, Georgia, had marked the only other significant action on the part of the French navy, a portion of which now lay frustratingly dormant at Newport at the southern end of Rhode Island's Narragansett Bay. By the fall of 1780, amid the aftershocks of devastating defeats at Charleston and Camden in South Carolina and Benedict Arnold's treasonous attempt to surrender the fortress at West Point to the enemy, Washington had come to wonder whether the ships of his salvation would ever appear.

For the last two years he'd been locked in an unproductive standoff with Sir Henry Clinton, the British commander in North America, in and around New York City. What fighting had occurred had been, for the most part, in the south, where British general Charles Cornwallis sought to build upon his recent victories by pushing into North Carolina. Between the northern and southern theaters of the war lay the inland sea of the Chesapeake, which had enjoyed a period of relative quiet since the early days of the conflict.

All that changed in December 1780, when Clinton sent his newest brigadier general, the traitor Benedict Arnold, to Virginia. Having already dispatched the Rhode Islander Nathanael Greene to do battle with Cornwallis in the Carolinas, Washington sent the young French nobleman whom he regarded as a surrogate son, the Marquis de Lafayette, in pursuit of Arnold.

Thus began the movement of troops that resulted nine months later in Cornwallis's entrapment at the shoreside hamlet of Yorktown, when a large fleet of French warships arrived from the Caribbean. As Washington had long since learned, coordinating his army's movements with those of a fleet of sail-powered men-of-war based two thousand miles away was virtually impossible. But in the late summer of 1781, the impossible happened.

And then, just a few days later, a fleet of British warships appeared.

The Battle of the Chesapeake has been called the most important naval engagement in the history of the world. Fought outside the entrance of the bay between French admiral Comte de Grasse's twenty-four ships of the line and a slightly smaller British fleet commanded by Rear Admiral Thomas Graves, the battle inflicted severe enough damage on the Empire's ships that Graves returned to New York for repairs. By preventing the rescue of seven thousand British and German soldiers under the command of General Cornwallis, de Grasse's victory on September 5, 1781, made Washington's subsequent triumph at Yorktown a virtual fait accompli. Peace would not be officially declared for another two years, but that does not change the fact that a naval battle fought between the French and the British was largely responsible for the independence of the United States.

Despite its undeniable significance, the Battle of the Chesapeake plays only a minor part in most popular accounts of the war, largely because no Americans participated in it. If the sea figures at all in the story of the Revolutionary War, the focus tends to be on the heroics of John Paul Jones off England's Flamborough Head, even though that two-ship engagement had little impact on the overall direction of the conflict. Instead of concentrating on the sea, the traditional narrative of Yorktown focuses on the allied army's long overland journey south, with a special emphasis on the collaborative relationship between Washington and his French counterpart the Comte de Rochambeau. In this view, the encounter between the French and British fleets was a mere prelude to the main event. In the account that follows, I hope to put the sea where it properly belongs: at the center of the story.

As Washington understood with a perspicacity that none of his military peers could match, only the intervention of the French navy could achieve the victory the times required. Six months before the Battle of the Chesapeake, during the winter of 1781, he had urged the French to send a large fleet of warships to the Chesapeake in an attempt to trap Benedict Arnold in Portsmouth, Virginia. What was, in effect, a dress rehearsal for the Yorktown campaign is essential to understanding the evolving, complex, and sometimes acrimonious relationship between Washington and Rochambeau. As we will see, the two leaders were not the selfless military partners of American legend; each had his own jealously guarded agenda, and it was only after Washington reluctantly—and angrily—acquiesced to French demands that they began to work in concert.

Ultimately, the course of the Revolutionary War came down to America's proximity to the sea—a place of storms and headwinds that no one could control. Instead of an inevitable march to victory, Yorktown was the result of a hurried rush of seemingly random events—from a hurricane in the Caribbean, to a bloody battle amid the woods near North Carolina's Guilford Courthouse, to the loan of 500,000 Spanish pesos from the citizens of Havana, Cuba—all of which had to occur before Cornwallis arrived at Yorktown and de Grasse sailed into the Chesapeake. That the pieces finally fell into place in September and October 1781 never ceased to amaze Washington. "I am sure," he wrote the following spring, "that there never was a people who had more reason to acknowledge a divine interposition in their affairs than those of the United States."

The victory at Yorktown was improbable at best, but it was also the result of a strategy Washington had been pursuing since the beginning of the French alliance. This is the story of how Washington's unrelenting quest for naval superiority made possible the triumph at Yorktown. It is also the story of how, in a supreme act of poetic justice, the final engagement of the war brought him back to the home he had not seen in six years. For it was here, on a river in Virginia, that he first began to learn about the wonder, power, and ultimate indifference of the sea.

PART I

"AGAINST THE WIND"

In any operations, and under all circumstances,
a decisive naval superiority is to be considered
as a fundamental principle, and the basis upon
which every hope of success must ultimately
depend.

—GEORGE WASHINGTON
to Comte de Rochambeau, July 15, 1780

The sea is not like the land. It deceives us
sometimes and we have not yet found out a
method of sailing against the wind.

—COMTE DE GRASSE
to George Washington, October 16, 1781

CHAPTER I

The Building Storm

On September 15, 1779, the newly appointed French minister to the United States, the Chevalier de la Luzerne, arrived on the banks of the Hudson River at Fishkill, New York. He and his entourage were on their way to the American fortress at West Point, where they were to meet with His Excellency George Washington. Much to Luzerne's surprise, the general himself arrived in the small vessel that was to take them the twenty-five miles down the river. Even more surprising, Washington was the one steering the boat.

They soon departed, and as they sailed south with the tide, the sky darkened and the wind began to shriek out of the surrounding mountains. Even though the vessel heeled ominously in the gusts, Washington refused to surrender the helm to a more experienced mariner. "The general held the tiller," the secretary to the French delegation recorded, "and during a little squall which required skill and practice, proved to us that this work was no less known to him than are other bits of useful knowledge." George Washington, a commander in chief who otherwise seemed rooted to his horse, was also a sailor.

He was born in Tidewater Virginia, a flat, water-laced land between the Blue Ridge Mountains to the west and the Chesapeake

Bay to the east. In the Tidewater, clear inland rivers blended with the turbid salt of the ocean as it ebbed and flowed along the marshy edges of the Chesapeake. On the Rappahannock River where Washington grew up (just across from the town of Fredericksburg), the tide's three-foot rise and fall was a daily reminder that even though he was more than fifty miles from the Chesapeake, he was connected to a distant and unseen sea.

When he was eleven years old, his father died, leaving his mother, who had been his father's second wife, with five young children to raise. Making their lot all the harder was his father's decision to leave his most valuable properties, on the Potomac River to the north, to his sons from his first marriage, Lawrence and Augustine. With money tight, the young Washington was unable to attend the school in England to which his older half brothers had been sent. Life in the fairly modest clapboard house on the Rappahannock, painted red to look like brick, offered few opportunities for an ambitious boy looking to make his mark on the world. And then in 1746, when Washington was fourteen years old, his elder half brother offered him a way out.

Lawrence Washington was twenty-eight years old and a veteran of the Siege of Cartagena, an unsuccessful attempt by the British to take the Spanish port on the coast of what is today Colombia. Although the siege had been a disappointment for the British, Lawrence had received so "many distinguished marks of patronage and favor" from Vice Admiral Edward Vernon that he'd chosen to name the house he'd inherited from his father Mount Vernon in the admiral's honor.

Lawrence and his stepmother, Mary Ball Washington, had differing ideas as to where George's future lay. Mary insisted that her first-born's place belonged with her on the Rappahannock, on what came to be known as Ferry Farm. Lawrence, on the other hand, determined that, like his idol Admiral Vernon, his brother was destined for the sea. A British naval vessel had arrived in the Chesapeake, and from Lawrence's perspective, a midshipman's appointment offered his younger brother not only the prospect of a promising and honorable career but the chance to escape the possessive clutches of his widowed mother.

What the fourteen-year-old Washington thought about all this is difficult to determine. Lawrence's father-in-law and neighbor William Fairfax, who delivered letters addressed to both George and his mother regarding Lawrence's proposal, reported that the boy "says he will be steady and thankfully follow your advice." This hardly sounds like an enthusiastic response on George's part to the prospect of a naval career. And yet, remaining with his willful and self-centered mother (Washington's cousin later confessed "he was ten times more afraid of Mary than he was of his own parents") also had its drawbacks.

After receiving Lawrence's offer, Mary allowed her son's plans to go to sea to reach the point that his "baggage [was] prepared for embarkation." In a scene that remained indelibly seared into the young Washington's memory, his mother waited until the last possible moment before intervening. "His mother interposed with her entreaties and tears so irresistibly," Washington's aide David Humphreys later recounted in an unfinished biography, "as to cause the project to be laid aside. Otherwise," Humphreys surmised, "instead of having led the armies of America to victory, it is not improbable he would have participated as an Admiral of distinction in the naval triumphs of Britain."

Rather than to the east, on the sea, Washington's future lay to the west. Within a few years' time, he'd begun a career as a surveyor. When he was sixteen, he set out into the frontier of the Blue Ridge, and with the support of Lawrence's in-laws, the powerful Fairfax family, he began to purchase tracts of land, accumulating close to two thousand acres by the time he had turned eighteen. Having negotiated the competing demands of his mother and half brother, he'd forged an identity that was not only congenial to his talents (by then he was over six feet tall, physically strong, and blessed with remarkable endurance), it was his and his alone.

All the while, a tragic sense of foreboding hovered over the young Washington's life. Lawrence, whom he called his "best friend," was dying of tuberculosis. ("I hope your cough is much mended since I saw you last," he wrote worriedly in the spring of 1749.) After trips to England and the hot springs of Virginia in search of a cure, Lawrence resolved to sail to the island of Barbados in the fall of 1751, with his brother, now nineteen years old, as his companion.

It was the first and last time Washington ever went to sea. The diary he kept during the voyage shows him both fascinated and appalled by the life of a sailor. Much of it came naturally to a boy who had grown up in the Virginia Tidewater, and in his journal he quickly adopted the shorthand of the sea to denote the day's sail changes, using the initials RMTS for reefed maintopsail and DRTS for double-reefed topsail.

As Washington soon discovered, however, this was very different from the circumscribed world of an inland river. On the Rappahannock and Potomac, a ship materialized almost instantly from around the nearest bend. On the ocean, a ship emerged slowly, indistinctly, from the seeming depths of the sea itself. First you saw only the uppermost sails rising out of the horizon ("hull down" in the phraseology of the sea) until there it was—the entirety of the ship—briefly beside you and then, as the distance between the two vessels increased, receding back into the rounded, wave-flecked obscurity from which it had come.

Mostly, however, you were alone with the waves and the pitiless wind. "Hard squalls . . . and rain with sea jostling in heaps," Washington wrote on October 19, "the seamen seemed disheartened, confessing they never had seen such weather before." This was not the sea of heroism and romance that Lawrence had promised him back when he was fourteen. This was an alien realm full of danger and fear. As they approached Barbados, he was disturbed to learn that the ship's navigator had misjudged their position by almost five hundred miles. Only by luck had they stumbled on their destination.

As it turned out, Washington's brief stay amid the tropical delights of Barbados almost killed him. Within a few weeks of his arrival, he was, in his own words, "strongly attacked with the smallpox." A month later, he emerged from his sickbed with barely a trace of pockmarks on his face and determined to go home. While his consumptive brother opted for the cooler breezes of Bermuda, Washington sailed for Virginia. By the following winter, Lawrence's condition had so worsened that he decided he must "hurry home to my grave." In the summer of 1752, he was laid to rest in the family vault at Mount Vernon, where forty-seven years later, he was joined by his brother George.

Washington seems to have been permanently influenced by this sea voyage to a distant island whose promise of rejuvenation had brought only illness and, in the case of his half brother, death. As he demonstrated on the Hudson River to the French minister Luzerne, Washington knew his way around boats and was even proud of his expertise. But that did not mean he *trusted* the sea and the rivers that flowed into it. For the rest of his life, he preferred the saddle of a horse to the deck of a ship, even when the quickest way to reach his destination was by water. Despite eventually inheriting a house that overlooked a beautiful, mile-wide river, he did his best to put the view, quite literally, behind him. While Lawrence's most impressive rooms had faced the Potomac, Washington added a large parlor and dining room on the opposite side of the ground floor that effectively flipped the house around so that it looked inland. The house might be named for a British admiral, but it now faced what Washington called the "infant woody country" of his future.

His experiences during the middle years of the Revolutionary War only confirmed his prejudice against the sea. The United States' efforts to create an ocean-going navy of its own had proven to be a disastrous waste of the country's nearly nonexistent resources. It has been estimated that close to 10 percent of Congressional spending during the war years was dedicated to building a navy that one historian has claimed "inflicted no more than a few pinpricks against the British navy." By the fall of 1780, with the royal navy in control of the Atlantic Seaboard and with his army cooped up amid the Hudson highlands north of British-occupied New York, Washington knew that only the French navy could break the deadlock. However, given the challenges of communication, the unpredictability of the ocean, and Britain's well-deserved reputation for naval dominance, could he realistically expect the French navy to make a difference? What good was the alliance with France if all it did was create what he called on October 4, 1780, "false hopes"? "I see nothing before us," he wrote despairingly from his headquarters on the west bank of the Hudson River at New Windsor, "but accumulating distresses. . . . We have lived upon expedients till we can live no longer."

Washington at the age of forty-eight was much as he'd been at fourteen: marooned on the banks of a river, wondering what, if anything, might come from the sea.

FRANCE HAD JOINED the War of Independence not to help America but to strike a blow against Great Britain. Ever since the humiliating conclusion of the Seven Years' War in 1763, which resulted in the loss of Canada to Britain as well as a disastrous loss of prestige among the powers of Europe, France had embarked on a strategy of *revanche,* or "revenge." She had no interest in conquering Britain; she simply wanted to restore the balance of power that had existed during the first half of the century when the two countries had functioned more or less as equals. By rebuilding her army and particularly her navy, France hoped to force her haughty rival (which had included a provision in the treaty that ended the Seven Years' War demanding that a British commissioner be installed at Dunkirk) to stop treating her as a subservient, second-tier nation. In 1775, with Britain becoming increasingly preoccupied with a colonial rebellion in North America, the French foreign minister, the Comte de Vergennes, had seen his opportunity, and three years later, after British general John Burgoyne suffered a mortifying defeat at Saratoga, France joined the war on America's behalf.

What the United States did not fully appreciate was that her new ally did not have to send a single soldier or ship to North America to start challenging an already militarily overextended Great Britain. With a mere twenty-one miles of water between her and the south-eastern edge of England, all France had to do was send a significant number of warships into the Channel from the naval port of Brest, and Britain would be forced to respond in kind.

Sure enough, in the summer of 1778, all of Britain watched in breathless suspense as her navy rushed to assemble the fleet required to meet the thirty warships under the command of the Comte d'Orvilliers. The Battle of Ushant, conducted at the southern edge of the English Channel, was ultimately indecisive, but it was now frighteningly obvious that with France in the war, Britain's naval resources were going to be stretched to the absolute limit. And then, with the entrance of France's ally Spain the following year, Britain found herself threatened in a way that had been unimaginable just a few years before. In the summer of 1779, a huge French-Spanish invasion fleet of 66 warships, 400 transports, and an army of 40,000 assembled in the waters to the south of Britain. Due to poor planning and uncooperative winds, a landing was never attempted, but even without a shot being fired, France, with the help of Spain, had succeeded in proving to her once vaunted antagonist that she could no longer take her dominance at sea for granted.

Since then, the waters between Britain and France continued to be the scene of numerous naval skirmishes while the war expanded into a truly global conflict with fighting as far away as India. But it was the waters surrounding the sugar islands of the Caribbean (which accounted for more than a third of France's overseas trade) that soon became the chief naval battleground of the war outside of Europe.

It may be difficult to appreciate today, but when the war for American independence broke out, Britain's possessions in the Caribbean were worth much more to her than all thirteen of her colonies in North America. Once France entered the war, Britain chose to concentrate a large portion of her naval resources in these commercially valuable and militarily vulnerable islands (an estimated 33 percent of her total navy compared with just 9 percent in the coastal waters of North America). France and Spain followed suit, and soon the Caribbean was engulfed in war.

It began with Britain taking the French island of St. Lucia, to which Admiral d'Estaing responded by capturing British Grenada. The Spanish, based in Cuba, were hopeful of winning back what they had lost to Britain in Florida during the Seven Years' War as well as taking back the island of Jamaica. Adding to the complexity of competing interests was the presence of the supposedly neutral Dutch trading post at St. Eustatius, whose opportunistic merchants furnished American coasting vessels with a steady stream of gunpowder, arms, and other supplies for the Continental army.

From the European perspective, the Caribbean (which was referred to as the West Indies in the eighteenth century), not North America, was where their navies were needed most. As a result, the island harbors in Cuba, Haiti (then known as Saint Domingue), Jamaica, Antigua, and Martinique remained filled to overflowing with warships while the lack of naval support in the north left the armies of both Washington and his British counterpart Sir Henry Clinton stranded in and around New York.

From Washington's perspective, it was as if "a chasm" divided him from the French fleet in the Caribbean. "There seems to be the strangest fatality and the most unaccountable silence attending the operations to the southward that can be conceived," he wrote in despair. Without the intervention of a large French fleet, the war in North America was likely to stagnate to the point that Britain could win what was proving to be a test of economic and political endurance rather than military might.

By the fall of 1780, it seemed as if France's preoccupation with the Caribbean might prevent a significant-sized fleet from ever making its way to the shores of the United States to aid the Continental army. Then, on October 3, one of the most powerful hurricanes in recorded history struck the waters between Jamaica and Cuba.

THE PHOENIX WAS A BRITISH FRIGATE, meaning that she was smaller and faster than the larger line-of-battle warships. Rather than blast

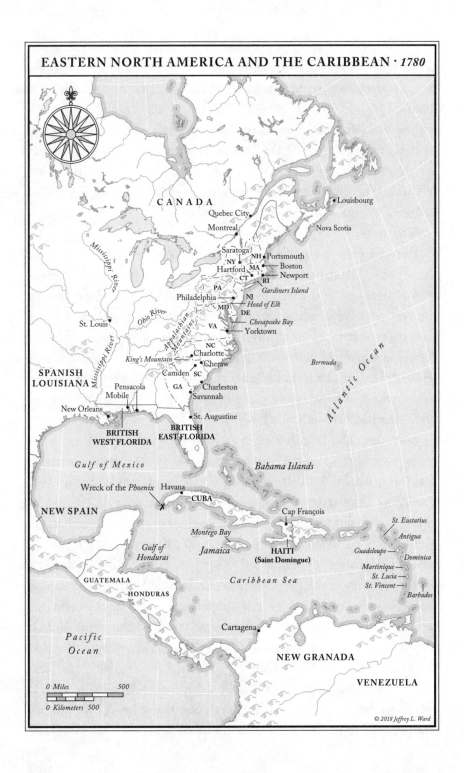

EASTERN NORTH AMERICA AND THE CARIBBEAN · 1780

CANADA

Louisbourg

Quebec City

Montreal

Nova Scotia

Saratoga

NH • Portsmouth

NY

Hartford

MA • Boston

CT

RI • Newport

Mississippi River

PA

Gardiners Island

Philadelphia

NJ

Head of Elk

MD

DE

Ohio River

St. Louis

VA

Chesapeake Bay

Yorktown

Appalachian Mountains

NC

Charlotte

Bermuda

Atlantic Ocean

King's Mountain

Cheraw

SPANISH
LOUISIANA

Camden

SC

Pensacola

GA

Charleston

Mobile

Savannah

New Orleans

St. Augustine

BRITISH
WEST FLORIDA

BRITISH
EAST FLORIDA

Gulf of Mexico

Bahama Islands

Wreck of the *Phoenix*

Havana

NEW SPAIN

CUBA

Cap François

St. Eustatius

Antigua

Montego Bay

Guadeloupe

Dominica

*Gulf of
Honduras*

Jamaica

HAITI
(Saint Domingue)

Martinique

St. Lucia

St. Vincent

GUATEMALA

Caribbean Sea

Barbados

HONDURAS

*Pacific
Ocean*

Cartagena

NEW GRANADA

VENEZUELA

0 Miles   500

0 Kilometers 500

© 2018 Jeffrey L. Ward

away at the enemy, the *Phoenix* had the speed and maneuverability to act as the eyes and ears of the British fleet. She had cannons to be sure, forty-four of them, but her chief role was that of a sentinel and scout.

She had left Jamaica on September 30, and after sailing north to British-held Pensacola on the Florida panhandle, which was bracing for an attack by the Spanish, the *Phoenix* sailed south to the coast of Cuba, where her captain, forty-one-year-old Sir Hyde Parker Jr., had seen evidence of a large fleet of Spanish ships gathering in Havana harbor.

Parker and his crew of 280 officers and men had been stationed in the western Atlantic since almost the beginning of the war. The *Phoenix* had been one of the first British warships to arrive in New York in the summer of 1776, when the city was still occupied by Washington's Continental army. Disdaining the barricade of sunken ships the Americans had laid across the Hudson, as well as the cannons clustered at the city's battery, Parker had sailed boldly past New York to the very verge of the Hudson highlands—an early setback to Rebel pride that had earned him a knighthood.

Soon after the British took New York, a printing press had been set up aboard the *Phoenix* to produce counterfeit American currency that was offered to loyalists (who were in on the scam) for the price of the paper. "The artists they employed performed so well," Benjamin Franklin later wrote, "that immense quantities of these counterfeits . . . were circulated among the inhabitants of all the states, before the fraud was detected." Not only did this provide the loyalists with some extra spending money, the injection of bogus dollars into the already shaky American economy greatly accelerated the currency's depreciation. Indeed, it might be argued that no vessel in the entire British navy had done more for the British cause in America than the *Phoenix*.

Now, on the evening of October 3, she was cruising between Cuba and Jamaica when, in the words of First Lieutenant Benjamin Archer, the wind began "to snuffle with a monstrous heavy appearance from the eastward." By eight the next morning, it was "blowing hard from the east-northeast with close-reef topsails . . . and heavy squalls." By the afternoon, after jibing, or "wearing" the ship across the wind (a tricky maneuver in any weather but especially difficult in a storm), it was blowing what Archer called "a hurricane," somewhere in the vicinity of seventy to eighty knots, and building fast. Realizing that "no canvas can stand against this a moment," Archer ordered all the sails to be taken in.

In addition to securing the triangular foresails at the bow and the gaff-rigged mizzen at the stern, a crowd of sailors leapt into the rigging to furl the *Phoenix*'s dozen or so rectangular sails as tightly as possible before securing them to the yards with gaskets. To reduce windage aloft, the upper segment of the mainmast, the topgallant, was brought down and tied to the deck. To keep the rain and spray from pouring through the gratings of the deck's hatchways, the carpenters secured tarpaulins to the lids by nailing battens to the hatches' sides.

By eight p.m., it was blowing so hard that birds began to seek refuge aboard the *Phoenix*. "The poor devils . . . dashed themselves down upon the deck without attempting to stir till picked up and when we let them go . . . they would not leave the ship, but endeavored to hide themselves from the wind." If the wind continued to build until the ship was in danger of capsizing, it might become necessary to cut away the masts. "Knowing from experience that at the moment you may want to cut away to save the ship an axe may not be found," Archer stationed a carpenter at each mast with a broad axe.

With no sails to steady her motion, the *Phoenix* wallowed wildly in the massive seas, creating an unearthly metallic squealing within the ship as the more than forty cannons secured to the vessel's sides shook in their carriages. When Archer went below for some supper, he found two marine officers (both landsmen) "white as sheets, not understanding the ship's working so much, and the noise of the lower deck guns, which by this time made a pretty screeching to people not used to it." Since the mattress on his bunk was saturated with water, Archer lay down between the two sea chests in his cabin and tried to fall asleep.

At midnight he was awakened by a young midshipman, who told him they must jibe the ship again to put some distance between them and Jamaica. He found Sir Hyde on the quarterdeck. "It blows damned hard, Archer," the captain said. "I don't know that I ever remember its blowing so hard before."

Even without a stitch of canvas set on the yards, the horizontal spars needed to be carefully manipulated during the jibe as the helmsman worked the ship across the eye of the wind. After a great struggle, which forced Archer to order most of the sailors into the forward rigging to help turn the ship, the *Phoenix* was finally on the other tack. The frequency and magnitude of the waves had increased to the extent that the ship "had not time to rise from one sea before another lashed against her." Even though the sails had been tied with extra care, the ever strengthening wind began to shred the canvas from the yards into what Archer called "coach whips"—something that not even the most experienced seamen had ever seen. "My God!" Archer wrote, "To think that the wind could have such force!"

So much water had leaked through the ship's seams that the lower gun deck was now virtually awash. To prevent the seawater from dislodging one of the cannons (a disastrous development since one wayward cannon, which weighed more than two tons, could punch a hole through the ship's side), Archer went below with an axe and chopped a hole through the gun deck. As the resultant surge of water flowed down into the well in the ship's hold, Archer searched out the men at the pumps and made sure they understood the urgency of the situation. For the next half hour, he stood at the pumps, "cheering the people" as they worked furiously to prevent the ship from sinking.

Once back on the quarterdeck, he discovered that Captain Parker had lashed himself to the windward rail to keep from being washed over the side, and he quickly followed suit. By now the wind was, according to Archer, "roaring louder than thunder (absolutely no flight of imagination)" as "a very uncommon kind of blue lightning" lit up the seas, "running as it were in Alps or peaks of Tenerife (mountains are too common an idea)." All the while "the poor ship [was] very much pressed, yet doing what she could, shaking her sides, and groaning at every stroke."

By four a.m. they had begun to approach the coast of Cuba. The wind had reached the point that the ship was almost completely on her side—"on her beam-ends, and not attempting to right again." Word came from below that the severe heel made it impossible for the men to work the pumps. Archer turned to his captain. "This is not the time, Sir, to think of saving the masts; shall we cut the mainmast away?" "Ay! As fast as you can." Before Archer had a chance to act, "a very violent sea broke right on board of us, carried everything upon deck away, filled the ship with water, the main and mizzen masts went, the ship righted, but was in the last struggle of sinking under us."

As soon as the two of them could, in Archer's words, "shake our heads above water," Captain Parker exclaimed, "We are gone at last, Archer! Foundered at sea!" "I then felt sorry that I could swim," Archer recalled, "as by that means I might be a quarter of an hour longer dying than a man who could not." Then they heard a "thump and grinding under our feet." To their astonishment, the ship had washed up onto the Cuban coast with her stern toward shore and her bow into the waves. By now, the quarterdeck, usually the domain of the captain and his officers, had become crowded with seamen, who scurried aft as the waves at the bow "wash[ed] clear over at every stroke." Captain Parker cried out, "Keep to the quarterdeck, my lads; when she goes to pieces it is our best chance!"

If they had any hope of survival, the bow had to remain pointed out to sea; should the ship turn broadside to the waves, it would immediately capsize, tossing them all into the rock-strewn sea. Unfortunately, the only mast left standing was the foremast, and the added windage of the spar threatened to force the bow around. The mast had to be cut down as soon as possible. Archer ordered a group of sailors forward, five of whom were almost immediately washed overboard when a huge sea swept the mast over the side. "That was nothing," Archer remembered, "[since] everyone expected it would be his own fate next."

At daybreak they discovered the *Phoenix* had come to rest "upon a bed of rocks, mountains of them on one side, and Cordilleras of water on the other; our poor ship grinding and crying out at every stroke between them, going away piecemeal." Over the course of the next several hours, "[t]hat unmerciful sea lifted and beat us up so high among the rocks that at last the ship scarcely moved. She was very strong, and did not go to pieces at the first thumping, though her decks tumbled in."

A relatively narrow span of water now lay between the stern and shore, and two sailors soon swam across with a line that they made fast to the rocks. By ten in the morning, everyone was ashore, with First Lieutenant Archer being the last man out of the ship. "Sir Hyde came to me," he remembered, "and taking me by the hand, was so affected that he was scarcely able to speak. 'Archer, I am happy beyond expression to see you on shore, but look at our poor *Phoenix*!' I turned about, but could not say a single word, being too full. My mind had been too intensely occupied before, but everything now rushed upon me at once, so that I could not contain myself, and I indulged for a full quarter of an hour in tears."

Eventually, once they'd brought across the necessary supplies and materials from the ship to build some crude shelters, they began to consider what to do next. They were stranded on the south shore of Cuba, about twelve miles to the east of Cape Cruz. There were 250 of them left alive, and "the prospect of being prisoners during the war at Havana, and walking 300 miles to it through the woods, was unpleasant." But Archer had an idea. There were still some pieces left of one of the ship's boats. What if they repaired it, and Archer sailed for Jamaica's Montego Bay (a voyage of more than 150 miles) with the hope of returning with a rescue party?

A few days later, Archer and a crew of four sailors set out for Jamaica. Four days after that, he was back off the coast of Cuba with three small vessels. "I thought the ship's crew would have devoured me on my landing," he remembered. "They presently whisked me up on their shoulders and carried me to the tent where Sir Hyde was."

But Archer had some disturbing news. The same hurricane that had destroyed the *Phoenix* had decimated Jamaica's Montego Bay to the extent that "scarcely a vestige remained" of the many houses that once lined the shore. In addition, every British warship anchored in the bay had been driven out to sea and lost. Clearly, they were very lucky to have escaped a watery death. "Thy works are wonderful, O God!" Archer wrote. "Praised be thy holy name!"

But as it turned out, another, even bigger storm was on the way.

ON OCTOBER 10, what came to be called the Great Storm of 1780 hit the island of Barbados. By the following day, virtually every house, including those built of stone, had been leveled to the ground, and six thousand inhabitants were dead. Many of the cannons at Fort James, which the young George Washington had visited almost thirty years earlier, were hurled more than a hundred feet through the air. The extraordinary surge of water and wind carried a ship so far onto shore that it landed on top of the island's hospital. The hurricane-whipped rain stripped the trees of bark, indicating that the winds at Barbados must have exceeded 200 mph.

A similar scene of destruction occurred at St. Lucia, St. Vincent, and Martinique, where a convoy carrying several thousand French troops was blown out to sea. One estimate puts the total death count of the Great Storm of 1780 at twenty-two thousand, making it the deadliest hurricane in recorded history.

And then, on October 18, two days after a Spanish fleet of seventy-four ships bearing four thousand soldiers under the command of General Don Bernardo de Gálvez departed from Havana to attack Pensacola, a third hurricane struck. Known today as Solano's Hurricane for José Solano, the admiral in charge of the fleet, the storm ravaged the Gulf of Mexico for three days and ultimately drove the remains of the Spanish fleet back to Cuba. With dozens of vessels

sunk and dismasted and hundreds of soldiers and sailors drowned, Solano and Gálvez reluctantly decided to postpone the attack until the
following year.

It would take the English, French, and Spanish months, if not
years, to recover from the three hurricanes of October 1780. When
British admiral George Rodney, who'd spent the late summer and fall
in New York, arrived at Barbados in early December, he was as-
tounded by what he saw. "Had I not been an eyewitness," he wrote to
his wife, "nothing could have induced me to have believed it. More
than *six thousand persons perished*, and all the inhabitants ruined. . . .
The hurricane proved fatal to six ships of my squadron."

The lesson was impossible to ignore. Given the seasonal dangers
of this storm-battered string of islands, the best place for a navy in the
summer and fall was anywhere but the Caribbean. Up until this point,
France had viewed a naval expedition to the north on the behalf of the
United States as a possibility but hardly a priority. After that horren-
dous October, a different attitude prevailed.

Once France had repaired her hurricane-ravaged ports and ships
and done what she could to further her objectives in the Caribbean
during the winter and spring of 1781, she must send a sizable fleet to
North America. Not only might the ships strike a helpful blow against
the enemy, the fleet's survival could very well depend on being away
from the Caribbean in August, September, and especially October.

As HURRICANES ROILED THE WATERS of the Caribbean in
1780, another kind of storm gripped the states of North and South
Carolina. Lord Charles Cornwallis was in command of the British
forces in the region. Ignoring the advice of his commander in chief,
Sir Henry Clinton in New York, who recognized the danger of venturing far from British naval support, he had decided to plunge into
the Carolina interior. Since it isolated him from the source of his army's supplies at Charleston, it was a risky move, but at least he was on
the offensive, and at this late stage in the war, King George III and

Secretary of State for the Colonies George Germain back in London had pinned their hopes on the subjugation of the south.

Initially, the news was good. Cornwallis's young cavalry commander Banastre Tarleton quickly established a reputation for brutal and terrifying efficiency, and on August 16, Cornwallis eviscerated a larger American army under General Horatio Gates at the Battle of Camden in South Carolina. But even with that resounding victory, Cornwallis had detected some disturbing signs that the people of the Carolinas were hardly awed by the power of the British military. "The approach of General Gates's army unveiled to us a fund of disaffection in this province of which we could have formed no idea," Cornwallis's second in command, Lord Francis Rawdon, wrote, "and even the dispersion of that force did not extinguish the ferment which the hope of its support had raised." Instead of being welcomed by enthusiastic loyalists, Cornwallis was shocked and perplexed to discover that "the majority of the inhabitants . . . are in arms against us."

That, however, did not prevent him from sending Major Patrick Ferguson and an army of 1125 loyalists even farther into the northern interior of South Carolina to "awe that district into quiet." Despite a reputation as a clever innovator (he had invented and patented the first breech-loading rifle in the British army and employed a silver whistle to better communicate his instructions to his troops in battle), Ferguson issued a proclamation that did little to enamor him with the local populace. "If you choose to be pissed upon forever and ever by a set of mongrels," it read, "say so at once and let your women turn their backs upon you, and look out for real men to protect you."

By the morning of October 7, Ferguson had set up camp on King's Mountain—a flat-topped, steep-sided, and heavily wooded ridge— unaware that a band of frontiersmen from the other side of the Smoky Mountains, who came to be known as the Overmountain Men, was approaching through the trees. Ferguson had had earlier premonitions of danger and even sent Cornwallis a request for reinforcements. His army temporarily immobilized by fever, the British commander had failed to send the extra troops, assuring Ferguson in a message he did not live to receive, "I now consider you perfectly safe."

About four in the afternoon, while 200 of Ferguson's soldiers were out looking for forage, 1790 Overmountain Men crept up the wooded sides of King's Mountain and caught the British army of just 900 men completely by surprise. Over the course of the next hour, Ferguson, dressed in a checked shirt with his silver whistle held tightly between his lips, rode back and forth across his flat-topped island amid the trees, attempting to beat back the Rebel hordes. Spurning his men's repeated requests to surrender, he was shot from his horse and killed while leading a desperate charge through the enemy line. The British casualties were horrific—290 killed, 103 wounded, and 688 captured, compared with just 29 Americans killed and 58 wounded.

Fearing the Overmountain Men might overwhelm his own army, Cornwallis retreated to Winnsboro, South Carolina, even as American militia leaders such as Francis Marion and Thomas Sumter led daring assaults on British and loyalist forces to the south and east. Brigadier General Charles O'Hara, presently in New York but soon to join Cornwallis in the south, had grave misgivings about the war in the Carolinas. "How impossible must it prove to conquer a country," he wrote, "where repeated successes cannot ensure permanent advantages, and the most trifling check to our arms acts like electrical fire by rousing at the same moment every man upon this vast continent to persevere upon the least and most distant dawn of hope."

Only later, once the war was over, did Henry Clinton realize that this "trifling check" in the Carolinas, coming as it did amid the setbacks suffered in the Caribbean, was "the first link in a chain of evils that . . . at last ended in the total loss of America."

EVER SINCE THE SUMMER, the five thousand soldiers, seven ships of the line, and six frigates of the French Expédition Particulière (Special Expedition) under the command of General Rochambeau and Admiral Charles-Henri Louis d'Arsac de Ternay in Newport,

Rhode Island, had suffered the same indignity they had known in France. Just as the French navy had been forced to contend with smothering enemy blockades at its naval ports in Brest and Toulon, now the expedition's fleet, anchored in a defensive half circle off Newport, was bottled up by a British squadron under the command of Admiral Mariot Arbuthnot.

Four different times Admiral de Ternay had attempted to send out dispatches to France, and each time they had been intercepted by the British. Now there was a message of extreme urgency that needed to be delivered. In late September, Washington had met with General Rochambeau in Hartford, Connecticut, where they had agreed on a plan for the following year that depended on two critical ingredients—money and naval support. Rochambeau's son, a lieutenant colonel in the French army, had been designated as the messenger; in case his ship should be captured and he be forced to destroy the dispatch, he had committed the entire memorandum to memory. With the end of the year approaching, time was of the essence. But what to do about the British ships hovering outside the entrance of Newport harbor? On October 28, as the remnants of Solano's Hurricane worked its way up coastal New England, scattering the British fleet, de Ternay saw his chance.

That evening, three French frigates sailed into the stormy night. Once it became clear they had eluded the enemy, the ships separated, and the *Amazone*, with the young Rochambeau aboard, headed east for France. On December 6, after a passage of only thirty-nine days, he was in Brest and on his way to the French court at Versailles.

CHAPTER 2

"An Enemy in the
Heart of the Country"

W HEN W ASHINGTON FIRST LEARNED of Benedict Arnold's
betrayal on September 25, 1780, he turned to Lafayette and asked,
"Whom can we trust now?" Based on what Washington did next, the
answer to that question was the thirty-eight-year-old major general
on whose good sense and clarity of thought he had come to depend:
Nathanael Greene.

Within days, he had chosen Greene to oversee the highly contro-
versial trial of John André, the captured British espionage chief with
whom Arnold had conspired to surrender West Point. Soon after André was hanged as a spy, Washington picked Greene to step into the
black hole left by Arnold and restore order at West Point. A few weeks
after that, he assigned Greene the most unenviable task of the war,
which was saying something given that Greene had already served as
the army's quartermaster during the terrible winter at Valley Forge.

On October 14, Washington ordered Greene to take command of
the beaten and demoralized Continental army in North Carolina. At
that moment, the enemy appeared poised to extend Britain's southern
dominion as far north as Virginia. News a few weeks later of the
American victory at King's Mountain certainly provided a flicker of
hope. But as Greene discovered during his hurried journey south,
which included stops at the Continental Congress in Philadelphia and

the residence of Virginia governor Thomas Jefferson in Richmond, the unexpected American triumph had given government officials the mistaken impression that the tide had already turned. As Greene's friend Lafayette wrote on November 10, "I wish [King's Mountain] had been postponed."

Relations between America's military and civil leaders had become increasingly strained as both the Continental Congress and the states failed to provide the bare essentials required to maintain a functional army. The American people had decided to rebel from the mother country because they did not want to pay the taxes insisted upon by a distant king and the Parliament. Now they refused to pay the taxes needed to fund the war to win their independence. By the fall of 1780, with Congress wallowing in debt and no apparent way to set things right, it seemed as if this five-year experiment in creating a republic was about to founder for a lack of will on the part of the people and their elected leaders. Greene had already established a reputation as one of Congress's more outspoken critics, and during his journey south, he found only confirmation of his already low expectations. When he asked for the soldiers, provisions, and supplies he needed if he had any hope of opposing a British army that was more than twice the size of the shattered remnant he was about to inherit from outgoing commander Horatio Gates, he received only shrugs and evasive replies.

Greene was a most unlikely soldier. A Quaker pacifist by birth, he suffered from asthma and had walked with a limp since childhood. He developed an early love of reading and often tended the family forge in Potowomut, Rhode Island, with a book in hand. Painfully aware of his lack of formal education, he cultivated younger and better educated friends who could contribute to his ongoing program of self-improvement. By the time of the Boston Tea Party, Greene was no longer a practicing Quaker and felt free to assume a leadership role in organizing his community's militia company. However, when the company voted to select its officers, Greene was overlooked. The reason: his physical disability detracted from the impression his company made when performing military exercises.

Initially devastated at being considered "an inferior point of light" ("I confess it is my misfortune to limp a little," he admitted, "but I did not conceive it to be so great"), he nonetheless continued to drill and parade with his company as a lowly private. All the while, Greene acquired as many works of military history and tactics as he could find (some of them purchased at the bookshop of future Continental artillery chief Henry Knox in Boston). By the spring of 1775, Greene had come to the attention of several influential lawmakers. That May the Rhode Island assembly voted to promote the thirty-two-year-old private who marched with a limp to the rank of brigadier general so that he could lead the fifteen hundred soldiers being sent to join the provincial army in Boston.

Greene quickly impressed Washington with his knowledge and judgment, and despite one, potentially career-ending lapse (when in the fall of 1776 he wrongly insisted that New York's Fort Washington could withstand a British attack), he had emerged as the Continental army's most capable and dependable major general. Adversity, it seemed, was something on which Nathanael Greene thrived. But even Greene, it turned out, had his limits.

It was in Richmond, on November 19, 1780, after a disheartening meeting with Governor Jefferson, that the utter impossibility of what he was about to undertake threatened to overwhelm him. "I cannot contemplate my own situation without the greatest degree of anxiety," he admitted to Washington. "I am far removed from almost all my friends and connections and have to prosecute a war . . . attended with almost insurmountable difficulties. . . . How I shall be able to support myself under these embarrassments God only knows."

"You have no doubt an arduous task on hand," Washington responded on December 13, "but where is the man charged with conducting public business in these days of public calamity that is exempt from it? Your difficulties I am persuaded are great; they may be insurmountable; but you see them now through a different medium than you have ever done before, because every department is now centered or combined in the commanding officer, exhibiting at one view a prospect of our complicated distresses." Greene, who had not seen his wife, Caty, and their two children since the previous winter, now knew what Washington had been living with for the last five years: the overpowering loneliness of command.

Throughout his travels south, Greene had been accompanied by Baron Friedrich Wilhelm von Steuben, the Prussian officer responsible for instilling some much needed order in the beleaguered Continental army at Valley Forge in the winter of 1778. Now, in Richmond in the late fall of 1780, Greene realized that his future fortunes in the Carolinas depended on what supplies and men he could get from Virginia. The state had, for the most part, not seen much fighting and therefore possessed ample quantities of the food and manufactured goods that would be impossible to find amid the burned-out farms of the Carolinas. Von Steuben must remain here, in Virginia, where he could oversee the recruitment of soldiers and supplies for the southern army.

If Greene did not have the benefit of von Steuben's personal counsel when he assumed command of the army in Charlotte, he did have a kind of surrogate. Von Steuben's stories of his former commander in Prussia, the military genius Frederick the Great, evidently inspired Greene to seek guidance from the king's writings. Over the course of the next few weeks, as he pondered how to contain Cornwallis's larger and better-trained army, his letters refer time and again to the Prussian monarch. Greene also realized that military strategy and tactics meant nothing without a thorough knowledge of the terrain, particularly the rivers that flowed out of the mountains to the west before tracing their meandering way across the more than five-hundred-mile length of North Carolina to the sea. With the Polish engineer Thaddeus Kosciuszko at the head, Greene sent out an advance guard to explore the possibility of constructing a fleet of small, portable boats to provide his army with a strategic advantage in negotiating the state's rivers.

Greene soon saw firsthand that a brutal civil war was raging in the Carolinas. "The whole country is in danger of being laid waste by the Whigs and Tories [patriots and loyalists]," he wrote to Congressional president Samuel Huntington, "who pursue each other with as much relentless fury as beasts of prey." The region around Charlotte was a "desert" that made it impossible to sustain an army for any length of time.

In early December, Greene hit on what one historian has termed "the most audacious and ingenious piece of military strategy of the war." Contrary to conventional military wisdom (which insisted that you never divided your army in the face of a larger enemy), the general resolved to send a portion of his army one way while the rest of his army went the other. From a purely practical standpoint, a divided army had a better chance of feeding itself in this war-ravaged region. But it also presented Cornwallis with a dilemma. "It makes the most of my inferior force," Greene explained, "for it compels my adversary to divide his and holds him in doubt as to his own line of conduct."

Soon Brigadier General Daniel Morgan was headed west with a "flying army" of between 800 and 1000 American soldiers in hopes of luring a significant portion of the enemy away from Greene's 1100-man force, which was headed east to Cheraw, South Carolina. Here, on a tributary of the Pee Dee River, Greene hoped to establish what he termed a "Camp of Repose" where he might rebuild the army into a force capable of meeting Cornwallis in the open field.

Over the course of the first two weeks of January, Greene's strategy set the stage for one of the most brilliant American victories of the Revolution. On January 17, at Cowpens in South Carolina, Morgan's army of mostly undisciplined militiamen defeated more than 1000 British soldiers led by Lieutenant Colonel Banastre Tarleton. It was an astonishing accomplishment, particularly given the enemy officer's reputation as an unrelenting and remorseless foe. Taking advantage of Tarleton's well-known impetuosity to entrap the vanguard of his cavalry within the lines of his surprisingly resolute mix of militiamen and Continental troops, Morgan succeeded in killing 110 enemy soldiers and capturing at least 500 more.

Greene was elated by the news of Morgan's coup. Unfortunately, developments in Virginia threatened to put a halt to his southern comeback even before it had properly begun. British brigadier general Benedict Arnold had arrived in the Chesapeake with a fleet of forty-six vessels and 1200 soldiers, and he was headed up the James River for Richmond.

THIRTY-FIVE MILLION YEARS AGO a meteor came screaming out of the sky and smashed into the waters near present-day Cape Charles at the entrance of the Chesapeake Bay. Billions of tons of seawater, mud, and bedrock were hurled hundreds of miles into the atmosphere as the force of the impact created a crater almost a mile deep and fifty miles wide. All evidence of the crater has long since been buried beneath an accretion of sediment (it was not until 1983, when fragments from the impact were discovered in the seabed off Atlantic City, that scientists first became aware of the possible existence of the crater), but we now know that the contours of the Chesapeake were shaped by this cataclysmic event.

The crater (larger than Rhode Island and almost as deep as the Grand Canyon) became a drain into which the bay's 150 rivers and creeks began to flow. About two hundred miles to the north, the Susquehanna River was drawn irresistibly in the crater's direction, ultimately carving the trough that established the bay's north-to-south orientation. To the south, the James River veered dramatically to the east, where it combined with the Elizabeth and Nansemond rivers to form the wide and protected body of water known today as the Hampton Roads. It was here, on December 31, 1780, in the anchorage created by an ancient meteor, that Benedict Arnold, the most hated man in America, arrived in the *Charon*, a 44-gun frigate named for the ferryman of Greek mythology who carried the souls of the dead into Hades.

It had been a horrific ten-day passage from New York. On December 26 and 27, a "hard gale" had separated Arnold's fleet. Several ships came close to foundering; one had been forced to jettison its cannons; a hundred of the expedition's cavalry horses had been hurled into the sea. When the fleet finally re-formed off the entrance to the

Chesapeake, four transports carrying a total of four hundred soldiers and one man-of-war were missing. That did not prevent Arnold from calling his remaining officers together on the deck of the *Charon*. They were to supply the troops with enough salted meat, biscuit, and rum for five days and start loading them into the open boats and sloops captured that morning by the advance guard of Arnold's fleet.

Arnold's commander in New York, Sir Henry Clinton, viewed the Chesapeake as essential to the ultimate defeat of the American insurgency in the Carolinas. All rebel communications between the north and the south had to go through the narrow corridor of land between the bulge of the bay's southwestern edge and the Blue Ridge Mountains. By establishing a fortified naval post in the Tidewater from which British patrols could be sent into the interior, Clinton hoped to block the passage of information and supplies along the western edge of the Chesapeake. If Arnold met with success in Virginia during the winter of 1781, Greene's forces in the Carolinas would be effectively starved into submission by the closure of their supply line to the north.

Clinton had reason to believe that Arnold, despite having suffered a severe leg injury at the Battle of Saratoga three years before, was ideally suited to lead this expedition. Described by Johann Ewald, the commander of the detachment's Hessian jaegers, as "a man of medium size, well built, with lively eyes and fine features," Arnold was energetic and, to Clinton's mind, motivated to succeed on this, his first command since becoming a British officer. "I was induced to select Arnold for this service," Clinton later wrote, "from the very high estimation in which he was held among the enemy . . . and from a persuasion that he would exert himself to the utmost to establish an equal fame with us in this first essay of his capacity."

What Clinton had not counted on, however, were the emotions Arnold would arouse among his former compatriots. Even if Virginia's officials proved woefully unprepared for what he was about to unleash upon them, the ordinary people of the Tidewater would ultimately demonstrate the kind of rage-stoked resolve that only a traitor could inspire.

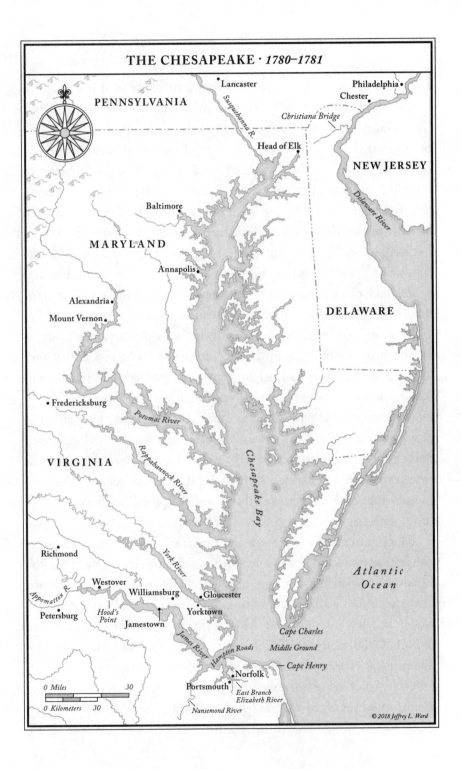

THE CHESAPEAKE · *1780–1781*

PENNSYLVANIA

Lancaster

Philadelphia
Chester

Susquehanna R.

Christiana Bridge

Head of Elk

NEW JERSEY

Delaware River

Baltimore

MARYLAND

Annapolis

DELAWARE

Alexandria
Mount Vernon

Fredericksburg

Potomac River

VIRGINIA

Rappahannock River

Chesapeake Bay

Richmond

York River

Westover
Williamsburg
Gloucester

Appomattox R.

Petersburg

Hood's
Point
Jamestown

Yorktown

*Atlantic
Ocean*

James River

Hampton Roads

Cape Charles

Middle Ground

— Cape Henry

Norfolk

Portsmouth

*East Branch
Elizabeth River*

0 Miles   30

0 Kilometers   30

Nansemond River

© 2018 Jeffrey L. Ward

. . .

IN ADDITION TO ESTABLISHING a fortified base at Portsmouth, a low, swampy settlement several miles up the Elizabeth River from Hampton Roads at the mouth of the James River, Arnold had been given the latitude to destroy "any of the enemy's magazines . . . provided it may be done without much risk." The ever aggressive Arnold chose to interpret this last caveat quite loosely. Knowing that the element of surprise gave him a window of only a handful of days before the state's militia had a chance to respond, Arnold resolved to sail quickly up the James, and if possible, attack the state at its new capital in Richmond—a town that Governor Jefferson had chosen because of its supposed safety more than a hundred miles upriver from Hampton Roads.

Working to Arnold's advantage was the region's vulnerability to an attack by water. Back in the seventeenth century, the Tidewater's long, navigable rivers had helped transform this part of Virginia into one of the most prosperous tobacco-producing areas in the colonies. Now the rivers that had been the making of the region were about to prove its undoing. With the aid of Arnold's fleet of sail-equipped boats (each of them packed so tightly with soldiers that Hessian commander Ewald complained of the sweltering heat generated within the confines of these overloaded cockleshells), the British were able to travel with frightening speed into the state's interior.

Making matters worse from an American perspective was Governor Jefferson's leisurely response to Arnold's appearance at Hampton Roads. When on the morning of December 31 he was first informed of the arrival of a large fleet of unknown origin, Jefferson seemed reluctant to view it as a threat. Years later, William Tatham, who had delivered the news to Jefferson, remembered that the governor "suppose[d] [the ships] were nothing more than a foraging party, [and] unless he had farther information to justify the measure, he should not disturb the country by calling out the militia."

Not until two days later did Jefferson, who had almost no military experience, decide to call out a portion of the militia. Not until two days after that, on January 4—by which time Arnold's fleet had sailed past the rudimentary fort at Hood's Point (which if it had been adequately prepared could have easily stopped the British dead in their tracks) and made short work of Virginia's small fleet of armed naval vessels—did Jefferson see fit to call out the "whole militia from the adjacent counties" even as he led a disorganized attempt to remove the military stores and state records from Richmond. Making matters all the worse was his increasingly antagonistic relationship with General von Steuben, the one Continental officer in Virginia with the experience to oppose an enemy of Arnold's caliber.

By January 6, as Governor Jefferson watched from a hill on the opposite bank of the river, Arnold had marched nearly unopposed into the state capital. By the following day, not only Richmond but the cannon foundry seven miles up the James were in flames. According to Arnold's official report to Clinton, "26 pieces of cannon, 310 barrels of gunpowder, a magazine of oats, and various other stores . . . , a valuable ropewalk, with all its materials and stock, a large depot of quartermaster's stores and several warehouses filled with rum, salt, sailcloth, and other goods" were destroyed.

Arnold clearly relished his role as the pillager of Richmond. On his arrival, an officer (who was, more than likely, Arnold himself) appeared at Jefferson's residence brandishing a pair of silver handcuffs in hopes of capturing the governor. Later in the day, Arnold attempted to contact Jefferson about the peaceful surrender of large quantities of tobacco, liquor, and other valuable goods. When Jefferson refused to negotiate, Arnold accused the "so-called governor" of being "inattentive to the preservation of private property" and added the goods to the bonfire.

It was later claimed that not until the destruction of the city during the Civil War was there "such a smell of tobacco in Richmond." Liquor from stove-in wine and rum casks flooded the town's streets, and one witness remembered that "even the hogs got drunk." According to Johann Ewald, "On the whole the expedition greatly resembled those of the freebooters, who sometimes at sea, sometimes ashore, ravaged and laid waste everything. Terrible things happened on this excursion: churches and holy places were plundered."

By the morning of January 7, Arnold's troops were in need of rest and sustenance. But Arnold insisted that they immediately begin the march back to Westover—a plantation thirty miles down the river where they had already established a base camp. Four years before, when he was an American general, he had led the Connecticut militia in an attempt to oppose a similar British raid on the inland town of Danbury. Arnold claimed that if the British "had marched two hours sooner from Danbury . . . they would have met without opposition; and if they had delayed it much longer they would have found it absolutely impossible to have regained their shipping." This was enough to convince Arnold's second in command, Lieutenant Colonel John Graves Simcoe, and soon the British, exhausted and famished, were marching through the rain to Westover. After a recuperative stay at the plantation, which happened to be owned by the widowed cousin of Arnold's wife, Peggy, the British were headed down the river. Ten days later, on the morning of January 20, Arnold's troops marched into the town of Portsmouth surrounded by the enveloping tendrils of the Elizabeth River.

Clinton claimed that Arnold's "active and spirited conduct on this service . . . justly merited the high military character his past actions with the enemy had procured him." While acknowledging that their commander was "bold, daring and prompt in the execution of what he undertakes," many of the officers serving under Arnold found it distasteful to be associated with a traitor.

"If he really felt in his conscience that he had done wrong in siding against his mother country," Ewald wrote, "he should have sheathed his sword and served no more, and then made known in writing his opinions with his reasons. This would have gained more proselytes than his shameful enterprise, which every man of honor and fine feelings—whether he be friend or foe of the common cause—must loathe." In the days and weeks ahead, as the British built a series of redoubts around Portsmouth, Ewald found it increasingly difficult to be in Arnold's presence. "This man remained so detestable to me," he wrote, "that I had to use every effort not to let him perceive, or even feel, the indignation of my soul."

Arnold tried to overlook the misgivings of his officers but found it impossible to ignore the hatred of the thousands of American militiamen who began to fill up the tangle of swamps and abandoned homes outside Portsmouth. Already he had been taunted by General Thomas Nelson, who threatened to "hang him up by the heels according to the orders of Congress." Governor Jefferson was rumored to have offered a reward of five thousand guineas for his capture and subsequent hanging.

At one point, Arnold asked a recently captured militia officer what he thought the Americans would do if they caught him. "If my countrymen should catch you," the officer replied, "I believe they would first cut off that lame leg, which was wounded in the cause of freedom and virtue, and bury it with the honors of the war, and afterwards hang the remainder of your body in gibbets." Ewald reported that Arnold "always carried a pair of small pistols in his pocket as a last resource to escape being hanged."

Making matters all the more tense for Arnold was the growing realization of how vulnerable he was in Portsmouth. For the time being, the redoubts protected him from an attack by land, but what if the French fleet of warships now anchored in Rhode Island's Narragansett Bay should appear in the Chesapeake, much as he had done just the month before? Unless a comparable British fleet should arrive to oppose the enemy ships, he would be cut off from his supply line to New York. He would also run the risk of being surrounded. On an isolated peninsula, with the American militia on one side of him and the French navy on the other, he would have nowhere to go. Nine months before Yorktown, Arnold found himself in almost exactly the same situation that would lead to the downfall of Cornwallis.

Soon after the British army's arrival at Portsmouth, Arnold received some encouraging news from New York. As he and his troops had been plundering the Tidewater, Continental troops wintering in New Jersey had mutinied. After more than a year without pay, sufficient food, and proper clothing, and with many of their terms of enlistment having long since expired, the soldiers of the Pennsylvania Line had risen up against their commanding officer, General Anthony Wayne. If their demands were not quickly met, they intended to march to Philadelphia and threaten Congress at gunpoint. In hopes the uprising might herald the wholesale defection that could end the war, Sir Henry Clinton had sent emissaries to the mutineers to encourage them to switch sides.

Arnold was ecstatic. Not only did the mutiny prevent Washington from "detaching troops to disturb" him in Portsmouth, it justified his own decision to turn to the British. "This event will be attended with happy consequences," he assured Clinton on January 23. "We anxiously wait in expectation of hearing that the malcontents have joined His Majesty's army in New York."

As it turned out, Benedict Arnold served as an example to the mutineers, but not in the way the turncoat general had anticipated. When presented with the prospect of siding with the British—who offered them all the financial rewards they could have ever hoped for—the soldiers, according to Anthony Wayne, indignantly spurned "the idea of turning *Arnolds* (as they express[ed] it)." Instead of undercutting the American cause, Arnold's treason had actually strengthened it by serving as a valuable cautionary tale during one of the darkest periods of the war. Without the vile example of Arnold staring them in the face, these despairing and angry Continental soldiers might have convinced themselves (as Arnold had done) that rather than an act of treason, turning to the British was a legitimate act of protest against a government that no longer functioned in their best interests. Several tense days lay ahead, during which Joseph Reed, the leader of the Pennsylvania legislature, negotiated a settlement with the soldiers, but for the time being the nation had withstood this ter-rifying challenge from within.

Washington worked tirelessly to ensure that the magnitude of the crisis was properly appreciated by both Congress and the states. Gen-eral Henry Knox was immediately sent on a tour of New England to inform the region's leaders of "the alarming crisis to which our affairs have arrived by a too long neglect of measures essential to the exis-tence of an army." As early as November, Washington had written to John Sullivan, a major general from New Hampshire who was now serving in the Continental Congress, about increasing the efficiency of the legislative body by "committing more of the executive business to small boards or responsible characters than is practiced at present." By February, with the example of the Pennsylvania mutiny before it, Congress began to lose its fear of investing too much executive power in any single individual and placed superintendents at the heads of the departments of war, marine, treasury, and foreign affairs. Instead of wasting time in ceaseless debate, Congress now had the potential to get something done.

As part of this last-ditch campaign to deal pragmatically rather than dogmatically with the momentous challenges facing the nation, one of Washington's former aides, Colonel John Laurens, was sent to France to provide, in Washington's words, "a military view" of the current state of affairs. Reinforcing the message already delivered by Rochambeau's son in December, Laurens was to emphasize the des-perate need for, in Washington's words, "effectual aid, particularly in money and in a naval superiority."

And then on January 21, just as it seemed the crisis created by the Pennsylvania mutiny had passed, Washington received word of a sec-ond mutiny, this time of the New Jersey Line. As Washington had feared, the excessively generous terms state officials had granted the earlier mutineers had emboldened another group of soldiers to follow suit. Although he could hardly blame these starving, unpaid soldiers for wanting some kind of respite from their sufferings, he knew he had to put down this second mutiny with a brutal show of force. Otherwise his entire army might desert. To put an end to this "very pernicious influence on the whole army," all negotiations involving civil officials must cease.

On January 25, with close to two feet of snow on the ground, he sent orders to Quartermaster Timothy Pickering for a "sleigh, pair of horses and driver." Two days later Washington and a detachment of Continental soldiers under the command of General Robert Howe were in Ringwood, New Jersey, close behind the mutineers, who had left their winter quarters and were on the way to Trenton. After giving Howe detailed instructions on how to subdue the rebels, Washington remained in Ringwood while Howe and his soldiers set out at midnight for the mutineers' encampment.

By dawn, Howe's soldiers had surrounded the huts of the mutineers, who were ordered out into the snow. Three of the ringleaders, Howe announced, would be "selected as victims for condign punishment." After being tried on the spot, they were sentenced to be immediately executed by a firing squad composed of "the most guilty mutineers." "This was a most painful task," a surgeon from Plymouth, Massachusetts, named James Thacher remembered; "being themselves guilty, they were greatly distressed with the duty imposed on them, and when ordered to load, some of them shed tears. The wretched victims, overwhelmed by the terrors of death, had neither time nor power to implore the mercy and forgiveness of their God, and such was their agonizing condition, that no heart could refrain from emotions of sympathy and compassion." After two of the men had been shot to death, Howe announced that the third was to be pardoned. "This tragical scene," Thacher wrote, "produced a dreadful shock, and a salutary effect on the minds of the guilty soldiers. Never were men more completely humbled and penitent; tears of sorrow, and of joy, rushed from their eyes, and each one appeared to congratulate himself that his forfeited life had been spared."

Later that day Washington informed the commissioners selected to "redress the grievances of the New Jersey Line" that their services were no longer required. "Unconditional submission," he wrote, "has been effected this morning; and we have reason to believe the mutinous disposition of the troops is now completely subdued and succeeded by a genuine penitence."

ON JANUARY 20, three French warships sailed out of Newport harbor. When British admiral Thomas Graves learned of the movement, he immediately assumed the enemy ships were headed to Virginia to attack Benedict Arnold's army in Portsmouth. Graves and his fleet of nine ships of the line were stationed almost sixty miles to the southwest of Newport at Gardiners Bay at the eastern end of Long Island. While sending word of the development to his superior, Admiral Arbuthnot in New York, Graves, fifty-five and married to the sister of Prime Minister Lord North, responded to the French challenge by dispatching three ships of his own—the *Culloden, Bedford,* and *America.*

It was an order he soon regretted. A winter storm that a British officer stationed in New York claimed was "the severest that has been felt here for many years" erupted over the waters off eastern Long Island. The 74-gun *Culloden* never made it past Montauk and was wrecked at the edge of Fort Pond Bay. The *Bedford,* another 74, lost all her masts to the gale and ultimately had to be towed back to Gardiners Bay, a shattered and leaking hulk. The *America* was the only ship to make it past the eastern tip of Long Island, where it was blown all the way to Virginia by the gale.

As it turned out, the French had had no intention of attacking Benedict Arnold; instead, the three ships had merely sailed out to meet two frigates returning from Boston and were safely back in Newport before they could fall victim to the storm. In just a day, naval superiority in the region had shifted from the British, who now had only six available ships of the line, to the French with seven ships. The question was, what would the French, whose spies in Connecticut provided them with precise and timely information about the status of the British fleet, do with this newfound advantage?

FOR WASHINGTON the answer was obvious: The French in Newport should send their entire fleet to the Chesapeake with an army of a thousand soldiers and the siege guns required to capture Benedict Arnold. For Washington, and the American people as a whole, it was intolerable to think that the "arch traitor" was free to plunder Virginia and was now industriously fortifying a British navy base at the southern end of the Chesapeake Bay that might stop the flow of supplies to Greene's army in the Carolinas. To seize and hang Arnold in the winter of 1781 would give Washington's recruitment efforts that spring an incalculable boost. It was the kind of opportunity that came along only once (or, as it would turn out, twice) in a war, and the French fleet in Newport must make the most of it while they still had the numerical advantage in warships.

Unfortunately, Washington had not yet received confirmation of the losses to the enemy fleet in Gardiners Bay. Until he knew for sure that the French fleet enjoyed a significant advantage, he could not formally request the naval expedition south. That, however, did not prevent him from deciding to send a twelve-hundred-man force of Continental soldiers overland to Head of Elk, a Maryland town at the northern tip of the Chesapeake, to reinforce a possible naval expedition to Virginia. "This will give a degree of certainty to the enterprise," he explained in a letter to General Rochambeau in Newport, "which will be precarious without it."

Tensions at the American headquarters in New Windsor, New York, mounted as Washington waited for the intelligence he needed to finalize his plan. The situation in Newport had been complicated by the recent death of French admiral de Ternay, whom Lafayette sardonically claimed had "found no way to bypass [the British blockade] except by way of the next world." Charles Destouches, de Ternay's second in command, inherited a poorly prepared fleet under (according to British intelligence) a "wretched system of discipline," and no one knew how quickly he could set sail—if, in fact, he was so inclined.

On February 7, Lafayette reported from headquarters that Washington "is waiting to form some kind of plan not only until the news is confirmed but until we know how much Destouches can take advantage of it and assure himself naval superiority. The *toast* of [the] general['s] headquarters is 'May M. Destouches soon be squadron commander!'"

It was a torturous time for Washington, who had watched in impotent rage as Arnold laid waste to his home state. For months Washington had been urging Governor Jefferson to prepare Virginia for the inevitable attack by water, even sending him detailed plans for a 25-foot flat-bottomed boat that fit into a standard-sized wagon for transport across the peninsulas of the Tidewater. "We could then move across from river to river with more rapidity than [the enemy] could go down one and up another," he explained to Jefferson, "and none of their detachments would be ever secure by having the water between them and us." Jefferson had demurred, postponing production of the very boats that might have prevented Arnold from reaching Richmond.

Now Washington worried that the presence of Arnold would cause Jefferson to neglect the supply needs of Greene's army to the south—a concern confirmed by General von Steuben's letters criticizing the governor's management of the war effort. "For while there is an enemy in the heart of the country," Washington wrote to Nathanael Greene, "you can neither expect men or supplies." Adding to his worries about the southern army was the unusually aggressive behavior of Lord Cornwallis, who had responded to the setback at Cowpens by pursuing Morgan's exhausted and prisoner-encumbered troops into North Carolina.

But it was the status of the French fleet that concerned Washington the most. Part of the problem was the agonizingly long time it took to get letters to and from Newport. A lack of funds had forced him to disband the system of couriers that had once linked the two headquarters, and the mails proved both slow and prone to theft by British agents. Not until February 15 was Washington finally able to write the letter with which he formally proposed sending the entire French fleet to Virginia.

In the days that followed, his headquarters became a hive of intense and tension-filled activity. He'd put Lafayette in command of the division that was to be in the Tidewater when the French fleet descended upon Arnold, and there were countless details to be worked out before the French marquis could start marching with his men to Head of Elk. At one point, it became necessary for Washington to visit West Point, ten miles down the river. Accompanying him were Lafayette and several members of Rochambeau's staff. It was cold and windy, and after a day of touring the fort, Washington noticed that Lafayette's leg, which had been injured at the Battle of Brandywine three years before, was giving him trouble. So as not to further tire the marquis, Washington suggested they return to New Windsor by water since "the tide will assist us in ascending against the stream."

A barge was found and once the necessary number of oarsmen had been assembled, they were off. As night came on, it began to snow. Coupled with the large floes of ice bobbing in the river, it made for a difficult passage, especially as the boat became increasingly filled with water. As had so often happened in Washington's experience, the water had proven to be a treacherous way to travel.

They were edging along the rocky shore near New Windsor in the darkness, looking for a place to land. "Perceiving that the master of the boat was very much alarmed," Washington took over the helm, proclaiming, according to an aide-de-camp to Rochambeau, "Courage my friends; I am going to conduct you, since it is my duty to hold the helm." Whether or not he was referring to his role as commander in chief of the allied forces, this was a man who insisted on being in control, especially in times of greatest peril. Soon after making this pronouncement, he steered them into a gap between the rocks and they pulled the boat onto the shore.

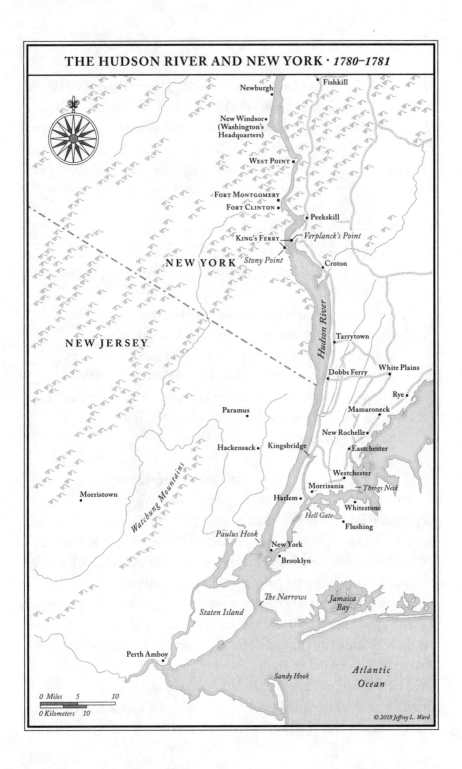

THE HUDSON RIVER AND NEW YORK · *1780–1781*

Fishkill

Newburgh

New Windsor
(Washington's
Headquarters)

WEST POINT

FORT MONTGOMERY
FORT CLINTON

Peekskill

KING'S FERRY — *Verplanck's Point*

NEW YORK *Stony Point*

Croton

Hudson River

Tarrytown

White Plains

Dobbs Ferry

NEW JERSEY

Rye

Mamaroneck

Paramus

New Rochelle

Hackensack • Kingsbridge

Eastchester

Westchester

Morrisania — *Throgs Neck*

Morristown

Harlem

Whitestone

Watchung Mountains

Hell Gate

Flushing

Paulus Hook

New York

Brooklyn

The Narrows

*Jamaica
Bay*

Staten Island

Perth Amboy

Sandy Hook

*Atlantic
Ocean*

0 Miles   5   10

0 Kilometers   10

© 2018 Jeffrey L. Ward

. . .

Back in November, French major general François Jean de Beauvoir Chastellux had visited Washington's headquarters at New Windsor. A highly sophisticated man of letters whose command of English would enable him to act as liaison officer between Washington and Rochambeau, Chastellux was deeply impressed by the American commander.

> His stature is noble and lofty, [he wrote], he is well made, and exactly proportioned; his physiognomy mild and agreeable, but such as to render it impossible to speak particularly of any of his features, so that in quitting him, you have only the recollection of a fine face. He has neither grave nor a familiar air, his brow is sometimes marked with thought, but never with inquietude; in inspiring respect, he inspires confidence, and his smile is always the smile of benevolence . . . ; a hero in a republic, he excites another sort of respect, which seems to spring from the sole idea, that the safety of each individual is attached to his person.

What Chastellux did not detect was the intensity of the passions—described by the New York lawyer Gouverneur Morris as "almost too mighty for man"—that seethed beneath Washington's usually placid exterior. Those who lived and worked with him, however, knew another, darker side, and on February 16, his aide-de-camp Alexander Hamilton became the target of his unchecked wrath.

Hamilton had just left Washington's upstairs office with a letter "of a pressing and interesting nature" for the army's commissary when he ran into Washington himself on the staircase. Anyone who has encountered a noted public figure has only an inkling of the charismatic force field Washington commanded. Three and a half years before, a British officer who found himself in Washington's presence had been, in the words of Henry Knox, "awestruck as if he was before something supernatural." Hamilton had spent enough time with the American commander to know that Washington's public persona (like all public personas) was, to a certain degree, an act. "It was not long," he confided to his father-in-law, Philip Schuyler, "before I discovered he was neither remarkable for delicacy nor good temper." That, however, did not diminish the sometimes terrifying potency of his commander's personality, and as they passed each other on the staircase, Washington told Hamilton he wanted to speak to him. "I answered," Hamilton wrote, "that I would wait upon him immediately."

But first he needed to deliver the letter to another one of Washington's aides, Tench Tilghman, who was working on the first floor. On Hamilton's way back to Washington's second-floor office, he was stopped by Lafayette. Although beloved by Washington, the young French nobleman could be highly emotional, willful, and impatient. Soon after the arrival of the Expédition Particulière, he had so pestered Rochambeau with his incessant cries for action against the British in New York that the French general had accused him of placing "private or personal ambition" ahead of the safety of the French army. "The warmth of your feelings," Rochambeau lectured Lafayette, who was less than half his age, "had somewhat overheated the calmness and prudence of your judgment."

On February 16, Lafayette's enthusiasm for the upcoming mission to the south threatened to prevent Hamilton from returning to Washington in a timely fashion. Hamilton did his best to extricate himself from the excitable marquis. "He can testify," Hamilton wrote, "how impatient I was to get back, and that I left him in a manner which but for our intimacy would have been more than abrupt."

Washington, Hamilton soon discovered, was waiting for him, not in his office, but at the head of the stairs, and he was in a towering rage. "Colonel Hamilton," he snarled, "you have kept me waiting at the head of the stairs these ten minutes. I must tell you, Sir, you treat me with disrespect."

"I am not conscious of it, Sir," Hamilton responded, "but since you have thought it necessary to tell me so, we part."

"Very well, Sir," he said, "if it be your choice."

So ended one of the great collaborations of the war. "For three years past," Hamilton confided to his father-in-law, "I have felt no friendship for him and have professed none. The truth is our own dispositions are the opposites of each other." During the winter of 1781, Washington was operating under tremendous stress. Hamilton was brilliant but also mercurial and desperate to move out of Washington's ever lengthening shadow. He had hoped to get the posting to France that had gone to his friend John Laurens. One has the sense that Hamilton was as much at fault as Washington in the rupture.

By February 19, Washington still had not heard from Rochambeau about the proposed naval expedition to the Chesapeake. "The destruction of the detachment under Arnold is of such immense importance," he wrote to the French commander. "I impatiently wait to be favored with Your Excellency's answer to these points."

Six days later, on February 25, Washington learned that the British warship *America* "had got into Gardiners Bay after being long out." Even worse, Arbuthnot, who had joined Graves at the eastern end of Long Island, was overseeing the repair of the dismasted *Bedford*, which was being outfitted with the wrecked *Culloden*'s undamaged spars. "This again gives Arbuthnot the superiority," he wrote sadly to Lafayette, who had already departed with his soldiers for the Chesapeake, "and puts it out of Monsieur Destouches's power to give us any further assistance."

But as Washington was to learn, it was a little more complicated than that.

EVEN BEFORE WASHINGTON HEARD that three British ships of the line had been taken out of action by the January storm, Virginia's Richard Henry Lee had written Congressional delegate Theodorick Bland in Philadelphia with a proposal to capture Benedict Arnold. If the French in Newport sent just one ship of the line and two frigates to the Chesapeake, "the militia now in arms [would be] strong enough to smother these invaders in a moment." Without consulting Washington, Congress then urged French minister Chevalier de la Luzerne, based in Philadelphia, to pass along the proposal to Destouches in Newport. Knowing that the enemy fleet in Gardiners Bay had been recently hobbled by the storm, Destouches decided to do as the politicians had requested. On February 9, having not yet heard from Washington about sending his entire fleet to Virginia and making no effort to check in with the American commander in advance, Destouches sent French captain Le Gardeur de Tilly to the Chesapeake with a single ship of the line and two frigates.

As Washington could have predicted, the three French vessels proved inadequate to the task at hand. Once alerted to the appearance of the French squadron in the Chesapeake on February 13, Arnold and Commodore Thomas Symonds in Portsmouth withdrew their fleet of frigates and smaller vessels into the shallows of the Elizabeth River, beyond the reach of Tilly's deep-drafted ship of the line. Since the two French frigates would have been cut to pieces if they had attempted to attack the British vessels gathered in the river and Tilly was without the soldiers to mount an assault on the fortifications at Portsmouth, he had no hope of taking Benedict Arnold. To "compensate for his inability to carry out his orders," he anchored his fleet at the entrance to the Chesapeake under a British ensign, "ready to fall upon the first ship that attempted to reach Arnold." In addition to capturing several valuable merchant vessels, Tilly succeeded in taking the *Romulus*, a 44-gun British frigate on its way to the Chesapeake from Charleston. Unfortunately from Washington's perspective, these well-intentioned efforts to salvage a failed expedition consumed a great deal of valuable time. Not until the end of February did Tilly return to Newport.

By then Destouches and Rochambeau had received Washington's proposal to send the entire French fleet to the Chesapeake. They'd also learned that with the return of the *America* to Gardiners Bay and the refitting of the *Bedford* with the *Culloden*'s masts, the British and French fleets were essentially even. Even though the delay imposed by the Tilly expedition had resulted in their losing the

numerical advantage they had once enjoyed, Destouches and Rochambeau decided to do as Washington had originally suggested:
Destouches would lead the entire French fleet to the Chesapeake.
"The great consequence that Your Excellency seemed to lay to the
establishment of Arnold at Portsmouth," Rochambeau wrote on February 25, "has determined Monsieur Destouches to sacrifice every
other object to this one." Also figuring into Destouches's thinking
was the acquisition of the *Romulus,* which if it did not tip the balance
in his favor, at least helped to even the odds.

Washington seems to have been more than a little perplexed by
the French commanders' sudden enthusiasm for an expedition that
was no longer the sure thing it would have been just two weeks before.
If the French hadn't thought to sail south with the entire fleet in early
February when they had a clear advantage over the British, why were
they so enthusiastic to do so now when the odds were no longer as
good? Lafayette believed he knew the answer. Once Rochambeau and
the other French officers learned that he was on his way south under
the command of a small army, they had been filled with jealous alarm
over the possibility that the young marquis might succeed in capturing the hated Benedict Arnold while they had been left loitering in
Newport. "I laugh at the arrangement as far as I personally am concerned," Lafayette wrote to Luzerne (whom he regarded as a confi-
dant), "and am very glad we have finally found a means to set Monsieur
de Rochambeau in motion, the more so because he decided on this
expedition after he had been told there was not so much need for it as
had been believed earlier."

Washington had no choice but to remain hopeful that this overdue
demonstration of French resolve would be worth the considerable
risk. Just to make sure his allies followed through with the projected
expedition, he decided to pay a personal visit to Newport. On the
morning of March 2, accompanied by his aides Tilghman and Hamilton (who had agreed to remain with him until a replacement could
be found that spring), Washington boarded a boat and set out across
the Hudson River.

CHAPTER 3

"Delays and Accidents of the Sea"

RIDING WITH WASHINGTON, Tilghman, and Hamilton across the winter rural landscape toward Newport was Baron Ludwig von Closen, an aide to Rochambeau sent to deliver the latest intelligence about the British fleet at Gardiners Bay. Von Closen reported that although the British warship *America* had returned to the anchorage in eastern Long Island, the refitting of the 74-gun *Bedford* was not yet complete. For now, the French fleet still held a narrow, one-ship advantage. However, given "the energy with which the British repaired their ships," the advantage was not going to last long. With time quickly running out, Washington was determined to do everything he could to hasten the departure of the French fleet, and he and his entourage rode toward Newport at a blistering pace.

Two days after leaving New Windsor, they were charging across a small wooden bridge in Connecticut when Washington's horse, "frightened by [the bridge's] springy action," lurched to the side and broke its leg. Even though it was one of his cherished saddle horses, Washington showed little outward emotion. "In seeing His Excellency's face at that moment," von Closen wrote, "you could appreciate very well this great man's very tranquil nature, for he was unmoved and not at all agitated by such an incident. He shrugged his shoulder and said, 'Well! We must leave him behind!'" Given the urgency of their mission, Washington hadn't the time for heartfelt goodbyes. By the end of the day they were in Farmington. Two days later, on the morning of March 6, they were being rowed from Narragansett Bay's Conanicut Island to Destouches's flagship, the *Duc de Bourgogne*.

Washington had hoped the French fleet would be on the verge of departure; instead the ships were dressed in ceremonial splendor in anticipation of his arrival. As they glided across the harbor in Destouches's magnificently appointed barge, the cannons of the assembled ships erupted in a thirteen-gun salute.

The previous month Rochambeau had celebrated Washington's birthday with a similar display of artillery along with a parade of French troops through Newport. When informed of the celebration by letter, Washington had thanked the French general for "the flattering distinction" even as he privately fumed over the time lost by the ill-conceived Tilly expedition. Now he wanted nothing more than to see the French fleet of eight ships of the line and assorted frigates and troop transports on its way to attack Benedict Arnold. Instead, he would have to suffer through a seemingly endless succession of meetings, dinners, balls, and troop reviews, all the while knowing that fewer than sixty miles away in Gardiners Bay the British were preparing their ships with all possible haste for the battle that might decide the fate of Arnold and, just perhaps, the war.

Making it all the more frustrating was the realization that this outward show of veneration on the part of the French high command was, to a certain extent, a lie. Even though Washington was the supposed commander in chief of the armies of the French-American alliance, Rochambeau and Destouches had shown no interest in including him in their decision making. It was true they now appeared intent on righting the wrong of the Tilly expedition by sending the entire fleet in pursuit of Arnold. But as Washington came to appreciate during a two-hour council of war aboard the *Duc de Bourgogne*, Rochambeau and Destouches had their own set of priorities when it came to the capture of Benedict Arnold.

Washington had assumed Lafayette would lead the land forces in

Virginia. Rochambeau had other ideas. As the Duc de Lauzun, a French cavalry officer, had explained to Washington during an earlier visit to New Windsor, many of the French officers resented Lafayette as a young upstart who had used his relationship with the American commander in chief to gain an influence beyond anything he deserved. Some officers had gone to the extreme of taking a vow never to serve under the young marquis.

Washington had expected Destouches to use his fleet's frigates to transport Lafayette's division from Head of Elk down the full length of the Chesapeake to Portsmouth. But the French naval commander insisted this was impossible. "Destouches," Washington wrote to Lafayette, "seems to make a difficulty, which I do not comprehend, about protecting the passage of your detachment down the bay." In other words, if Lafayette did not find a way to get himself and his soldiers from Head of Elk to Portsmouth, a voyage of some two hundred miles, his French compatriots planned to leave him stranded at the top of the Chesapeake.

Even if Lafayette succeeded in getting himself to Portsmouth, Rochambeau had, by selecting a higher-ranking general, the Baron de Vioménil, to command the French ground forces sent south, denied the marquis the chance of leading the expedition against Arnold. "This arrangement was peculiarly distasteful to [Washington]," Lauzun claimed, "and he did not conceal his annoyance." He fell short of insisting that Rochambeau change his decision, but he did make it clear that in the future "his requests were to be regarded as orders."

Already exasperated by the maneuvering Rochambeau and Destouches had done behind his back, Washington could barely contain himself as the French insistence on pomp and circumstance postponed the departure of the fleet by another day. Finally, at midday on March 8, the French fleet set sail as Washington and Rochambeau looked on from the hill at Brenton Point. But even that long anticipated event was temporarily delayed. The *Fantasque*, which had been converted into a troop ship by the removal of her upper-deck guns, ran aground on Brenton Point, in full view of Washington and

Rochambeau and the entire town of Newport. With the help of some small boats, she was eventually set free, but not until six in the evening was the fleet able to clear the harbor mouth in a light northwesterly breeze.

In the weeks ahead, as he waited anxiously for word of the expedition, Washington complained repeatedly in letters to friends, fellow officers, and politicians about the "unfortunate and to me unaccountable delay of twenty-four hours in their quitting Newport after it was said they were ready to sail; the wind being as favorable to them and as adverse to the enemy as heaven could furnish." Rochambeau later insisted that what Washington had perceived as a delay was, in actuality, the time required to fully prepare the fleet. Destouches went so far as to claim the fleet should have never set out in such a light and fluky breeze and that it was only because of Washington, "who had the strongest desire to see us set out," that he reluctantly allowed his ships to depart on the evening of March 8. Whatever the case may be, almost a month after Washington had first proposed the operation, the French fleet had finally set sail.

BRITISH ADMIRAL ARBUTHNOT was in his seventies and desperately unhappy with spending a winter at the eastern end of Long Island, which he described as "an uninhabited land [with only] a few Indians." As he had repeatedly requested in letters to the head of the Admiralty, Lord Sandwich, he wanted to be relieved of command. He and Henry Clinton, who commanded the British army, had been at each other's throats for more than a year. His health was not good. Just a few weeks before Arbuthnot had listed his symptoms to Sandwich. "My constitution is destroyed," he wrote from Gardiners Bay on February 16. "I have lost almost totally the sight of one eye, and the other is but a very feeble helpmate, constantly almost obliging me to call in assistance to its aid in discovering particular objects. Besides this I have lately been seized with very odd fits, resembling apoplexy. . . . I faint, remain senseless and speechless sometimes four hours and sometimes longer and when I recover I am ignorant of the past but remain very low with cold sweats for two or three days after."

And yet somehow, this rheumy-eyed, half-blind excuse of a British admiral, who was regularly derided by Clinton as a do-nothing fool and who would never have secured his current position had he not been a personal friend of Sandwich's, had found a way to rise to the occasion. After more than fifty years of service in the British navy, he had learned a thing or two about seamanship. When presented with the problem of turning two broken ships of the line—one wrecked on the Long Island coast, the other dismasted—into a single workable vessel, he had, contrary to the expectations of almost everyone in the British army and navy, leapt into action. The prospects were grim, he wrote to Clinton, but he would "put up a bold countenance."

On March 5, while Washington and his entourage were riding hell-bent for Rhode Island, Arbuthnot oversaw the installation of the *Culloden*'s masts into the *Bedford*—a difficult task in the best of times but all the more challenging when stationed in the lee of an island along a storm-ravaged coast in winter. And yet, by bringing the *Bedford* alongside the largest ship in his fleet, the 90-gun *London,* he was able to use the *London*'s masts as cranes that gently lowered the *Culloden*'s reconditioned spars into place. When he learned four days later that the French fleet had sailed from Newport, the *Bedford* was only twenty-four hours away from being ready, and on March 10, Arbuthnot and eight ships of the line set sail.

The following day Washington was passing through New London, Connecticut, on his way back to his headquarters in New Windsor, when he received word of the British departure. "I think the French had so much the start that they will first reach [Chesapeake] Bay," he wrote to Lafayette. And yet, as he had learned through long and bitter experience, "there is no accounting for the delays and accidents of the sea."

ARBUTHNOT KNEW THE FRENCH FLEET had left at least a day (actually thirty-six hours) before him. He also knew that the bottoms of the entire British fleet had been sheathed in plates of copper, which gave them a significant speed advantage (some claimed as much as a knot and a half) over vessels whose bottoms had grown shaggy with sea growth. Only a portion of the French warships had received this latest technological improvement, and since the enemy fleet could sail only as fast as its slowest ship, Arbuthnot had a distinct chance of making up distance on Destouches's squadron; the question was how far ahead were they?

On March 12 Arbuthnot learned the answer. He and his eight ships of the line and four frigates were laboring under a light and variable breeze off the coast of New Jersey when they came upon a packet ship from Ireland bound for New York. Just the day before the vessel had been briefly chased by one of the frigates attached to the French fleet. The packet's captain reported that the French were twenty-four leagues (approximately seventy-two nautical miles) to the south. "Immediately after this man was dismissed," Arbuthnot wrote to Sandwich, "a smart wind sprung up at north-north-west." Steering a course "as would best enable me to intercept the enemy," the British fleet headed south with the wind on its beam. The race was on.

Flowing north along the Eastern Seaboard of the United States is a dark-blue river of Caribbean-heated water that today we call the Gulf Stream. As early as 1735, a Maryland tobacco farmer and mariner named Walter Haxton drew the first large-scale chart of the Chesapeake that included a detailed written description of what he called the "Northeast Current," based on his experiences during twenty-three voyages to England. "The knowledge of its limits, course, and strength," he wrote, "may be very useful to those who have occasioned to sail in it."

In addition to mariners in the tobacco trade, whalers from Nantucket Island, who regularly pursued sperm whales along the current's edges, gained an intimate familiarity with the stream. Benjamin Franklin's mother, Abiah Folger, had been born on Nantucket, and in

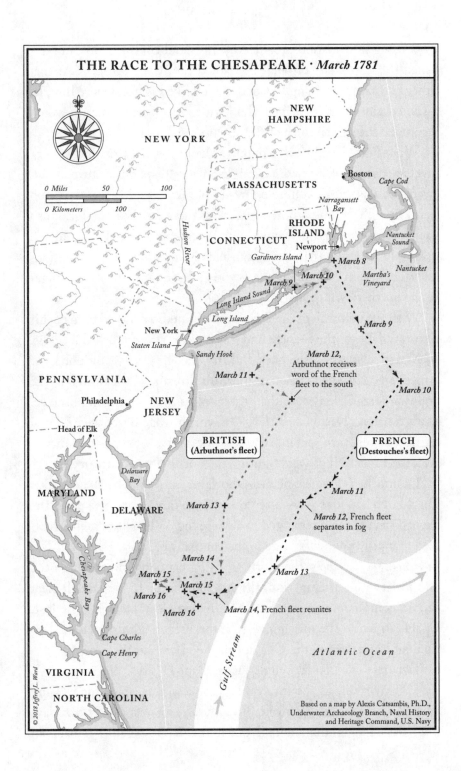

THE RACE TO THE CHESAPEAKE · *March 1781*

NEW HAMPSHIRE

NEW YORK

Boston

Cape Cod

0 Miles   *50*   *100*

0 Kilometers   *100*

MASSACHUSETTS

Narragansett Bay

RHODE ISLAND

CONNECTICUT

Newport

Nantucket Sound

Gardiners Island

March 8

March 10

March 9

Martha's Vineyard

Nantucket

Long Island Sound

March 9

Long Island

New York

Staten Island

Sandy Hook

March 12, Arbuthnot receives word of the French fleet to the south

March 10

PENNSYLVANIA

March 11

Philadelphia

NEW JERSEY

Head of Elk

BRITISH (Arbuthnot's fleet)

FRENCH (Destouches's fleet)

Delaware Bay

March 11

MARYLAND

DELAWARE

March 13

March 12, French fleet separates in fog

March 14

March 13

March 15

March 15

March 16

March 14, French fleet reunites

March 16

Chesapeake Bay

Cape Charles

Cape Henry

Gulf Stream

Atlantic Ocean

VIRGINIA

NORTH CAROLINA

© 2018 Jeffrey L. Ward

Based on a map by Alexis Catsambis, Ph.D., Underwater Archaeology Branch, Naval History and Heritage Command, U.S. Navy

1769, using information provided by an island cousin, Franklin published the first chart of what he named the "Gulf Stream." At that time, Franklin was living in London, and like Haxton before him, he assumed any British mariner who regularly sailed to America would recognize the significance of the stream.

What Franklin did not take into account was the British mariners' inveterate sense of superiority. English packet captains, it turned out, "were too wise to be counseled by simple American fishermen," and Franklin's chart was ignored. As a result, westerly bound English packet ships continued to take more than two weeks longer to sail across the Atlantic than American merchant vessels, whose captains knew enough to cut quickly across the Gulf Stream rather than linger in the north-flowing current.

With the outbreak of the Revolution, Franklin resolved to make his chart available to the French, and it was eventually published in Paris. In March 1781, as Destouches and his fleet headed south along the American coast, the location of the Gulf Stream, which flowed in the opposite direction at more than three knots, was of vital importance. Unfortunately, Destouches elected to make what Baron von Closen termed "a great turn" out into the Atlantic, and for at least a day, maybe two, the French ships were fighting the north-flowing stream.

Destouches's greatest nemesis, however, proved to be the weather. On March 12, four days after their departure from Newport, the French fleet became separated in a dense fog. When Destouches realized that just three ships were in the company of his flagship, the *Duc de Bourgogne,* he spent the morning firing cannons and tacking back and forth in an attempt to "rally his squadron." If the British fleet should come upon a portion of his divided fleet, all would be lost. Unable to locate the missing vessels, the French admiral had no option but to proceed to the Chesapeake and hope for the best.

Two days later, on March 14, just as Cape Henry at the entrance of the Chesapeake was about to come into view, they spied the missing part of the French squadron. Finally, after a passage of six days (two days longer than it had taken the Tilly expedition back in

February), Destouches was poised to implement his plan: "arrive first at Chesapeake Bay and so entrench myself in the James River that I could not be chased out by any naval force, and cut off all retreat and communications by sea for Mr. Arnold's fleet." Then it started to blow hard out of the southwest, putting Cape Henry directly upwind of the newly reunited French fleet.

A square-rigged vessel in the eighteenth century could not sail effectively against the wind. For the next two days, with land almost within sight, Destouches's ships actually lost distance as they attempted to work their way toward the Chesapeake. By March 16, eight days after leaving Newport, they had been blown well to the east of the bay entrance. At 6:30 that morning, they were on port tack (meaning the wind was coming over the ship's port, or left, side) sailing toward the Maryland shore in a rain-filled mist and heavy sea when the frigate *Hermione* signaled that up ahead, in the direction of the bay, she had seen a sail.

WHILE THE FRENCH had been struggling for the last two days in a southerly, Arbuthnot's copper-sheathed fleet—pushed along for a time by a violent northwester—had caught up to and actually passed the French. Worst of all, from the French perspective, the British were in the coveted windward position, giving them what was known as the weather gage, the naval equivalent of a soldier's high ground. Now that they were closer to the direction of the wind, or "upwind," of the French, the British were ideally positioned to reverse course and sail with the wind, or "downwind," to attack their enemy.

Centuries of tradition had determined that the best way for two opposing fleets of warships to engage in combat was by means of the line of battle: Following a series of maneuvers orchestrated by the two opposing admirals (who usually positioned their own ships at the center of their respective lines and communicated their wishes with signal flags), the two lines of battle edged close enough to start hammering away with their artillery.

The line of battle was an essentially defensive configuration by which a fleet of warships attempted to create an ocean-borne imitation of a land-bound fortress. For the line of battle to work, each ship had to maintain its station by providing support to the ships ahead and behind even as it blasted away at its opponent on the enemy line. A ship of the line needed to be both powerful and maneuverable, and by the latter part of the eighteenth century, it had been determined that the 74—meaning that the ship had 74 cannons arranged on two decks (24 pounders below, 18 pounders above)—represented the perfect compromise between agility and firepower.

While the smaller frigate was built for speed, a 74, which had a crew of between 500 and 750 men, was more like a large floating tank constructed of wood. It took two thousand oak trees, or fifty-seven acres of forest, to build a single 74, whose ribs and planking were so thick that cannonballs, if shot from a distance, regularly bounced off the ship's sides. The 74s were large and powerful but they were by no means the biggest of the battleships. Destouches's flagship, the *Duc de Bourgogne,* was a two-decker with 84 guns; even more massive was British admiral Thomas Graves's *London,* a 90-gun three-decker with the biggest cannons of them all, the 32 pounders (each measuring nine and a half feet in length and weighing close to three tons) mounted in her lower deck. The smallest ship of the line that day was the *Romulus,* which Destouches had pressed into service after her capture during the Tilly expedition. With just 44 guns, she was 16 guns shy of qualifying as a legitimate line-of-battle ship, but she was better than nothing. Largely because of the disparity between the *London* and the *Romulus,* the British fleet held a slight, 22-gun advantage over the French.

Since opposing ships often positioned themselves within less than a pistol shot (fifty yards) of each other, a typical naval battle brought to bear a far higher concentration of artillery at far closer quarters than ever seen on land. And yet fleet actions in the eighteenth century, which generally lasted several hours but could continue for a day or more, were rarely conclusive. Part of the problem was that while the hull of a line-of-battle ship was incredibly strong, her rigging of wooden spars, cloth sails, and hemp ropes could be seriously damaged by a single cannon shot. To take advantage of this weakness, the tactically minded French tended to fire high. The more aggressive British, on the other hand, preferred to kill as many of the enemy sailors as possible by firing low. In either instance, the mobility of a warship allowed the fleet that was getting beaten to avoid complete destruction by simply sailing away. According to one British captain, "Two fleets of equal force never can produce decisive events unless they are equally determined to fight it out, or the commander in chief of one of them bitches it, so as to misconduct his line."

Of the two commanders, Destouches was less inclined to fight. Now that the British were between him and his objective, he believed he had no choice but to abandon his original plan. Even if he was able to work his way into the Chesapeake, how was he to disembark his troops under the guns of the enemy? From his perspective, there was nothing to be gained by engaging the more powerful and faster British fleet in battle. Arbuthnot, however, had other ideas.

An admiral in the age of sail had the ability to control the movements of his ships, but there was one thing he could not control: the wind. No matter how expertly he maneuvered his fleet relative to the enemy, all it took was one detrimental shift of wind to negate everything. This is what happened to British admiral Arbuthnot over the course of the next two hours as the southwesterly wind veered to the right by almost 180 degrees. The effect of this monumental change of wind direction was to reverse the relative positions of the two opposing fleets. With the wind out of the northeast, the French now had the weather gage, requiring that the British sail upwind if they were to continue the pursuit.

The coppered ships of the British were faster, but the weather gods had finally begun to work in Destouches's favor. Instead of simply chasing the French, the British now also had to battle the wind—tacking back and forth at an angle of approximately 60 degrees as they attempted to decrease the distance (approximately five miles) between them and the enemy to windward. To capitalize on his newfound advantage, Destouches ordered his fleet to tack in succession so that the order of his ships would be the same as they sailed upwind on the starboard tack (with the wind coming over each ship's right side) toward the Maryland shore.

Tacking a square-rigged ship (which took between five and fifteen minutes) was never easy, especially in the jumbled seas following a major wind shift. If the yards were not manipulated correctly as the ship's bow worked its way through the eye of the wind in the disorganized waves, damage to the spars could result. While the British announced the final, most perilous stage of a tack with the order "Helm's a-lee!" the French shouted *"Adieu-va!,"* or "Go with God!"—which one naval historian describes as a prayer "reflecting the uncertainty of the outcome attending tacking."

Whether or not Destouches's men used this soulful ejaculation (by the end of the eighteenth century, *"Envoyez!"* or "Away you go!" was in more common usage), two of the French ships did indeed run into trouble, with both the *Eveillé* and *Ardent* breaking the yards of their maintopsails. This seriously impeded their ability to sail to windward. According to Destouches, the damage to the two ships "made me lose hope of keeping upwind of the enemy, whose sailing capacity was infinitely superior to that of my squadron." Before long, the French would have to fight.

Within minutes of the French tack to starboard, the British followed suit. Over the course of the next hour, in what the log keeper of the *Royal Oak* described as a "drilling rain," the British piled on sail and "gained sensibly upon the rear of the French fleet." While Destouches kept his fleet in an orderly line, Arbuthnot allowed the faster and more weatherly ships of his fleet to climb ahead toward their prey. According to the Bavarian nobleman Guillaume de

Deux-Ponts, "The inequality of the speed in the enemy's ships separated them into two divisions."

As the ships pounded through the waves in the rain, the officers and crews of both fleets prepared for battle. The sailors' hammocks were brought up from below and stuffed into netting over the ship's gunnels, where they formed a barricade against small arms fire. The thin partitions that formed the walls of the officers' cabins in the aft portion of the ship were removed along with any furniture. The small boats stowed between the quarterdeck and foredeck were packed with nonessential items, lowered over the side, and towed behind the ship, safely out of harm's way. The boatswain and his mates secured the yards with extra rope to prevent them from tumbling down onto the men in the midst of a cannonade. The carpenter and his crew prepared plugs of wood to close up any holes in the ship's sides below the waterline. The gunner and his mates busied themselves with the cannons, making sure that in addition to being ready to fire, there were adequate supplies of powder. Down in the lightless bowels of the ship, just above the sloshing, malodorous bilge water of the hold, was the cockpit, where the surgeon laid out his instruments in preparation for the grim harvest of legs and arms to come.

By one p.m., after a series of tacks, the two fleets were on port tack with the British advancing rapidly from behind. The ships were heeling so much in the freshening breeze that their lower gun ports on the leeward side were underwater. This prompted Arbuthnot to order the captain of the leading British ship, the 74 *Robust*, to begin the attack not from the usually preferred windward position but from to leeward of, or below, the enemy. By attacking with the windward sides of his ships facing the French, Arbuthnot's fleet would be able to fire both rows of cannons while the lower gun ports of the enemy would be buried beneath the waves. "Nothing could bear a more pleasing prospect than my situation," Arbuthnot wrote.

But as he was about to discover, Destouches saw an opportunity of his own.

. . .

So far, all had gone according to the usual British script: through an exemplary display of seamanship and aggression, Arbuthnot's fleet had made a mockery of Destouches's attempts to take advantage of the setback the British had suffered during the January storm at Gardiners Bay. In keeping with the reputation established by the royal navy during the Seven Years' War, when the British had handed the French a series of lopsided defeats (the most humiliating of which had been suffered before the eyes of their own countrymen at Brittany's Quiberon Bay in 1759), Arbuthnot seemed on the verge of both saving Benedict Arnold and annihilating the French fleet.

There were reasons, however, for the British admiral to give pause as he watched the *Robust* climb toward the stern of the last French ship, the 64-gun *Provence*. Since France's entry into the American War of Independence, its navy had shown unsettling signs of improvement, especially when it came to tactics. Rather than following the British model—which emphasized tradition and seamanship and encouraged officers to learn by doing—the French set out to approach naval combat analytically. Embracing the Enlightenment's belief in the power of reason, the French established in 1752 the Académie de Marine in Brest, where instructors such as Vicomte de Morogues produced groundbreaking treatises on naval tactics that enabled students to think of a naval battle in terms of a chess game rather than a brawl. While British ships communicated with a relatively limited series of signal flags dating back to the previous century, the French instituted what was called a numerary system of signals, which gave their admirals the ability to relay a much wider range of orders. To increase its officers' familiarity with the new signaling system and the tactics promulgated by Morogues, the French navy created an "Evolutionary Squadron" that practiced fleet maneuvers over the course of several extended cruises.

With the outbreak of war between France and Britain, it became almost immediately evident that this was a new, revitalized French navy. On June 17, 1778, a French frigate with what turned out to be the wonderfully ironic name of *Belle Poule* ("Beautiful Chicken") fought the much larger HMS *Arethusa* to a brutal draw off the coast of Brittany. (The excitement caused by this early encounter was so great that the fashionable ladies of Paris invented the "Belle Poule" hairstyle, featuring a model of the frigate balanced atop a pile of carefully arranged hair.) When a month later at the Battle of Ushant, the French fleet displayed a crispness and cohesion that made the poorly directed British look like amateurs, the alarm was sounded. "There is something surprising," Captain Richard Kempenfelt wrote in January 1780, "that we, who have been so long a famous maritime power, should not yet have established any regular rules for the orderly and expeditious performance of the several evolutions necessary to be made in a fleet. The French have long set us the example." For the first time in centuries, a whisper of doubt had entered the collective psyche of the British navy.

DESTOUCHES'S ORIGINAL PLAN had been to sail unmolested into the Chesapeake and disembark the soldiers who were to capture Benedict Arnold. The appearance of the British squadron had, to Destouches's mind at least, destroyed those plans. If it had been possible, he would have simply sailed away from the enemy and returned to Newport. Unfortunately, the British ships were significantly faster, enabling them to force a confrontation. Since Destouches had no choice but to fight and had little to no chance of completing his mission, what concerned him now was "the problem of preserving the honor of the King's arms without endangering his fleet." With the British vanguard about to open fire on his rearguard, a battle was inevitable. To improve his odds against a faster and more powerful opponent, he must deny Arbuthnot the advantage of the leeward position.

So Destouches ordered his fleet to reverse direction. First the lead ship in the squadron, the *Conquérant,* commanded by Charles-Marie de la Grandière, bore down and jibed to starboard; then each subsequent ship followed in succession, until the entire French fleet was to leeward of the British line of battle and approaching on starboard. As Destouches later noted with considerable satisfaction, it was a "movement which the enemy had not foreseen." Just when Arbuthnot thought he had the French in his grasp, Destouches had seized the initiative. The French were now racing toward him in the favored leeward position, the heel of their ships keeping both rows of cannons well above the choppy seas, while the lower gun ports of the British were buried underwater. Suddenly, the French had an almost two-to-one advantage in firepower. It was a brilliant move on Destouches's part that, in his own words, "threatened to batter the head of [the British] line against two scythes."

Adding to Arbuthnot's woes was the disorganized state of his line of battle. Up until just a few minutes before, he had been in dogged pursuit of the enemy, and the three leading British ships, the *Robust*, *Prudent*, and *Europe*, had worked themselves significantly ahead of his flagship, the *Royal Oak*, which occupied the fourth position in the British line. Arbuthnot was about to signal for the *Robust* to shorten sail and "to continue to press the enemy on the larboard [or port] tack" when Captain Phillips Cosby decided to retake the initiative.

Cosby was supposed to have passed just to windward of the leading French ship (the *Conquérant*) as the rest of the British squadron followed him in running the length of the enemy line. Instead, he bore dramatically away from the direction of the wind until the *Robust*'s bow was pointing directly at the *Conquérant*. To avoid a collision, the leading French ship also bore away until her starboard side and all her cannons were facing the bow of the leading British ship.

Cosby's aggressively spontaneous move was well intentioned but ill advised. With his ship's bow pointed toward the French ship's side, Cosby was virtually defenseless against the *Conquérant*, which almost immediately unleashed a frightening rain of cannonballs and canister shot (clusters of smaller balls capable of clear-cutting a ship's deck of men), along with an evil cloud of langridge (bolts, nails, bars, and other pieces of iron) that began to wreak havoc with the *Robust*'s sails and rigging. In the parlance of naval warfare, Cosby's T had been crossed, and the subsequent raking fire inflicted a hurt upon the leading British ship from which she never recovered.

Making matters worse, from a British perspective, the captains of the two ships behind Cosby (who both assumed Cosby was following Arbuthnot's orders) also bore off and were quickly subjected to similar treatment by the next two ships in the French line, the *Jason* and the *Ardent*. "For a long while," Destouches wrote, "three vessels from their van were in a head-on position athwart mine, which took advantage of this by brisk, sustained fire." For the first three British ships, time must have seemed to have stopped as the French artillery blasted splintered chunks out of their spars, topsides, and hulls while riddling the sails with holes.

Arbuthnot had lost control of his squadron. But what to do? Reluctantly, the British admiral decided he had no choice but to follow in the wake of his wayward vanguard and attack the nearest French ship. What Arbuthnot should have done at this point was raise the blue and yellow checked flag that ordered "every ship . . . to engage the enemy as close as possible." Instead he kept up the signal for forming a line of battle, which ordered his captains to close up any gaps between their ships but made no reference to attacking the enemy. And so, with the captains of his rearguard "in a quandary, whether to continue to windward or bear away," Arbuthnot followed his vanguard into battle.

The British flagship was soon in the midst of the same firestorm that had afflicted the three British ships ahead of her. And with a large gap between the *Royal Oak* and the British vanguard, the enemy, led by Destouches's flagship, the *Duc de Bourgogne*, and what Arbuthnot described as the French admiral's "two seconds," the *Neptune* and the tiny *Romulus*, had plenty of time to make a mess of the *Royal Oak*'s spars and rigging. "My ship's foresail was so torn with shot," Arbuthnot wrote, "that it hung to the yard by four cloths and the earings [small ropes that attached the upper corners of the sail to the yard] only; the maintopsail halyards, braces, ties, also the foretop and fore braces and bowline [were also damaged], and . . . for a little space . . . the ship was ungovernable."

In the meantime, Cosby in the *Robust* continued to push forward the attack. After surviving the first onslaught of fire, he drew to within fifty yards of the *Conquérant* and, having jibed onto starboard tack, forced his French opponent to turn away from the direction of the wind until both ships were sailing side by side with the wind directly behind them. Now that they were on a run, the ships were rolling back and forth with the rise and dip of the waves instead of heeling to one side. This allowed Cosby to use both decks of cannons, and he was soon giving as he had so far received.

For the next half hour, the vanguards of the French and British lines went after each other in a wild melee. Since they were sailing with the wind, the powder smoke followed the fleet in a smothering, fire-licked cloud. The recoil of the great guns shook the ships to their keels; cannonballs shot at point-blank range tore into the vessels' sides, sending jagged splinters of oak pinwheeling through the crowded gun decks where men cheered and screamed and died.

Up above on their quarterdecks, the ships' captains and their fellow officers, immaculate in their dress uniforms, attempted to maintain a surreal sense of serenity amid the bloody chaos that surrounded them. Claude Blanchard, the French army's commissary, stood on the quarterdeck of the *Duc de Bourgogne* beside Destouches and a group of officers. "I displayed a coolness," Blanchard recorded proudly in his notebook. "I remember that in the midst of the hottest fire, Mr. de Menonville having opened his snuff box, I begged a pinch of him, and we exchanged a joke upon this subject."

Six were killed and five wounded aboard Destouches's flagship, but it was the *Conquérant*, which found herself in the midst of the fighting from first to last, that suffered the highest casualties of the battle. Before long, every man on the poop deck (the raised deck at the ship's stern) was either killed or wounded. "A hundred soldiers and sailors . . . were hit," Blanchard wrote, "among them forty were killed on the spot and an equal number mortally wounded." One of the grenadiers of the Soissonnais Regiment, dressed in a uniform with crimson lapels, a sky-blue collar, yellow buttons, and with a fur hat on his head, "especially distinguished himself" when a cannonball ripped off one of his legs. "Thank heaven," he was reputed to have cried out in a story that was repeated several times in the French press, "I still have two arms and a leg to serve my King!" Since the soldiers aboard Destouches's ships had nothing to do during the battle other than fire blindly into the smoke with their muskets and provide the sailors with moral encouragement, their heavy losses were, in Blanchard's words, "glorious, but useless."

After forty-five minutes of fighting, Destouches realized that thanks to the ambiguity of the signals flying from the British flagship, the last three ships of the enemy line had not yet come within cannon range of the French rear. Before the fight could extend across his entire line of battle, Destouches decided to give the enemy vanguard, which had already suffered mightily, the equivalent of a kick in the gut. "I gave the signal to reestablish the line of battle on port tack, without regard for position." By spinning around to the opposite tack and looping past the *Robust, Prudent,* and *Europe* (which were so heavily damaged that evasive maneuvers were now impossible), the first five ships in Destouches's line did their best to end the battle as it had begun. Once again, the *Robust* got the worst of it. Particularly memorable, according to Destouches, was when "[t]he *Neptune* placed itself in musket range of [the *Robust*'s] poop and raked it with its entire broadside, while [the British ship] was unable to respond with a single gunshot."

As the tail end of the French line followed in the wake of the leaders sailing off on port tack to the east, several ships in the British rearguard tried to mount one final attack. Unfortunately for the British, this attempt at a last-minute rally did not go well. As the largest ship in the fleet, the *London,* bore down menacingly on the tiny *Romulus,* a gunner on the French ship got off a lucky shot that took out the *London*'s maintopsail yard. To have such a small ship (and a former British ship at that) "disable and beat our London of 90 guns" was a

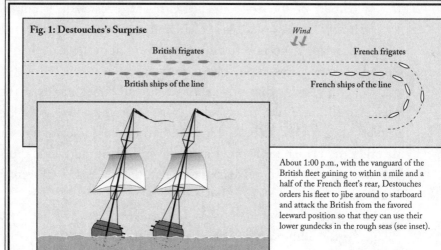

Fig. 1: Destouches's Surprise

Wind

British frigates

French frigates

British ships of the line

French ships of the line

Windward   *Leeward*

The advantage of the leeward position in high winds and seas

About 1:00 p.m., with the vanguard of the British fleet gaining to within a mile and a half of the French fleet's rear, Destouches orders his fleet to jibe around to starboard and attack the British from the favored leeward position so that they can use their lower gundecks in the rough seas (see inset).

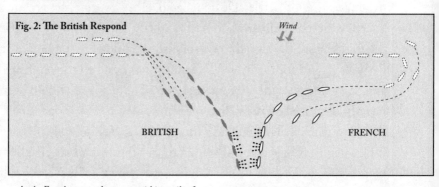

Fig. 2: The British Respond

Wind

BRITISH

FRENCH

As the French vanguard comes to within a mile of the enemy, the British vanguard suddenly bears off and heads at the leading French ships, which respond by bearing off as firing begins. Soon the vanguards of the two fleets are heavily engaged and sailing directly downwind.

Fig. 3: The Battle Rages

Wind

BRITISH

FRENCH

The fighting extends back to the middle of both lines, both fleets sailing downwind.

Fig. 4: Destouches Retakes the Initiative

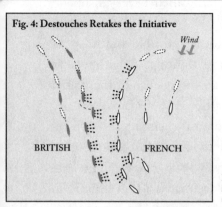

Wind

BRITISH   FRENCH

Destouches orders his fleet to jibe to port tack and head up in a looping movement that allows the entire French squadron to file past (and fire on) the British vanguard.

Fig. 5: Destouches Delivers the "Kick in the Gut"

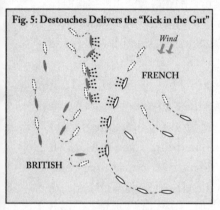

Wind

FRENCH

BRITISH

The leading British ships suffer heavy damage as the British rear attempts to engage the rear of the French.

Fig. 6: The Humiliation of the *London*

Wind

BRITISH   *London*   FRENCH

Conquérant

Robust   *Romulus*

As the French fleet sails off on port tack, the heavily damaged *Conquérant* draws the fire of the *London*, which loses its maintopsail yard to the much smaller *Romulus*. Meanwhile, the *Robust*, also heavily damaged, sails away on starboard.

Fig. 7: Destouches Fails to Follow Through

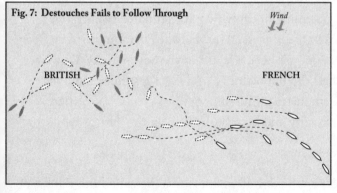

Wind

BRITISH   FRENCH

Firing having ceased, the French fleet forms a line of battle on port tack and sails off to the south while the British head west. Unaware of the extent of the damage he has inflicted on the enemy, Destouches returns to Newport while the British, despite having been bested, sail into the Chesapeake.

sadly fitting end to what one British captain called a "very dishonorable humiliating day's disgrace."

Destouches prepared his fleet for another possible attack by the British, but after more than two hours of fighting, Arbuthnot had no interest in continuing the battle. As a consequence of the British tendency to fire low, the French had suffered more casualties (164 killed and wounded to 97 for the British), but their ships—with the exception of the *Conquérant* (which had temporarily lost control of her rudder) and *Ardent*—had received relatively little damage. The British ships, on the other hand, had been decimated. "If Admiral Arbuthnot tells the truth," a British officer later wrote, "he must confess to the eternal disgrace of our navy, that with a much superior fleet both in number and size of ships, he behaved as shamefully ill as the French behaved gallantly well."

Destouches had done what he, and certainly his opponent, had not thought possible: beat a superior British fleet to the point that if Destouches chose to resume the fight, he stood a more than even chance of "totally destroying this stronger squadron." Even the British acknowledged that the French admiral could have "done as he pleased." He would have then been free to sail into the Chesapeake and capture the traitor Benedict Arnold. This was exactly the kind of daring and improbable victory the British had inflicted on the French at Quiberon Bay in 1759, when Sir Edward Hawke had sailed boldly, if not recklessly, into the wave-battered verge of a rocky lee shore and destroyed six enemy ships, killing or drowning an estimated twenty-five hundred French sailors in the process. After Hawke's stunning victory, the French navy had no longer been a factor in the Seven Years' War.

Destouches now had the opportunity to deliver a similar blow to the British. He had demonstrated his superior grasp of naval tactics. But did he have the audacity and bloodlust to finish the job?

ON MARCH 16, 1781, the day of what came to be called the Battle of Cape Henry, Benedict Arnold was in Portsmouth, Virginia, overseeing the construction of what was to be a British naval base in the Chesapeake. It was also turning out to be a kind of self-created hell. After his initial successes along the James River—crowned by the burning of Richmond—he and the expedition's naval commander had fallen into a violent argument about the distribution of prize money, and the two were no longer talking. In the meantime, his own army officers had made it increasingly clear that they detested him as a traitor. Johann Ewald, the captain of the jaegers, was better than most about keeping his feelings hidden, but amid his personal papers was a poem that spoke to how he and his fellow officers felt about their commander.

> *Honor is like an island,*
> *Steep and without shore:*
> *They who once leave,*
> *Can never return.*

On the day of the clash between the British and French fleets, Arnold received word that an enemy ship of the line had been seen near the entrance of the Chesapeake. "This caused some anxiety among us," Ewald wrote, "since we knew the [French] fleet, which had three thousand troops on board, was off the coast of Virginia, and that . . . [the American general John] Muhlenberg had reinforced the Southern army with a strong corps [of militia]. From this, one could conclude that if this French fleet was not beaten, it intended to undertake something against Portsmouth."

The following day, Ewald wrote, "every minute a bearer of evil tidings arrived." First they received word that Lafayette "approached at quick step with a corps of ten thousand men." Then they heard that the French fleet was off the coast of Virginia, followed by the report of a "union between Rochambeau and Lafayette." Ewald remembered, "Now the water rose up to our necks." Up until then Arnold had regularly entertained his officers at the dinner table with tales of his exploits as an American general. He also talked about "his ingenious trick at West Point, a story which he could make ridiculous with much wit."

But on the day he learned of the imminent approach of the combined French and American forces, Arnold suddenly lost his sense of humor. "General Arnold, who had constantly beaten the French and Americans at table," Ewald wrote, "lost his head and wanted to make up all at once for what had been neglected up to now. We now worked hastily to make his post impregnable, although the entire place consisted of miserable works of only six to eight feet on the average."

The very next day, March 18, they learned that a fleet of warships had entered the Chesapeake. A naval officer was sent by land to investigate. He returned that afternoon with "the bad news that he had seen the French flag."

Destouches had apparently done it. Not only had he defeated Arbuthnot; he was about to disembark his soldiers and begin operations against Arnold. "General Arnold," Ewald wrote, "the former American Hannibal, now stayed on horseback day and night. . . . Everyone . . . continually asked him [questions], which he answered with another one, until a cold sweat broke out over him, [saying,] 'What do you think of this fine works? By God! The French will not take it by assault! By God they cannot!'"

The next morning at dawn, three days after the Battle of Cape Henry, Ewald's pickets captured an American soldier who claimed that "a corps of five thousand men under the Marquis de Lafayette, Baron Steuben, and General Muhlenberg was on the march toward Portsmouth to join the French troops which were on board the French fleet in the Chesapeake, and then to take Portsmouth by storm." Ewald instructed his men to notify him the moment of the enemy's arrival and went back to report to Arnold, "who could not be indifferent to this news, because he ran the risk of being hanged." The two of them were about to sit down to dinner when Ewald heard "many shots in succession . . . and rushed toward my picket," where he discovered "to my astonishment that the entire opposite bank of the creek was occupied by the enemy." The much anticipated American-French assault was about to begin.

During the fighting that followed, Ewald received a bullet to the knee and had to be carried to his quarters for medical attention. On the way, he came upon Arnold, who asked "if the enemy would possibly take the post." Ewald was exasperated by the question. "I said, 'No!,'" he remembered. "'As long as one jaeger lives, no damned American will come across the causeway!'"

Soon after returning to his lodgings, Ewald received the news that the American soldiers had, for no apparent reason, retreated. "Like everyone else," he wrote, "I was transported with joy." That evening, he learned the reason behind the enemy's sudden withdrawal. In hopes of deceiving the Americans on shore, Arbuthnot's fleet had sailed into the Chesapeake flying the French colors. It was the British—not the French—who were anchored inside Cape Henry at the mouth of the Chesapeake.

LAFAYETTE COULD NOT BELIEVE IT. After leaving his detachment in Annapolis, he had sailed down the Chesapeake in a small boat and eventually joined the American forces surrounding Arnold's army in Portsmouth. Everything seemed to be in place to take the British works by storm. And then he had received the heartbreaking news. Even though Destouches's fleet had bested the British, "they did not pursue their advantage" and had sailed for Newport.

On March 27, Lafayette wrote to Governor Jefferson. "How much the disappointment is felt by me, Your Excellency will better judge than I can express. This however may be a satisfaction that on our part we have been perfectly ready, and that with a naval superiority our success would have been certain."

Destouches later claimed he had been unaware of the extent of the damage he had inflicted on the British, and given the losses his fleet had sustained, he felt it would have been unwise to continue the fighting. Having only recently become commander of the French squadron after the death of Admiral de Ternay in December, Destouches, in the words of the artilleryman Comte de Clermont-Crèvecoeur, "did not wish to compromise himself since he held only a temporary command. He could not bring himself to renew the battle when prudence indicated a retreat." Destouches's replacement, Admiral de Barras, later defended his predecessor's decision to abandon the contest and return to Newport for repairs: "It is a principle in war that one should risk much to defend one's position and very little to attack those of the enemy. Destouches, whose object was purely offensive, could and should, when the enemy opposed him had superior forces, renounce a project which could no longer succeed unless, contrary to all probability, it ended not only in beating but also destroying entirely that superior squadron."

That did not change the fact that all Destouches had to do was resume the fight and he would have, in all likelihood, destroyed the British fleet. Instead he chose, in de Barras's words, to "retreat with honor after punishing the enemy's arrogance and establishing the reputation of French arms in the eyes of the people of America." Unfortunately, that did nothing to further the war effort. Even though the British had been soundly trounced, they were the ultimate victors since Arbuthnot, who was forced to tow two of his ships from the scene of his ignominy, was free to continue into the Chesapeake the following morning. Thus, a battle that might have resulted in the capture and hanging of Benedict Arnold had come to what has been called "a farcical end."

In the weeks to come Lafayette tried to put the debacle in the best possible light. However, his commander in chief, George Washington, was less forgiving.

CHAPTER 4

Bayonets and Zeal

Washington did not receive word of the Battle of Cape Henry until two weeks later, on March 30. The French had fought bravely and well, he was told, but never had a chance of accomplishing their objective due to the appearance of the British fleet.

At first Washington did his best to take the high road, assuring Destouches that "the winds and weather had more influence than valor or skill." And then the British published irrefutable evidence of what he really believed had happened.

Back when Washington was still awaiting word of the French squadron, he had written a letter to his cousin Lund, who managed his plantation at Mount Vernon. Between paragraphs about the state of the property, Washington inserted the same tirade he had been repeating throughout the month about the interminable delays associated with the departure of the Destouches expedition. If the French had only done as he'd first suggested, "the destruction of Arnold's corps would have been inevitable before the British fleet could have been in condition to put to sea."

Unfortunately, the letter was intercepted by the British and published in the loyalist *Gazette* in New York on April 8. The French were not amused. In a private letter to Washington, Rochambeau pointed out that he and Destouches had not received Washington's request to send the entire French fleet until well after the Tilly expedition had departed for the Chesapeake—an expedition requested by both the state of Virginia and the Continental Congress. Even the ever loyal Lafayette felt compelled to inform Washington that the letter to Lund "gives me pain on many political accounts." What Lafayette could not understand was how Washington—renowned for his tact and restraint—could have been so careless. Hadn't he been lectured by Washington countless times in the past about the "many things I had to say not being of a nature which would render it prudent to entrust them to paper"?

Washington went through the motions of explaining himself, insisting that the letter had been dashed off after learning that the French fleet had not arrived in the Chesapeake as of March 15. What he failed to tell both Lafayette and Rochambeau was that the letter to Lund was one of five he had written complaining about the French. Washington knew better than anyone that the mails were not safe. Either anger had made him reckless, or, more likely, he had embarked on a conscious campaign to broadcast the fact that the French had once again wasted an opportunity to establish naval superiority, this time by not sending out the entirety of the fleet at Newport until more than a month after the three British ships at Gardiners Bay were scattered and wrecked by the January storm.

Washington's tightly coiled response to Rochambeau reveals that he was far from contrite. While claiming the letter's publication had caused him "extreme pain," he fell short of disavowing its contents, stating that "it would be disingenuous in me not to acknowledge that I believe the general import to be true." He concluded, "With this explanation, I leave the matter to [Destouches's] candor and to yours, and flatter myself it will make no impressions inconsistent with an entire persuasion of my sincere esteem and attachment." These are hardly the words of abasement and regret.

It may have proved messier than he would have liked, but Washington had found a way to let Rochambeau (and the rest of the world) know the true extent of his frustrations. There was such a thing as a chain of command. At some point the French in Newport needed to start taking their cue not from the state of Virginia or even the Continental Congress in Philadelphia but from their commander in chief on the west bank of the Hudson.

LORD CORNWALLIS, the forty-two-year-old commander of the British forces in the south, was devoted to his wife, the beautiful and sad-eyed Jemima Tullikens. When he had learned in the fall of 1778 that she was critically ill, he rushed from New York back to their home in Culford, a small town about a hundred miles to the northeast of London, arriving shortly before her death at the age of thirty-two. Never happy about her husband's decision to leave her and their two children in England while he fought the war in America, Jemima had requested that a thorn tree be planted over her grave to signify "the sorrow which [had] destroyed her life." Cornwallis made sure her wishes were fulfilled, and as late as the middle of the nineteenth century, a thorn tree still flourished over the grave of Jemima Cornwallis.

In a letter to his brother, Cornwallis confessed that his wife's death had "effectually destroyed all my hopes of happiness in this world." Unable to remain in Culford with his grief, he determined to return to the war and his regiment. "I am now returning to America," he explained, "not with views of conquest and ambition [since] nothing brilliant can be expected in that quarter; but I find this country quite unsupportable to me. I must shift the scene; I have many friends in the [British] army [in America]; I love that army, and flatter myself that I am not quite indifferent to them." Cornwallis would never remarry. Unlike other British generals, who were notorious for their affairs, he appears to have remained faithful to the memory of his wife. Instead of another woman, he would devote the rest of his life to what was perhaps his first love, the British army.

By the time Cornwallis returned to America, he had already established a reputation as a dedicated and energetic officer whose eagerness for battle could, on occasion, blind him to the strategic possibilities that lay before him. At the second Battle of Trenton, on January 2, 1777, which followed up Washington's unexpected victory against the Hessians on Christmas Day, Cornwallis had neglected to send out the flanking movement that might have trapped the Americans on the bank of Trenton's Assunpink Creek. Instead, he launched a series of unsuccessful frontal assaults across a narrow stone bridge that resulted in the deaths of dozens of British and Hessian soldiers before learning the following morning that Washington's army had escaped in the dead of night. After serving as William Howe's loyal second in command during the taking of Philadelphia in 1777 and his sad farewell to his wife in England in 1779, Cornwallis had served under Sir Henry Clinton during the taking of Charleston in 1780. Although that campaign had been a success, Cornwallis's relations with Clinton had begun to deteriorate soon after the British commander in chief returned to New York.

It was Clinton's understanding that Cornwallis would pursue a gradual process of reestablishing His Majesty's authority in South Carolina—a strategy developed by Secretary of State Germain's administration in London to address the obvious inadequacies of what had occurred during the previous five years of the war. Even though the British army had won virtually every battle it had fought (with the notable exception of the Battle of Saratoga in 1777), it had not succeeded in destroying Washington's Continentals. It had also made no apparent progress in persuading the American people to return to the welcoming embrace of the British Empire. If Britain could not subdue the colonies militarily, perhaps it was possible to do it politically. Rather than fight, conquer, and move on, it was time for the British army to remain in place for a while, especially in a colony with as many loyalists as South Carolina was reputed to have. If the army could restore order to the extent that the colonists began to enjoy even a portion of the English liberties and economic benefits they had known before the Revolution, perhaps South Carolina could serve as an example to the rest of America. According to a 1780 memorandum in the Germain papers, "[this] would with ease bring about what will never be effected by mere force."

The gist of this new approach was to promote the benefits of British rule by persuasion rather than by conquest. The successful implementation of this plan would have required a general with the demeanor of a diplomat. That was not Lord Cornwallis, whose restless and aggressive temperament was ill suited to the execution of a largely defensive strategy. Given the tremendous distance between his army in the interior of the Carolinas and Clinton in New York, Cornwallis felt free to do as he saw fit. Almost as soon as the commander in chief had sailed from Charleston for New York, his army was on the move. As his young and merciless subordinates (most notably, the cavalry commander Banastre Tarleton) cut a wide and bloody swath across the region, Cornwallis began hatching plans to extend the military presence of the British Empire into North Carolina, even if that left the preexisting outposts in South Carolina dangerously exposed. Tarleton's defeat at Cowpens on January 17 was certainly a setback ("the late affair has almost broke my heart," he admitted), but even the loss of close to a third of his army was not enough to deter him from seizing the offensive. He had to pursue Daniel Morgan's army across the North Carolina border, retrieve his five hundred British prisoners, and then turn his sights on the army of Nathanael Greene to the east on the Pee Dee River in South Carolina. "All was to be risked," wrote Brigadier General Charles O'Hara, who had recently joined the British army in the south, "as the only event that could possibly . . . retrieve our affairs in this quarter was the beating or driving of Greene's army out of the Carolinas." This was completely contrary to the original plan in the region, but it provided Cornwallis with the satisfaction of doing what he did best: attack with little regard for the consequences.

Encouraging Cornwallis in this determination to run wild across the region was the official whose administration had hatched the policy that his lordship was about to abandon: Secretary of State

Germain. The inherent problem with the ministry's southern strategy was that it took time and patience—neither of which made good headlines back in England. It was battles (the more desperately fought the better) that created the impression that progress was being made. Cornwallis might be inviting the same fate that had claimed detach-ments of his army at King's Mountain and Cowpens, but at least he was *doing something.* Henry Clinton, on the other hand, hadn't moved from New York in years. Who cared if he had good reasons for that inactivity (such as the British army's absolute dependence on the navy)? By contrast, Cornwallis had the derring-do. And since it took as many as three to four months for a letter from Clinton in New York to reach him in the interior of the Carolinas, Cornwallis was free to pursue whatever strategy he felt was appropriate, especially since one of his subordinates, who had spoken directly to Germain during a recent trip to England, reported that he had the ministry's support.

Cornwallis hardly looked the part of a swashbuckling risk taker. He was overweight and had a deviated left eye due to an injury as a student at Eton. As his earlier letter to his brother indicated, he was deeply skeptical of Britain's ability to put an end to the American re-bellion. By late January 1781, however, he had embraced a fatalistic determination to give it a try nonetheless. Fueled by his deeply felt sense of loss for his wife and his equally passionate love for his army, and emboldened by the ministry back home, he was about to confront the conundrum that had so far stymied every one of his predecessors: how to subdue a wilderness. While Washington hoped to beat the British by using the French fleet to establish naval superiority on the sea, Cornwallis was determined to take the war into the tangled heart of the enemy's own country.

With every step north, he was putting more distance between his army and its source of supply in Charleston. Although he had hopes of rallying the local loyalists to his cause, he could not ignore the threat posed by the Overmountain Men from the west (the band who had annihilated Major Patrick Ferguson's army at King's Mountain) and the militiamen in Virginia, whom Governor Jefferson and Baron von Steuben were attempting to rally in support of Nathanael Greene. But perhaps the severest challenge Cornwallis faced came from the land itself. Nowhere in eighteenth-century colonial America were the roads as terrible as they were in North Carolina, where, in the words of one frustrated traveler, "the red clay abounds." What roads existed were transformed into "linear bogs" by the relentless winter rains. Soldiers on foot found it easier to walk through the dense undergrowth on either side of a road than wallow in the knee-deep clay; wagon wheels became so clotted with reddish-brown muck that the spokes had to be turned by hand; even horses floundered in the clinging mire. And then there were the many rivers. Since bridges and boats were a rarity, Cornwallis's army would more than likely have to wade across the shallows of long established fords that might be ankle-deep in summer but were waist-high (if not deeper) in winter.

On January 27, as his army paused at Ramsour's Mill on the south fork of the Catawba River, forty miles northwest of Charlotte, North Carolina, Cornwallis decided he and his men must make the ultimate sacrifice. To increase their speed and ease of movement in pursuit of Morgan's army, which was less than twenty miles to the east on the opposite side of the Catawba, they must rid themselves of their "superfluous baggage." All of it—not only the baggage but the wagons that carried it—must be hurled into a huge bonfire.

One can only wonder what was going through the minds of his two thousand or so soldiers as they pitched their belongings into the flames. With this strangely ritualistic, ultimately self-defeating act, Cornwallis had deprived them of what were commonly regarded as essential to an army: food, shelter, and rum. From here on in, they must live off the land, sleep in the rain, and (perhaps the greatest sacrifice of all) remain sober.

Cornwallis later downplayed the magnitude of what he had demanded of his army, insisting in a letter to Germain that his officers and men displayed "the most general cheerful acquiescence" as they watched the billows of smoke rise through the gray rain. General Charles O'Hara, on the other hand, was fully aware of the deprivations that awaited them. "In this situation," he wrote, "without baggage, necessaries, or provisions of any sort for officer or soldier, in the most barren, inhospitable, unhealthy part of North America, opposed to the most savage, inveterate, perfidious, cruel enemy, with zeal and with bayonets only, it was resolved to follow Greene's army to the end of the world."

LIKE HIS BRITISH OPPONENT, Lord Cornwallis, Nathanael Greene, then stationed with the eastern portion of the American army at Cheraw, South Carolina, was acting with only minimal input from his commander in chief. For all intents and purposes, he was operating on his own, and on January 28, the day after Cornwallis burned his baggage train, he committed what his first biographer described as "the most imprudent action of his life." Knowing that the British were in pursuit of Daniel Morgan's prisoner-burdened army in the west, he decided he must leave the main portion of the American army at Cheraw and go to support Morgan. Instructing General Isaac Huger to march the army to a meeting place at the town of Salisbury in the center of North Carolina, he set out with just an aide, a guide, and a sergeant's guard of cavalry. Given the lack of roads and the presence of a significant number of loyalist militiamen, plus the fact that he had more than a hundred miles to cover, Greene ran a high risk of capture. Three days later, however, at 2:30 p.m. on January 31, he rode into Morgan's camp on the eastern bank of the Catawba. That afternoon Greene, Morgan, William Washington (a cavalry officer and distant relative of the commander in chief), and William Davidson, the local militia general, sat down on a log beside the river and conducted an impromptu council of war.

In addition to learning about Cornwallis's decision to burn his baggage train, Greene received tangible proof of just how close the enemy was when a British officer, who may have been Cornwallis himself, was spotted on the opposite bank of the river studying them through a spyglass. Only the extreme depth of the newly risen Catawba (which had just begun to recede after several days of rain) prevented the British from crossing the river and attacking Morgan's tiny and exhausted army.

Greene soon realized he and Morgan had differing ideas about what to do next. There were only about 100 miles between them and the mountains to the west and close to 300 miles of river-ribbed country extending eastward to the coast. Morgan felt their only chance was to retreat into the mountains, where the topography was better adapted to keeping Cornwallis at bay. Heading west would also reduce the number of rivers they needed to cross. For the present, the flooded Catawba was shielding them from the British; however, if they continued to work their way east, the rivers that lay ahead were just as likely to block their path and force a confrontation with the British—exactly the scenario that had led to the Battle of Cowpens. Although Morgan had pulled off a stunning victory in that instance, he knew better than anyone that his army could have just as easily been destroyed on the banks of the impassable Broad River. Morgan, for one, had had enough of rivers.

Greene, in contrast, saw North Carolina's many waterways as a potential asset, especially if his army had boats. Unfortunately, logistical difficulties would make it impossible for General Huger to bring the many flat-bottomed craft built during the army's encampment in Cheraw. That, however, did not prevent boats from working to his army's strategic advantage. They weren't as abundant as they'd been before the war, but watercraft—from canoes to raftlike vessels known as "flats"—could still be found on the rivers of North Carolina. It would require an extraordinary amount of planning and coordination, but with Edward Carrington, his highly capable quartermaster, traveling in advance, Greene was confident they would find the boats they needed to cross each river at a point that was too deep for the British to follow on foot. Assuming they could stay ahead of the enemy (which was a very big assumption), rivers would provide his troops with the opportunity to increase the distance between them and their pursuers.

With this as his guiding principle, Greene proposed they march northeast, meet up with Huger and the main army at Salisbury, and, when the time was right, attack Cornwallis. It would involve a march of more than fifty miles to Salisbury, during which Cornwallis might catch up to them at any time, but it was, Greene felt, worth the gamble, especially since they could always slip across the next river to the east, the Yadkin, if it was in their best interests to avoid a battle.

Morgan was hardly averse to risk, but this, he felt, was simply hazarding too much, and he declared "he would not be answerable for consequences." Many commanding officers in Greene's position would have had difficulty contradicting Morgan, who had just won one of the most decisive victories of the war. But Greene was not to be dissuaded, assuring Morgan that he would "take the measure upon myself." As events soon proved, Greene had hit upon the only strategy capable of buying the time his army needed before it could face the British in battle.

Greene was a pessimist by nature. "I am of the Spanish disposition," he admitted to his wife, Caty, "always most serious when there is the greatest need of good fortune . . . for fear of some ill-fated stroke." Now, however, at what was the most desperate point of the campaign, he projected an aura of quiet confidence, much of it based on his opponent's willingness to turn a blind eye to the logistical realities of supporting an army in the hinterlands of North Carolina. "I am not without hopes of ruining Lord Cornwallis if he persists in his mad scheme of pushing through the country," he wrote to General Huger, who was in motion with the main army to the east, "and it is my earnest desire to form a junction [with you] as soon as possible for this purpose."

Already Morgan had sent ahead his five hundred British prisoners toward Virginia; soon the rest of the army was marching toward Salisbury. It would be left to General William Davidson and his three hundred North Carolina militiamen to prevent the British from crossing the Catawba River for as long as possible.

Cornwallis had camped near Beatty's Ford, which was the most commonly used crossing point in the area. Greene, however, suspected that the British commander actually planned to cross elsewhere. Three miles to the south was Cowan's Ford. The water was deeper and faster-flowing at this portion of the river, but Greene was convinced that Cornwallis's outward interest in Beatty's Ford was only a feint. Davidson should divide his force and place a significant number of men at the ford to the south.

On the way down to Cowan's Ford, William Davidson turned to a twenty-one-year-old captain named Joseph Graham and expressed his astonishment at their commander's knowledge of the region, all of it apparently acquired by looking at a map. "Though General Greene had never seen the Catawba before," he marveled, "he appeared to know more about it than those who were raised on it."

Greene's monthlong study of North Carolina's geography was already proving to be of immense value. If he had his way, there would not be another dramatic battle at the edge of a flooded river. This was to be a war fought in bits and pieces.

EARLY THE NEXT MORNING, events unfolded almost exactly as Greene had anticipated. While a small portion of the British army unleashed an artillery barrage at the militiamen on the east side of Beatty's Ford—a cannonade that soon had every inhabitant within a twenty-five-mile radius on the run—Cornwallis led the rest of his force down the right bank of the river to Cowan's Ford. It was a windless, foggy morning, and as the sound of the cannons rolled down "the river like repeated peals of thunder," the British troops assembled on the edge of the mist-shrouded shore. Ahead of them, the river was a seething torrent of brown, debris-filled water. To prevent being swept off their feet in the current, the soldiers held eight-foot poles in their right hands. In addition to the knapsacks on their backs and the leather cartridge boxes tied around their necks (to keep the gunpowder from getting wet), they carried their bayonet-equipped muskets over their left shoulders. They could see the campfires of the American militiamen on the opposite shore about four hundred yards away. They had to march through the rushing, breast-high water knowing that a steep, overhanging bank was between them and the enemy.

Sergeant Roger Lamb remembered how "Lord Cornwallis, according to his usual manner, dashed first into the river, mounted on a very fine spirited horse." As wave after wave of troops followed in his wake, Cornwallis led them into the deepest part of the river. About halfway across, the enemy began to fire. "Amidst these dreadful oppositions," Lamb remembered, "we still urged through this rapid stream, striving with every effort to gain the opposite shore." At one point the horse of General Charles O'Hara, commander of the elite Brigade of Guards, lost its footing on the rocky bottom. For forty yards, "O'Hara's horse rolled with him down the current." According to Rebel militiaman Joseph Graham, the bodies of several British soldiers were later "found down the river some distance, lodged in fish traps and in the brush about the banks on rocks."

For the most part, however, "our divisions waded on," Lamb remembered, "in a cool intrepid manner." Although Cornwallis's horse was shot at least once during the crossing, the animal managed to stay alive until it reached the water's edge, where it collapsed in a quivering heap. By then the British regulars had reached the shallows and were firing at the militiamen. As more and more regulars climbed the bank, resorting in some instances to pulling themselves up by bushes and the roots of trees, the militiamen's confidence quickly began to erode—especially when their leader, General Davidson, was felled by a musket ball to the heart. Soon the militiamen were running for their lives.

Years later, Nicholas Gosnell, a loyalist serving in the British army, recalled Cornwallis's dramatic arrival on the east bank of the Catawba. The British soldiers were, in Gosnell's colorful words, "a snortin', an hollerin' and a drownin' until his Lordship reached the . . . bank; the Rebels made straight shirt tails and all was silent—then I tell you his Lordship . . . when he rose the bank he was the best dog in the hunt, and not a Rebel to be seen."

. . .

By the time Cornwallis's army assembled on shore, the surrounding roads were crowded with militiamen and families on the run. "Hitching up their teams in great haste," Graham wrote, "and packing up their most valuable goods and some means of subsistence, the men who were not in service and women and children abandoned their homes and drove off in different directions." By the middle of the day, hundreds of refugees, along with dozens of militiamen who'd been posted at the two fords, had gathered at Torrence's Tavern, about ten miles to the east. Torrence's was dangerously close to the British army, but this mixture of citizens and soldiers were so cold and tired that they judged the stop worth the risk. Wagons piled high with mattresses and other household goods jammed the road as pails of whiskey were passed around in the rain.

Into this chaotic scene charged Banastre Tarleton and the British cavalry, crying out "Remember Cowpens!" "The militia fled in every direction," Graham remembered. "Those who were on horseback and kept the roads were pursued about half a mile. Ten were killed, of whom several were old men, unarmed, who had come there in the general alarm, and a few were wounded, all with sabers. . . . On the return of the dragoons from the pursuit, they made great destruction of the property in the wagons . . . ; ripped up beds and strewed the feathers, until the lane was covered with them. Everything else they could destroy was used in the same manner." Soon Torrence's Tavern and all the nearby buildings were in flames.

Through this panicked, shattered land, over roads the color of rain-washed blood, Lord Cornwallis marched in pursuit of Nathanael Greene.

On the following day, February 2, Morgan's men arrived at Salisbury, which served as the state's supply depot for the Continental army. With Cornwallis hot on their heels and unsure of what progress

Huger and the main part of the army had made, Greene now realized he must come up with an alternative place to rendezvous. Between the two American armies was the Yadkin River. At Trading Ford, a day's march to the north, an advance party from the quartermaster's department was already assembling a small fleet of boats to transport the Americans across the river, which was, like the Catawba before it, on the rise. If they could get Morgan's army across the Yadkin by the next night, the swollen river would once again serve as a barrier against the British, especially since Quartermaster Edward Carrington would make certain there was not a boat to be found on the west side of the river. That would give the two American armies the opportunity to meet at a small hamlet to the north called Guilford Courthouse, on the outskirts of modern-day Greensboro.

That night, Greene sent off letters not only to Huger but to political and military leaders throughout the region in an effort to rally the militia at Guilford Courthouse. After Davidson's death at Cowan's Ford and the rout of the militia at Torrence's Tavern, local opposition to the British army had virtually disappeared. If Greene had any hope of defeating Lord Cornwallis, he needed to more than double the size of his army with an infusion of at least two thousand militiamen. Until then, he must get Morgan and his army across the Yadkin.

The following day proved to be yet another brutal slog through the mud, made all the more harrowing by the torrential rain and the knowledge that the British, led by the Guards under General O'Hara, were gaining on them. Late that night, they arrived at Trading Ford. The deluge had raised the water level to a dangerous height and the raging current made it extremely dangerous to navigate a boat across the river. But Greene knew they had no choice but to proceed with the crossing.

By the time O'Hara and his Guards arrived at the banks of the Yadkin at midnight, after a march of twenty miles in knee-deep mud, almost all of Morgan's army had crossed. In fact, O'Hara could see the boats secured on the opposite shore. His frustrations only increased when his men were fired upon by a small group of North Carolina militia that included Captain Graham. After two or three volleys, the militiamen scampered off to the south, eventually crossing the river in canoes they'd concealed in the haw and persimmon bushes at the water's edge. When Cornwallis arrived at Trading Ford several hours later, he ordered the artillery to fire a few ineffectual blasts at the American army on the eastern shore, but the truth was all too apparent. Even though he had burned his army's baggage in a desperate bid to catch Morgan's army before it crossed the Yadkin, the Americans had eluded the British general's grasp.

On his arrival at Guilford Courthouse on February 7, Greene realized that even after the union with Huger's portion of the army (which staggered into camp the following day), he did not have enough men to face Cornwallis. Making matters worse, Daniel Morgan could no longer go on. For weeks he had been tormented by sciatica. But now he had a new complaint—hemorrhoids. "To add to my misfortunes," he wrote to Greene, "I am violently attacked with the piles, so that I can scarcely sit upon my horse. This is the first time that I ever experienced this disorder, and from the idea I had of it, sincerely prayed that I might never know what it was." He must leave the army and find "some safe retreat, and try to recover."

It was a terrible loss. "Great generals are scarce," Greene lamented. "There are few Morgans to be found." No one was better at motivating the undisciplined ranks of the militia than Daniel Morgan, whose back was still crisscrossed by the hundreds of lashes he'd suffered at the hands of a British officer while serving as a wagoner during the Seven Years' War. The night before the Battle of Cowpens, he had walked among his troops and assured them that he "would crack his whip over Ben [Tarleton] in the morning." To his men he was "the Old Wagoner"—a battle-scarred veteran who looked and talked a lot like them. Greene, on the other hand, was more comfortable studying military treatises and maps than swapping tales around the campfire. He possessed an almost godlike ability to sort through the myriad details of feeding, equipping, and moving an army, but he lacked the common touch. He also shared with Washington an oft-repeated distrust of the militia. Both had watched in helpless anger as time and time again during battles in New York, New Jersey, and Pennsylvania, these "irregular troops" had bolted in fear just when they were needed most. But now, in North Carolina, Greene knew he needed the militia if he had any hope of facing Cornwallis in battle. And yet, without Morgan to inspire them, how would he get these farmers and frontiersmen to fight? The Old Wagoner would be dearly missed.

On February 9, Greene held his second council of war. In attendance were Morgan (who would soon be headed home to Virginia), Huger, and Greene's adjutant general, Otho Holland Williams, a thirty-one-year-old from Maryland. So far, the hoped-for influx of militiamen had not yet occurred. It was only a matter of time before Cornwallis, who had crossed the Yadkin to the north and was now securing food for his men among the Moravian communities clustered around Salem, resumed the chase.

Greene hated to do it, but they must continue their retreat—all the way to the Dan River on the Virginia border. Once in that state, he could rebuild the army with reinforcements and equipment provided by General von Steuben and Governor Jefferson in Richmond. Then he would recross the river and go after Cornwallis.

The easiest and closest place to cross the Dan was at Dix's Ferry near modern Danville, Virginia, about seventy miles northeast of the Rebels' current position. That, of course, was where Cornwallis assumed they'd cross. But Greene had found an alternative. About twenty miles downriver of Dix's Ferry, near modern South Boston, Virginia, Quartermaster Carrington and his staff had located six boats. There, at two nearby ferry landings named Boyd's and Irwin's, they would attempt to cross the Dan.

In an effort to conceal his intentions from Cornwallis, Greene created a separate seven-hundred-man flying army, under the command of Otho Williams, which included William Washington's cavalry as well as the newly arrived legion under Henry "Light Horse Harry" Lee. As Greene and the main army of over a thousand soldiers marched toward the downriver fords, Williams and his cavalry would stay to their left in hopes of convincing Cornwallis that Greene was headed upriver. At some point, of course, the British would realize their mistake and set out after the American army. That was when the decoy would become a shield, as Williams and his cavalry placed themselves between Greene and the ever advancing British. The tensest and most critical time would come at the end, after Greene's army had forded the Dan, when the cavalry would have to find a way to cross the river without being overtaken by the hard-charging British vanguard under Banastre Tarleton.

Morgan, Huger, and Williams agreed with Greene's plan, and the next day the American army (minus Morgan) set out on what came to be known as the Race to the Dan.

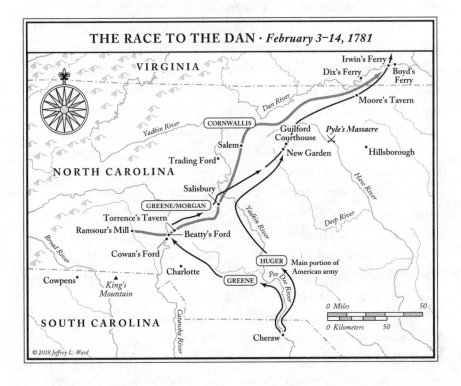

THE RACE TO THE DAN · *February 3–14, 1781*

. . .

EVEN BEFORE THE RACE HAD BEGUN, Cornwallis wasted a day, if not more, on what proved to be a wild goose chase. Hoping to intercept Huger and the main portion of the army before they reached Guilford Courthouse, he pushed his army south, only to learn that Huger had already reunited with Greene and the entire force had left the rendezvous point. Once again, Cornwallis had underestimated the Americans, and he resumed the chase with a furious will.

Over the course of the next four days, as Greene and his army marched toward Irwin's and Boyd's ferries, Otho Williams and his cavalry attempted to draw the attention of the British vanguard without becoming ensnared by it. The biggest threat to the American army existed at night, when it was feared Cornwallis might attempt a forced march that would place him between Williams and Greene, which would enable the British to attack the main portion of the American army without interference from Williams's cavalry. To guard against the maneuver, half of Williams's troops remained on duty each night, requiring that each man averaged only three hours of sleep a day. Finding the time and opportunity to feed themselves was also difficult. Every morning at three o'clock Williams roused his troopers, and after a brief ride to put some extra distance between themselves and the enemy, they stopped for their only meal of the day—a breakfast of cornmeal and bacon.

Despite these precautions, Tarleton's cavalry was able to catch the Americans by surprise in at least one instance, and skirmishes between the two armies were frequent and often bloody. However, as the days clicked past and exhaustion began to set in, the dragoons in the British vanguard, who were often in sight of Lee's rearguard, lost much of their aggressiveness. "The demeanor of the hostile troops became so pacific," Lee wrote, "that a spectator would have been led to consider them members of the same army." Contributing to the passivity of the British was the knowledge that the Americans' horses were larger and healthier than their own. As with the copper-bottomed ships of the British navy, the American cavalry enjoyed a significant speed advantage that allowed them to hover in the face of the British column with impunity. "Only when a defile or a water course crossed our route," Lee remembered, "did the enemy exhibit any indication to cut off our rear. . . . [Soon, however,] their useless efforts were gradually discontinued."

The speed advantage did not apply to Greene's twelve hundred foot soldiers, many of whom had worn out their shoes after more than 250 miles of almost continuous marching. They were tired, but they were also hungry, and one of Greene's greatest challenges was finding a way to provide his army with food. Every night between eleven and twelve, while just about everyone around them was lost to sleep, Greene and his commissary general, William Davie, a North Carolinian graduate of what is now Princeton University, spread out a map and analyzed "the expected movements of the enemy and the positions proposed to be taken by our own army." With his finger on the map, Greene would "observe," Davie remembered, "'if the enemy move in this direction, I must take position there. Can subsidence be procured?'" More often than not, the answer was no. And yet, somehow, Greene, with Davie's help, always seemed to find a way to solve the problem. "His mind naturally of the most firm texture," Davie wrote, "and rich in its own resources never despaired for a moment under these appalling circumstances."

By this time, Cornwallis had begun to realize where Greene was headed. It was now an all-out sprint for the Dan, with fewer than thirty miles between the vanguard of Cornwallis's army and the rear of Greene's, with Williams's cavalry in between. Greene depended on Williams for information about the enemy, and the two officers exchanged several letters a day. Early on February 13, Greene wrote to Williams from Moore's Tavern, about twenty-five miles from the ferry crossings. It was evident that "the enemy intended to push us in crossing the river." That said, Williams must not take any unnecessary risks. "You have the flower of the army," Greene reminded him. "[D]on't expose the men too much, lest our situation should grow more critical."

Williams estimated that Cornwallis's soldiers had advanced to within just twenty-two miles of Greene's army. "Rely on it, my dear sir," Williams wrote to Greene, "it is possible for you to be overtaken before you can cross the Dan even if you had 20 boats." Since Greene had only six watercraft and had marched only eleven miles the previous day, Williams estimated it would take him at least another two days to reach and cross the river. "In less time than that," he warned, "we will be driven into your camp or I must risk the troops I've the honor to command and in doing that I risk everything."

That night, Henry Lee became convinced their worst fears were about to be realized. Up ahead they saw the "numerous fires" of an encampment. "Not a doubt was entertained," he wrote, "that the descried camp was Greene's." The time had come, he and his officers believed, that their "self-sacrifice could alone give a chance of escape to the main body." As it so happened, Williams had just learned of Greene's actual position, about eleven miles to the northeast. The fires must have been left by Greene's army when they abandoned the campsite the previous morning. The time for the dreaded last stand had not yet arrived.

There was no denying, however, that the British were now terrifyingly close to Greene's army. At four the following morning Greene confessed in a letter to Otho Williams that he was preparing for "the worst." He'd slept only four hours in the last four days and was convinced a British officer had been in his camp "the night before last." Had they come all this way only to be overtaken almost within sight of the Dan?

And then, ten hours later, at two p.m. on February 14, Greene finally had some good news to report. After a desperate push for the river, he was at the ferry landing. Most of the army's wagons were already across and the troops were just now piling into the boats.

Three and a half hours later, at 5:30 p.m., Greene wrote that all the troops had crossed, and "the stage is clear." When Williams received Greene's letter at noon the following day, he quickly shared the news with his officers. Henry Lee remembered how the "whole corps became renovated in strength and agility." They immediately set out at a much faster pace, only to realize that the British vanguard was staying right with them. By three that afternoon they were within fourteen miles of the river. In an attempt to stall the British, Williams ordered Lee and his legion "to wait on the enemy," while he and the rest of the cavalry galloped for Boyd's Ferry.

Just before sunset, Williams arrived at the banks of the Dan, where he found Greene waiting for him. By the time Lee's cavalry reached the river, it was almost eight p.m., and the boats were just returning from the northern shore. Once their horses had been "turned into the stream," Lee's dragoons threw their equipment into the boats and followed their horses across the river.

Not until the next morning at daybreak, after driving his army more than forty miles in thirty-one hours, did Lord Cornwallis arrive at the riverbank. Yet again, he had been outgeneraled by Nathanael Greene, whose army had managed to stay ahead of him even though burdened with the supply wagons Cornwallis had opted to burn. Had the deprivations he had inflicted on his men been for naught? In a letter to Germain, he blamed the failure to catch the Americans on faulty intelligence from the loyalists, who had assured him there were not enough boats for an army of Greene's size to cross the lower fords of the Dan.

As he looked across the river at the little fleet pulled up onto the opposite shore, Cornwallis must have realized that it had all come down to boats. Fixated on bringing the Americans to battle, he had failed to take into account the advantage Greene's army enjoyed by being the first to reach each river. By repeatedly securing the inland equivalent of naval superiority, Greene had found a way to lure the British army ever farther toward what Charles O'Hara had called "the end of the world."

Cornwallis was now almost 250 miles from the nearest British base. Greene, on the other hand, had crossed into the safe haven of southern Virginia, where throngs of militiamen were making their way in his direction. But Cornwallis was not about to give up just yet.

He hadn't destroyed Greene's army, but he had forced it out of North Carolina. While the Americans attempted to recruit and rebuild in Virginia, he would rally the Carolina loyalists, who could not help but be encouraged by the Continental army's dramatic exit from their state. If all went according to plan, Lord Cornwallis would more than match Greene's recruitment efforts and be in an even better position to crush the Americans when (and if) they ventured back into North Carolina.

GREENE MADE SURE CORNWALLIS'S recruitment efforts did not go as the British general had hoped. To "repress the meditated rising of the loyalists," Greene sent Lee's regiment of cavalry and the mounted militia under a South Carolinian commander named Andrew Pickens back into North Carolina. Cornwallis had retired fifty miles to the south, to the town of Hillsborough, where he "erected the King's standard and invited by proclamation all loyal subjects to repair to it." Learning that "a considerable body of friends" lived between the Haw and Deep rivers, about twenty miles to the west, he sent Tarleton and his cavalry into the area "to prevent their being interrupted in assembling."

Soon Lee and Pickens were on their way toward Tarleton. The American dragoons under Lee wore green jackets that were almost identical to the ones worn by Tarleton's regiment, and as they rode through the largely loyalist countryside they were hailed by the inhabitants as British saviors, a deception Lee was happy to encourage if it allowed him to approach Tarleton's camp unmolested. They were closing in on their prey when they came upon a group of about four hundred mounted loyalists, under the command of Dr. John Pyle, who were on their way to join Tarleton and who assumed they were being passed by none other than the British cavalry commander himself.

It was almost surreal as the loyalists moved to the side of the path and paused while Lee, at the head of the American cavalry, "passed along the line . . . with a smiling countenance, dropping occasionally expressions complimentary to the good looks and commendable conduct of his loyal friends." It was the same ruse Arbuthnot had played when his fleet arrived at the Chesapeake under the French colors, and Lee remembered how the loyalists "rejoiced in meeting us."

Lee later claimed he had intended to offer the loyalists "exemption from injury" if they agreed to either return home or join his own force. Before he could make the offer, his second in command, Joseph Eggleston, who seems to have been as bewildered as the loyalists as to what was actually going on, asked one of Pyle's men, "To whom do you belong?" (Since the only way to distinguish a loyalist from a patriot was the strip of red he wore in his hat, Eggleston's confusion was understandable.) When the loyalist responded a "friend of his Majesty," Eggleston immediately whacked him over the head with his saber. According to Joseph Graham, who was there that day with Pickens's militia, "That prompted the militia to rush the loyalists and begin slashing."

By the time they were finished, close to a hundred loyalists, whose weapons had been slung over their shoulders when Lee's soldiers began the attack, had been hacked to death, many of them crying out to the end "To the king!" under the mistaken impression they were being attacked by Tarleton's cavalry. The encounter spoke to the terrible savagery of partisan warfare in the south; it also put an end to Cornwallis's recruitment efforts. Militia leader Andrew Pickens was not known for his volubility. ("He would first take the words out of his mouth with his fingers," a friend remembered, "and examine them before he uttered them.") But even Pickens was ebullient in describing what came to be known as Pyle's Massacre. "This affair . . . has been of infinite service," he wrote to Nathanael Greene. "It has knocked up Toryism altogether in this part."

GREENE'S ORIGINAL PLAN had been to remain on the other side of the Dan until the arrival of his expected reinforcements. Certainly his men could use the rest. But the longer he lingered in Virginia, the more he began to worry about Cornwallis's recruitment efforts in North Carolina, Pyle's Massacre notwithstanding. Eventually, he decided that even though he did not yet have enough men to bring the British to battle, his army's presence in the state would be a continued damper on British recruitment. He must follow Lee and Pickens into North Carolina.

Over the course of the next three weeks, Greene and Cornwallis engaged in an exhausting game of hide-and-seek among the winding creeks and rivers of central North Carolina, with the Americans, in the words of Charles O'Hara, "constantly avoiding a general action" and the British "as industriously seeking it." To make sure Cornwallis had no way of knowing where his army was headed next, Greene kept his plans "a profound secret with himself," before moving the army at night. By the middle of March, his men had covered more than 230 miles, marching in two instances an incredible 60 miles a day. Perpetually baffled by Greene's maneuvers, with his own army growing increasingly tired and hungry, Cornwallis cut off the chase and moved his men to the Quaker community of New Garden, where he hoped the many abundant farms would provide his army with much needed sustenance.

From Greene's perspective, the timing could not have been better. By March 11, the last of his reinforcements had arrived from Virginia, swelling his army to 4242 soldiers, more than twice the size of Cornwallis's. The time for the long awaited battle had arrived. Back in February, during the brief pause that preceded the Race to the Dan, he had noticed a promising patch of ground to the west of the village of Guilford Courthouse. There, on a heavily wooded hill through which ran the road from New Garden (just eight miles away), he would await the approach of Lord Cornwallis.

THE BRITISH MARCHED out of New Garden on the morning of March 15. Cornwallis's men had not been able to find the expected provisions and had received no breakfast. Greene's men, on the other hand, had eaten well that morning, and even enjoyed the unexpected gift of a gill (a quarter of a pint) of rum.

Following Morgan's example at Cowpens, Greene had posted his army in three defensive lines. In the very front, where the road from New Garden ran through a recently plowed field before entering the trees at the bottom of the hill, he placed the North Carolina militia behind a rail fence. Since they were the most likely to run in the face of a bayonet charge, the militiamen had been assured they need only fire two volleys at the approaching British before they retreated into the dense woods behind them—the same directive Morgan had given his front line at Cowpens. Four hundred yards up the hill were the Virginia militia. There amid the tall trees and dense undergrowth the British would have a difficult time retaining any semblance of a formation. Assuming the Virginia militia put up a fight, Cornwallis's soldiers would emerge from the woods badly mauled and disoriented, with the American army's most experienced soldiers waiting for them on the other side of an irregularly shaped clearing. At the far edge of this bowl of grass, partially hidden in the trees, would be the Continentals from Delaware, Maryland, and Virginia, who should have the discipline and resolve to put a stop to whatever was left of Cornwallis's army. On either side of the battlefield Greene placed the cavalry, with William Washington to the right and Henry Lee to the left. They were to support the soldiers in between them as the British fought their way, line by line, to the hollow of grass at the top of the hill.

Greene had based the disposition of his army on the template Morgan had created at Cowpens, but there were inevitably some differences. This was a much larger and much more heavily wooded battlefield, which made it impossible for Greene, or anyone else, to see what was actually going on throughout the course of the fighting. At Cowpens, Morgan had ranged about the field and personally intervened as the battle progressed; Greene, astride a horse at the rear of the battlefield, would be unable to adjust the components of his force until the very end, when the British emerged from the trees and faced the Continentals. Greene had created a three-step gauntlet

under the assumption that Cornwallis would do exactly what Tarleton had done at Cowpens and follow the collapsing first line of militia
into the trees. Greene's biggest fear was that instead of attacking their
front, Cornwallis would "change his position and fall upon their
flanks."

He needn't have worried. By the time the battle began with a
twenty-minute cannonade as Cornwallis struggled to assemble a line
long enough to span the entire width of the American front, the British general wanted nothing less than to hurl his beloved army into the
cataclysmic fight of their lives. He later admitted that as he stared
into the margin of the wooded hill, he had no idea of what lay ahead.
From the rumors he'd heard there might be as many as 10,000 American soldiers waiting for his army of just 2000 men. But no matter, his
loyal and well-disciplined men would do whatever was asked of them,
even if it resulted in their complete and utter destruction.

Despite the example of William Howe at Bunker Hill and John
Burgoyne at Saratoga, Cornwallis was fully prepared to offer his army
as a sacrifice to the ministry's continued belief that the rebellion could
be ended with one decisive blow. History has made him synonymous
with the defeat at Yorktown seven months later, but Cornwallis's ultimate undoing was set into motion at 1:30 p.m. on March 15, 1781, when
after chasing the American army across the interior of North Carolina, he ordered his men to charge into Nathanael Greene's trap.

As might have been expected, many of the North Caro-
lina militiamen fled without a fight, but a significant portion of the
Virginia militia held their ground as the woods around Guilford
Courthouse became a smoke-filled glade of deafening sound. "The
roar of musketry and cracking of the rifles were almost perpetual,"
Otho Williams remembered, "and as heavy as any I ever heard." On
the British side, Cornwallis wrote, "The excessive thickness of the
woods rendered our bayonets of little use, and enabled the broken
enemy to make frequent stands with an irregular fire."

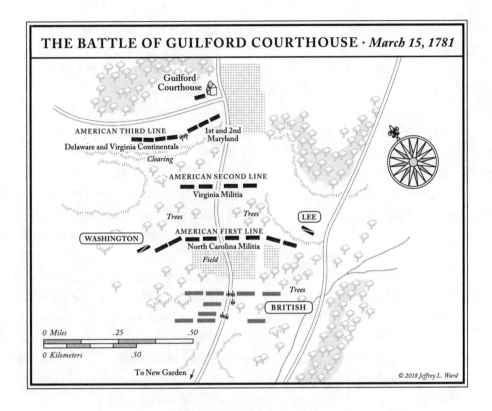

THE BATTLE OF GUILFORD COURTHOUSE · *March 15, 1781*

Guilford
Courthouse

AMERICAN THIRD LINE
Delaware and Virginia Continentals
Clearing
1st and 2nd
Maryland

AMERICAN SECOND LINE
Virginia Militia

Trees   *Trees*   LEE

WASHINGTON
AMERICAN FIRST LINE
North Carolina Militia
Field

Trees

BRITISH

0 Miles   .25   .50
0 Kilometers   .50

To New Garden

© 2018 Jeffrey L. Ward

Sergeant Roger Lamb, like many of the British soldiers, became separated from his regiment in the dense underbrush and smoke. Militiamen were all around him as he bent down to replenish his supply of cartridges from the box of a dead comrade. "I saw Lord Cornwallis riding across clear ground," he remembered, "mounted on a dragoon's horse (his own having been shot); the saddle-bags were under the creature's belly, which much retarded his progress . . . his lordship was evidently unconscious of the danger." Lamb could see Cornwallis was headed directly for the enemy, who were concealed from his view by the trees, and was on the verge of being "surrounded . . . and perhaps cut to pieces or captured." Lamb leapt to his feet, ran to grab the horse's bridle, and led the animal and his disoriented rider away from the militiamen. Cornwallis and Lamb soon came upon Lamb's regiment, the Twenty-third, "drawn up in the skirt of the woods" after an unsuccessful attempt to break the Continental line on the far side of the grassy hollow.

Just minutes before, Lieutenant Colonel James Webster had led the regiment in a mad dash across the open ground, only to discover that a line of American Continentals was waiting for them in the trees on the other side. Sent reeling by the enemy fire, Webster (who sustained what proved to be a mortal injury to his leg) and his men had been forced to retreat back to where Cornwallis and Lamb had found them. Soon they were joined by O'Hara's Guards, who emerged from the trees to their right. O'Hara had also been wounded, so it was left to Lieutenant Colonel Duncan Stuart to lead them on a second attempt to break the Continental line.

Just as had occurred to Webster and the Twenty-third, the Guards, after seizing two of the Rebels' cannons, found themselves just yards from an American regiment, the First Maryland led by Lieutenant Colonel John Eager Howard. "This conflict . . . was most terrific," an American soldier named Nathaniel Slade remembered, "for [the Guards and the First Maryland] fired at the same instant, and they appeared so near that the blazes from the muzzles of their guns seemed to meet." Before the Guards could reload, William Washington and his cavalry burst out of the trees and, "leaping a ravine," plowed into the British. This, Cornwallis realized, was the pivotal moment. If the Guards should be forced to retreat, all would be lost. The British artillery, directed by Lieutenant John McLeod, had just arrived via the road from New Garden. Even though McLeod didn't have a clear shot, Cornwallis ordered him to fire. When Guard commander Charles O'Hara objected, claiming the artillery was likely to kill as many British as American soldiers, Cornwallis insisted they had no other choice if they were to avoid "impending destruction." The cannons fired, soldiers fell on both sides, but disaster was averted when Washington and his cavalry gave up their pursuit.

As it turned out, Greene had already ordered a retreat. Unaware of how close Cornwallis's Guards had come to annihilation and fearful that his own Continentals were about to become surrounded, he made the difficult decision to err on the side of caution rather than risk losing what he had earlier called "the flower" of his army. The British retained the field and could therefore claim victory, but at a terrible cost. "Nearly one half of our best officers and soldiers were either killed or wounded," O'Hara lamented, "and what remains are so completely worn out by the excessive fatigues of the campaign. . . . No zeal or courage is equal to the constant exertions we are making." It didn't actually matter who "won" since Greene had effectively eviscerated Cornwallis's army. In addition, Cornwallis's technical victory helped convince the ministry in England that progress was being made when exactly the opposite was the case, a misapprehension that would lead to the concentration of British troops in Virginia in the months ahead.

That night it began to rain. "I never did and hope I never shall experience such two days and nights as these immediately after the battle," O'Hara wrote. "We remained on the very ground on which it had been fought covered with dead and with dying and with hundreds of wounded, rebels as well as our own." Without tents or food or any way to succor the wounded, an estimated fifty men died before morning. "The cries of the wounded and dying who remained on the field of action during the night exceeded all description," Sergeant Lamb remembered. "Such a complicated scene of horror and distress, it is hoped for the sake of humanity, rarely occurs even in a military life."

Over the course of the days to come, Greene gradually came to realize what he had accomplished. "The action has been long, obstinate, and bloody," he wrote to Joseph Reed in Philadelphia. "The enemy has been so soundly beaten that they dare not move toward us since the action. They have gained no advantage, on the contrary they are little short of being ruined." It had been more than a month of unremitting tension. "I have never felt an easy moment since the enemy crossed the Catawba," Greene admitted. Just a few days before, he'd fainted from exhaustion. Having spent his nights beside a succession of smoky campfires, his eyes had become badly infected. But finally, now that Cornwallis's seemingly invincible army had been all but destroyed, he had found some peace. "Now I am perfectly easy," he wrote, "being persuaded it is out of the enemy's power to do us any great injury."

In the weeks ahead, Cornwallis retreated as far south as the town of Wilmington on the Carolina coast, where provisions could be shipped up from Charleston. "I assure you that I am quite tired of marching about the country in quest of adventures," he wrote to his friend General William Phillips, who had succeeded Benedict Arnold as leader of the British forces in Virginia.

While Cornwallis lingered on the coast, Greene headed into South Carolina. One by one, in the months ahead, he attacked the fortified posts upon which British control of the state depended. Victory on the battlefield once again eluded him, but the sheer pugnacity of his presence eventually forced the British to abandon the state's interior and retreat to Charleston. "We fight, get beat, rise, and fight again," he commented with grim satisfaction.

In the days immediately following the Battle of Guilford Courthouse, Greene wrote to his wife, Caty. After noting that he hadn't "had my clothes [off] for upwards of six weeks" (a complaint perhaps inspired by thoughts of his beautiful wife), he became uncharacteristically optimistic for someone of his naturally pessimistic nature. "I should be extremely happy if the war had an honorable close," he wrote; "and I on a farm with my little family about me. God grant the day may not be far distant when peace with all her train of blessings, shall diffuse universal joy through America."

THE DAY AFTER WASHINGTON learned of the disappointment at Cape Henry, he received word of the Battle of Guilford Courthouse—yet another engagement that had come teasingly close to a victory. There was an important distinction between the two, however. Destouches had decided not to capitalize on his initial victory against Arbuthnot even though the French fleet was, relative to the British, close to full strength. Greene's army, on the other hand, had been more than cut in half by the desertion of the militia, who began fleeing the field even before the battle began. Unlike Destouches, Greene would have been hard-pressed to continue the fight even if he had wanted to. "Although the honors of the field did not fall to your lot," Washington wrote to Greene on April 18, "I am convinced you deserved them. . . . [T]he most flattering prospects may, and often do, deceive us, especially while we are in the power of the militia."

Greene, Washington knew, was determined to avoid the one catastrophic mistake that might mean the destruction of his army. If this careful approach had denied Greene the chance to crush Cornwallis, that was just fine with Washington. "We ought not to look back unless it is to derive useful lessons from past errors and for the purpose of profiting by dear-bought experience," he wrote. "To inveigh against things that are past and irremediable is unpleasing; but to steer clear of the shelves and rocks we have struck upon is the part of wisdom."

CHAPTER 5

The End of the Tether

THE MONTHS OF March and April 1781 were not kind to George Washington. Not only was the war not going particularly well; his family was giving him trouble. His twenty-six-year-old stepson Jacky Custis, a newly elected state legislator, had let it be known he was going to boycott future sessions of the Virginia assembly. Jacky had a history of erratic and infuriating behavior, none of which had diminished his exalted status in the eyes of his mother. Washington had to be careful when it came to his pampered and hotheaded stepson, whom he gently reprimanded with a word of advice: "hear dispassionately and determine coolly."

And then there was Washington's mother, Mary, who seems to have been the only person in the United States unimpressed by the accomplishments of her eldest son. Mary had announced to the world that because of the neglect of her children, she was in need of financial help. There was even talk in the Virginia legislature of setting aside some public money for her support. Deeply humiliated by "a presumptive want of duty on my part," Washington assured his friend Benjamin Harrison that his mother "has not a child that would not divide the last sixpence to relieve her from *real* distress. This she has been repeatedly assured of by me; and all of us, I am certain would feel much hurt at having our mother a pensioner while we had the means of supporting her; but in fact she has an ample income of her own."

Finally there was the case of his cousin Lund Washington, whom he'd left in charge of Mount Vernon. In April the British sloop of war *Savage* sailed up the Potomac, burning plantations everywhere it went. Mount Vernon, however, had been saved, largely because Lund provided the enemy with food and drink. Washington was outraged. "It would have been a less painful circumstance to me," he wrote, "to have heard that in consequence of your non-compliance with their request, they had burnt my house and laid the plantation in ruins. You ought to have considered yourself as my representative, and should have reflected on the bad example of communicating with the enemy."

While Mount Vernon had been saved, Washington had lost seventeen slaves to the British, who had offered them freedom if they chose to desert their master. Although Washington claimed to have already resigned himself to both "the destruction of my houses" and "the loss of all my Negroes," that did not prevent him from doing everything possible in the years ahead to recapture the slaves he had lost. For Washington in the spring of 1781, the *Savage*'s appearance on the Potomac was a source of embarrassment not because of the dubious light it cast on his own role as the supposed champion of American liberty and freedom, but because his cousin had dared to pander to the enemy.

These personal matters were distressing, but as his correspondence that spring makes clear, it was the setback suffered at the Battle of Cape Henry that hurt the most. "The failure of this expedition . . . is much regretted," he wrote to John Laurens, the former aide-de-camp who was now in France attempting to secure an urgently needed loan. Not only had Destouches's unconsummated mission against the British fleet and ultimately Arnold wasted precious resources, it had raised and then dashed the country's expectations just when "we stood in need of something to keep us afloat. . . . Without a foreign loan, our present force (which is but the remnant of an army) cannot be kept together this campaign." Washington went on to list some of the other challenges facing the country and its exhausted army (such as Congress's inability to exert "a controlling interest over the states"), then stopped himself. "But why need I run into the detail when it may be declared in a word that we are at the end of our tether and that now or never our deliverance must come."

One can only wonder how, after six years of war, after so many disappointments, both personal and professional, Washington was able to go on. As his letter to Laurens reveals, the prospect of "a superior fleet" from the French was all that he had left. "Alas!" he wrote wistfully, "The ruin of the enemy's schemes would then be certain; the bold game they are now playing would be the means to effect it for they would be reduced to the necessity of concentrating their force at capital points, thereby giving up all the advantages they have gained in the Southern States, or be vulnerable everywhere."

His attention that winter had been directed toward the Chesapeake, but Washington had far grander ambitions for the spring and summer. Assuming the French could once again achieve naval superiority, he saw New York, not the Chesapeake, as the prize that might force the British government to renounce its claim on the American colonies. He estimated that there were approximately ten thousand British soldiers in New York—almost five times the size of the enemy force currently in Virginia. Assuming the states provided him with even a portion of the recruits he'd requested and the French fleet appeared at the harbor entrance at Sandy Hook, he would then be in a position to combine with Comte de Rochambeau's army and take New York. Even if circumstances ultimately prevented him from attacking the city, the presence of a strong allied army outside New York would force the enemy to divert troops away from Virginia. "The most powerful diversion that can be made in favor of the Southern states," he insisted to the Virginian Benjamin Harrison, "will be a respectable force in the neighborhood of New York." He would send

Lafayette's small army of less than a thousand soldiers (who were now in Baltimore) to Virginia, but that was all.

It was true the majority of the fighting was occurring in the south. But with the enemy's forces divided between Virginia and the Carolinas into two armies of about two thousand soldiers each, there simply wasn't, as of yet, the opportunity for a French-American victory of sufficient magnitude to end the war.

Five hundred and fifty miles to the south of Washington's headquarters on the Hudson, in Wilmington, North Carolina, Lord Cornwallis was about to make a decision that changed all that.

HE HAD GAINED GREAT HONOR at Guilford Courthouse, but he had destroyed his army. By retreating all the way to the Carolina coast at Wilmington, he had left the interior open to Nathanael Greene, who was now working his methodical way from post to post as he attempted to dismantle what remained of British rule in South Carolina.

Cornwallis could have loaded his footsore army into a small fleet of transports and sailed for Charleston. There he could have personally led the defense of South Carolina. But like John Burgoyne before him, he judged any move that might be perceived as a retreat to be "disgraceful." He must resume the offensive, this time in Virginia.

It was exactly what George Germain and the rest of the ministry in London wanted to hear, but as Henry Clinton in New York and William Phillips in Virginia realized, the summer was no time to initiate any kind of offensive operation in the Tidewater. First of all, there was the heat, which made active military operations virtually impossible in July and August. Yes, the region's many wide and navigable rivers were, as Cornwallis maintained in a letter to Henry Clinton, "advantageous to an invading army," but as Benedict Arnold had discovered, those same rivers meant that Virginia remained vulnerable to attack from the sea. Until a defensible naval base was established in the

Chesapeake (which had been the original objective behind Arnold's and now Phillips's missions), the Tidewater was a very dangerous place for the British army.

And besides, what, exactly, would an offensive war in Virginia accomplish that had not already been attempted elsewhere? As Cornwallis had just proven in North Carolina—and had been proven time and again over the last six years, at Bunker Hill, Long Island, Brandywine, Germantown, Charleston, and Camden—even the most heroic of British victories did little to win the support of the people if nothing was done to ensure the security of the loyalists after the British army left to fight in another part of the country. The cumulative effect of "taking possession of places at one time and abandoning them at another" was to disaffect the loyalists and embolden the patriots to the point that it would have been better if the British army had never made an appearance in the first place. Admiral Samuel Graves, who had been in Boston for the Battle of Bunker Hill, likened the movements of the British army to "the passage of a ship through the sea whose track is soon lost." In this instance, the absence of a strong federal government actually worked to America's advantage. Broken up into thirteen largely self-sufficient entities, the United States was a segmented political organism that was almost impossible for the British army to kill.

Even Cornwallis had to admit to the futility of what he had attempted in North Carolina. But that did not mean "the experiment" could not be attempted somewhere else. Increasingly fanatical in his determination to bring the Americans to battle, he convinced himself that Virginia was where the final apocalyptic encounter of the war should be fought. In fact, if he had his way, virtually all of His Majesty's forces in North America would be diverted to the Tidewater. "If we mean an offensive war in America," he asserted, "we must abandon New York and bring our whole force into Virginia. We then have a stake to fight for, and a successful battle may give us America." To cede New York back to the enemy after an almost five-year occupation was, of course, absurd. These were not the words of an officer soberly attempting to further the interests of Great Britain; these were the wild and exaggerated claims of a punch-drunk brawler looking for one last fight.

At this late stage of the war, with the Americans, to use Washington's phrase, at the end of their tether, it behooved the British simply to wait it out until the high cost of this protracted war forced the French to the negotiating table at the end of the year. Instead, the fortunes of the Empire were in thrall to a dangerously reckless field general who defiantly disregarded the perils presented by the sea. A forceful commander in chief might have contained Cornwallis. Not Henry Clinton, who might quibble halfheartedly about his subordinate's aggressiveness but had so far refused to take any steps to curb his behavior. In truth, Clinton's hands were tied by the ministry's enthusiasm for whatever Cornwallis wanted to do. "I am very well pleased to find Lord Cornwallis's opinion entirely coincides with mine," Germain enthused to Clinton, "of the great importance of pushing the war on the side of Virginia with all the force that can be spared until that province is reduced."

Cornwallis had become the increasingly desperate embodiment of Germain's and the king's determination to win the war at all costs. He must leave Wilmington as soon as possible, he announced, before "the return of General Greene to North Carolina . . . put a junction with General Phillips out of my power." But that was not the real reason he needed to depart in such a hurry. It had come to his attention that a vessel was on its way from Charleston bearing dispatches from Henry Clinton. Having spent the winter doing exactly as he pleased, he was not about to be overruled by his superior. So on April 25, knowing that the dispatches were due any day, Cornwallis began the long march to Virginia.

FOR THE MARQUIS DE LAFAYETTE, who had reunited with his detachment in Maryland after the failure of the Destouches expedition and was about to head back into Virginia, this was personal.

Twenty-one years before, on August 1, 1759, when he was not yet two years old, a cannonball fired from the battery directed by the present commander of the British forces in Virginia, Major General William Phillips, had killed his father at the Battle of Minden in Prussia. "General Phillips's battery at Minden having killed my father," he wrote to Nathanael Greene from Baltimore on April 17, "I would have no objections to contract the latitude of his plans."

Eight days later Lafayette and his army were in Fredericksburg; five days after that they were in Richmond, just in time to prevent Phillips and his force of 2300 regulars from taking the city. That he accomplished this with an army he estimated to be just a third of the enemy's caused him infinite delight. "Phillips is my object," he wrote to Washington, "and if with less than a thousand men I can oppose three thousand in this state, I think I am useful to General Greene."

Greene was indeed grateful for whatever Lafayette could do to keep the farms and manufacturing centers in Virginia producing the provisions and equipment on which his army in South Carolina depended. But he also knew the young marquis had to be careful. "I have only one word of advice to give you," Greene wrote to Lafayette on May 1, "that is not to let the love of fame get the better of your prudence and plunge you into a misfortune in too eager a pursuit after glory. This is the voice of a friend, and not the caution of a general." Doing his best to contain his naturally impetuous personality, Lafayette studiously avoided the confrontations that might mean the annihilation of his little army.

By early May, Phillips had moved his army to Petersburg, Virginia, in anticipation of the arrival of Lord Cornwallis from the south. "When I look to the left," Lafayette wrote to the Chevalier de la Luzerne, the French minister in Philadelphia, "there is General Phillips with his army and absolute command of the James River. When I turn to the right, Lord Cornwallis's army is advancing as fast as it can go to devour me, and the worst of the affair is that on looking behind me I see just 900 Continental troops and some militia . . .

never enough not to be completely thrashed by the smallest of the two armies that do me the honor of visiting."

Although some relief was on the way (General Anthony Wayne was marching south from Pennsylvania with an army about the size of Lafayette's), the marquis knew that once the two British armies had combined he would be powerless to prevent Cornwallis's troops and Tarleton's cavalry from rampaging across Virginia. Outnumbered and outgunned, all he could do was exactly what Greene had done during the Race to the Dan: stay out of Cornwallis's way until the time was right to meet the British general under more favorable circumstances. What he never could have imagined in the spring of 1781 was how favorable those circumstances would ultimately be.

O N   M AY   13, Washington learned of the long awaited return of Rochambeau's son. Not only did the Vicomte de Rochambeau have the latest word from France, he was accompanied by the new commander of the French naval forces in Newport, the Comte de Barras. It was time, at long last, for Rochambeau and Washington to discuss the coming campaign. Since the Connecticut state legislature was in session in Hartford (where the two generals had met the year before), a meeting was arranged for May 22 at the home of Joseph Webb in the nearby town of Wethersfield.

Washington had suffered through a difficult spring, but so had Rochambeau. In April the British had published Washington's letter criticizing the Destouches expedition. Then came the news from France—almost all of it unsatisfactory. After a great deal of deliberation, the ministers in Versailles had decided not to provide Rochambeau with the promised second division of soldiers, meaning that the force under his command would remain at half of what it should have been according to the original plan. This did not mean the ministers had lost confidence in him; quite the opposite, in fact, for he also learned that if he had been in France that winter the king would have, in all likelihood, appointed him minister of war. Unfortunately, this news only made his present situation in America all the more galling. In addition, many of his officers had been writing letters to their friends in France criticizing him. According to the Duc de Lauzun, Rochambeau was infuriated to learn that those "whom he had treated most kindly had by no means spared him in their letters."

There was, however, some positive news. In lieu of soldiers, the French government would provide the Americans with a gift of six million livres; it wasn't as much as John Laurens had wanted, but it was at least something. There was also the promise of significant naval support. In a confidential message that he was instructed not to share with Washington, Rochambeau learned that in March the newly promoted Comte de Grasse had sailed from Brest with a large fleet of warships bound for Martinique. When combined with the French ships of the line already in the Caribbean and those at Newport, France should be able to attain naval superiority in American waters when de Grasse sailed north in July or August to escape hurricane season. Where he was to meet up with the French and American land forces was left to de Grasse's discretion; however, the French ministers had already indicated they had little enthusiasm for an operation against New York. Not only did the sandbar at the harbor mouth present a problem for the French ships (which tended to be deeper drafted than the enemy's), the British had spent the last five years fortifying the city. No matter how large a force Washington and Rochambeau were able to put together (and they needed a force at least twice the size of the British army's to make the attack feasible), it was likely to result in a long and bloody siege, and time was not on the allies' side.

The French ministers had included a disturbing caveat in their letters to Rochambeau. If, despite Washington's best efforts, the American army should start to fall apart, thus eliminating any hope of a successful campaign, Rochambeau should use de Grasse's fleet to transport his army to the Caribbean. The resulting scene in Newport as the French soldiers were loaded into the ships, and America was left to return to the British Empire, can only be imagined. No wonder the French government wanted Rochambeau to keep the particulars of de Grasse's fleet a secret for as long as possible.

That the French commander in chief saw the collapse of the American war effort as a distinct possibility is indicated by the testimony of the Marquis de Beauvoir Chastellux, the highly educated major general and writer who, in the absence of Lafayette, would serve as Washington's translator at Wethersfield. According to Chastellux, Rochambeau "sees everything darkly . . . , never *foreseeing* anything but a total defection on the part of the Americans." Given how events ultimately turned out, there has been a tendency to portray Rochambeau as Washington's ideal helpmate: the benign and fatherly general who worked from the start to ensure the independence of the United States. In truth, the French general had grave doubts about the Americans' ability to finish what they had started. (Henry Clinton's spies claimed Rochambeau was "utterly against the American Alliance," while Chastellux insisted that "he has taken an aversion to this whole country.") Already, Rochambeau and Washington had worked at cross-purposes during the planning of the failed Destouches expedition, and despite mutual protestations to the contrary, both inevitably brought a sense of wariness and distrust to the meeting in Wethersfield. Instead of the glorious melding of two patriotic spirits, this was to be the collaboration that triumphed in spite of itself.

WASHINGTON, it turned out, had a mole within Rochambeau's staff. The Marquis de Beauvoir Chastellux had been greatly impressed by Washington ever since first meeting him in November. As his comments about Rochambeau suggest, Chastellux feared his commander lacked the necessary enthusiasm for America. He must provide Washington with access to the information Rochambeau (and the French government) refused to make available. "As my zeal for your country and my attachment for Your Excellency knows no limits," he wrote on May 12, "I hazard a step that may be conceived as a transgression, acting but an under part in the French army, but I rely on the secrecy of your excellency, as one of [your] numerous virtues." Chastellux then proceeded to inform Washington that "a large fleet of 26 ships of the line sailed from Brest, March 22, bound for the West Indies." When they met in Wethersfield, "I should be glad to have some private conversation with Your Excellency, but we must avoid giving suspicion of a peculiar [impression]." In other words, Washington must conceal all evidence of knowing anything about de Grasse's fleet; he must also, Chastellux instructed, "burn this letter," a request that Washington chose to ignore.

He may have been well intentioned, but Chastellux, like most informants, had an inflated sense of his own importance. Other than placing Washington in a tremendously awkward position, Chastellux had done little to prepare the American commander in a constructive way for the negotiations ahead. Washington was thankful for whatever information he could get, but he also did not want to imperil his relationship with Rochambeau. As events subsequently revealed, one of his greatest strengths was his ability to keep his own counsel amid the building cacophony of increasingly urgent and often contradictory appeals.

THE CONFERENCE BEGAN AWKWARDLY when Washington learned that de Barras was not able to attend. The appearance of some British warships off Block Island required the admiral to remain in Newport. Given that problems of communication had plagued the previous French naval expedition from the start, this was not a good sign, particularly when Washington learned that de Barras claimed he did not have enough ships to transport Rochambeau's army by water.

In his memoirs, Rochambeau depicted Washington as stubbornly attached to the concept of attacking New York despite the obvious problems with the plan and the just as obvious advantages of looking to Virginia. However, it would be another two months before Cornwallis took up the position at the tip of an isolated point that made the

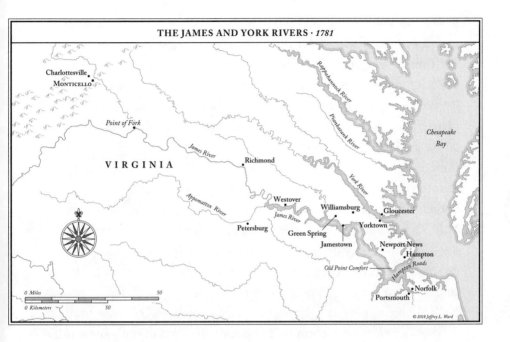

THE JAMES AND YORK RIVERS · *1781*

Charlottesville
MONTICELLO
Point of Fork
Rappahannock River
Pianbatank River
Chesapeake
Bay
James River
VIRGINIA
Richmond
York River
Westover
Williamsburg
Gloucester
Appomattox River
James River
Yorktown
Petersburg
Green Spring
Jamestown
Newport News
Hampton
Old Point Comfort
Hampton Roads
Norfolk
Portsmouth
0 Miles   50
0 Kilometers   50
© 2018 Jeffrey L. Ward

victory at Yorktown possible. The appearance of a large French fleet while the British general was still ranging about the interior of the Tidewater would, in all likelihood, have done little more than force him to retreat into North Carolina. Clinton, on the other hand, dug in at New York, had nowhere to go. It is only hindsight that makes Rochambeau's early preference for the Chesapeake look so prescient. Without the help of Cornwallis, the Chesapeake gambit would have never unfolded as it did. In late May of 1781, Washington was completely justified in his preference for New York.

And besides, given France's three-year history of failure in providing naval superiority, Washington had reason to wonder whether he would ever see a large French fleet on the North American coast. As he had learned to his repeated regret, the vagaries of wind and weather, along with a lack of resolve on the part of a naval commander, could make even the most assured prospect of success come to nothing. If a superior French fleet was unlikely and de Barras was unwilling to transport any soldiers by water, the only option Washington had was to mass as many soldiers as possible around New York in the hope of taking some of the pressure off Lafayette in Virginia.

It must have been an infuriating exercise on Washington's part as Rochambeau expressed doubts about New York and yet provided no legitimate reason to believe that Virginia was a better option. Ultimately, they agreed that given "the insurmountable difficulty and expense of land transportation—the waste of men in long marches (especially where there is a disinclination to the service, objections to the climate, etc.) with other reasons too numerous to detail," their only option, at this time, was "to commence an operation against New York." It was also agreed that Rochambeau's army would begin marching south from Rhode Island as soon as possible while de Barras (for reasons of safety) moved his fleet from Newport to Boston until his ships were needed to support the joint American-French force in New York. If conditions should change, however, Washington agreed it might be in their best interests "to extend our views to the southward."

WHEN WASHINGTON RETURNED to the "plain Dutch house" that served as his headquarters in New Windsor, he discovered that his wife, Martha, who had been with him since the beginning of the year, had grown dangerously ill. Although her condition improved in the weeks ahead, Washington remained concerned about her health. "Her complaint was in the stomach, bilious," he wrote to her son Jacky, "and now turned to a kind of jaundice; but she is better than she has been, though still weak and low." He had a favor to ask his stepson: "As she is very desirous of seeing you, and as it is about the period for her returning to Virginia, I should be glad if it does not interfere with any important engagements if you could make her a visit." Jacky did have "important engagements," and his sick mother would have to fend for herself.

Word of Martha's illness prompted the widow of a British paymaster in New York (in whose house the Washingtons had lived at the beginning of the war) to send a selection of fruits and "hyssop tea" to assist in her recovery. To avoid a repeat of the *Savage* incident and be accused of accepting special treatment from the enemy, Washington felt compelled to return the gifts to New York. Not until the end of June would Martha be well enough to begin the journey back to Virginia, accompanied by Dr. James Craik, their family doctor from Alexandria who now served as a physician general in the Continental army.

IN THE IMMEDIATE AFTERMATH of the meeting in Wethersfield, Washington wrote letters to the states' political leaders requesting the soldiers he needed for a siege of New York. "Our allies in this country expect, and depend upon being supported by us in the attempt we are about to make," he warned, "and those in Europe will be astonished should we neglect the favorable opportunity which is now before us." Much as he'd done around the time of the Destouches expedition, Washington sent out letter after letter to a wide range of friends and political leaders, this time detailing the plans to attack New York. And just as happened in the earlier instance, the British intercepted several of those letters. Given the unlikelihood of the French fleet appearing any time soon, there was nothing to be lost and everything to be gained by letting Henry Clinton know a combined French and American operation against New York was in the offing. Just as Washington intended, the British commander subsequently ordered the withdrawal of a significant number of soldiers from Virginia to New York. He would get no credit for it from the politicians in his home state, but Washington was doing everything he possibly could on their behalf.

Soon after his return to Newport, Rochambeau had second thoughts about one of the stipulations of the Wethersfield conference. Rather than move de Barras's squadron to Boston (as had been decided at Wethersfield), the ships should remain in Newport, where they would be closer to the ultimate scene of action, whether it be in New York or Virginia. To change one of the central tenets of the agreement so soon after the conference was guaranteed to anger the already disgruntled American commander, especially since it would require a significant number of American militia to remain in Newport manning the town's fortifications once the French army marched south. According to the Duc de Lauzun, who delivered Rochambeau's letter to Washington, the proposal "put him in such a rage that he refused to answer it." Eventually, of course, Washington had to respond. "I must adhere to my *opinion*," he wrote, "and to the plan which was fixed at Wethersfield as most eligible, all circumstances considered." That said, he knew he had no choice other than to do whatever the French decided, and to no one's surprise, the French fleet remained in Newport.

Adding to the humiliation of being a commander in chief in name only was Rochambeau's continued refusal to provide him with any information regarding the whereabouts of de Grasse's fleet. Why all this mystery, Washington couldn't help but wonder, if France really had the United States' best interests at heart? There even were those, such as Washington's friend George Mason in Virginia, who suspected that the French were purposely holding back naval support with the intention of "spinning out the war." The longer the war dragged on, Mason maintained, the more dependent the fledgling United States would be upon France once her independence was ultimately won. "France sure intends the separation of the states forever from Great Britain," he wrote; "but by drawing out the thread too fine and long, it may unexpectedly break in her hands."

On June 7, Washington received a newspaper account of Admiral de Grasse's recent activities in the waters surrounding Martinique, which he immediately forwarded to Rochambeau's headquarters in Newport. Now that Washington had irrefutable proof that a large French naval force had long since arrived in the Caribbean, Rochambeau had no choice but to confess to knowing much more than he had so far revealed. Yes, Rochambeau admitted, he had been in correspondence with de Grasse, but not to worry, he had been careful to communicate everything he and Washington had discussed in Wethersfield. "I have apprized him," he assured the Virginian, "that the only means which seem practicable to your Excellency is a diversion upon New

York." What he chose not to tell Washington was that the French general had also made it clear that he did not necessarily agree with his American counterpart. "The southwesterly winds and the state of distress in Virginia will probably make you prefer Chesapeake Bay," Rochambeau had written to de Grasse on May 28, "and it will be there where we think you may be able to render the greatest service."

This was, of course, completely contrary to what he and Washington had agreed to. In his letter to Washington, Rochambeau felt compelled to at least hint at what he had actually written. "I have [also] spoken to him of the enemy's naval forces and told him that by reason of the constant [southerly] wind, I thought it would be a great stroke to go to the Chesapeake Bay in which he can make great things against the naval forces that will be there, and then the wind could bring him in two days . . . [to] New York."

For Washington, it must have felt like the Destouches expedition all over again: No matter what he said, the French were going to do exactly as they pleased. And yet, with so much at stake, now was not the time to surrender to his mounting anger and frustration. "Your Excellency will be pleased to recollect," Washington reminded Rochambeau, "that New York was looked upon by us as the only practicable object under present circumstances; but should we be able to secure a naval superiority, we may perhaps find others more practicable and equally advisable." Washington's fear was that by going to the Chesapeake first, as Rochambeau suggested, de Grasse would lose the element of surprise he might enjoy "by coming suddenly" to New York, where "he would certainly block up any fleet which might be within; and he would even have a very good chance of forcing the entrance before dispositions could be made to oppose him."

What concerned Washington most in the spring of 1781 was not *where* they were going to attack, since "it could not be foreknown where the enemy would be most susceptible of impression," but how he and Rochambeau were going to get the allied army there. It was his assumption that "having command of the water with sufficient means of conveyance . . . , [the French fleet] could transport ourselves to any spot with the greatest celerity." This—the ability to transport the Continental and French armies by water—was, from Washington's perspective, the key component to victory. That was how the British had taken both New York and Charleston and how Benedict Arnold had ravaged Virginia—by transporting their armies with lightning speed to wherever the enemy was open to attack. No matter what part of the country proved to be the enemy's "most vulnerable quarter," the French fleet should first sail to Sandy Hook at the entrance to New York harbor, where de Grasse could embark at least a portion of the allied army.

Making it increasingly difficult for Washington to insist that Rochambeau adhere to their mutually agreed plan was the realization that he was not going to receive anywhere near the number of recruits he had requested from the states. Unable to hold up his end of the bargain, he was in no position to loftily chastise his ally, especially if that ally could make up for the American troop deficit with French soldiers from the Caribbean. The campaign ahead might not unfold as he wished, but that, he had long since learned, was the way of the world. As he'd written five years before, at the conclusion of the Siege of Boston, which ended not with the attack on the city he had yearned for but with the anticlimactic placement of several cannons atop Dorchester Heights, "I will not lament or repine at any act of Providence, because I am in a great measure a convert to [the poet] Mr. Pope's opinion that whatever is, is right."

By the time Cornwallis arrived in Petersburg, Virginia, General William Phillips had died of a fever, his last days made even more miserable than they otherwise might have been by the cannonballs that kept ripping through the house in which he lay. Lafayette wasn't aware of it at the time, but by ordering his artillery to fire on Petersburg from the opposite shore of the Appomattox River, he had succeeded in exacting at least a measure of revenge on the man who had killed his father.

With the conjunction of the two British armies, along with the addition of some recently arrived reinforcements, Cornwallis now had somewhere in the neighborhood of seven thousand soldiers in Virginia, making his force more than two-thirds the size of Clinton's army in New York. Virginia was renowned for its horses, and Tarleton quickly equipped his four hundred dragoons with the finest mounts he could find. "We have everything to fear from their cavalry," Lafayette wrote. "They will overrun the country and our flanks; our stores, our very camp will be unsecure." When Cornwallis learned that Lord Rawdon had beaten Nathanael Greene's larger army at Hobkirk's Hill near Camden, South Carolina, and that three British regiments had recently sailed from Ireland for Charleston, the news, Tarleton remembered, "eased his anxiety for South Carolina and gave him brilliant hopes of a glorious campaign [in Virginia]."

The first order of business was to destroy Lafayette's army before it could link up with Anthony Wayne's force on its way south from Pennsylvania. "The boy," Cornwallis reportedly boasted, "cannot escape me." But Lafayette, who had absorbed the counsel of both Greene and Washington, was not about to subject his little army to unnecessary risk.

For Cornwallis, it must have been frustratingly reminiscent of his pursuit of Greene's army in North Carolina. He might burn and destroy everything in his path as he pursued Lafayette toward Fredericksburg to the north, where the French leader hoped to meet Wayne, but his prey always remained out of reach.

Part of Cornwallis's problem was self-created. This was no longer the lean, fast-moving army he had led in North Carolina. Ever since the retreat to Wilmington, he had encouraged his officers and men to acquire as many horses and escaped slaves (who were enlisted as servants) as they wanted. By the time Cornwallis's force had combined with Phillips's, the British army in Virginia resembled what Hessian captain Johann Ewald described as "a wandering Arabian or Tartar horde." When he first saw Cornwallis's army, Ewald was so stunned by its unmilitary appearance that he "could not grasp it. . . . Every officer had four to six horses and three or four Negroes, as well as one or two Negresses for cook and maid. . . . Every soldier had his Negro, who carried his provisions and bundles." This meant that behind the army of seven thousand soldiers and their baggage train followed what Ewald estimated to be at least four thousand former slaves. "Any place this horde approached was eaten clean," he wrote, "like an acre invaded by a swarm of locusts. . . . I wondered as much about the indulgent character of Lord Cornwallis as I admired him for his military abilities. I wished I could reconcile these qualities." As Ewald sensed, something inside the British general had snapped since the bloody encounter at Guilford Courthouse.

Making matters worse was the notorious southern heat, which Ewald described as "so unbearable that many men have been lost by sunstroke or their reason has been impaired . . . , [our clothes] soaked as with water from the constant perspiration. The nights are especially terrible, when there is so little air that one can scarcely breathe." Add to that "the torment of several billions of insects, which plagued us day and night," and Cornwallis had reason to regret his decision to move the war into Virginia.

The British general might have been having second thoughts, but that did not prevent him from continuing to ravage the Virginia countryside. Not only did his soldiers burn and loot; in more than one instance they also raped and murdered, inevitably spreading fear and hatred everywhere they went. "We have made people miserable by our presence," Ewald wrote in disgust. "So, too, have we constantly deceived the loyally-disposed subjects by our freebooting expeditions, and yet we still want to find friends in this country!"

By early June, Cornwallis had given up his pursuit of Lafayette and begun a gradual movement down the James River toward Williamsburg. As a kind of parting shot, he sent his cavalry in the opposite direction on a two-pronged lightning strike. The state legislature had recently relocated to Charlottesville, which was thought to be a safe enough distance from the British army. Cornwallis ordered Tarleton to ride to Charlottesville and round up as many of the legislators as he could find, including the outgoing governor, Thomas Jefferson, whose home of Monticello stood on a nearby hill. At the same time, John Graves Simcoe, leader of the Queen's Rangers, headed to Point of Fork on the James, where General von Steuben and a detachment of soldiers guarded a magazine of valuable military stores.

Riding seventy miles in just twenty-four hours, Tarleton and 180 dragoons captured eight legislators and came within minutes of seizing Jefferson. The governor's popularity had plummeted since his lackadaisical response to the appearance of Benedict Arnold in January. His subsequent decision to retire from office just when his state needed him the most caused the legislature to launch an investigation into his conduct as governor.

Neither would it be von Steuben's finest hour. Rather than confront Simcoe's smaller force, he abandoned the magazine in a hasty retreat that only confirmed the reputation for ineffectual bluster he had already acquired. "The baron is so *unpopular*," Lafayette lamented several days later, "that I do not know where to put him."

Virginia was in turmoil, but Lafayette recognized the ultimate futility of Cornwallis's depredations in the state. "You can be entirely calm with regards to the rapid marches of Lord Cornwallis," he wrote in a letter intercepted by the British. "Let him march from St. Augustine to Boston. What he wins in his front, he loses in his rear. His army will bury itself," he predicted, "without requiring us to fight him."

While Lafayette saw Cornwallis's campaign in Virginia for what it was, this did not apply to many of the state's leading citizens, who feared that in the vacuum left by Jefferson's departure, and with the legislature temporarily unable to meet because of Tarleton's surprise attack, only George Washington could save their state from ruin.

It began with a direct appeal from Virginia's outgoing governor, who insisted "your appearance among [your countrymen] I say would restore full confidence in salvation. . . . [T]he difficulty would then be how to keep them out of the field." Even Richard Henry Lee, one of Washington's political enemies, claimed "that your personal call would bring into immediate exertion the force and recourse of this state and its neighboring one." Lee went so far as to suggest that Washington be "possessed of dictatorial powers," a far cry from the days of the Conway Cabal back in 1778, when Lee and a number of delegates to the Continental Congress talked of replacing the beleaguered general with Horatio Gates.

It was the Temptation of George Washington: the offer to return to the homeland he hadn't seen in six years as a general with supreme political power. Adding to the urgency of the situation were the recent reports from Europe of a proposed peace conference between France and Britain. Once the two European powers agreed to an armistice, the reports claimed, the thirteen former colonies would be divided between the United States and Great Britain on the basis of *uti possidetis,* meaning that each side kept whatever territory its army controlled at the time peace was declared. Since the British presently occupied Charleston, New York, and parts of modern Maine, those would go to the enemy, but so, too, might Virginia. "From the most recent European intelligences," Washington believed the British were "endeavoring to make as large seeming conquests [in Virginia so] that they may urge the plea of *uti possidetis* in the proposed mediation." In the likely event of negotiations at the end of the year, he stood to lose his home at Mount Vernon. And with several bastions of British rule contained within its boundaries, the United States would, in all probability, cease to exist. Given all this—especially in light of Rochambeau's preference for a campaign in the Chesapeake—shouldn't he heed the call and immediately head to Virginia?

But as Washington realized, this was not the time to march south, especially with the mantle of dictatorial authority draped across his shoulders. In addition to being wrong militarily (as commander in chief of the allied forces, he must not desert his present post before the arrival of Rochambeau and the French army from Newport), it was wrong from a political perspective. The very existence of a republic depended on the supremacy of civil government. For the military to seize the reins of government, even for a brief period, was the wrong precedent to set—no matter how dismal the present prospects.

"Nobody," Washington wrote, "can doubt my inclination to be immediately employed in the defense of that country where all my property and connections are, but there are powerful objections to my leaving this army at this time. . . . [N]o other person has power to command the French troops who are now about to form a junction with this army. Let it suffice for me to add that I am acting on the great scale, that temporary evils must be endured where there is no remedy at hand; that I am not without hopes the table may be turned; but these being contingent, I can promise no more than my utmost exertions." Even as events in Virginia threatened to reach a personally disastrous climax, he refused to let self-interest supersede what he perceived to be the greater good.

For the present, he would remain on the Hudson, awaiting the arrival of Rochambeau's Expédition Particulière from Newport, while Lafayette's army, now twice its original size since the junction with Wayne, followed Cornwallis toward Williamsburg. In the meantime, more than two thousand miles to the south, the warships on which everything depended were gathering amid the islands of the Caribbean.

PART II

"The Ocean of History"

It is easy to understand that while ever
the ocean of history remains calm, a
pilot-administrator in a little bobbing boat
holding on to the ship of the people with a tiny
boathook, and moving along with it, might
easily think *he* is driving the ship that he is
clinging to. But the moment a storm comes up,
with the sea heaving and the ship tossing
about, this kind of delusion immediately
becomes impossible. The great ship on its vast
course is a free agent, the boathook can no
longer reach the moving vessel, and the pilot
who had been in charge, providing all the
power, finds himself transformed into a
creature that is pathetically useless.
　　　　—Leo Tolstoy, *War and Peace* (1869)

Great indeed must be the resources of that man
who can render himself the most formidable to
an enemy when apparently he is the most
destitute of power.
　　　　　　　　—James Thacher,
　　　　on his way to Yorktown, August 22, 1781

CHAPTER 6

"A Ray of Light"

IN THE YEAR 1781, the Caribbean might as well have been the Mediterranean of Homer's *Odyssey:* an island-speckled sea of swirling currents and wayward winds, where unseen gods made sport with the vain ambitions of mortal men, especially if you were British admiral George Rodney. In his youth he had been one of the most adept and lucky young captains in the British navy and had quickly amassed enough prize money from capturing enemy vessels to make him financially independent for life. But Rodney, who had the pedigree of a nobleman without the inherited income, lived life extravagantly, building himself a manor house, gambling, and launching a costly political campaign that ultimately forced him to flee to Paris to escape his creditors.

By the time France entered the American War for Independence in 1778, the once winning and handsome British admiral had become a shrill old man, hungry for one last chance to restore his reputation and bank account, only to be stranded in the capital of the enemy, where he had been jailed for debt. Then came one of those improbable interventions that make life a never-ending surprise. Even though France was at war with Britain, the Parisian nobleman Marshal de Biron loaned Rodney the money he needed to settle with his creditors. Soon he was back in England and, at the age of sixty-two, placed in command of the British fleet in the Caribbean.

Almost instantly Rodney became, once again, a hero. Even before crossing the Atlantic, he had destroyed or captured five Spanish men-of-war and brought much needed relief to the British forces at Gibraltar. Once in the Caribbean, he attacked the fleet commanded by French admiral the Comte de Guichen. Although the battle proved indecisive, his unrelenting pursuit drove de Guichen to the brink of an emotional breakdown, and the enemy commander soon returned to France. Rodney was wracked by the pains associated with gout and an enlarged prostate, but no admiral then serving in the British navy had his energy and his ability as a fighter. Unfortunately, there was also no British admiral who could match his lust for money, and on January 27, 1781, he learned that Britain had declared war on Holland. Before the news spread across the Caribbean, he had to attack the island of St. Eustatius, a Dutch trading center teeming with enough contraband to make him, once again, rich.

The French, he knew, were due to send a large fleet of warships to Martinique under the command of Admiral de Grasse. As the British naval commander in the Caribbean, Rodney must try to intercept the French fleet before the convoy they were escorting reached the base at Fort Royal Bay. And then, come July and the advent of the hurricane season, de Grasse would likely take a significant portion of his fleet north to assist the Rebel army in New York or the Chesapeake. It would be Rodney's duty to send his own fleet of ships in pursuit so as to maintain British naval superiority along the North American coast.

These were his primary responsibilities in the winter and spring of 1781. Once he'd taken St. Eustatius (which fell in a day, on February 3), he could have delegated the occupation of the island to his second in command, Rear Admiral Samuel Hood, or to British general John Vaughan. Instead he remained on the island for the next three months, tallying up the booty and loading it into a convoy bound for England.

It would be left to Samuel Hood to intercept the French fleet under Admiral de Grasse.

. . .

WHEREAS RODNEY WAS SPINDLY and delicate, de Grasse was a great bear of a man with a Rodney-like hunger to succeed. He was so intent on crossing the Atlantic in a timely fashion that he ordered his warships to tow the slower merchant vessels of the convoy, successfully completing the passage in an unheard-of thirty-six days. By the time the French reached the windward side of Martinique on April 28, 1781, the British fleet of eighteen ships had been on blockade duty for almost two months, and their commander, Admiral Hood, was not happy about it. Rodney had ordered him to position his fleet not on the windward side of Martinique, as he had requested, but to leeward so as to provide St. Eustatius with some cover. The likely consequence was clear: because of Rodney's self-indulgent preoccupation with St. Eustatius (where "the lures . . . were so bewitching as not to be withstood by flesh and blood"), Hood would be placed at a clear disadvantage when de Grasse appeared with his larger fleet of twenty warships.

Sure enough, de Grasse, whose officers spoke of his "brutal character" and "grim appearance," quickly put Hood's fleet on the defensive. By the end of the first day of fighting, four of Hood's ships had been seriously damaged, with the *Russell* taking on so much water that she was forced to sail for St. Eustatius for repairs. Hood insisted that de Grasse "has, I thank God, nothing to boast of," and yet the French admiral had succeeded in delivering every one of the ships in his large and vulnerable convoy to Martinique.

Luckily, from the British perspective, Hood's copper-bottomed ships had the same overwhelming speed advantage that Arbuthnot's fleet had enjoyed the month before at Cape Henry. When de Grasse ordered his warships to pursue the fleeing British, he watched in agonized frustration as the uncoppered vessels in his own fleet, despite being "covered with sails," fell so far behind that "some were out of sight." "I saw with grief," he wrote, "that it was only too true that the sailing of the English was superior to ours." With only half his ships in range to attack, he was forced to abandon the chase.

De Grasse's frustrations were compounded by his belief that several of his captains had been slow to respond to his commands. Even though he had, in this instance, gotten the better of the enemy, an element of bitterness had entered into his relations with his officers that would only increase in the months ahead.

From a naval standpoint, France needed Spain. Without Spanish warships, France had no hope of defeating Britain, whose fleet was much larger than her own. If France was to count on Spain's continued support later in the year for an expedition to North America, she had to make sure her ally's expectations were being met. In the winter of 1781, it was absolutely essential that Spain win back British-occupied Pensacola in West Florida.

To ensure that its interests were being attended to, the Spanish government sent a thirty-four-year-old envoy named Francisco Saavedra de Sangronis to the Caribbean. A former army officer turned diplomat, Saavedra was the consummate fixer. He had enormous discretionary powers when it came to financial matters. Most important, he was intelligent, tactful, and decisive. "It was indispensable," he recorded in his journal, "that I gain for myself the goodwill of the general officers, not with artifices or intrigues . . . but with a frank and impartial policy." With Saavedra in the room, even the most antagonistic group of military leaders could be brought to see what was in their mutual best interests.

Saavedra immediately realized that Spanish general Bernardo de Gálvez needed more troops for the expedition against Pensacola. "I was always of the opinion that the forces he was counting on were not adequate for the purpose," Saavedra wrote. "The general knew better than I the insufficiency of his resources, but in order not to delay the launching of the expedition, he did not dare to request more troops." In addition to making sure Gálvez had the troops he needed when the Spanish fleet departed from Cuba on February 28, Saavedra promised to provide him with reinforcements in April.

For the last three years, France's conduct of the war in North America and the Caribbean had been characterized by confusion at almost every turn. Beginning in the spring of 1781, however, events started to unfold with an almost preternatural precision, and much of the credit belongs to Saavedra. In addition to coordinating the actions of his own generals for the attack on Pensacola, he would play, as we shall soon see, an indispensable role in French admiral de Grasse's subsequent expedition to the Chesapeake. His name has been virtually lost to American history, but no one short of Washington and de Grasse, it could be argued, would do more to make the Yorktown campaign a success than Francisco Saavedra.

On April 5, word reached Spanish headquarters at Havana that Gálvez's attack on Pensacola had stalled. Despite single-handedly leading the Spanish fleet through the narrow and well-guarded entrance to Pensacola Bay, Gálvez had encountered more resistance from the British and their Native American allies than he had anticipated, and the assault had lapsed into a bloody standoff. When Saavedra arrived with reinforcements on April 19, Gálvez expressed his fears that with the approach of the hurricane season he might be forced to abandon the siege. In seeming confirmation of those fears, on May 6 a tornado accompanied by "terrifying claps of thunder" temporarily forced the Spanish fleet anchored off the entrance to Pensacola Bay out to sea.

Two days later, Saavedra and several Spanish officers headed into the dense underbrush surrounding Pensacola to perform some reconnaissance. They had just found a piece of high ground from which they could see all three British fortifications when one of the forts exploded "with a terrifying noise" that sent hundreds of bodies hurling into the air. A lucky shot from one of the Spanish cannons had hit the fort's powder magazine and killed almost every man in the garrison. Soon all three forts had fallen, and Bernardo de Gálvez (who adopted the motto *"Yo solo"*—"I alone"—to memorialize the bold move with which the siege had begun) was the hero of Pensacola. Now that the Spanish had won back Pensacola, Saavedra could turn his attention to assisting the French.

On June 9, Admiral Rodney squandered the opportunity of his life. Over the course of the previous few months, de Grasse had taken advantage of Rodney's preoccupation with St. Eustatius and captured Tobago. He was now on his way back to Martinique with twenty-three ships of the line. Rodney had finally finished with the Dutch island and reassumed direct command of the British fleet. He was cruising off British-held Barbados with twenty ships of the line when he sighted de Grasse. The French had the advantage in firepower but Rodney's fleet was coppered and thus swifter. Given Rodney's history as a fighter, it might have been assumed he would attack, especially since he enjoyed the favored windward position. But this was not the Rodney of old.

His health was not good. Gout had been a perennial problem for Rodney, but what he called "a stricture" caused by his enlarged prostate had become so painful that he seriously considered returning to England for treatment. "From the unsteadiness of the commander in chief," Samuel Hood complained, "[it is difficult] to know what he means three days together. One hour he says his complaints are of such nature that he cannot possibly remain in this country and is determined to leave the command with me; the next day he says he has no thought of going home." As his letters reveal, Rodney was not thinking clearly during the spring and summer of 1781. He later claimed that a concern for the safety of Barbados had prevented him from attacking de Grasse. Whether or not Rodney's worries were justified, it was as if some kind of protective aura hovered over the French fleet as it threaded its way through the islands of the Caribbean.

While Rodney dithered, de Grasse continued on to Martinique. On July 5, he left that island with a convoy of 160 merchantmen. Ten days later he sailed into the magnificent anchorage at Cap François on the north coast of Haiti, where he learned that a Spanish envoy named Francisco Saavedra was waiting to meet with him.

FOR THE MOST PART, Rochambeau's march from Rhode Island to New York went off without a hitch. The troops were first transported to Providence by water, then they departed sequentially in four divisions along a carefully prepared route. The first division left at four a.m. on June 18, and after a march of between twelve and fifteen miles began to arrive at the next campsite, near Waterman's Tavern in Coventry, before the heat of the day had set in around noon. The next morning, the first division was on its way to the next stop as the second division began its march to the campsite just vacated by its predecessor. And so it went until June 30.

By then, Rochambeau was in Newtown, Connecticut, with forty miles left to go before he joined Washington's Continental army at White Plains, New York. The French general intended to remain in Newtown for a few days as he reorganized his army into two divisions before marching for White Plains on July 2. Then he received the dispatch from Washington that upended all his plans.

The American general had a plan of his own. It had been three years, almost to the day, since Washington had led an army in battle. For more than half the Revolutionary War, while fighting raged to the south in Georgia, the Carolinas, and now Virginia, he had presided over a stalemate in and around British-occupied New York. ("Things drag on like a cart without wheels," he lamented.) As far back as the fall of 1778, he had devised plans for an attack on the city, only to see them dashed by a lack of French naval support. In the summer of 1781, he yearned to take New York.

There was no immediate prospect of naval support, but perhaps the sudden appearance of Rochambeau's army of more than four thousand soldiers would be enough to establish a strategic toehold on Manhattan island. On July 2, the waxing moon would still be slender enough to attempt a night attack on the three British fortifications guarding the north edge of the island. Once those had been taken, his forces would ambush the British division of cavalry guarding Kingsbridge at Spuyten Duyvil Creek. Given that he had only eight hundred soldiers under Benjamin Lincoln to lead the assault and would depend on Rochambeau's troops for reinforcements if he had any hope of holding the forts (assuming, of course, they could be taken), the highly complicated operation had only the slightest likelihood of success. "I am not highly sanguine in my expectations," he confessed to Rochambeau. But Washington felt it was worth a try. "Should we be so happy as to succeed in this attempt," he wrote, "it would give us exceeding great advantage in our future expectations."

Rochambeau seems to have recognized the venture for what it was: the desperate attempt by a deeply frustrated general to kick-start a siege that he knew was already viewed with skepticism by his ally. To the French general's credit, he agreed to participate in Washington's plan by accelerating his troops' march toward New York while sending forward Lauzun's cavalry for the projected capture of the British cavalry at Kingsbridge. If the plan worked, all the better; if it didn't, Washington would have no choice but to acknowledge the futility of his ambitions on New York.

As might have been expected, Washington's plan quickly fizzled when a British foraging expedition stumbled on some of Lincoln's troops. But this setback was not enough to discourage Washington's hopes of capturing New York. Two subsequent scouting expeditions revealed just how formidable the British fortifications actually were. The thousands of hoped-for American recruits failed to materialize even as the British in New York received two convoys of reinforcements. Not only Rochambeau but also French minister Luzerne, who made the trip up from Philadelphia, spoke of the opportunities in the Chesapeake. And still Washington continued to obsess on New York.

Hindsight would make Washington look stubborn and myopic, but he had legitimate reasons for continuing to focus on the city, and they had to do with the key ingredient to a potential victory: naval superiority. On July 21, the British fleet under the command of Admiral

Thomas Graves (who had replaced Arbuthnot) departed from Sandy Hook with hopes of intercepting a French convoy bound for Boston. Not until August 16 would they return, leaving New York, from a naval point of view, entirely defenseless for almost a month.

It was an extraordinary lapse on the part of the British. If a French fleet of almost any size were to sail into New York harbor, the city, in all likelihood, would fall. Washington immediately requested that Admiral de Barras in Newport take advantage of Graves's departure and sail for Sandy Hook. Even Rochambeau recognized the opportunity, and seconded Washington's plea for French naval support. But de Barras, who had already declined to transport Rochambeau's troops by sea, refused, claiming he should remain in Newport until de Grasse made his intentions known. Realizing the futility of "urging a measure to which [de Barras's] own judgment was opposed," Washington's only solace was the hope that de Grasse would sail not to the Chesapeake but to New York. Even if the Chesapeake proved to be the ultimate objective, the only way for the French fleet to transport the allied army south was if de Grasse first sailed to New York. What Washington didn't know was that Rochambeau's letters to de Grasse had already made the admiral's appearance at Sandy Hook highly unlikely.

THROUGHOUT THE MONTH OF JULY, British commander Henry Clinton in New York and Lord Cornwallis in Virginia spent more time warring with each other than with the enemy. Clinton, who never thought Cornwallis should have marched into Virginia in the first place, wanted him to establish a naval base on the Chesapeake as quickly as possible and then transport a significant portion of his troops to New York, where it looked as if he was about to be attacked by Washington's and Rochambeau's two armies. Cornwallis had no interest in establishing a naval post, "which cannot have the smallest influence on the war in Carolina, and which only gives us some acres of an unhealthy swamp." In reluctant obedience to

Clinton's orders, he made his dilatory way to Portsmouth, which only infuriated Clinton all the more since Benedict Arnold's experience a few months earlier had already demonstrated that large ships of the line could not be accommodated by the shallow waters surrounding this "sickly post." Cornwallis should look to Yorktown, where a second, subsidiary post across the river at Gloucester would provide the protection necessary for "a naval station for large ships as well as small." After a brief examination of an alternative site on the opposite side of the James River from Portsmouth at Old Point Comfort, Cornwallis reluctantly agreed that Yorktown was the proper place for a British naval base.

All the while Lafayette, stationed across the James River from Portsmouth, watched the British activities with exceeding, if somewhat baffled, interest. Over the last month, he had developed great respect for Cornwallis, who had almost succeeded in ambushing a significant portion of his army at Green Spring before crossing the James River to Portsmouth. "This devil Cornwallis is much wiser than the other generals with whom I have dealt," he wrote. "He inspires me with a sincere fear, and his name has greatly troubled my sleep."

That said, Lafayette could not understand what Cornwallis was attempting to accomplish by retreating to Portsmouth. He'd heard rumors that the British general was not happy with being subordinate to Clinton. Perhaps he was about to sail home? "Should he go to England, we are, I think, to rejoice for it. He is a bold and active man, two dangerous qualities in this Southern war."

By July 23, forty-nine British ships had sailed into Hampton Roads. Initially Lafayette believed they were to transport a portion of Cornwallis's army to New York. But by July 29, he was no longer so certain about the destination of the British convoy. For several days a brisk northwesterly breeze had been blowing—just the direction to sail out of the Chesapeake from Hampton Roads—and yet the British fleet had remained at anchor.

By August 4, he was even more confused. "From the moment the enemy embarked," he wrote General Anthony Wayne, "I was certain

New York would be the object and a part of Lord Cornwallis's army would attempt going to Carolina." But now there was evidence that a portion of the British army had landed at Yorktown, of all places. Was it a feint to draw Lafayette "very low down" the peninsula between the York and James rivers so that Cornwallis and the majority of his troops, still in Portsmouth, "might push for Carolina"?

Only time would tell.

On July 12, just four days before the appearance of de Grasse's fleet from Martinique, the *Concorde* arrived at Cap François, Haiti. The speedy French frigate had completed the passage from Boston in an impressive twenty-two days. In addition to dispatches from General Rochambeau, Admiral de Barras, and French minister Luzerne (which may have included a copy of the British navy's signal book secured by a highly placed spy in New York), the *Concorde* carried more than a dozen American pilots to assist de Grasse's fleet in navigating the unfamiliar coast of North America.

Soon after breaking the letters' seals, de Grasse realized he had an incredibly daunting task ahead of him—assuming, of course, he was willing to take up the challenge. Rochambeau's assessment was particularly dour. "I must not conceal from you, Monsieur," the French general had written, "that the Americans are at the end of their resources, that Washington will not have half of the troops he is reckoned to have . . . ; it is therefore of the greatest consequence that you will take on board as many troops as possible; that 4,000 or 5,000 men will not be too many, whether you aid us to destroy the works at Portsmouth, Virginia . . . [or] to force the Hook in seizing [New York]. . . . [T]here, Monsieur, are the . . . actual and sad pictures of the affairs of this country." But that was not all. In addition to a lack of allied soldiers, Rochambeau's army was about to run out of money. If the projected expedition was to go forward, he would need 1.2 million livres in specie, and it was up to de Grasse to find the cash.

Then there was the question of establishing naval superiority. De

Grasse had to assume that Rodney would send a significant portion of his fleet north to join the half-dozen ships under the command of Admiral Graves in New York; in addition, British admiral Robert Digby was reported to be bound for America from England with a squadron of his own. Clearly, de Grasse would need every possible ship if he had any hope of success. But how was he to provide for the protection of Haiti, the richest sugar-producing island in the Caribbean, as well as a merchant convoy to France? And then there was the matter of time. If all of this was to unfold before operations were to resume in the Caribbean in November, he must get his fleet to either Virginia or New York by the end of August at the absolute latest.

Finally, there was the question of how this would be viewed by the government in France, which had given him only the vaguest of instructions regarding his actions to the north. Did the ministers have "the confidence in him to hope that this project, useful and glorious as it might be to the French navy, would not be reproached by all in case of failure; he had to create all the means, and had only twenty days to provide for everything"?

First he must decide where he was headed. Assuming everything else fell into place, he would sail for the Chesapeake, since that was where Rochambeau obviously wanted him to go. But how was he to come up with the necessary ships? For that, he needed Francisco Saavedra.

THE MEETING BEGAN ON JULY 18 at six in the morning aboard de Grasse's flagship, the *Ville de Paris*. After showing each other their governmental credentials, de Grasse and Saavedra "talked about the cordiality and good faith with which the Spaniards and the French must cooperate toward the humiliation of a nation that so openly claimed dominion of the seas." Already France had lent its support to Spain's operations in Pensacola by providing Gálvez's army with troops and warships under the command of Chevalier François-Aymar Monteil, whose fleet had joined de Grasse's at Cap François.

Now it was Spain's turn to further France's interests in North America. Assuming he succeeded in capturing Cornwallis's army (thus forcing "the English cabinet [to] lose the hope of subduing [the Americans]"), de Grasse would turn his attention in the fall to assisting Spain in taking Jamaica.

When it came to the operation in the Chesapeake, de Grasse had decided to take no more than twenty-four ships of the line, because "it was necessary to leave five or six to protect the commerce of [Haiti]." As Saavedra had done during his discussions with Bernardo de Gálvez, the Spanish emissary urged de Grasse to increase the size of his force to its absolute maximum. He should take all thirty of the ships he then had under his command. To ease his concerns about leaving Haiti unguarded, Saavedra proposed that four Spanish ships of the line presently stationed at Havana be sent to Cap François. "This expedient pleased the comte enormously," Saavedra recorded in his journal, "and from that moment I noted on his part a great reliance on everything I proposed to him." Saavedra also encouraged de Grasse to take the 3400 French troops stationed at Haiti (which had been reserved for use in the upcoming operation against Jamaica), since they would be back in the Caribbean by the fall. With the Spanish envoy's help, de Grasse now had the ships and soldiers he needed.

All seemed to be going well as Saavedra prepared the documents outlining what he and de Grasse had agreed upon when, on the morning of July 23, attention shifted to the harbor at Cap François. One of de Grasse's ships, the *Intrepide*, had raised a signal of distress. A fire had broken out, and given the amount of gunpowder she had aboard and the proximity of the more than three hundred vessels crowded into the anchorage, most of the French admiral's ships were in danger of being blown to smithereens.

IN ALL LIKELIHOOD, Saavedra watched the unfolding drama from his residence overlooking the harbor. By then he had acquired considerable experience with both the Spanish and French navies.

The French, he knew, did things a little differently from the other navies of the world, particularly when it came to food and drink. Instead of hardtack, the French provided their crews with freshly baked bread, which required their warships be equipped with large ovens that, according to Saavedra, had the effect of "concentrating there a foul-smelling smoke that pervades the entire ship."

Instead of rum laced with water, which the British called grog, the French gave their men wine twice a day; it was also a French tradition when in the Caribbean to start the morning with a brandylike liquor known as tafia. On the morning of July 23, the clerk of the *Intrepide* was deep within the interior of the ship with a lantern in one hand as he worked the pump to the cask of tafia with the other. Suddenly the lantern's flame brushed against the spigot and ignited the cask. Soon the center portion of the ship was engulfed in flames.

"A fortune in this misfortune," an officer later recalled, "was that the bulkhead of the after room had been masoned with bricks in order to prevent the very thing which now happened." This gave the *Intrepide*'s crew the time to mitigate the impending disaster. As the ship was towed away from the other vessels toward shore, the officers and crew frantically threw casks of gunpowder into the sea while others cut holes into the ship's sides below the waterline. Soon the fire had spread to the masts and rigging, prompting a sailor to shout, *"Sauve qui peut!"* ("Save yourself, if you can!")

"Then everyone rushed to the boats," another officer remembered. So much thick black smoke poured out of the burning ship that "the sun disappeared from us—we could only see the flames bursting from the portholes." The intensity of the heat caused the barrels of the ship's cannons to glow a bright red as they began to discharge into the town, which according to the officer, "received her whole broadside." Seconds later, what remained of the ship's powder magazine erupted with such force that the entire stern "sprang into the air" as a deadly shower of splinters rained down on the waterfront. As if this tragedy were not enough, a few days later de Grasse learned that yet another of his ships, *L'Inconstante,* anchored at a small island four miles to the northwest, had also been destroyed in almost exactly the same manner. One could only wonder whether the French sailors' thirst for tafia might consume the entire fleet before it became time to leave Cap François.

O N J U L Y 2 8, five days after the loss of the *Intrepide*, the frigate *Concorde* departed for Boston with copies of a dispatch for the allied generals in White Plains. "I have thought myself authorized," de Grasse wrote, "to take everything on myself for the common cause." He would be sailing for the Chesapeake, "the place which seems to me to have been indicated by [you] as the surest to operate best as you propose. . . . By these efforts which I have made, you may realize the desire that I have to effect a change in our position and in the condition of affairs."

What de Grasse chose not to mention in his dispatch was that yet another, potentially fatal problem had emerged. Haiti's governor had announced that the colony's coffers were empty. If de Grasse was to come up with the million-plus livres needed to fund Rochambeau's army, let alone pay for his own voyage, the funds would have to be provided through loans from the island's planters.

There was no doubt they had the money. In 1781, Cap François, with its newly built stone houses and wide, crowded streets, was "the Paris of the isles," and its white residents were some of the wealthiest people in the world. Whereas Cuba's Havana owed much of its riches to the Spanish gold and silver mines of Mexico and South America, Cap François's prosperity was based on Haiti's highly profitable sugar industry, which was in turn based on what has been called the most brutal manifestation of African slavery in the Western Hemisphere. Of the estimated thirty thousand slaves shipped to Haiti annually, more than a third were worked to death within the first years of their arrival. De Grasse and his officers might pride themselves in furthering the cause of freedom through their efforts on America's behalf, but the unsettling truth was that even if the United States should win its independence, African slavery would remain a reality not only here in Haiti but also in Virginia and the rest of the thirteen states. And in what is a consummate historical irony given America's self-proclaimed role as the upholder of human liberty, the slaves of Haiti would win their freedom (through a bloody revolution of their own) more than a half century before those of the United States.

The planters of Cap François might have been rich in the summer of 1781, but that did not mean they were willing to loan Admiral de Grasse the money. Although the terms were favorable, the French government had been slow to honor its commitments in an earlier instance. There were also grumblings about de Grasse's refusal to provide any warships for a convoy slated to sail for France. Even when he offered his own considerable property on the island as collateral, the planters declined to cooperate. By July 31, de Grasse had come to fear that due to a lack of funds, "his fleet [must] remain idle in port." But, once again, Saavedra had an idea. What if the Spanish envoy sailed to Cuba in advance of the French fleet and solicited the colony's government in Havana for the loan?

It required him a night to think it over, but de Grasse ultimately decided to go ahead with what he realized was becoming an increasingly "risky operation." Saavedra would depart on a "swift frigate" for Havana while de Grasse led his fleet up the Old Bahama Channel, a dangerous and rarely used passageway along the northeast coast of Cuba. Assuming Saavedra was able to raise the cash, he would meet de Grasse off Matanzas, about 70 miles to the east of Havana, before the French fleet sailed for Virginia.

"His plan seemed good to me," Saavedra wrote, and on August 3, he boarded the frigate *Aigrette* and was soon on his way to Cuba.

On July 7, Admiral George Rodney, then stationed at Barbados and close to incapacitated with the pain caused by his swollen prostate, learned that de Grasse was planning to sail up the American coast that summer. He quickly dispatched the *Swallow* with a

George Washington and his enslaved manservant Billy Lee beside the Hudson River with the fortress at West Point in the background. Washington became intimately familiar with the Hudson over the course of the war, often taking the helm of the vessel that was transporting his entourage up or down the river.

The Comte de Rochambeau, commander of the French Expédition Particulière. In the summer of 1780, a year after arriving at Newport, Rhode Island, Rochambeau and his army joined Washington at White Plains for the long march to Yorktown.

François Jean de Beauvoir Chastellux visited Washington's headquarters in November 1780 and was greatly impressed by the American commander in chief. The following spring he provided Washington with information about the French fleet under the command of the Comte de Grasse that Rochambeau had been ordered to withhold from the Americans.

The French cavalry officer Duc de Lauzun also visited Washington at his headquarters on the Hudson and bore witness to the American commander's frustrations with the French high command.

Sir Henry Clinton, commander of the British forces in North America. As a subordinate of Thomas Gage and William Howe, Clinton had been full of daring and imaginative ideas, but once he became commander in chief he grew considerably less adventuresome, never straying from his base at New York City throughout the year of Yorktown.

As secretary of state for the colonies, George Germain oversaw the British war effort in North America. Despite considerable evidence to the contrary, he clung to the mistaken belief that most Americans remained loyal to the king and, if given the opportunity, would rise up to free themselves from patriot oppression.

King George III in 1771,
ten years before Britain
suffered her crushing defeat
at Yorktown.

Raised as a Quaker in Rhode
Island, Nathanael Greene proved
to be one of the great strategists
of the Revolutionary War.
Although he never achieved
victory on the battlefield, his
pugnacious presence in North
and South Carolina helped to lay
the groundwork for the victory
at Yorktown.

While Greene battled the British in the Carolinas, Friedrich von Steuben remained in Virginia, where he helped to assemble the troops and provisions needed by the American army to the south.

Daniel Morgan achieved one of the most spectacular victories of the war by defeating Banastre Tarleton at Cowpens, South Carolina, in January 1781. A series of health problems forced him to retire to his home in Virginia before the Battle of Guilford Courthouse two months later.

Before his defeat at Cowpens, the British cavalry officer Banastre Tarleton had established a reputation for brutality and arrogance that made him one of the most hated men in America.

Tarleton may have been despised, but no one could match the traitor Benedict Arnold when it came to arousing the passions of the American people. By sending Arnold, a newly minted British general, to Virginia in December 1780, Sir Henry Clinton initiated the movement of troops that would culminate in Lord Charles Cornwallis's defeat at Yorktown less than a year later.

Jaeger captain Johann Ewald, shown here at the end of his long and distinguished career, served under both Benedict Arnold and Lord Cornwallis during the British campaign in Virginia in 1781.

Virginia governor Thomas Jefferson's curiously lackadaisical response to Benedict Arnold's appearance at the mouth of the James River in January 1781 would remain a source of controversy throughout his long political career.

Coeffure à la Belle Poule

A fashionable Parisian woman wearing what was known as the "Belle Poule" hairstyle in tribute to the French frigate that took on a much larger British ship off the coast of Brittany in June 1778, soon after France's entry into the war.

Situation of the British fleet in Gardiners Bay.
Two days ago there arrived a 64 gun ship that had cut her cables, in the night that the Gale came on, being them at the East of Fisher's island, a little visiting vessel has brought 80 and upwards fathoms of the cables, 22 inches in circumference.

The ship (4) is the Admiral, the flag is at the little top gallant mast.
(5) flag at mizen mast three Decker
(6) Dismasted, (8) last arrived,
(9) either 50 gunship, or frigate.
the vessel left off the island cannot be seen

16th February 1781   8 o'clock A.M.

The Vessel most at the North as well as the rest of them have Lengthened out a great deal of cable to the Northward, have an anchor S.E. ward, another N.O. ward, the Northern most ship is upon the edge of the current, which sets from Gardner's point, goes to the N.O and N.O ½ N at the rate of 4 or 5 knots an hour, so that all the ships in case they be attacked can get into the middle of the current stream, they seam most to be attacked on the East side, according to their Laying

This sketch made by an allied spy detailing the position of the British fleet anchored off Gardiners Island near Montauk, Long Island, was sent to Washington by Rochambeau on February 16, 1781.

Mariot Arbuthnot, commander of the British fleet at the Battle of Cape Henry on March 16, 1781. Although French admiral Charles Destouches got the better of him in that instance, Arbuthnot was still able to save a besieged Benedict Arnold at Portsmouth, Virginia, six months before British general Cornwallis found himself in a similar situation at Yorktown.

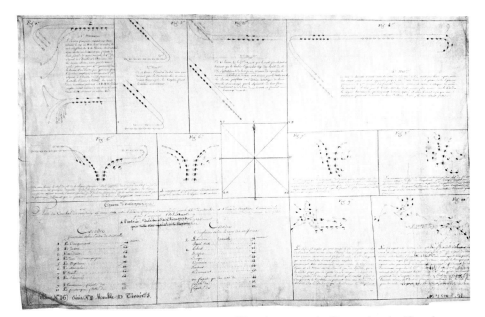

A series of diagrams made under the direction of French commander Destouches detailing the encounter between the French and British fleets at the Battle of Cape Henry.

An engraving of the French grenadier aboard the *Conquérant* who lost a leg to a British cannon ball during the Battle of Cape Henry. According to one account, the soldier cried out, "Thank heaven I still have two arms and a leg to serve my King!"

The French fleet anchored in Newport harbor in the spring of 1781 soon after its return from the Battle of Cape Henry.

Although Lord Cornwallis was just the kind of aggressive officer the ministry in London wanted, his reckless pursuit of Nathanael Greene across North Carolina, followed by the bloody Battle of Guilford Courthouse on March 15, 1781, marked the beginning of the end for British fortunes in the south.

Some of Cornwallis's desperate aggression in North Carolina may have been in response to the death of his beautiful wife, Jemima, which, he claimed, had "effectually destroyed all my hopes of happiness in this world."

British General Charles O'Hara commanded the elite Guards in Cornwallis's army and served as his commander's surrogate during the surrender ceremony at Yorktown.

Henry "Light Horse Harry" Lee's cavalry jousted repeatedly with Tarleton's dragoons during the Race to the Dan. His youngest son, Robert E. Lee, would lead the Confederate forces during the Civil War.

Before France could send a fleet from the Caribbean to North America, she had to attend to the needs of her ally Spain by supporting General Bernardo de Gálvez's attack on the British outpost at Pensacola, Florida. When Gálvez succeeded in defeating the British on May 8, 1781, the way was clear for the French naval commander Comte de Grasse to begin planning an expedition to the north.

Francisco Saavedra, the largely unheralded Spanish emissary who assisted both General Gálvez and Admiral de Grasse with the complicated financial and logistical details that proved essential to their successes.

message for Admiral Graves in New York. "I shall keep as good a look out as possible on their motions," he promised, "by which my own shall be regulated." However, by the time the *Swallow* arrived in New York on July 27, Graves had already sailed for Boston in hopes of intercepting the convoy from France. Leaving a copy of the dispatch in New York, the captain of the *Swallow* headed out to find Graves and his fleet, only to be driven ashore on Long Island by some American privateers.

By the end of July, Rodney had decided he must seek medical treatment. On August 1, he sailed for England with two ships of the line and a frigate, leaving Samuel Hood in command of the British squadron in the Caribbean. Rodney had left instructions for Hood to stop at the Chesapeake and Delaware on his way north and if he did not find any signs of de Grasse's fleet, rendezvous with Graves in New York. On August 3, Hood sent out another dispatch for Graves informing him of his impending departure. Unfortunately, this vessel also ran afoul of the Americans and never made it past Philadelphia. This meant that when Graves returned to New York on August 16 (after spending much of the month in a fog bank off Georges Bank futilely searching for the French convoy) and found a copy of Rodney's dispatch, he had no word of Hood and knew only that back in early July Rodney had promised that at some undetermined time a British fleet would be sent up the coast.

Most extraordinary of all in this ever lengthening list of failed British opportunities is the one involving Rodney himself. On the night of July 31, before his departure from St. Eustatius for England, he received the most vital piece of intelligence to date. Up until that point, he knew de Grasse was about to sail up the North American coast, but he didn't know to where. From the Danish island of St. Thomas came the news that the French were headed for the Chesapeake. For reasons that are difficult to understand, Rodney neglected to pass along the news to Hood, who sailed from Antigua on August 10. Rodney may have been too overcome with pain to process the importance of the intelligence at the time of his departure on

August 1; he also held out hope that once out of the sweltering heat of the Caribbean, his condition might improve to the point that he could rejoin the British fleet on the American coast. Twelve days later, while sailing on the latitude of Bermuda, he determined that, no, he must continue on to England. He did, however, decide to communicate, at long last, the intelligence he had received before his departure from the Caribbean. Not until September 8, far too late to be of any help to Graves, did the frigate *Pegasus* arrive at Sandy Hook with information Rodney had first received more than a month before.

One is struck by the contrast between the British and the French during these crucial months. Whether it was the feuding between Clinton and Cornwallis or the dubious and sometimes unfathomable behavior of Rodney, the British were plagued by discord and miscommunication. The French also had their share of problems, but there was something—whether it be as loftily intangible as fate or as prosaic as the steadfast competence of Francisco Saavedra—that kept them on course. And then there was Washington, aligned with a general he did not entirely trust, waiting to know when and where he could expect de Grasse. On August 14, he got the answer.

L ONG BEFORE HE LEARNED that the French admiral was sailing for the Chesapeake, Washington had begun to have his doubts about the wisdom of attacking New York. As early as June 28 he had admitted to artillery chief Henry Knox, then in Philadelphia, "I am every day more and more dubious of our being able to carry into execution the operations we have in contemplation." On July 30, he wrote to Lafayette in Virginia that it was "more than probable that we shall . . . entirely change our plan of operations." Two days later, on August 1, he recorded in his diary: "I turned my views more seriously (than I had ever before done) to an operation to the southward."

When it came to his communications with Rochambeau, however, he revealed none of these misgivings about attacking New York. Indeed, he seems to have been unwilling even to discuss the possibility of a southern option. This also applied to his own officers in White Plains, particularly his quartermaster, Timothy Pickering, whom he continued to pester with impatient demands for the boats needed for an amphibious attack on New York. So far as almost everyone around him was concerned, Washington was implacable in his resolve to attack New York.

The reason for the discrepancy between what he told intimates such as Lafayette and Knox and what he told both the French and American officers at or near his headquarters was the absolute importance of secrecy. As soon as Rochambeau learned that Washington had decided on the Chesapeake instead of New York, the French would inevitably begin to prepare for the nearly five-hundred-mile march south to Virginia—preparations that would quickly tip off the British as to what was really afoot. Rochambeau might have been concealing the truth about his correspondence with de Grasse, but Washington was being just as cagey and, in his own way, manipulative. There is even evidence he had gone to the lengths of establishing his own line of communication with de Grasse. Years later, Allan McLane, who was a thirty-five-year-old Continental officer in 1781, claimed he had been dispatched from Philadelphia aboard the privateer *Congress* for a secret mission to Haiti. According to McLane, he met with de Grasse aboard the *Ville de Paris* at Cap François, where he passed along messages from Washington. Whether or not this is entirely true, Washington was not about to reveal the full extent of his thinking to Rochambeau, because the future success of any land-based movement of troops to the Chesapeake depended on its being as much a mystery to the French as to the British.

What Washington held out hope for was that the allied army would not have to travel the entire way by land. On August 2, he wrote to Robert Morris (who was now the equivalent of the country's finance minister) in Philadelphia about the possibility of finding enough ships on the Delaware to transport his troops. Once again, his chief concern was secrecy. "The principal difficulty which occurs," he wrote, "is obtaining transports at the moment they may be wanted;

for if they are taken up beforehand, the use for which they are designed cannot be concealed and the enemy will make arrangements to defeat the plan." The good part about assembling the fleet in Philadelphia was that it was removed from the cloud of British spies surrounding New York. "I can direct certain preparations to be made in Philadelphia and at other convenient places," he explained, "without incurring any suspicions."

His best option, however, involved de Grasse. If the French fleet should suddenly appear at Sandy Hook as he had earlier recommended, he and Rochambeau could immediately march their men to New Jersey and embark them for the Chesapeake. But as de Grasse made clear in his July 26 letter, it had been represented to him that he should sail directly to Virginia. According to Richard Peters, president of the Continental Congress's Board of War and an old friend of Washington's who was at headquarters with Robert Morris on the morning Washington learned of de Grasse's dispatch, "The general . . . [responded] with expressions of intemperate passion (which I will not repeat), [then] handed me [the] letter. . . . 'Here,' said the general, 'read this; you understand the French'; and turning away, 'so do I now better than ever.'"

As Lafayette had learned that spring, marching an army from New York to Virginia was fraught with difficulties. How Washington and Rochambeau were supposed to do it in the heat of summer, with an American army that had not been paid in over a year and was without the necessary provisions, uniforms, and arms, was anyone's guess. No wonder Washington was enraged when he learned that because of de Grasse's decision to sail to the Chesapeake rather than first stopping at Sandy Hook, they had lost the opportunity to transport their armies by water. As he complained to Pickering, "I wish to the Lord the French would not raise our expectation [of] a cooperation, or fulfill them!"

His anger was short-lived, however. After being "not a little astonished" by Washington's initial response to the letter, Peters and Morris returned to their rooms to prepare for breakfast. Once at Washington's table for the morning meal, they were just as amazed to find him "as composed as if nothing extraordinary had happened." Having unleashed his emotions privately, he was now ready to assume his public role as commander in chief and continue to do his best to win the war. Later in the morning, once breakfast was finished, Washington turned to Peters. "Well," he said, "what can you do for us, under the present change of circumstances?"

What none of them knew was that as late as only a few days before, de Grasse's arrival in the Chesapeake was anything but assured.

At 600 miles from east to west, with a coastline of 2200 miles, Cuba is the largest of the Caribbean islands. For about 140 miles along Cuba's northeast coast extends the Old Bahama Channel, a narrow curving passage between Cuba to the south and the Bahamas to the north. In the sixteenth century it had been used by the Spanish treasure fleet but had long since fallen out of favor due to the dangers posed by the many coral reefs and sandbars. This especially held true during the hurricane season, exactly when de Grasse decided to take his twenty-eight ships of the line and assorted frigates through a channel that no other French fleet had ever attempted.

He had several reasons for this bold decision. First, it greatly increased the chances of his fleet's making the voyage from Haiti to the outskirts of Havana without being detected by the enemy. Not only did it put the entire island of Cuba between his fleet and the prying eyes of the British in Jamaica, the sheer outrageousness of the maneuver meant that enemy frigates were unlikely to be looking for the French fleet along this portion of the Cuban coast. The other benefit was that assuming his ships could successfully negotiate the channel, it would deliver them to the safest and most inconspicuous place possible to meet up with the hopefully money-laden *Aigrette*.

As it turned out, the wind deserted them at the narrowest part of the channel, where they were "surrounded by reefs on every side, experiencing an unsupportable contrariety of winds." At one point the

Northumberland came terrifyingly close to crashing into the breakers when the helmsman mistakenly turned the wheel in the wrong direction. Then, on August 14, a strong breeze finally began to blow from the prevailing southeasterly direction, and the fleet sailed to the designated rendezvous point three leagues (almost ten miles) off Matanzas. Now the great question was whether Saavedra had been successful in securing the 1.2 million livres.

Almost as soon as Francisco Saavedra had arrived in Havana, he learned the terrible news. As chance would have it, the only convoy Spain would send across the Atlantic during the entire war had just left a few weeks earlier, taking with it most of the gold and silver in Cuba. A new shipment was expected soon from Mexico, but at present the public money that Saavedra had been counting on was not available. "Amidst all this difficulty," he recorded in his journal, "a decision urgently had to be made because without money de Grasse could do nothing, and to allow him to wait off Matanzas for a long time was to expose his fleet to great danger." Saavedra had only one option: attempt exactly what de Grasse had unsuccessfully tried at Cap François and "turn once again to the citizenry, making known the urgency of the case, so that each man would give what he could." But why would the residents of Havana be willing to fund a French expedition in support of the Americans, especially when the French in Haiti had refused to help?

Circumstances, however, were considerably different in Cuba. Rather than having to deal with a distant governmental official in Europe, as would have been the case at Cap François, the residents of Havana would be repaid (at 2 percent interest) as soon as the next treasure ship arrived from Mexico. Two French naval officers were sent out into the streets of Havana to collect the funds on the morning of August 16, and in just six hours they had come up with 500,000 pesos, the equivalent of 1.2 million livres. According to a legend promulgated by de Grasse, who referred to "the million that was supplied by *'las damas de la Havana,'*" a portion of the money came in the form of diamonds donated by the well-to-do ladies of the town. Unfortunately, existing documentation demonstrates that instead of from *"las damas,"* most of the money came from a handful of local businessmen with a history of lending to the Spanish government, as well as several regiments of Spanish soldiers who donated what was in their military coffers. No matter who stepped forward to support the French expedition, it cannot be denied that the Spanish residents of Cuba provided what one commentator has called "the bottom dollars upon which the edifice of American independence was raised."

On August 18, the *Aigrette,* loaded with six tons of coins but without Francisco Saavedra, who remained in Havana to make sure the promised Spanish men-of-war were sent to guard Haiti, rendezvoused with de Grasse's fleet. The money was distributed throughout the fleet to ensure that the loss of one ship did not sink the entire treasure. The Spanish pilots were sent ashore, and by that evening the fleet had started tacking up Old Bahama Channel toward America, whisked along by the Gulf Stream.

ON AUGUST 16, two days after he'd learned that de Grasse was destined for the Chesapeake, Washington received a letter from Lafayette. The young general had been having a difficult time figuring out what Cornwallis was up to. "You must not wonder, my dear general, that there has been a fluctuation in my intelligences," Lafayette wrote. "I am positive the British councils have also been fluctuating." However, it was now safe to say, the Frenchman had determined, that Cornwallis was in fact establishing his army on the high bluffs of Yorktown and across the river at Gloucester. "Should a fleet come in at this moment," he speculated, "our affairs would take a very happy turn."

Washington was intimately familiar with the geography of this peninsula between the York and James rivers. Back in 1777, he had received a letter from Thomas Nelson, then a brigadier general and now Thomas Jefferson's replacement as governor of Virginia, proposing that he establish a small base at Yorktown, where his soldiers could monitor the movements of British ships. Washington had advised against it. Nelson's troops, he warned, "by being upon a narrow neck of land, would be in danger of being cut off. The enemy might very easily throw up a few ships into York and James's river . . . and land a body of men there, who by throwing up a few redoubts, would intercept their retreat and oblige them to surrender at discretion."

Now, in the summer of 1781, it was, Washington later remembered, "as clear to my view as a ray of light": if Lafayette could contain Cornwallis—and de Grasse's fleet arrived as promised—the British general would be trapped. So much could still go wrong: Just as had happened in March, the British fleet might beat the French to the Chesapeake and force them to retire to the Caribbean. Cornwallis might realize the risk he was running and retreat into North Carolina before Washington and Rochambeau arrived with reinforcements. Clinton could put an immediate halt to the operation by attacking the allied forces as they attempted to cross the Hudson.

And yet, just when it seemed the American cause might be irredeemable, Washington now saw a way the war could be won. It required him to begin a five-hundred-mile trek under the very noses of the British, but it was worth the gamble. As soon as possible, they were marching for Virginia.

CHAPTER 7

"The Spur of Speed"

IT WAS THE CHANCE of a lifetime. But as revealed by his impassioned response to de Grasse's letter, there was a part of Washington that writhed with anguished rage over the position in which he'd been placed by the French alliance. The bitter truth was that by the summer of 1781 the American Revolution had failed. With thousands of able-bodied citizens refusing to serve, with the thirteen states refusing to fund the meager army that did exist, and with the Continental Congress helpless to effect any constructive change, the very existence of the United States now rested with the soldiers and sailors of another nation. Washington had only 2500 men to take to the Chesapeake; Rochambeau had more than double that number, and there were 3100 additional French soldiers en route with de Grasse. "How will it sound in history," Captain Samuel Shaw, aide-de-camp to American artillery commander Henry Knox, had written the year before, "that the United States could not, or rather would not, make an exertion, when the means were amply in their power, which might at once rid them of their enemies, and put them in possession of that liberty, and safety, for which we have been so long contending? By Heaven! If our rulers had any modesty, they would blush at the idea of calling in foreign aide! 'Tis really abominable, that we should send to France *for* soldiers, when there are so many sons of America idle."

Washington, ever the pragmatic survivor, had done his best to lay this sense of humiliation aside in his dealings with Rochambeau, something that had been easier to do when the Expédition Particulière was still in Newport. But now, as the march to Yorktown commenced with a French army that was twice the size of his own, on their way to meet a French naval force beyond imagining, it was impossible to ignore that the American army was, in essence, a fly on the back of an elephant, and he, as that fly's commander, was in no position to claim credit for a plan that had been essentially forced on him by the French.

In the letter Washington received on August 14, Admiral de Grasse had insisted he could stay in the Chesapeake only until October 15 before returning to the Caribbean. That gave Washington and Rochambeau just two months to get the allied army to Virginia and (assuming Cornwallis was still dug in at Yorktown when they arrived) begin a siege. As they all knew, sieges took time.

Unlike a battle, in which two armies fought it out until one side declared victory, a siege involved the methodical process of surrounding an enemy, cutting him off from the source of supply, and using artillery to gradually break down his defenses. Assuming Cornwallis had done everything possible to fortify his position, it could take months, not weeks, to dislodge his army. If de Grasse were to abandon them prematurely, they would be left open to attack by a British fleet. This was almost exactly what had occurred three years before, when de Grasse's predecessor, Admiral d'Estaing, had abruptly ceased operations against Newport and forced the American army, left unprotected from the sea, to fight its way out of Rhode Island.

And then there was the matter of Admiral de Barras, stationed in Newport. Not only were his eight ships of the line needed to maintain naval superiority in the Chesapeake, he would be transporting the heavy artillery and provisions essential to conducting a siege. And yet de Barras had announced he had no intention of sailing south. To avoid the indignity of serving under Admiral de Grasse, whom he outranked, de Barras had decided to take his fleet north to, of all places, Newfoundland. With a British fleet in New York and, most likely, an even larger enemy fleet headed up the coast from the south (not to mention a third fleet of British warships expected any day from England under Graves's replacement Admiral Digby), it was imperative that the French consolidate rather than scatter their naval resources. Rochambeau had already voiced his objections to de Barras's proposal; now it was Washington's turn. "I cannot avoid repeating," he wrote on August 15, "in earnest terms the request of General Rochambeau that you form the junction, and as soon as possible, with Admiral de Grasse in Chesapeake Bay." De Barras ultimately agreed to sail south, and on August 23 departed from Newport.

Washington had decided he must leave half his army at West Point under General William Heath. Once Clinton realized the allies had departed for the Chesapeake, he would almost certainly attack what was left of the American forces along the Hudson. Heath's army would be outnumbered by nearly four to one by the British in New York, but at least the fortifications at West Point would give them a fighting chance in the face of a British onslaught. That left 2500 of the Continental army's best soldiers for the march south under the command of Benjamin Lincoln, the general who had been forced to surrender Charleston to the British the year before and who had rejoined the American army in a prisoner exchange. Included in these ranks would be Washington's former aide, Alexander Hamilton. Given their past history, Hamilton had assumed Washington would refuse to assign him to the field, and he had turned in his commission. But Washington chose not to accept it. Using his aide Tench Tilghman as an intermediary, he assured Hamilton that every effort would be made to secure him the appropriate command, and Hamilton was now a part of the army that was about to head south.

Washington might be on occasion snappish and overbearing, but as even Hamilton must admit, he was also something more: one of those rare individuals with the capacity to rise above the emotions of the moment and, given time, recognize what really mattered. In the summer of 1775, when he first arrived at Boston to assume command of the American army, he had been horrified by the slovenly crew of New Englanders he had inherited, describing them as "an exceeding dirty and nasty people." Six years later, he had come to respect these same New Englanders—particularly the African American soldiers from Rhode Island—as some of his best and most disciplined men. As the French had realized after the skirmishes that accompanied the two reconnaissance missions to the edges of British-held New York, the Americans might not look like much, but they could fight. "It is incredible," Baron von Closen commented, "that soldiers composed of men of every age, even of children of fifteen, of whites and blacks, almost naked, unpaid, and rather poorly fed, can march so well and withstand fire so steadfastly." This was perhaps Washington's greatest accomplishment. As one after the other of his British opponents, from Thomas Gage to William Howe (with Clinton and Cornwallis soon to follow), returned to England in disgrace, he had found a way, despite having lost more battles than he had won, to keep his army, and by extension his country, together.

Central to his durability was the aura of reserve that clung to him like a protective cloak, a rigorously maintained aloofness that no one—with the possible exceptions of Martha and Lafayette—could penetrate. "Be easy and condescending in your deportment to your officers," he had advised one of his newly minted colonels back in 1775, "but not too familiar, lest you subject yourself to a want of that respect, which is necessary to support a proper command." As the historian Edmund Morgan has written, "The remoteness that still surrounds [Washington] was a necessary adjunct of the power he was called upon to exercise." And yet there was also a likeable humility about the commander in chief, a humanizing lack of pretension that saved him from the pomposity that afflicted so many of his contemporaries. "The calm and calculated measure of General Washington," von Closen observed, "in whom I discover daily some new and eminent qualities, are already well known, and the entire universe accords him the homage of its highest esteem. . . . Everyone regards him as his friend and father."

. . .

B<small>Y THE SUMMER OF</small> 1781, the cast of Founding Fathers with which the Revolution had begun had largely dispersed, with Thomas Jefferson currently out of public office in Virginia and with Benjamin Franklin, John Adams, and others in Europe. In the absence of a viable federal government, that left Washington to hold together both the army and the country on his own. Finally, however, Congress was making belated efforts to provide him with some support, particularly with the appointment of Robert Morris as superintendent of finance.

As Morris had explained to Washington when he visited the commander in chief at his headquarters in White Plains earlier in August, he was willing to extend his considerable personal credit as far as it might go to assist the nation in the ensuing campaign. (Back in 1776, it had been Morris who came up with the emergency funds Washington needed to cross the Delaware and secure victory at Trenton.) Morris also hoped to consolidate the supply operations of both the American and French armies. Up until then the two armies had been competing with each other for provisions, and since the French were able to pay in gold and silver as opposed to the worthless credit the American commissary agents had to offer, it was a competition the Americans were guaranteed to lose, even as it drove up the prices of goods for both armies. Unfortunately, Rochambeau refused to cooperate, and the Americans were left to their own devices. "The French agents have their riders all round the country," Colonel James Hendricks complained, "buying flour and beef with specie. This will effectively prevent the [American] commissioners from procuring any, as there is not a probability of the people letting the state agents have an ounce on credit while they can get the French crowns and Louis."

Despite this handicap, Morris took over much of the responsibility of securing supplies and established depots for the American army between New York and Yorktown. This enabled Timothy Pickering, Washington's quartermaster, to concentrate on selecting the best route and campsites. Making Pickering's efforts all the more challenging was Washington's insistence on secrecy.

It was essential that Clinton be left in doubt for as long as possible as to where the French and Americans were headed. For now, the British commander assumed they were about to launch an attack on his army in New York via Staten Island, with naval assistance to be provided by de Grasse's fleet at Sandy Hook. Luckily, the army's first three days' march through New Jersey was along the same route they would have taken to Staten Island. Any preparations made for the allied armies beyond those first three days' march (as they veered off for Princeton and beyond that Trenton) might alert the British prematurely to their ultimate destination. As a consequence, Pickering would be left with only four days' advance notice before he and his staff could begin to attend to the myriad details of getting the army to Philadelphia.

In the meantime, Washington used every means at his disposal to convince Clinton they were headed for Staten Island. In addition to making sure official correspondence alluding to an attack on New York was captured by the British, Washington insisted that his army lug forty carriage-mounted boats across New Jersey. Perhaps the most effective ploy concerned the French army's well-known reliance on fresh-baked bread. French agents were sent out to New Jersey to purchase flour in communities along the west bank of the Hudson while bricks were collected along the Raritan River (a waterway that flowed into Arthur Kill near the southwestern tip of Staten Island) for the construction of ovens in Chatham, far enough inland that they were beyond the reach of the British but well situated to supply an army whose ostensible purpose was to attack New York.

But first the two armies needed to cross the Hudson River at a spot sufficiently removed from the British that it could be accomplished in relative safety. This required them to backtrack forty miles to King's Ferry, a march over rain-soaked roads that took the French six tortuous days. The American army was the first to reach the ferry, completing the two-mile crossing in a day. The French, on the other hand, required three. Since the British had sent several warships up the river earlier in the summer, it was generally assumed they would do so again, especially given the easy target presented by a mass of slow-moving, soldier-packed boats. But for reasons known only to Sir Henry Clinton, the British let the two armies pass the river unimpeded.

To screen the size of the force from the enemy, the American and French armies were divided into separate columns that took different but parallel routes down the length of New Jersey toward the Delaware River. This overland portion of the march required hundreds upon hundreds of horses and oxen to pull the heavily loaded wagons and artillery, with each column extending for two to three miles as it made its dusty way through the relatively lush New Jersey countryside.

Only a select group of American and French officers were aware of the army's true destination. Most believed they were, as all signs seemed to indicate, headed for Staten Island to begin an attack on New York. But no one knew for sure. As the surgeon James Thacher observed, since Washington "makes the great plans and designs under an impenetrable veil of secrecy . . . , our own opinions must be founded only on doubtful conjectures." And with each step into New Jersey, the speculation mounted. "Our situation reminds me of some theatrical exhibition," Thacher wrote, "where the interest and expectations of the spectators are continually increasing, and where curiosity is wrought to the highest point."

The faster Washington could move his army through New Jersey, the more likely they were to get far enough south that Clinton could do nothing to stop them. However, given the logistical demands of moving more than seven thousand men, along with all their munitions and equipment, they were lucky to cover fifteen miles a day. As a consequence, the race was being conducted in agonizingly slow motion. That, however, did not change the need to quicken the pace. "The success of our enterprise," Washington reminded Lincoln on August 24, "depends upon the celerity of our movements; delay therefore may be ruinous to it." And yet, if de Grasse and his fleet did not arrive as promised in the Chesapeake, all would be for naught.

Washington had hopes he would have word from the French admiral by the time the armies reached the vicinity of Springfield, which was almost even with the southern tip of Manhattan. But by August 29, he had heard nothing of the French fleet. Rather than continue and "discover our real object to the enemy," he ordered the first division of the French army to halt and bring up the column's rear.

Washington's anxiety level continued to build as he sent out orders to Colonel Samuel Miles in Trenton and Robert Morris in Philadelphia to start assembling boats in anticipation of the army's arrival. "I have delayed having these preparations made until this moment," he explained to Miles, "because I wished to deceive the enemy with regard to our real object as long as possible. Our movements have been calculated for that purpose, and I am still anxious the deception should be kept up a few days longer, until our intentions are announced by the army's filing off towards the Delaware."

And yet still no word from de Grasse. Inevitably, Washington's temper began to fray. On August 28, he fired off an admonitory note to twenty-five-year-old William Colfax, the captain of his Lifeguards: "The enclosed are the instructions which I meant to deliver verbally, with some explanation, but your absence has prevented it! When business or inclination (especially on a march) calls you from your command I should be glad to know it, that I may regulate myself and orders accordingly." Commissary general Pickering was also castigated for his unavailability. But all of them, of course, were doing the best they could.

And then Washington learned that a large fleet of British warships had arrived at Sandy Hook, most likely from the Caribbean. Had they attacked and defeated the French fleet? Was that why he had not yet heard from de Grasse?

On August 10, eight days after his commander in chief, Admiral Rodney, sailed for England, Rear Admiral Samuel Hood departed from the British base at Antigua with fourteen ships of the line. By then Hood knew de Grasse had sailed from Cap François to Havana. What he did not know was how many ships the French admiral had taken with him. Assuming a significant number of French ships of the line had been left in the Caribbean to defend Haiti and Martinique, as well as to escort the convoy of merchant ships bound for France, Hood was confident that his and Graves's fleets were sufficient "to defeat any designs of the enemy, let de Grasse bring or send what ships he may in aid of those under Barras."

Rodney had left orders for him to stop at the Chesapeake and Delaware on his way to New York to make sure the French fleet had not arrived at either place ahead of him. Hood, who had left the Caribbean as quickly as possible "lest the enemy should get to America before me," appeared confident that he was far enough ahead of de Grasse that there was no need to make the intermediary stops Rodney had required. Although Hood claimed he'd found "no enemy . . . either in the Chesapeake or Delaware," Graves later insisted Hood had never actually stopped at either place, and logbook records from Hood's fleet appear to bear out the claim. For an officer with a reputation as a stickler, it was a curious lapse in judgment, especially since the French fleet had actually left the Caribbean several days ahead of him. As Graves was soon to discover, now that Hood had been temporarily freed from the overbearing presence of Rodney, he was displaying a rebellious, verging-on-insubordinate tendency to ignore the wishes of his superiors.

On his arrival at Sandy Hook, Hood discovered that a strange sort of languor had gripped British military leadership in New York. Instead of focusing on the imminent naval threat from the south, Admiral Graves and General Clinton (who had not yet learned that the French fleet in Newport had set sail) were preoccupied with plans to attack de Barras. Graves had spent the summer in a literal fog off the coast of Massachusetts searching for a French fleet he never found. Clinton had cycled through a long list of possible initiatives (one of which had included attacking Philadelphia) but had never been able to settle on a single objective, preferring instead to devote the majority of his energies to criticizing Cornwallis's actions in Virginia. "Sir Henry is all mystery," William Smith, the British chief justice of New York, recorded in frustration, "seems to approve [of a plan] but changes and resolves nothing."

As a subordinate, Clinton had been full of bold and daring ideas, but now, midway into his third year as commander in chief, he was quite content to coast. Not only was he well paid (his salary was higher than the prime minister's), he had the use of no less than five sumptuous houses in and around New York and seemed disinclined to begin a campaign that might take him away from his afternoon fox hunt. He was prone to what Smith described as "such gusts of passion that no gentlemen of spirit and independence will long continue in his [military] family." The sycophants who served under Clinton, Smith continued, "study only to make a use of their general for their own interests. . . . None of the set seeks information. . . . Poor Sir Henry! His want of parts renders him insensible of his dangers."

Clinton later insisted that there was nothing he could have done to interfere with the allied army's crossing of the Hudson and subsequent march across New Jersey since the largest force he could have mounted against them (four thousand men) would have been easily defeated by the combined American and French armies. With the exception of the naval expedition to Newport, his best option was to sit tight and prepare for a siege, even though he was daily receiving intelligence reports (despite Washington's attempts at subterfuge) that the Americans and French were actually preparing to march to Virginia. From Clinton's perspective, Cornwallis had nothing to fear from Washington and Rochambeau since the British admiralty had assured him "of our having a naval superiority." Because of his confidence in the British navy, it would have been wrong of him, he further insisted, to "entertain the most distant suspicion that General Washington really intended to march his army to the Chesapeake, where I knew it was impossible for such a number of troops to be fed without his having command of those waters."

Admiral Graves was in a similar state of denial, even proposing that de Grasse was really headed back to France. When Hood first arrived at Sandy Hook, Graves suggested that, for reasons of safety, he bring his fleet over the bar and into New York harbor, a process that would have delayed the fleet's sailing for several days. Troubled by the lack of urgency, Hood decided he must speak with his superiors face-to-face. "I got into my boat," he recalled, "and met with Mr. Graves and Clinton on Long Island, who were deliberating upon a plan of destroying the ships at Rhode Island. . . . I humbly submitted the necessity which struck me very forcibly of such of Graves's squadron as were ready coming without the bar immediately, whether to attend Clinton to Rhode Island or to look for the enemy at sea."

When they learned the next day that the French had sailed from Newport several days before, it became clear even to Clinton and Graves that the British navy must be sent to the Chesapeake. And yet when Hood insisted that they should sail as quickly as possible, the general and the admiral equivocated. "Graves and Sir Henry not fond of it," William Smith recorded in his journal, "but Hood pressed it, declaring that the French are gone to Havana and will be coming here." Graves wanted to wait until the *Prudent* and *Robust,* the two 74s that had been so badly damaged during the Battle of Cape Henry, were ready to sail. Hood, however, asserted that they already possessed an adequate force. "He is sure they will be superior to the united force of French and Spaniards after their detachment for the trade home," Smith wrote. "He is confident of their ill condition, and for fighting them wherever they can be met with."

Hood, full of arrogant impatience, had already roared up the coast of North America without giving the Chesapeake a serious look. He now disdained the need to bring along as many ships of the line as possible. Graves was hardly the man to impose his will upon an impetuous subordinate. At the beginning of the Seven Years' War, in 1757, he'd elected not to attack a French merchant vessel because he feared it might be a more powerful ship of the line, an exercise in caution that had earned him a court-martial and public reprimand. At the Battle of Cape Henry, just six months before, his ship, the

London, the largest in the action, had been disabled by the smallest vessel in the French fleet.

On August 31, these two very different admirals and their nineteen warships departed for the Chesapeake.

WHEN WASHINGTON LEARNED the British had sailed from Sandy Hook, he had still heard nothing from either de Grasse or de Barras. He feared that "by occupying the Chesapeake," the British fleet "should frustrate all our flattering prospects in that quarter." With so much riding on the appearance of the French fleet, Washington confessed to Nathanael Greene that "the present time is as interesting and anxious a moment as I have ever experienced." There was nothing he could do, however, but "hope . . . for the most propitious issue of our united exertions."

By the end of August both the French and American armies had made enough progress south that it was impossible to hide that they were not headed for Staten Island and New York. "Our destination can no longer be a secret," James Thacher wrote in his journal. "Lord Cornwallis is unquestionably the object of our present expedition. It is now rumored that a French fleet may soon be expected to arrive in Chesapeake Bay. . . . The great secret respecting our late preparations and movements can now be explained."

For Washington, the final leg of the march through New Jersey, from Princeton to Trenton, must have brought back a flood of memories from the winter of 1776–1777, when victories at those two towns had saved the American war effort from collapse. Now, almost five years later, in the sweltering heat of summer, he had a chance to finish what he had started. But first he had to get his army down the Delaware River to Philadelphia and ultimately to Christiana Bridge in Delaware, where they would disembark for a short, twelve-mile march to Head of Elk at the top of Chesapeake Bay.

Colonel Samuel Miles had rounded up twenty-three sloops, four schooners, and four bargelike scows to transport the army down the

Delaware from Trenton. Unfortunately, there was room for only about four thousand men. If the American army (which was in advance of the French) transported all its soldiers by water, there would be enough boats for only a portion of the French army. "Some delicacy must be used," Washington advised General Lincoln, "without . . . giving umbrage to our allies by taking more care of ourselves than them." Luckily, the French were more than willing to march by land to Philadelphia, and since the river was much lower than it had been during that stormy Christmas night in 1776 when Washington and his men had crossed the Delaware in the opposite direction, Rochambeau's soldiers were able to wade across at a fording place just upriver from Trenton.

By September 1, Washington was in Philadelphia, where he and Rochambeau and their staffs stayed at Robert Morris's house on Front Street. After having kept the destination of their march a secret for the last two weeks, it was now time to announce that they were headed to the Chesapeake. When Lieutenant Colonel Jean Baptiste Gouvion was sent ahead to assess "the state and condition of the intermediate roads and the measures proper to repair them," he was also told to "excite the inhabitants" in an effort to "facilitate the movement of our wagons." Washington sent letters to the leaders of the affected states, calling for their help in providing his army with provisions and livestock. His "strongest fears," he confessed in a circular sent to New Jersey, Delaware, and Maryland, were that even though the farmers in the region had enjoyed an excellent growing season, his army would be forced to disband for a lack of food.

To assist the American army in the purchase of these supplies now that the "Continentals" issued by Congress had depreciated to the point that they were worthless, Morris had gone to the extraordinary length of issuing his own currency. Just as Washington held together the American army, Morris was single-handedly providing the country with a way to pay for the war. Known as Morris notes ("Bobs" for short), this unusual, desperately last-ditch form of currency would prove indispensable in getting the army to Yorktown.

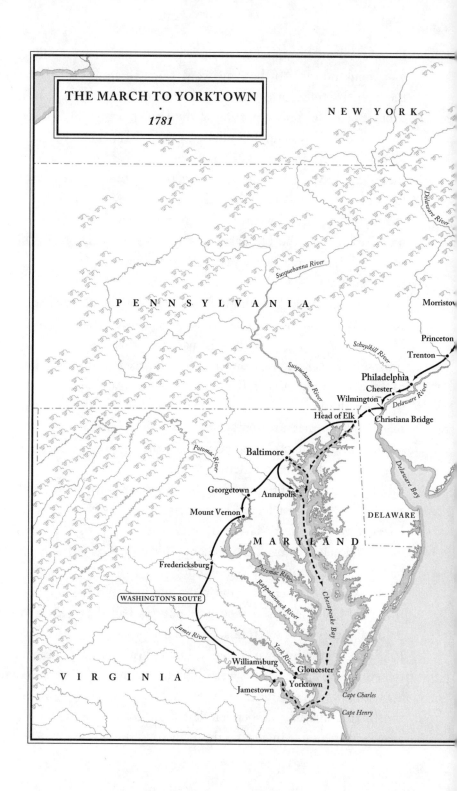

THE MARCH TO YORKTOWN
·
1781

NEW YORK

PENNSYLVANIA

Susquehanna River

Delaware River

Morristo[wn]

Princeton

Schuylkill River

Trenton

Philadelphia

Chester

Wilmington

Susquehanna River

Delaware River

Head of Elk

Christiana Bridge

Potomac River

Baltimore

Delaware Bay

Georgetown

Annapolis

Mount Vernon

DELAWARE

M A R Y L A N D

Fredericksburg

Potomac River

Rappahannock River

Chesapeake Bay

WASHINGTON'S ROUTE

James River

York River

Williamsburg

Gloucester

Jamestown

Yorktown

Cape Charles

Cape Henry

V I R G I N I A

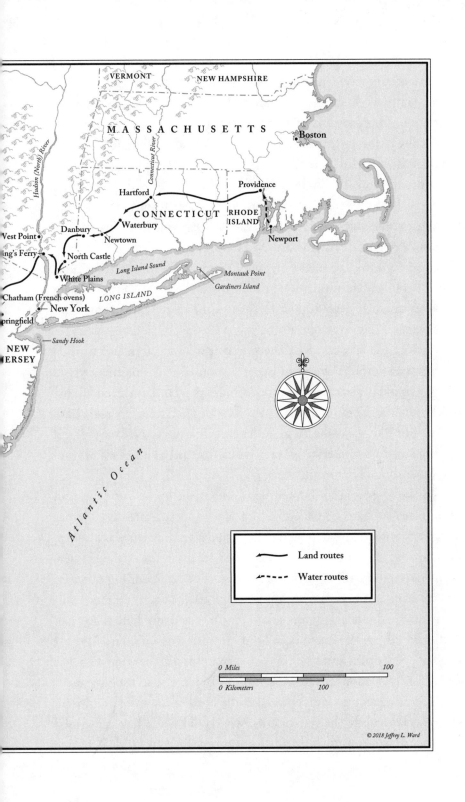

VERMONT   NEW HAMPSHIRE

M A S S A C H U S E T T S   •Boston

Hudson (North) River

Connecticut River

Hartford•   •Providence

C O N N E C T I C U T   RHODE ISLAND

Vest Point• •Danbury   •Waterbury

ng's Ferry• •Newtown   •Newport

•North Castle

•White Plains   Long Island Sound   Montauk Point

Chatham (French ovens)   Gardiners Island

•New York   LONG ISLAND

pringfield

—Sandy Hook

NEW JERSEY

Atlantic Ocean

Land routes

Water routes

0 Miles   100

0 Kilometers   100

© 2018 Jeffrey L. Ward

The citizens of Philadelphia (who had enjoyed several years out of the line of fire) were jubilant about the exciting turn the war had taken. Many of Washington's soldiers, however, were less than enamored with the prospect of marching several hundred miles into a region known for its infernal temperatures and killing fevers. The Americans were also more than a little envious of their better-supplied comrades in arms, the French. In addition to being paid on a regular basis, the French were allotted a pound and a half (or half a loaf) of bread each day. Back in July and early August, when the two armies were encamped side by side on the Hudson, some of the French soldiers had even tried to sell a portion of their rations to the Americans, who, of course, had no money of their own. Fights had erupted, and the resentment had continued to build until many Continental soldiers were on the verge of mutiny.

Washington had foreseen the problem weeks before and warned Morris that without the promise of a month's pay, his men would more than likely desert before proceeding into Maryland. And "Bobs" would not do. They must be paid, for the first time, in real, hard money, just like the coins they could hear clinking in the knapsacks of the French. But where was Morris going to find more than twenty-five thousand dollars in specie?

On the afternoon of September 2, the majority of the American army marched into Philadelphia "in slow and solemn step," James Thacher wrote, "regulated by the drum and fife." Since it was a warm, dry day and the line of march extended for two miles, the soldiers soon "raised a dust like a smothering snow storm, blinding our eyes and covering our bodies with it." The next day, it was the French soldiers' turn. About a mile outside of town, the army halted so each soldier could powder his hair and put on fresh white gaiters. And instead of just a drum and fife, they were accompanied by what Thacher described as "a complete band of music." Baron von Closen recalled, "Rochambeau and his staff entered at the head of the troops and were much acclaimed by the inhabitants, who could never have imagined that the French troops could be so handsome. All the gilded contingent was drawn up between the lancers and the hussars of Lauzun's legion to salute with all the grace possible the Congress, which was stationed with the president at its head, on the balcony of the hall of Congress." Thomas McKean, president of the Continental Congress, dressed in a black velvet suit, asked Rochambeau "if it would be proper for him to salute the field officers." When Rochambeau replied that the king of France usually did, McKean determined that "he might do likewise without demeaning himself" and raised his hand to his forehead.

While Philadelphia buzzed with anticipation, Washington was desperate for news of the French fleet. "I am distressed beyond expression," he wrote to Lafayette, "to know what is become of the Count de Grasse. . . . You see how critically important the present moment is: for my own part I am determined still to persist with unremitting ardor in my present plan, unless some inevitable and insuperable obstacles are thrown in our way. Adieu my Dear Marquis! If you get anything new from any quarter send it I pray *on the Spur of Speed*, for I am almost all impatience and anxiety at the same time."

NOT UNTIL SEPTEMBER 2, by which time Washington and Rochambeau were in Philadelphia, with the two armies soon to follow them into the city, did Henry Clinton have incontrovertible proof that the Americans and French were not about to attack New York. "By intelligence which I have this day received, it would seem that Mr. Washington is moving an army to the southward with an appearance of haste," he wrote to Cornwallis, "and gives out that he expects the cooperation of a considerable French armament."

Clinton had been completely bamboozled, and his officers knew it. "Thus by threatening us with a siege," British officer Frederick Mackenzie wrote, "the enemy have been suffered to come within sight of our posts, to retire thence again, to pass the Hudson, and to advance a good way into Jersey, without molestation or obstruction; while the army in Virginia . . . is now entirely unprepared for being attacked by a fleet and an army." It may have been Rochambeau's idea to head south, but without Washington's insistence on secrecy and subterfuge, they never would have gotten out of New Jersey. "If this is their scheme," Mackenzie continued, "the only thing we can do at present is to move with all our force into Jersey, so as to keep close to Washington and prevent him from moving southward and attack him. If the rebel army passes the Delaware unmolested, it will be then in vain to attempt stopping them." But, of course, by September 2, it was too late.

ON SEPTEMBER 5, three days after Clinton sent a message to Cornwallis about the approach of the enemy army from the north, Washington set out for Head of Elk, Maryland, about fifty miles southwest of Philadelphia. Now that the rear of the French army had reached the city and "everything in a tolerable train here," he must see firsthand how many boats had been assembled at the northern tip of the Chesapeake to transport the troops to Virginia. He had still heard nothing from de Grasse, an increasingly inexplicable silence that, if his previous experiences with the French were any indication, foretold no good.

While Washington traveled by land, Rochambeau and his entourage chose to go by water. Several French officers serving in the American army had played a prominent part in the heroic but ultimately unsuccessful defense of Philadelphia in the fall of 1777, when three riverside forts had been the only thing preventing the British navy from sailing into Philadelphia. With Thomas-Antoine de Mauduit du Plessis, a veteran of the action, as their guide, the French high command set out in a cutter from Philadelphia for a tour of the forts before disembarking at the town of Chester and proceeding by land to Head of Elk.

After stops at Fort Mifflin, Red Bank, and Billingsport, where they enjoyed some bread and butter and tea with the fort's elderly commandant, they continued on to Chester. While still a good distance from the town's landing, they noticed a man standing on the water-front, gesticulating wildly with his hat in one hand and a white hand-kerchief in the other. He was dressed in blue and buff regimentals and was leaping about like a man possessed. Could this be the commander in chief? Of course not. His Excellency was, in the words of Guillaume de Deux-Ponts, "of a natural coldness and of a serious and noble approach." He would never allow himself to act this way.

But sure enough, it was Washington.

H E H A D B E E N A B O U T T H R E E M I L E S to the south of Chester when he was handed a packet of letters forwarded to him by General Mordecai Gist in Baltimore just the day before. De Grasse and a fleet of twenty-eight ships of the line had arrived at the Chesapeake with 3100 French soldiers, more men than in the entire Continental army then encamped outside Philadelphia.

"One must experience such circumstances," Baron von Closen later wrote, "to appreciate the effect that such gratifying news can have." When word of de Grasse's presence in the Chesapeake reached Philadelphia later in the day, the city went wild with jubilation. "Some merry fellows mounted on scaffolds and stages," James Thacher wrote, "pronounced funeral orations for Lord Cornwallis. . . . The people ran in crowds to the residence of the minister of France and 'Long live Louis the Sixteenth!' was the general cry."

But as Washington had come to learn, the realization that a long coveted goal was almost within reach was one of the most dangerous feelings in the world. To be distracted by the prospect of an outcome that had not yet been achieved could be disastrous. How many times had he been on the cusp of victory only to watch in horrified astonishment as his opponent capitalized on a moment's complacency and his army had gone down in defeat? (The battles of Brandywine and Germantown, both fought within less than twenty miles of his present location, were just two of the more notorious examples.) Now, with the French fleet in the Chesapeake and Cornwallis trapped at the end of a solitary point, was when Washington needed his powers of concentration at their highest. Under no circumstances should he succumb to the self-indulgent urgings of expectation. He should continue to Head of Elk and attend to business.

But Washington could not help himself. The unrelenting pressures leading up to this moment had made it an almost physical necessity that he surrender himself to his emotions. He turned his horse around and rode back to Chester to tell Rochambeau the good news.

I have never seen a man more overcome with great and sincere joy than was General Washington," the Duc de Lauzun wrote with wonder. "His features, his physiognomy, his deportment," Guillaume de Deux-Ponts remembered, "all were changed in an instant. He put aside his character as arbiter of North America and contented himself for the moment with that of a citizen, happy at the good fortune of his country. A child, whose every wish had been gratified, would not have experienced a sensation more lively, and I believe that I am doing honor to the feelings of this rare man in endeavoring to express all their ardor."

The cutter nudged up to the wharf, and Rochambeau and Washington "embraced *warmly* on the shore." Soon the news had spread to both armies. "The soldiers from then on spoke of Lord Cornwallis as if they had already captured him," Baron von Closen observed, adding ominously, "one must not count his chickens before they are hatched."

Even before Washington learned of de Grasse's arrival in the Chesapeake, Henry Clinton had received disturbing intelligence of the sighting of a large French fleet off the American coast. And then on September 6, the day after Washington and Rochambeau's emotional embrace, he received a fifteen-word message from Cornwallis written in cipher on a note of Continental currency: *"An enemy's fleet within the Capes, between 30 and 40 ships of war, mostly large."*

"I can have no doubt that Washington is moving with at least 6000 French and rebel troops against you," Clinton responded on September 6. "I think the best way to relieve you is to join you as soon as possible, with all the force that can be spared from hence, which is about 4000 men." Washington might have gotten the jump on him, but since Clinton had access to troop transports, he could still get an army of reinforcements to Cornwallis before the arrival of the American and French land forces. The only problem was the issue of naval superiority. If the French fleet was as large as Cornwallis claimed, Clinton could not set out until he knew that Graves and Hood had met and defeated de Grasse. Clinton assured Cornwallis that the reinforcements "are already embarked and will proceed the instant I receive information from the admiral that we may venture." Washington had outgeneraled Clinton for the moment, but all it would take was a British naval victory to turn the tables on the enemy, and as Frederick Mackenzie recorded in his journal, "There is little doubt [that] an action must ensue."

While the citizens of Philadelphia applauded and cheered, a whole different mood gripped the British high command in New York. "This is an hour of anxiety!" the loyalist William Smith wrote on September 4. "A week will decide perhaps the ruin or salvation of the British Empire!"

BY SEPTEMBER 6, Washington was at the wide tidal creek Head of Elk, where a fleet of eighty vessels, including eighteen schooners, twelve sloops, and a few dozen smaller vessels, most of them oyster boats, had been appropriated for use by the allied army. There weren't enough vessels to come close to accommodating both armies, but given that the British had done their best to destroy as many watercraft as possible on the bay, this "mosquito fleet" was not a bad showing. Soon 1450 Continentals and their equipment began boarding; in the days to come another 1200 French soldiers and their artillery would be loaded aboard, leaving 4000 French and 1000 American soldiers to start the march to Baltimore and beyond that Annapolis, where it was hoped additional shipping could be secured from de Grasse.

Already word of the impending campaign against Cornwallis had started to spread across the nation. "The country through which we have passed," Washington's aide Jonathan Trumbull wrote, "[was] greatly pleased with the prospect of our expedition." That morning Washington officially announced the news of de Grasse's arrival to his troops. "As no circumstance could possibly have happened more opportunely in point of time," the general orders of the day read, "no prospect could ever have promised more important successes, and nothing but our want of exertions can probably blast the pleasing prospects before us. The general calls upon all the gallant officers, the brave and faithful soldiers he has the honor to command to exert their utmost abilities in the cause of the country and to share with him (with their usual alacrity) the difficulties, dangers, and glory of the present enterprise."

In truth, Washington realized that many of his "brave and faithful soldiers" had reached the breaking point. As the American army marched through Philadelphia, Robert Morris had worriedly noticed "great symptoms of discontent" among the ranks. Desertions were on the rise and might become wholesale if Morris didn't come up with the money Washington had requested to pay the soldiers a month's salary. Before he continued on to Virginia, Washington felt compelled to remind Morris "in the warmest terms to send on a month's pay at least, with all the expedition possible. I wish it come on the Wings of speed."

From Morris's perspective, the most important part of the news about de Grasse's arrival in the Chesapeake was knowing the admiral had the 500,000 pesos collected by Saavedra in Havana. With that amount of money waiting for the French army in Virginia, Rochambeau was now willing to loan Morris the twenty-five thousand dollars in coins needed to pay Washington's soldiers. Not only were the French providing the United States with a navy, they were paying its army.

The day after Washington reached out to Morris, kegs of silver dollars began to arrive at Head of Elk. The soldiers watched in wonder as the paymaster knocked the heads off the barrels and the coins spilled out across the ground. "I received the only pay that I ever drew for my service during the war," thirteen-year-old private John Hudson of the First New York Regiment later remembered, "six French crowns."

By September 8, Washington was on his way to Baltimore, a ride of sixty miles that he completed in a single day. "Great joy in town," Jonathan Trumbull noted, "illuminations, addresses, etc." Washington was determined to keep pushing south. Although Williamsburg (where Lafayette was now headquartered) was his ultimate destination, he had decided to visit Mount Vernon on the way. Both Nathanael Greene and Lafayette had stopped there during recent trips through the state, and Washington now longed to see the patch of ground that meant more to him than any in the world, a place he had not set eyes on in six years and four months.

So much had happened during those years—both throughout the United States and at Mount Vernon. Even before he married Martha, he had doubled the size of the house by adding a story. In 1773, he had decided to embark on a second major renovation, which would double the house's size once again with the addition of two large spaces at either end while adding the features that have come to define what we think of today as Mount Vernon: a central pediment in the front, a cupola on top, covered arcades (which Washington called "ways") connecting the sides of the house to buildings on either side of it, and a relatively new architectural feature for the late eighteenth century—a piazza on the back overlooking the river. More than a decade after shifting the orientation of the house inland, Washington had decided, at long last, to provide himself with a view of the Potomac.

With the outbreak of the war in 1775, it seemed ludicrous (at least to his caretaker Lund Washington) to continue with these costly and very complicated plans for a house that might be burned to the ground by the enemy at any moment, particularly since its owner was notorious as the leader of the American army. But Washington pushed forward with the renovations, badgering Lund with a ceaseless stream of instructions and questions.

It was when Washington's fortunes were at their lowest that he hungered most greedily for news of his distant and much loved house. In September 1776, after losing the Battle of Long Island and on the verge of being forced to retreat across New Jersey to the Pennsylvania side of the Delaware River, he had written Lund an extraordinary letter in which he admitted to never having been "in such an unhappy, divided state since I was born," only to turn his thoughts to the new room being built on the north end of the house. "The chimney . . . should be exactly in the middle of it, the doors and everything else to be exactly answerable and uniform—in short the whole executed in a masterly manner." The following year, after losing Philadelphia to the British and undergoing the tortuous political machinations surrounding the Conway Cabal as his troops languished at Valley Forge, he remotely oversaw the construction of the cupola and piazza. By March 1781, amid the frustrations of the failed Destouches expedition and myriad other woes, he had written his most recent existing letter about Mount Vernon: "Is your cover[ed] ways done?" he had plaintively asked Lund. "What are you going about next? Have you any prospect of getting paint and oil? Are you going to repair the pavements of the piazza? . . . An account of these things would be satisfactory to me, and infinitely amusing in the recital, as I have these kind of improvements very much at heart."

On the night of September 8, with Baltimore in a jubilant uproar, he resolved to leave early the next morning for Mount Vernon, another sixty miles away.

So as to travel as quickly as possible, he brought with him only a single aide, David Humphreys, as well as his enslaved manservant Billy Lee, who had been at his side throughout the war. The rest of his military family would catch up to them at Mount Vernon the following day, as would Rochambeau and his entourage.

All along the dusty road, past Annapolis, and across the Potomac into Virginia, Washington was pleased to observe what he described, in a letter to Maryland governor Thomas Sim Lee, as "a spirit of exertion." At long last, the American people were taking an interest in the outcome of the war.

By evening, in the last light of day, after riding a total of 120 miles in forty-eight hours (a figure Washington proudly noted in his diary), he made the familiar turn to Mount Vernon. Over the course of the last six years he had ordered Lund to supervise the replanting of trees on either side of the house so that it no longer stood alone on the top of its bare hill. He must have looked with a certain satisfaction on the changes he had made to the house. Thanks to the angular formality of the new pediment projecting from the roof (with an oval "oxeye" window in the center) and the cupola rising above, the horizontal additions were now balanced by a much needed upward reach into the sky above.

His first series of renovations, started back in 1758, had turned Mount Vernon into a conventional southern house. But now it was something else altogether: a wonderfully idiosyncratic (Washington called it "not quite orthodox") expression of a planter who, after being denied the English education of his father and half brother, had fully embraced the wayward freedom of a country at the edge of a wilderness. His neighbor Bryan Fairfax had been immediately struck by the changes Washington had made, writing in the spring of 1778, "I like the house because it is uncommon for there has always appeared too great a sameness in our buildings."

We know that Washington found the time that evening to write a letter requesting that the local militia be immediately employed in improving the roads in anticipation of the army's supply train of 1500 horses, 800 oxen, and 220 wagons. But we know nothing else of his first night at Mount Vernon. In addition to Martha and his stepson Jacky Custis and Jacky's wife, Eleanor, there were four new grandchildren—three girls and an infant boy—all of whom had been born since the beginning of the war.

The house renovations were by no means finished—the large public room in the north end of the house had not even been plastered. The new roof had already begun to leak and much else was left undone, but at some point he must have taken a seat on his new piazza with its soaring, two-story-high columns and looked out on the starlit serenity of the Potomac. Now, twenty-two years after the renovations that had turned the house away from the river, he was able to gaze upon its waters with the knowledge that more than 150 miles to the southeast a fleet of French warships was anchored just inside Cape Henry.

By the next afternoon, the rest of Washington's military family had arrived; later that evening came Rochambeau and the following day General Chastellux and his retinue. "A numerous family now present," Trumbull recorded on September 11. "All accommodated. An elegant seat and situation, great appearance of opulence and real exhibitions of hospitality and princely entertainment." At one point Washington wrote to Lafayette about their travel plans, adding in an uncharacteristically cheerful postscript, "I hope you will keep Lord Cornwallis safe, without provisions or forage until we arrive. Adieu."

After a day of rest on September 12, Washington left for Williamsburg, still more than 150 miles away. He had gone only 15 or so miles when, halfway between the towns of Colchester and Dumfries, he received an express. "The French were gone out from the bay in pursuit of the English," Trumbull recorded. What had happened after that "was not known."

Suddenly all vestiges of the elation Washington had felt the previous week had vanished. If the French fleet had been beaten and the British regained control of the Chesapeake, the dozens upon dozens of allied vessels heading down the bay were at risk. He must order them to seek shelter until the results of the battle were known. Trumbull had only two words to describe Washington's response to the news: "Much agitated."

On they rode through the familiar countryside toward Williamsburg, not knowing what lay ahead.

CHAPTER 8

"Ligne de Vitesse"

ON AUGUST 30, 1781, Admiral de Grasse's squadron of twenty-eight ships of the line and five frigates sailed into the Chesapeake. Finally, after three years of trying, the French had established naval superiority along a portion of the North American coast.

By assembling a fleet of close to thirty ships of the line and successfully anchoring them inside the Chesapeake, de Grasse had made possible what looked to be a great victory. As Louis Lebègue Duportail, the engineer Washington had sent to the Chesapeake to prepare for the army's arrival, wrote from the *Ville de Paris,* de Grasse's flagship, on September 4, "We must take Lord Cornwallis or be all dishonored."

And yet the French fleet still faced at least one significant challenge. It was only a matter of time before the British sent a large fleet of their own to the Chesapeake. De Grasse's highest priority was to prepare for that inevitable confrontation. He must keep his fleet of battleships poised and ready at the bay entrance while his frigates patrolled the waters beyond the Virginia capes for any signs of the enemy. Once Washington and Rochambeau reached Virginia, it would then be time to cooperate with the land forces in securing Cornwallis's defeat. Until that point (which was weeks away), his fleet must remain ever vigilant at the bay entrance, since to lose control of the Chesapeake was to lose everything.

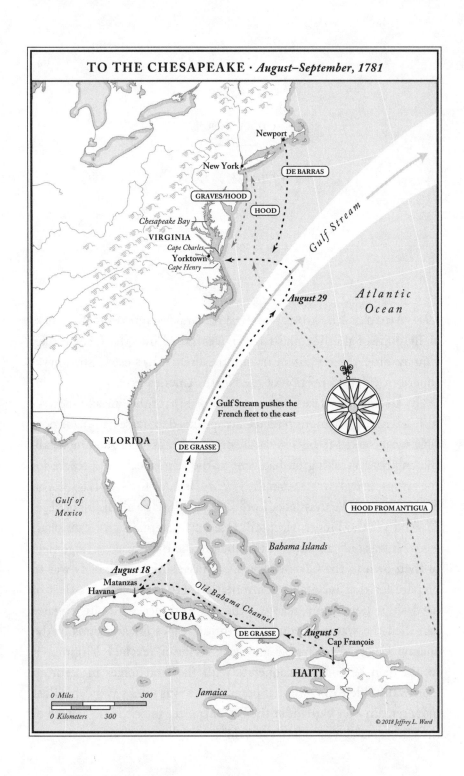

TO THE CHESAPEAKE · *August–September, 1781*

Newport

New York

DE BARRAS

GRAVES/HOOD

HOOD

Chesapeake Bay

VIRGINIA

Cape Charles

Yorktown

Cape Henry

Gulf Stream

August 29

Atlantic Ocean

Gulf Stream pushes the French fleet to the east

FLORIDA

DE GRASSE

Gulf of Mexico

HOOD FROM ANTIGUA

Bahama Islands

August 18

Matanzas

Havana

Old Bahama Channel

CUBA

DE GRASSE

August 5

Cap François

HAITI

Jamaica

0 Miles   300

0 Kilometers   300

© 2018 Jeffrey L. Ward

Almost a decade before, during a training cruise off the coast of France, de Grasse had impressed his superiors as "the best skilled captain in the squadron." But there had been a caveat. "His frequent collisions with other ships during the cruise seems to demand something more perfect in his estimate of a situation at a glance." As Washington would come to recognize in the weeks ahead, de Grasse's considerable talents as a naval commander were "marred by his own impetuosity."

Even before his fleet had dropped anchor, de Grasse was preparing to disembark the more than three thousand soldiers under the command of the Comte de Saint-Simon. "Feeling the full cost of time," de Grasse longed to begin the assault on the British posts at Yorktown and Gloucester and even considered attacking Cornwallis before the arrival of the armies from the north. Luckily, a conversation with Duportail convinced him that the enemy's fortified positions "shall be forced with difficulty," and that he better wait for Washington and Rochambeau. Once the two generals had arrived in Williamsburg and joined with the army under Lafayette, the allied land forces could begin the thirteen-mile march across the peninsula formed by the James and York rivers to Yorktown.

By September 4, the French fleet's longboats and cutters, accompanied by the ship of the line *Experiment* and two frigates, had begun to transport Saint-Simon's troops up the James River to combine with Lafayette's army in Williamsburg. This meant that almost two thousand of the squadron's officers and sailors (close to 30 percent of the ship's crew in at least one instance) were away from their vessels as they rowed the soldiers more than sixty miles upriver. Depending on the weather, it could take as much as a week for these officers and sailors (whom de Grasse described as "the best drilled part of the crew") to complete the voyage up and down the James.

De Grasse then sent three additional ships of the line and a frigate to the mouth of the York River to prevent Cornwallis's army from escaping by water. As a result of these detachments, the French fleet stationed at the entrance of the Chesapeake was now down from twenty-eight ships of the line and five frigates to twenty-four ships of the line and just two frigates to act as roving pickets. On September 4, in response to a request from Washington to assist in transporting the American and French troops down the bay, de Grasse agreed to send seven additional men-of-war to Baltimore. The fleet upon which French naval superiority depended was about to be reduced by almost a third.

At ten the next morning, before he had a chance to send the ships up the bay, de Grasse learned that sails had been sighted off the entrance of the Chesapeake. At first it was hoped these were the ships under the command of Admiral de Barras, already overdue from Newport.

And then the truth began to set in. The fleet was far too big for this to be de Barras's squadron—at least twenty-five sails were now visible on the horizon. This could only be the British.

No one in the British Admiralty had ever wanted Rear Admiral Thomas Graves to be where he was now—in command of a fleet of nineteen ships of the line and eight frigates approaching an even larger fleet of French warships in possession of the Chesapeake. Even before Graves's predecessor, Mariot Arbuthnot, had resigned back in July, the Admiralty had decided to move Graves to a subordinate position in the Caribbean while Rear Admiral Digby replaced him as commander of the North American squadron in New York. Unfortunately, Digby had not yet arrived from England, and since Graves outranked Hood, it fell to Graves to lead the present expedition.

Graves was the antithesis of Hood's former commander, the forceful and temperamental George Rodney, who once reminded a subordinate that "the painful task of thinking belongs to me." Instead of dictating to his captains, Graves encouraged his officers to do their own thinking—partly because that was how it had been done where he had previously served (the Channel Fleet in England) and partly because decisiveness had never been a part of his makeup. As his superiors in the Admiralty understood, Graves lacked the force of character to command a large squadron of ships of the line. But thanks to Rodney's swollen prostate and Arbuthnot's defective eyes, here he was.

He had been led to believe by his second in command, Samuel Hood, that de Grasse's fleet would be considerably smaller than his own. Hood had been confident that given the French navy's long-standing commitment to escorting convoys of merchant vessels back to France, the most ships de Grasse would take north was twelve, or "about the number they had coppered."

But de Grasse had fooled them all. By bringing every ship of the line he had available, he had caught the British completely by surprise. One can only imagine the sickening sense of dread that washed over Rear Admiral Thomas Graves when on the morning of September 5 he "discovered a number of great ships at anchor, which seemed to be extended across the entrance of the Chesapeake." Not only had the French beat him to the Chesapeake but they had twenty-four ships of the line—five more than he had under his command—and as Hood noted, "their topsail yards [were] hoisted aloft as a signal for getting under sail."

DE GRASSE'S SQUADRON was anchored just inside the Middle Ground—the wide shoal between Cape Charles to the north and Cape Henry to the south. In addition to being depleted by four ships of the line and three frigates, the squadron was missing a significant portion of its officers and crew—a deficiency of which the British were thankfully unaware. Of the two frigates performing lookout duty, one had run aground on Cape Henry that morning and spent several hours attempting to free itself. Instead of a frigate, the 74-gun *Marseilles,* anchored inside the Middle Ground, was the first to sight the enemy.

As a consequence, de Grasse did not receive word of the British fleet until it was almost upon him. Worst of all, the tide was flowing in, making it impossible for his ships to sail out of the bay until the tide changed at noon. With luck, the French ships would be able to clear Cape Henry before the vanguard of the British fleet arrived, but it would be close.

De Grasse might have elected to remain at anchor and make the enemy come to him—a strategy that made a great deal of sense given the foul tide and missing crew members. But that would have required the impulsive de Grasse to sit and wait for the enemy. No matter what disadvantages he was operating under, he resolved to set sail and attack.

By 10:30 a.m., de Grasse had ordered his ships (still tethered to their anchors as they waited for the tide to shift) to clear for action. By 11:15 he had given the signal to heave in their cables until their bows were directly above their anchors. Since the majority of the longboats and cutters were dozens of miles up the James River, the ships' crews lacked the small vessels required to get their larger anchors aboard, and at 11:45 de Grasse ordered his ships to leave their anchors behind and slip their cables (to which they attached buoys for later retrieval) and set sail.

Under normal circumstances, de Grasse would have overseen the painstaking process of assembling his fleet into the line of battle—a preestablished order in which he positioned himself in the center of the line, with designated captains commanding the vanguard and rearguard. But these were not normal circumstances. For only the second time in the history of the French navy, de Grasse ordered a *"ligne de vitesse,"* or line of speed, calling for his captains to form a line according to their ships' relative speeds rather than their assigned positions. Since the ships that sailed out of the bay the fastest would have the honor of leading the fleet into battle, this turned the usually ponderous and often frustrating process of forming the line into an exhilarating race.

Making it all the more exciting, if not downright terrifying, was the challenge of maneuvering a ship of the line at close quarters without her full complement of crew. The Chevalier de Thy was the captain of the 74-gun *Citoyen*. De Thy had hoped to begin sailing out of the anchorage on port tack, but the captain of the frigate *Aigrette,* which had run aground earlier that morning, warned him "that if I didn't put about I ran the risk of running aground on Cape Henry." Reluctantly de Thy set out on starboard, heading north through the French anchorage. He soon found himself coming up on de Grasse's *Ville de Paris,* which was just getting under way. De Thy was tempted to shoot up to windward of the giant flagship, but not wanting "to disturb" the admiral (who was renowned for his temper), de Thy wisely bore off to leeward.

Finally at 1:15 p.m., "finding myself free of all ships that were under sail to exit the bay," de Thy tacked to port. De Grasse was "a little ahead of me," signaling the leading ships "that had gone out and were forming up, to keep close to the wind." At 1:30, having finally secured his smaller anchor to the cathead on the bow, de Thy "crowded sail," and he passed Cape Henry about fifteen minutes later. Once he had manned his two batteries of cannons "as well as I could," he reduced sail so he could take up a position behind the *Northumberland.* Suddenly another ship, the *Palmier,* made it clear she wanted "that station." In addition, the *Solitaire* was "crowding sail" and threatening to overrun all three of them. "To avoid disputing further," de Thy headed up, made sail, and went looking for yet another place in the line. It was a no-holds-barred competition to secure the best possible position. At one point the *Caton* attempted to force her way into an apparently nonexistent space between the *César* and the *Destin.* "The latter only saved its bowsprit by backing all sails." As it was, the *Destin* lost a foretopsail mast and punctured a sail.

Up until now, Admiral de Grasse—a tall, imposing figure from one of the oldest families in France—had established a reputation as a demanding leader. After the indecisive engagement against Hood off Martinique on April 29, he'd called his captains together and "with the sharpest reproaches made known the dissatisfaction he felt with [their] behavior . . . , adding that another time he would lay down his command unless they showed a better conduct in obeying signals and fulfilling their duties." In the early afternoon hours of

September 5, as those same captains raced one another out of the Chesapeake toward the approaching enemy, de Grasse was going to have to settle for whatever line of battle they created.

As might have been expected, given the tumultuous circumstances of the fleet's leave-taking, the French fleet was, according to one officer, "in a very bad order." The normal distance between two ships varied between one and two cable lengths, or between 600 and 1200 feet. Now there was a mile and a half between the first cluster of four French ships and the next group of two. Then it was another three miles to the fourteen ships that made up the rest of the fleet, with de Grasse's *Ville de Paris* commanding the center and Baron de Monteil's *Languedoc* in charge of the rear.

It was hardly an encouraging way to begin a battle. With huge, irregular gaps in the French line, with their ships drastically undermanned, and with the British approaching on the opposite tack "in the best possible order, bowsprit to stern, bearing down on us," de Grasse's fleet—despite having once enjoyed an overwhelming numerical and strategic advantage—now appeared to be at the mercy of the enemy.

The way to win a naval battle in the eighteenth century was to isolate a portion of the enemy's fleet and attack it with a greater number of your own ships, a process that could be repeated as the opponent was defeated piece by piece or decided to end the battle by sailing away. In the early afternoon hours of September 5, there was more than a mile between the French vanguard and the rest of de Grasse's squadron. As the British fleet approached on starboard tack under foresails and topgallant sails, the French vanguard was there for the taking. According to Samuel Hood, whose *Barfleur* commanded the vanguard of the British line, the half-dozen or so enemy ships might have been "demolished . . . a full hour and [a] half . . . before any of the [French] rear could have come up."

Several French captains sailing out of the Chesapeake feared that was exactly what the British were about to do. When the ships in the British van began to bear off toward the French vanguard, Balthazar de Gras-Préville, captain of the *Zélé*, assumed the British were about to "cross [our] ships' course" and place the leading French ships between two lines of fire.

Admiral Graves also recognized that "the French van had extended themselves considerably too much from their own center and seemed to present the favorable moment for an attack." He, however, chose to take a different, more conservative course, and given the realities of communication at that time in the British navy, one can hardly blame him. While the French used a system of signaling that was consistent throughout their entire navy, there was no such uniformity among the British. The commands, as well as the flags Graves used to signal them (a system he'd inherited, for the most part, from Arbuthnot), were in several critical instances different from those used by the captains in Hood's fleet from the Caribbean. Given that the two fleets had only recently been combined, there was a high likelihood of confusion when it came to signaling (which, as it turned out, proved to be the case). Rather than pounce on the enemy's vanguard and begin a series of maneuvers that would have been difficult, if not impossible, to communicate given the limitations he was operating under, Graves elected to do the more conventional thing: adjust his line of battle so as to "bring his Majesty's fleet nearly parallel to the line of approach of the enemy."

Seeing that his own vanguard was approaching the shoal water of the Middle Ground at the bay's entrance, Graves ordered his fleet to wear (or jibe) so that they were now sailing on the same tack as the enemy. Unlike Destouches at the Battle of Cape Henry, Graves did not order his fleet to jibe in succession, which would have preserved the existing order of the British line. Instead, his fleet jibed in unison, which placed Rear Admiral Francis Samuel Drake (and some of the oldest ships in the fleet) in the van and put Hood in the rear. Soon after, Graves ordered his ships to cease all forward motion so as to "let the center of the enemy's ships come abreast of us."

After two hours of adjusting his ships' relative positions as they gradually edged downwind toward the enemy to leeward, Graves began to realize that he was running out of time. Even though de Grasse had not yet been able to form a proper line of battle (his center and rear still lagged far behind and below the vanguard), he must begin the fighting. "The enemy's ships advancing very slow, and evening approaching," the log of the *London*, Graves's flagship, reads, "the Admiral, judging this to be the moment of attack, made the signal for the ships to bear down and engage their opponents."

Unfortunately, like Arbuthnot before him at the Battle of Cape Henry, Graves neglected to lower the signal for line ahead, a signal that contradicted the order to engage the enemy, a simple but potentially fatal human error. Most of the ships in the British line followed Graves's example and headed for the French. But not Samuel Hood and the rest of the rearguard, who continued to follow in his commander's wake rather than peel off for the enemy. Whether the result of honest confusion or an act of passive-aggressive protest, Hood's actions (or lack thereof) ultimately had little impact on the result of the battle. Because by four p.m., when Graves ordered the attack, the wind had begun to shift.

Over the course of the next two hours, the wind clocked more than 30 degrees to the right. The effect of this shift from north to east was to squeeze the two opposing vanguards together while increasing the distance between the rearguards, which never came within effective range of each other during the battle. Even the lines' two centers, from which Graves and de Grasse issued their orders, had a difficult time engaging with any effectiveness. As a result, the Battle of the Chesapeake would be fought almost entirely between the ships of the two vans. As the Chevalier de Gras-Préville recorded in the log of the *Zélé*, "From the center the [rest of the] two navies looked on."

ONE OF THE FIRST FRENCH SHIPS out of the anchorage that afternoon had been the 80-gun *Auguste* commanded by the fifty-one-year-old Louis-Antoine de Bougainville. Bougainville had begun his military career in the army, and after serving under Montcalm during the fall of Quebec in the Seven Years' War, transferred to the navy, where he'd led exploring expeditions to the Falkland Islands and, most famously, to the South Pacific, becoming the first Frenchman to circumnavigate the globe. (It was during this voyage that one of his naturalists discovered the flower that was ultimately named Bougain-villea.) Besides being a military officer, Bougainville enjoyed a con-siderable intellectual reputation (the writer and philosopher Denis Diderot described him as "ballasted to starboard by a treatise on dif-ferential and integral calculus and to port by a voyage around the world"), and when not at sea, he frequented the salons of Paris, where the intellectual elite of the Enlightenment gathered to discuss litera-ture and science, and to gossip.

Despite Bougainville's considerable accomplishments as a mariner, his humble birth (his father had been a notary) limited his options in the French navy, where aristocratic, academy-trained officers (known as "the Reds" for the color of their uniforms) looked down on "the Blues," auxiliary officers recruited from either the merchant service or the army who tended to come from less distinguished families. Ac-cording to the Spaniard Francisco Saavedra, who was shocked by the class warfare he witnessed in de Grasse's squadron, "These factions have the navy divided into scandalous bands; each ship of the line; each vessel is a battlefield. The nobility defends the cause of the old navy, the commoners that of the auxiliary officers." Being a confirmed Red, de Grasse (who had regarded his predecessor, the army-trained Comte d'Estaing, with "irreconcilable enmity") was predisposed to view Bougainville as an "intruder," and the two had been on "un-friendly terms" ever since the engagement off Martinique on April 29, when de Grasse blamed Bougainville for not bringing up the fleet's rearguard in a timely fashion.

But the afternoon of September 5 promised to be different. Out of the Darwinian competition unleashed by the line of speed, Bougain-ville, one of the smartest, most talented mariners on the water that day, had taken his rightful place at the head of the fleet. History has

THE BATTLE OF THE CHESAPEAKE · *September 5, 1781*

Fig. 1: The British Approach

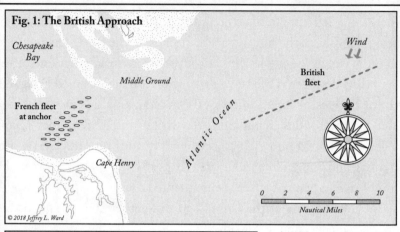

Chesapeake
Bay

Middle Ground

Atlantic Ocean

French fleet
at anchor

Cape Henry

Wind

British
fleet

0   2   4   6   8   10
Nautical Miles

© 2018 Jeffrey L. Ward

Fig. 2: *Ligne de Vitesse*

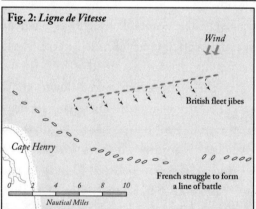

Wind

British fleet jibes

Cape Henry

French struggle to form
a line of battle

0   2   4   6   8   10
Nautical Miles

At 10:00 a.m., the French sight the British approaching on starboard tack. De Grasse must wait until noon, when the tide begins to ebb, before he can order his fleet to leave the anchorage.

Without the time to form the standard line of battle, de Grasse orders his captains to form the line according to their ships' relative speeds. By 2:15, there is a three-mile gap between the French vanguard and the rest of the fleet, providing British admiral Graves with the opportunity to isolate and destroy the leading French ships.

Fig. 3: The Battle Begins

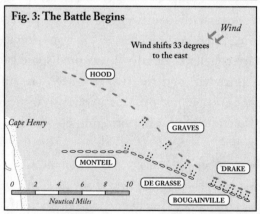

Wind

Wind shifts 33 degrees
to the east

HOOD

Cape Henry

GRAVES

MONTEIL

DRAKE

DE GRASSE

BOUGAINVILLE

0   2   4   6   8   10
Nautical Miles

Instead of immediately attacking the French vanguard, Graves spends the next two hours waiting for the French fleet to emerge from the Chesapeake and form a line of battle. At 4:15, just as the wind begins to shift to the east, Graves orders his fleet to engage the enemy. Since only the leading ships are within effective range, the battle is fought almost entirely by the two vanguards, commanded by Drake and Bougainville.

made de Grasse the hero of the Chesapeake, but it would be Bougain-ville and the French vanguard that did the fighting.

THE ONCE FRESH BREEZE had begun to die as the leading Brit-ish ships bore down on the French. Since the enemy's bows were pointed at their port sides, Bougainville and his vanguard had the opportunity to "fight them with advantage." Once the British were within what an ensign aboard the *Auguste* described as "a very small half-cannon range," the undermanned French batteries (Bougain-ville's usual 700-man crew was down by 200 officers and sailors) be-gan to fire, and soon both vans were "fiercely engaged." Almost immediately, the ship at the head of the British van, the *Shrewsbury,* had "her fore and main topsail yards shot away" and was disabled. As the *Shrewsbury* drifted off station, the second in the British line, the *Intrepid,* found herself besieged by the more powerful *Pluton* and *Marseilles.* One of the first French casualties of the battle was Captain Brun de Boade of the *Reflechi,* who was killed by the initial British broadside. "All that could be seen," the Chevalier de Thy recorded from the rearguard, "was fire and smoke on either side."

By 4:30, Drake's flagship, the 80-gun *Princessa,* had begun to fire at close range on the French 74 *Diadème,* captained by the Marquis de Montecler. The ships were so close to each other that the wadding from the British cannons "set fire to [the *Diadème*] at every shot." Their vessels surrounded by a disorienting cloud of fire and smoke as the constantly shifting breeze continued to shuffle the ships' posi-tions, the crews of the two vans blasted away at whatever vessel was beside them, and instances of friendly fire were almost inevitable.

To better align the French van with the rest of the fleet, which had an increasingly difficult time reaching the leading ships because of the more easterly direction of the wind, de Grasse ordered the van to bear off more than 20 degrees. However, since such a maneuver would have, in the words of one French officer, "presented the stern [to the enemy]" and caused the van to receive an even more "severe handling" than it already had, the captains found the order "impracticable" and remained side to side with their British opponents. Too closely involved with the enemy to bear off and with the rest of their fleet too far to leeward to provide any assistance, "[t]he four ships in the van soon found themselves . . . entirely cut off from the rest of the fleet and constantly engaged with seven or eight vessels at close quarters." It may have taken longer than it should have, but Graves had finally succeeded in bringing a larger number of his own ships against the enemy's isolated vanguard.

At one point, with the British at what an ensign aboard the *Auguste* described as "the infinitesimally small range of langridge shot, nearly rifle range," Bougainville drew so close to Admiral Drake's *Princessa* that even de Grasse was impressed. "That is what I call fighting," the admiral later enthused; "I thought you had boarded!" Although the *Princessa* was able to elude capture, this allowed Bougainville to turn his undivided attention on the *Terrible,* which he quickly pounded into a barely floating wreck. Two cannonballs were later found buried in the British 74's foremast, one of which weighed a reported thirty-nine pounds—four pounds more than the supposed maximum size of a naval cannonball. According to Bougainville, the gunners aboard the *Auguste* fired an impressive 654 cannon shots that day.

In the midst of this furor, a British cannonball cut through the bowline of the *Auguste*'s foretopsail (one of the primary sails used in battle). Without the bowline (which pulled the forward edge of the sail tight when sailing close-hauled), the foretop was "rendered incapable of service," and Bougainville would have a difficult time remaining on the attack.

The way to repair the bowline was to lower a man from the yardarm—a challenging procedure at the best of times but close to impossible in the midst of a battle. Twice a man ventured onto the foretopsail yard to make the repair and twice that man was killed. Assuming "no one would make a third attempt," Bougainville offered, with what the officer Karl Tornquist described as "his usual kindness," the contents of his "purse to the one who would put the bowline in shape." A sailor immediately leapt onto the yard and calling out, "'My captain, we do not go there for money . . . ,' tackled his work and fortunately carried it through."

Because of the time it took to repair the bowline, Bougainville's *Auguste* dropped too far to leeward to assist the beleaguered *Diadème,* "which could scarcely hold out . . . , having only four 36 pounders and nine 18s fit for use and having all on board killed, wounded, or burnt." Just when it seemed the *Diadème* might be in danger of being totally destroyed, Chabert Cogolin, captain of the *Saint Esprit,* "seeing the imminent danger of the *Diadème,* hoisted sail and was soon in her wake; then . . . opened a terrible fire" that forced the British 74 *Albion* to "haul her wind" to escape.

Taking up the rear of the French vanguard was the 64 *Caton,* the only uncoppered ship to make it to the front of the fleet. By the end of the fighting this smallest of the ships of the line had suffered, according to Captain Framond, "more than fifty gunshots in the planking of my . . . bottom, including several under the water, one in my rudder, at least three times as many in my sails, mast, and rigging." With no ships to support her from behind, the *Caton,* "whose natural position was . . . the 28th ship in the rearguard," endured "continual fire" for an hour and forty-five minutes "without bending or yielding by a line."

By 5:30, after an hour and a half of intense fighting, both the French and British vanguards had reached the point of exhaustion. "For our part," an officer aboard the *Saint Esprit* recorded, "we were so tired that though within gunshot, the vans no longer fired." While sporadic fighting continued between the centers of the two lines for the next half hour, the cessation of combat in the front of the line allowed the leading French ships to start complying, at long last, with de Grasse's order to bear away from the wind. As the French vanguard sailed almost directly downwind, the French center and rear, "by crowding sail . . . closed our line to the extent possible." By six, de Grasse had finally succeeded in closing the gaps in the French line of battle and had hopes of renewing the fight, but in thirty minutes, with the approach of darkness, all firing had ceased.

The vessels in both vans had suffered mightily, and yet, given the ferocity of the fighting, it was amazing how little overall damage the French had experienced, especially compared with the British. The *Diadème* was in need of assistance, but the rest of the fleet was still capable of continuing the fight. Not so their opponents: Admiral Graves soon learned that "the *Shrewsbury, Intrepid,* and *Montague* [were] unable to keep the line, and the *Princessa* [was] in the momentary apprehension of the maintopmast going over the side."

That night, as sailors throughout the French squadron worked frantically to repair their ships' rigging, de Grasse had no choice but to acknowledge that "the honors of the day" belonged to Louis-Antoine de Bougainville. "These two gentlemen had since April 29 been on unfriendly terms," Tornquist wrote, "but now and thereafter became attached to one another."

For the next four days the two fleets kept in sight of each other as they sailed farther and farther from the Chesapeake. Above all else, de Grasse wanted to attack the British. "My dear Bougainville," he wrote on September 7, "if the wind continues and the English do not escape us tonight, we shall meet them at closer range tomorrow morning. . . . I have great hopes based upon the damages to the enemy which I can see. I judge by them that they are not as well-outfitted as we are, and by the slowness of their movements that they are not as ready for battle."

While de Grasse wished for a rematch with the British, Bougainville believed they should have long since given up the chase and returned to the Chesapeake. "It is what we ought to have been doing since the battle," he wrote in his journal on September 9. "Perhaps we would also find the squadron of M. de Barras." As Bougainville realized, occupation of the Chesapeake—not attacking Graves—should be the top French priority. If the British fleet should slip away in the night and get into the bay first, de Grasse would have, like Destouches before him, squandered the victory that might have won the war.

. . .

IN THE DAYS AHEAD, the two fleets attempted to take advantage of the constantly shifting wind. While de Grasse tried to gain the weather gage and attack, Graves did his best to keep the French fleet a safe distance to leeward while he and Samuel Hood, his second in command, traded politely worded barbs. Hood made it clear he thought Graves had failed to take advantage of what he called "a most glorious opening." Graves made it clear he thought Hood had willfully failed to engage the French rearguard and thereby "a most glorious victory was lost."

It all came to a head during a conference aboard Graves's flagship, the *London*. According to an account published the following year, "Admiral Graves asked Admiral Hood why he did not bear down and engage? The answer was: 'You had up the signal for the line.' Admiral Graves then turned to Admiral Drake, and asked him how he came to bear down? He replied: 'On account of the signal for action.' Admiral Graves then said: 'What say you to this, Admiral Hood?' Sir Samuel answered: 'The signal for the line was enough for me.'"

By the night of September 9, the British had lost sight of the enemy. That same night William Clement Finch, the captain of the *Terrible*, reported that the pumps were having difficulty keeping up with his leaky ship. Two days later, at a council of war, Graves, Hood, and Drake decided they must sink the *Terrible*. But when a sea cock was opened, the old and broken ship refused to go down. So on September 12, Graves ordered her burned. "At half past 8 saw the *Terrible* on fire," the logbook of the *Royal Oak* reads, "at 2 am saw the explosion of the *Terrible*, all the fleet in company."

The following day, Graves learned from one of his frigates that while he'd been focusing on the state of the *Terrible* and the lack of support he'd received from Hood, de Grasse had finally decided to head back to the Chesapeake. To add insult to injury, the enemy fleet now included de Barras's squadron from Newport, which had snuck into the bay the day before de Grasse's return. Even worse, two British frigates had been captured after pausing in the Chesapeake to clip the buoys attached to the French fleet's anchor cables.

Once again, Graves called a council of war. "Upon this state of the position of the enemy, the present condition of the British fleet . . . , and the impracticability of giving any effectual succor to Lord Cornwallis in the Chesapeake, it was resolved that the British squadron . . . should proceed with all dispatch to New York, and there use every possible means for putting the squadron into the best state for service." Until the British fleet's return, Cornwallis was on his own. And so, after more than a week of hesitancy and hand-wringing, the Battle of the Chesapeake ended with the British in retreat and a newly fortified French fleet in possession of the Chesapeake.

The following night, September 14, George Washington and Rochambeau rode into Williamsburg.

Lafayette had been stricken by a fever, but when he learned of Washington's approach, he immediately rode out to meet his commander in chief. St. George Tucker, a twenty-nine-year-old lawyer and lieutenant colonel in the Virginia militia, watched wide-eyed as Lafayette "caught the general round his body, hugged him as close as it was possible, and absolutely kissed him from ear to ear once or twice . . . with as much ardor as ever an absent lover kissed his mistress on his return."

Word of de Grasse's victory had not yet reached Williamsburg, but at some point that night Washington learned the good news. "I am at a loss to express the pleasure, which I have in congratulating your Excellency on your return to your former station in the bay," he wrote to de Grasse the following day. "I take particular satisfaction in felicitating your Excellency on the glory of having driven the British fleet from the coast, and taken two of their frigates. These happy events, and the decided superiority of your fleet, gives us the happiest presages of the most complete success in our combined operations in this bay."

But as Washington soon learned, de Grasse was not as sanguine about the progress of the allied armies. "I am annoyed by the delay caused by the first division," he wrote on September 16; "time is passing, the enemy is profiting by it, and the season is approaching when, against my will, I shall be obliged to forsake the allies for whom I have done my very best and more than could be expected." Washington and Rochambeau must get themselves to de Grasse's flagship—a voyage of some sixty miles down the James River—and persuade the French admiral to remain in the Chesapeake for as long as the siege lasted.

On September 17, Washington, along with Rochambeau, Chastellux, Duportail, and artillery chief Henry Knox, boarded what the aide Jonathan Trumbull referred to as "the fine little ship *Queen Charlotte*." Captured by de Grasse during the passage from Cuba to the Chesapeake, the *Charlotte* had been modified to accommodate Cornwallis's second in command, Lord Rawdon, for a voyage back to England. Having been "fitted for his lordship" (who was now a prisoner of the French), this was just the luxury craft to transport them down the James on what may have been Washington's longest voyage by water since sailing to Barbados with his half brother Lawrence.

Despite Washington's lack of saltwater experience, he was intimately familiar with the rivers of the Tidewater. Up until it was stolen by the British earlier that spring, he'd owned a copper-bottomed schooner that he docked in front of his home at Mount Vernon. In addition to growing crops, Mount Vernon's slaves busied themselves every spring with harvesting huge numbers of shad from the Potomac, using seines to capture the wriggling fish much as Washington now hoped to use the combination of sea and land forces to trap Cornwallis. It might be argued that the commander in chief of the Continental army had a more nuanced understanding of the importance of naval superiority than Admiral de Grasse, who'd seemed strangely indifferent to the dangers posed by the British fleet both before and after the Battle of the Chesapeake.

By the next morning, the *Queen Charlotte* was within sight of the French fleet, which with the addition of de Barras's squadron now totaled thirty-six ships of the line. No piece of eighteenth-century technology could compare in complexity, sophistication, and heart-stopping beauty to a ship of the line, and here were three dozen of them anchored inside Cape Henry. Washington would have no doubt agreed with Trumbull's description of the fleet as "a grand sight."

Elation, at least on the part of de Grasse, appears to have been the predominant mood of the meeting aboard the *Ville de Paris*. According to legend, de Grasse wrapped the over-six-foot-tall Washington in a hug while crying out, *"Mon cher petit general!"* If true, this marked the third time in two weeks the American commander in chief found himself in the arms of a Frenchman. By the end of the conference, de Grasse (who had already sent several ships up the bay to retrieve the remaining American and French soldiers) had agreed to remain in the Chesapeake an extra two weeks, until the end of October. He was also willing to contribute as many as two thousand of his own men, if needed, in a coup de main against Cornwallis.

Dinner was followed by a tour of the ship. At 104 guns and 177 feet in length, the *Ville de Paris* was the largest ship of the line in the French navy. "[T]he world in miniature," Trumbull recorded in his diary. After "receiving the compliments of the officers of the fleet," Washington and his retinue were back on the *Queen Charlotte*. The sail through the anchorage at sunset must have made for a magnificent spectacle. Sailors clustered on the yards, shouting, *"Vive le Roi!"* as below them the powder smoke from a thirteen-gun salute billowed across the water. By nightfall, the *Charlotte*, whose captain would one day father a son named John James Audubon, had turned up the river and was headed back toward Williamsburg.

Joseph Plumb Martin was twenty years old. Although born in Massachusetts, he'd been raised in Connecticut and as a private and now a sergeant in the Continental army had been present at virtually every major battle of the Revolution. Now he was headed for Yorktown. His voyage south had begun at Philadelphia in a schooner so loaded with gunpowder that he feared a random bolt of lightning might "compel me to leave the vessel sooner than I wished." Once he'd sailed down the Delaware and gone overland to Head of Elk, he'd found "a *large* fleet of *small* vessels waiting to convey us and other troops, stores, etc. down the bay."

Martin was a member of the Sappers and Miners, a corps of soldiers specially trained in the art of digging the trenches and fortifications used in conducting a siege. As a consequence, he was aboard one of the first groups of vessels to begin sailing down the Chesapeake. "We passed down the bay making a grand appearance with our mosquito fleet to Annapolis," he remembered. There they paused to await the outcome of the Battle of the Chesapeake. On September 15, they learned of de Grasse's victory, and pushed by the same northeasterly gale that would make Washington and Rochambeau's return to Williamsburg a four-day ordeal, they were soon approaching the mouth of the James, where they enjoyed an excellent view of the French fleet. One of Martin's compatriots described the ships as "the most noble and majestic spectacle I ever witnessed." Martin, the ever sardonic New Englander, was less impressed, comparing the French ships' hundred or so masts to "a swamp of dry pine trees."

After riding out the worst of the storm in a sheltered cove, they put into another cove near Jamestown and were soon in Williamsburg. Martin's military career had begun in 1776 at the Battle of Long Island, and he looked forward to paying "our old acquaintance, the British, at Yorktown, a visit." The one thing Martin had not lost after five years of war was his sense of humor. "I doubt not but their wish was not to have so many of us come at once, as their accommodations were rather scanty," he wrote. "They thought, 'The fewer the better cheer.' We thought, 'The more the merrier.'"

ON SEPTEMBER 16, Cornwallis learned that the French fleet had returned to the Chesapeake and the British fleet was headed back to New York. Having heard from General Clinton that Admiral Digby was due to arrive in New York with his own fleet of ships, he clung to the belief that all was not lost. "If I had no hopes of relief, I would rather risk an action than defend my half-finished works," he wrote to Clinton on September 17. "But as you say Admiral Digby is hourly expected, and promise every exertion to assist me, I do not think myself justifiable in putting the fate of the war on so desperate an attempt. By examining the transports, and turning out useless mouths, my provisions will last at least six weeks from this day."

Later that day Cornwallis learned that the French fleet now included de Barras's squadron, bringing the total number of enemy battleships in the bay to thirty-six. A French fleet of this size would be virtually impossible to dislodge from the bay. With the French controlling the waters surrounding Yorktown, the allied army would be free to begin siege operations by land—creating an ever constricting cordon of artillery and soldiers that eventually would batter down his defenses and make surrender inevitable. Cornwallis was no longer so optimistic: "This place is in no state of defense," he wrote to Clinton. "If you cannot relieve me very soon, you must be prepared to hear the worst."

Commodore Thomas Symonds commanded the fleet of British vessels anchored between Yorktown and Gloucester. For the last few weeks he'd been helping Cornwallis prepare for what now looked to be the inevitable siege. In addition to offloading cannons and sailors to assist with the construction of land-based batteries, he'd anchored the *Guadaloupe* opposite a creek "to enfilade a gulley should the enemy attempt to cross it." All of these measures were defensive, but on September 20, with the wind beginning to blow a near gale out of the northeast, he prepared to launch the fireships.

In the early morning hours of September 22, with both the wind and the tide running out of the York, five unmanned vessels packed with combustible materials were guided by longboats into the center of the river, just upwind of the French warships anchored at the river's mouth. At two a.m., the ships' sails were set, their helms lashed, and their cargoes ignited in hopes they would fetch against the enemy and set fire to the French fleet. "In the dark night it was a beautiful and at the same time devastating sight," Karl Tornquist remembered, "five burning ships with full sails floating down the stream." Most of the French ships were able to avoid destruction by slipping their cables, but not the *Triton*, which ran aground on a nearby shoal just as a fireship threatened to ram into her side. In desperation, the *Triton*'s crew fired "a whole broadside with a double load of round bullets" that succeeded in altering the fireship's course. "It passed, however, so close to the square stern," Tornquist wrote, "that no one could remain on the afterdeck."

De Grasse believed Cornwallis had hoped to gain "possession of the river York for at least one night . . . that he might . . . get out of the river with his boats and sailing close to the shore come to land on the right bank of the James." From there, the British would have fought their way south into the Carolinas. The next day, de Grasse ordered two of his frigates to anchor at the entrance of the James, "so as not to allow a single boat to approach." In the meantime, the admiral's modest reserves of patience had once again begun to wane. "It is time to begin to close in on the enemy," he wrote to Washington on September 22, "and to give him a taste of our combined strength."

THE FOLLOWING DAY, Washington received some potentially disturbing intelligence from the president of the Continental Congress, Thomas McKean. British admiral Digby, it was reported, was about to arrive in New York with ten ships of the line. Washington remained confident that even with this influx of enemy ships, de Grasse would still enjoy a "considerable" superiority and had nothing to fear. Then on September 25 came the thunderbolt. Baron von Closen had delivered the intelligence about Digby to de Grasse. Instead of taking the news in stride, the French admiral was "alarmed and disquieted." After having almost lost the Battle of the Chesapeake because of an inexcusable lack of vigilance on September 5, de Grasse decided "it would be imprudent of me to put myself in a position where I could not engage [the British] in battle should they attempt to come up with relief." He must recall "all the ships at York except two" and wait for the British outside the Capes, where "I can engage them in a less disadvantageous position." He was even contemplating sailing to New York "where, perhaps, I could do more for the common cause than by remaining here, an idle spectator."

Because of a rumor (which ultimately proved untrue; Digby had only three ships of the line), de Grasse was about to shut down a combined land-sea operation that depended on his squadron's presence in the Chesapeake. Without the support of the French fleet, efforts against Cornwallis would come to a standstill due to a lack of water transportation, thus sacrificing everything that had been accomplished by the Battle of the Chesapeake. Now—not back on September 5— was the time for de Grasse to risk the possibility of losing control of the Chesapeake so that he could assist Washington's and Rochambeau's armies in achieving the victory that ended the war.

"I cannot conceal from your Excellency," Washington responded, "the painful anxiety under which I have labored since the receipt of [your] letter. . . . I must earnestly entreat your Excellency . . . to consider . . . that if you should withdraw your maritime force from the position agreed upon that no future day can restore to us a similar occasion for striking a decisive blow."

Washington's concern was so great that he asked Lafayette to accompany von Closen on his second visit to the French fleet. As it turned out, by the time the baron and the marquis arrived at the *Ville de Paris*, de Grasse had changed his mind. After a council of war with his captains, he'd decided to remain in the Chesapeake. Although he claimed his plan to sail for New York was "the most brilliant and glorious," he acknowledged that it "did not appear to fulfill the aims we had in view." Washington chose to take the high road in his reply the following day. "The resolution that your Excellency has taken," he wrote, "proves that a great mind knows how to make personal sacrifices to secure an important general good." "By the vivacity of his head," Rochambeau later said of de Grasse, "he did take always violent parts."

By the end of September, the allied forces had started to accumulate the men, provisions, equipment, and cannons they needed to start the thirteen-mile march to Yorktown. No one could quite believe they'd reached this point. There were at least 8000 French soldiers, a similar number of Continentals, and over 3000 American militia, for a total of almost 19,000 soldiers. (Even Washington's twenty-six-year-old stepson, Jacky Custis, who had shown no previous interest in participating in the Revolutionary War, had decided that now was the time to join his stepfather's army.) On top of that, approximately 20,000 French sailors were stationed on the ships scattered across the lower portions of the Chesapeake. In total, close to 40,000 French and Americans were temporarily gathered in this portion of Virginia to face Cornwallis's army of between 7000 and 9000 soldiers. For a few brief weeks in the autumn of 1781, the largest concentration of people in North America (more than half of them French) existed not in Philadelphia (the most populous city in America) but on and around a peninsula between the York and James rivers.

Writing on September 28, Jonathan Trumbull called it "a most wonderful and very observable coincidence of favorable circumstances." That morning the army marched out of Williamsburg and approached to within two miles of the British fortifications. "The line being formed," Washington recorded in his diary, "all the troops, officers, and men lay upon their arms during the night."

The Siege of Yorktown was about to begin.

CHAPTER 9

Yorktown

YORKTOWN WAS SITUATED atop a line of bluffs at the end of the peninsula formed by the York River to the north and the James to the south. Across the York, more than a half mile to the north, was the town of Gloucester, which the British also fortified. In the waters between Gloucester and Yorktown, the British had assembled a fleet of armed vessels that included two frigates. This meant that even though de Grasse had established naval superiority throughout most of the Chesapeake, he had failed to provide Washington with the direct support he needed where it really mattered—the York River. Despite the presence of several French warships at the river mouth, Cornwallis's frigates still controlled the waters between Yorktown and Gloucester Point as well as the waters above Yorktown, providing Cornwallis's army with possible avenues of escape to the north and west. To Washington's mind, de Grasse's job was not complete until he had sent some of his warships up the York and established command of the river. Only then would Cornwallis's army be completely surrounded.

But de Grasse, laid low by a bout of asthma, refused to send his ships up the York. He made halfhearted claims about the threat posed by British fireships, but as the weeks passed it became increasingly clear the French admiral believed he had already done more than enough to assist the allied army. Like "a blind man discoursing on colors," he simply did not recognize the benefits of doing as Washington requested. De Grasse was in command of the fleet that had made it possible for the allied army to surround the British at Yorktown by land, but he remained strangely oblivious to the importance of establishing naval superiority in the immediate vicinity of the enemy. As a result, September 29 was spent, Washington recorded with considerable bitterness, "reconnoitering the enemy's position and determining upon a plan of attack and approach which must be done without the assistance of the shipping above the town as the admiral (notwithstanding my earnest solicitations) declined hazarding any vessels on that station."

That night Cornwallis went a considerable way to making de Grasse's assistance unnecessary. The British commander had originally chosen Yorktown because of its strategic location on the high ground overlooking the river. By fortifying those bluffs, as well as the opposite shore at Gloucester, his army was well positioned to defend itself against an assault by water. Attacking Yorktown by land was also no easy matter since the terrain to the south of the village was cut up by a series of easily defended creeks and ravines. Because this land was slightly higher than the bluffs along the shore, the British had built a series of fortifications well outside the town. Before the allies could begin the time-consuming process of taking Yorktown by siege, they had to take this roughly semicircular network of outer defenses.

On the morning of September 30, the allies discovered that the British had abandoned several key redoubts in their outer perimeter. Instead of battling the enemy at every turn, Cornwallis had decided to surrender these strategically placed entrenchments so he could devote more of his resources to improving the works immediately surrounding Yorktown. He claimed the enemy had been in danger of flanking his outer defenses, but as the cavalry officer Banastre Tarleton later asserted, "great time would have been gained by holding and disputing the ground inch by inch, both to finish the works of Yorktown, and to retard the operations of the combined army." Washington could not have agreed more. "We . . . find ourselves very unexpectedly upon very advantageous ground," his aide Jonathan Trumbull recorded in his diary. "At night our troops begin to throw up some works and to take advantage of the enemy's evacuated labors."

Over the course of the next five days, as the British cannons directed a steady but largely ineffective fire on the newly acquired allied redoubts, the Americans and French labored to assemble the artillery and equipment required to conduct a siege. Unlike the Americans, the French had extensive experience in just this kind of operation, in which a series of concentric and interconnected trenches, known as parallels, were dug to facilitate the gradual advance of artillery toward an enemy stronghold.

From the French perspective, there was nothing exceptional about the task ahead of them. Since Cornwallis had seen fit to concede his outer defenses, the allies had to build only two (as opposed to the usual three) parallels. Washington and Rochambeau (for whom this was his fifteenth siege) determined that the Americans would occupy the right half of the parallel (beginning at the York River to the east) while the French took the left (ending at a deep ravine to the west). Although most of the soldiers in the Continental army were unfamiliar with the art of conducting a siege, there was one exception: the members of the recently formed Sappers and Miners, of which the young Joseph Plumb Martin was a member.

By the night of October 5, the allies had stockpiled enough artillery, ammunition, gunpowder, digging implements, and other materials to start laying out the first parallel. Luckily, the full moon was hidden behind a thick screen of clouds as a steady rain masked the sounds of the soldiers making their way across a broad, undulant field plowed into deep furrows by the enemy's cannonballs. "A third part of our Sappers and Miners were ordered out this night," Martin remembered, "to assist the engineers in laying out the works."

Once they'd been directed to the appropriate place, they began placing narrow strips of pine along the line marked by the engineers, just six hundred yards from the enemy's fortifications. "We had not proceeded far in the business," Martin wrote, "before the engineers ordered us to desist and remain where we were and be sure not to straggle a foot from the spot while they were absent from us." Standing motionless in an open field within easy cannon shot of the British was not a pleasant duty. Making it even worse was the knowledge that should they be discovered by the enemy and identified as sappers, they would invariably be killed.

Not long after the departure of the engineers, a tall man in a long overcoat appeared out of the blackness. "The stranger inquired what troops we were," Martin remembered, "[and] talked familiarly with us a few minutes." Before leaving to find the engineers, the stranger reminded them not to reveal "what troops we were" if they should be taken prisoners. "We were obliged to him for his kind advice," Martin wrote, "but we considered ourselves as standing in no great need of it; for we knew as well as he did that Sappers and Miners were allowed no quarters, at least are entitled to none by the laws of warfare."

Eventually the engineers returned in the company of "the aforementioned stranger." "By the officers often calling him 'Your Excellency,' we discovered that it was George Washington. Had we dared, we might have cautioned him for exposing himself too carelessly to danger at such a time, and doubtless he would have taken it in good part if we had." Like the young warrior king in William Shakespeare's play *Henry V,* Washington had left an indelible impression on his men as he chatted with them on a dark night before battle.

By the following night, all was ready to begin digging the first parallel. Once a line of armed soldiers had been assembled a hundred yards ahead of them for protection from enemy patrols, the troops laid down their muskets and took up their spades, shovels, and other implements. To help screen their activities from the enemy, fires were lit on the extreme left of the allied line to convince the British that "we were about some secret mischief there." As a consequence, Martin remembered, the British "directed their whole fire to that quarter, while we were entrenching literally under their noses."

By throwing the sandy dirt into three or more rows of gabions (baskets constructed of sticks interwoven with brush), the men not only dug a trench but built up a parapet to shield them from the enemy. By daybreak, they had succeeded in completing a trench about two thousand feet long, which was to include four batteries for cannon emplacements. "It was a sight to see a plain old field with men in it working with spades making a ditch," wrote Daniel Trabue, a sutler who sold liquor to the allied soldiers. "[M]en could walk around in it and . . . not be seen by the enemy."

The British, needless to say, were not pleased by the sudden appearance of the enemy just six hundred yards from their fortifications. "As soon as it was day, they perceived their mistake and began to fire where they ought to have done sooner," Martin remembered. "They brought out a fieldpiece or two without their trenches and discharged several shots at the men who were at work erecting a bomb battery; but their shot had no effect, and they soon gave it over."

One of the traditions associated with a siege was the Opening of the Trenches, a ceremony in which the troops of the day marched to their appointed places with drums beating and banners flying before planting their flags in the rampart ahead of them. Leading the battalion of light infantry that day was Alexander Hamilton. Having spent most of the war as an aide to Washington, the ambitious Hamilton was intent on winning as much military glory as possible in what might be the last significant action of the war. Unfortunately, sieges offered relatively few opportunities for flashy heroics since, as Napoleon would later comment, "it is the artillery that takes a stronghold, the infantry simply assists." That morning, Hamilton made sure that at least for a few minutes his troops were the center of everyone's attention. Even though it placed them directly in the line of fire, he ordered his men up onto the ramparts, where in full view of the astonished enemy (who temporarily ceased firing), they performed a series of evolutions known as the manual of arms. It was a gratuitous act of bravado reminiscent of how six years before at the Battle of Bunker Hill, Colonel William Prescott had leapt onto the ramparts of his little earthen fort and bid defiance to the British. "Colonel Hamilton gave these orders," Captain James Duncan wrote, "and although I esteem him one of the first officers in the American army, I must beg in this instance to think he wantonly exposed the lives of his men." It would not be the last time Hamilton made a point of placing himself (and his men) in harm's way.

Over the course of the next four days, as the Americans and French labored to complete the first parallel and its batteries, the British kept up a steady fire. To provide the workers with some warning of an incoming cannonball or explosive shell, a man was kept on watch on the ramparts. As soon as he saw one of the enemy gunners place a burning match to a cannon's vent, he shouted out a word of warning and the soldiers would, Daniel Trabue remembered, "fall down in the ditch, and you could hear the ball go by. Sometimes it would skip along on the ground and bury the men in the ditch, but in general they would not be hurt."

By October 10, just four days after the completion of the first parallel, forty-one cannons, mortars, and howitzers had been placed inside the allied batteries. Only after the American flag had been hoisted above the Grand Battery, containing half a dozen large pieces of artillery near the York River, was the firing to begin. "All were upon the tiptoe of expectation and impatience," Martin remembered. "About noon the much-wished-for signal went up. I confess I felt a secret pride swell my heart when I saw the star-spangled banner waving majestically in the very faces of our implacable adversaries; it appeared like an omen of success to our enterprise."

As the army's commander in chief, Washington was given the distinction of firing the first shot, aimed at a cluster of houses that included the home of sixty-five-year-old Thomas Nelson, granduncle of the Virginia governor of the same name. In the days to come, Nelson, who would be granted a parole by the British, described how Washington's 18-pound cannonball scored a direct hit, crashing through several houses before it killed the British commissary general as he sat at the dinner table with his wife and a group of officers that included Lord Cornwallis.

There were more than six thousand British and German soldiers, along with hundreds if not thousands of escaped slaves, cooped up in a space just 500 yards wide and 1200 yards long. With the beach at their backs and a steep bluff between them and the front of their fortifications, there were few places to hide as the allied cannonballs and bombshells rained down on them over the course of the afternoon and evening. A cannonball could do more than its share of damage as it ricocheted through the town and, in some cases, skipped across the water before crashing into the sides of the ships anchored off the beach. But it was the bombshells—huge, openmouthed orbs of iron filled with gunpowder and other combustibles and fired from the mortars in high, lazy arcs—that wreaked the most havoc.

"I followed with my eye, in its parabolic path, the slow and destructive bomb," a French chaplain recounted, "sometimes burying itself in the roofs of the houses, sometimes when it burst, raising clouds of dust and rubbish from the ruins of the buildings, at other times blowing the unfortunate wretches that happened to be within its reach, more than twenty feet high in the air, and letting them fall at a considerable distance most pitiably torn." Johann Doehla, a German soldier, was standing on the beach when several bombs plunged into the water beside him. A full five minutes passed before the bombs began to explode. "[I]t felt like the shocks of an earthquake," he remembered. In addition to showering the beach with sand and mud, "the fragments and pieces of these bombs flew back . . . and fell on the houses and buildings of the city . . . where they . . . robbed many a brave soldier of his life or struck off his arm and leg. I had myself a piece of an exploded bomb in my hands which weighed more than thirty pounds and was over three inches thick."

Their homes rendered uninhabitable by the incessant fire, the citizens of Yorktown, along with a considerable number of British soldiers, fled in desperation to the beach, where they began to burrow into the sandy cliffs. "But there also they did not stay undamaged," Doehla remembered, "for many were badly injured and mortally wounded by the fragments of bombs which exploded partly in the air and partly on the ground, their arms and legs severed or themselves struck dead."

A few days before, Cornwallis had decided to rid the army of its horses. Unable to feed the animals and unwilling to give them up to the enemy, he ordered them slaughtered and dragged into the river. Initially, the hundreds of carcasses had washed out with the tide, but now they were back. "Several days after their death these poor animals came back in heaps," the jaeger captain Johann Ewald recounted. "It seemed as if they wanted to cry out against their murder after their death."

By far the worst fate had been reserved for the army's former slaves, who had worked day and night building and repairing the British fortifications in anticipation of winning their freedom. Their rations reduced to virtually nothing and without shelter from the enemy's fire, many had died in what the Virginia militia officer St. George Tucker described as "the most miserable manner." The surviving African Americans' only consolation was that they still had the British fortifications between them and a return to slavery. But as they were about to discover, now that Cornwallis's army was running out of provisions, freedom was no longer an option.

To prevent a possible amphibious assault, the British had sunk a large number of captured sailing vessels in the shallows beside the beach, their masts canted at haphazard angles amid the billows of smoke and dust that kept rolling off the shore. On the morning of October 9, a double-ended open boat with fourteen oars, four swivel guns, two lateen sails, and sixteen British sailors was seen making its way through this reef of sunken vessels toward the beach. The French occupied the Chesapeake, but that did not prevent the British from maintaining a steady flow of "express boats" between Yorktown and New York capable of completing the five-hundred-mile passage in as little as four days.

The following morning, with the express boat about to leave that evening, Cornwallis began a letter to Sir Henry Clinton: "I have only to repeat what I said in my letter of the third, that nothing but a direct move to York River, which includes a successful naval action, can save me. The enemy made their first parallel on the night of the sixth at the distance of 600 yards, and have perfected it, and constructed places of arms and batteries with great regularity and caution. On the evening of the ninth, their batteries opened and have since continued firing without intermission. . . . We have lost about seventy men and many of our works are considerably damaged; with such works on disadvantageous ground against so powerful an attack we cannot hope to make a very long resistance."

Several hours later, Cornwallis, who had retired to what was described as a "grotto" in the cliffs behind Nelson's house, added a postscript: "Since my letter was written we have lost thirty men."

SOME OF THE MOST EFFECTIVE British fire came not from the batteries built into the defenses surrounding Yorktown but from the frigate *Charon*, anchored so it could, in the words of Jonathan Trumbull, "greatly . . . annoy" the battery on the extreme left of the French line. Adding to the allies' irritation was the knowledge that just a single French man-of-war might have long since silenced this and the other enemy vessels. Early on the evening of October 10, the French gunners decided it was time for the firing from the *Charon* to stop.

The way to destroy a wooden ship was with hotshot—cannonballs heated in a furnace until they were literally red-hot. Once the ball had been removed with tongs, it was deposited into the cannon's muzzle, which had been prepared with a wadding of water-soaked hay. Soon the cannons of the leftmost French battery were hurling several of these hotshots in the frigate's direction.

Bartholomew James was a proud lieutenant on the *Charon*, who, along with most of his fellow officers, was stationed at the batteries in front of Yorktown. James watched in horror as fire erupted aboard his ship "in three different places, and in a few minutes [was] in flames

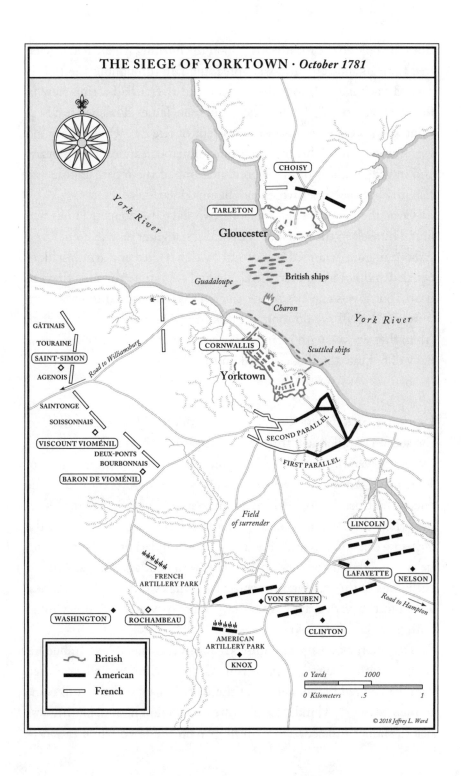

THE SIEGE OF YORKTOWN · *October 1781*

CHOISY

TARLETON

Gloucester

York River

Guadaloupe

British ships

Charon

York River

GÂTINAIS

TOURAINE

SAINT-SIMON

AGENOIS

Road to Williamsburg

CORNWALLIS

Scuttled ships

Yorktown

SAINTONGE

SOISSONNAIS

VISCOUNT VIOMÉNIL

DEUX-PONTS

BOURBONNAIS

BARON DE VIOMÉNIL

SECOND PARALLEL

FIRST PARALLEL

*Field
of surrender*

LINCOLN

FRENCH
ARTILLERY PARK

LAFAYETTE

NELSON

VON STEUBEN

Road to Hampton

WASHINGTON

ROCHAMBEAU

AMERICAN
ARTILLERY PARK

CLINTON

KNOX

	British
	American
	French

0 Yards   1000

0 Kilometers   .5   1

© 2018 Jeffrey L. Ward

from the hold to the mastheads." Soon the burning frigate had broken free from its mooring and was spreading fire throughout the tightly packed anchorage. "From the bank of the river I had a fine view of this conflagration," the American surgeon James Thacher recalled. "The ships were enwrapped in a torrent of fire . . . while all around was thunder and lightning from our numerous cannon and mortars and in the darkness of night presented one of the most sublime and magnificent spectacles which can be imagined."

Over the course of the previous two days, Lieutenant James had found himself in the midst of "a dreadful slaughter" as the French and American guns pounded his battery "with a degree of warmth seldom equaled and not to be described." He had seen more than his share of death, but it was the loss of the *Charon* that threatened to move him to tears. "I shall say no more on this head," he wrote in his journal, "than that we saw with infinite concern one of the finest ships in the navy of her rate totally destroyed on this day."

On the night of October 11, allied soldiers began work on the second parallel, just three hundred yards from the British fortifications. Over the course of the previous few days, the number of French and American cannons, howitzers, and mortars trained on the enemy had nearly doubled, to seventy-six pieces. Lieutenant James estimated that "upwards of a thousand shells" were thrown into the British works that night. "The noise and thundering of the cannon," he wrote, "the distressing cries of the wounded, and the lamentable sufferings of the inhabitants, whose dwellings were chiefly in flames, added to the restless fatigues of duty, must inevitably fill every mind with pity and compassion."

Despite the carnage and misery, Cornwallis was able to imbue his soldiers with a sense of optimism. General Clinton had promised him, he assured his soldiers, that the British navy was about to come to their rescue. "[A]midst all this dire destruction no murmuring was heard," James insisted, "no wish to give up the town while the most distant hope was in view of being relieved. On the contrary, this very distinguished little army, taking example from their chief, went through the business of the siege with a perfect undaunted resolution, and hourly discovered proofs of their attachment to the general, who had so often led them to the field with success."

The appearance of the second parallel on the morning of October 12 within virtual musket shot of their own fortifications was a clear setback to the British, but all was not yet lost. Two formidable British redoubts, referred to as numbers 9 and 10, blocked the enemy from extending their parallel all the way to the bluffs on the York River. As long as those redoubts held, there was still a modicum of hope.

Many of Washington's officers were getting impatient with the pace of the siege and wanted to burst out of the trenches and take the British fortifications with a bloody coup de main. "The troops of both nations chafe at the slowness of the approach works and ask permission to shorten the time by taking this point or that with drawn swords," Lafayette wrote to French minister Luzerne, "but the general, who knows his success is assured, is determined to conserve the blood of his troops." Or as Rochambeau was overheard to say after inspecting the defenses surrounding British redoubts 9 and 10 in anticipation of a possible attack, "We shall see tomorrow whether the pear is ripe."

On October 14, after two days of unremitting fire on the surrounding defenses, Washington decided the time had come to take the two redoubts by storm. The infantry finally had a chance to do something more than just dig. The American forces under Lafayette were to attack the smaller of the two fortifications on the far right; the French, under Baron de Vioménil, would take the one on its immediate left. Much to the frustration of Alexander Hamilton, Lafayette chose Lieutenant Colonel Jean-Joseph Sourbader de Gimat, his trusted subordinate throughout the Virginia campaign (and fellow Frenchman), to lead the attack. Hamilton (who outranked de Gimat) was not about to let this chance for glory slip through his fingers. Even though he considered Lafayette a friend, he decided to appeal directly to Washington.

For four years these two men had worked side by side, with

Hamilton becoming not just an aide but the written voice of his commander. Eight months earlier, that relationship had ended with the angry encounter at Washington's headquarters on the Hudson. By awarding Hamilton his current position at the head of the light infantry, Washington had proven capable of rising above their past differences. But to request that he overrule Lafayette, who enjoyed a personal relationship with his commander that no officer could match, was, in all likelihood, asking the impossible.

Already, however, Washington had proven capable of denying Lafayette. When the marquis learned that Benjamin Lincoln was to command the troops at Yorktown, he had suggested that Washington send Lincoln across the river to Gloucester, so that Lafayette could become the second-ranking general in the main theater of the engagement. Washington loved the young French general like a son, but he also recognized that his affection could not be unconditional. As long as he remained commander in chief, he must keep "all men . . . at a proper distance," for to "grow upon familiarity" was to "in proportion sink in authority." Lincoln, Washington told Lafayette in no uncertain terms, was staying in Yorktown.

To Hamilton's surprise and ultimate delight, Washington decided in his favor. "We have it!" Hamilton gleefully announced to his friend Nicholas Fish on returning to the tent the two officers shared. While Hamilton led the assault on the British redoubt, his other good friend and former aide to Washington, John Laurens, would command a small group of soldiers who worked their way to the back of the fortification to cut off the enemy's escape. After a year of deferring to the sometimes infuriating demands of the French, Washington had decided it was finally time to give two of his most promising American officers the opportunity they deserved.

Captain Stephen Olney commanded a company of soldiers in the First Rhode Island Regiment, a significant number of whom were African American. The Rhode Islanders were some of the toughest, best-disciplined soldiers in the Continental army, and a portion of them were selected for the assault on redoubt number 10. Olney remembered that they were "paraded just after daylight in front of our works. General Washington made a short address or harangue, admonishing us to act the part of firm and brave soldiers.... I thought then that His Excellency's knees rather shook, but I have since doubted whether it was not mine."

To eliminate the possibility of a soldier spoiling the element of surprise by firing his musket too early, Lafayette had ordered that their guns remain unloaded. They would take the redoubt with only the "cold steel" of the bayonet. "The column marched in silence," Olney remembered, "many, no doubt, thinking that less than one quarter of a mile would finish the journey of life with them."

Also there that night was Sergeant Joseph Plumb Martin, who, as a member of the Sappers and Miners, was at the very front of the column with an axe in hand. Before the light infantry could attack the redoubt, it was the sappers' job to cut a passage through the abatis, a dense thicket of treetops, their branches cut with what Martin called a "slashing stroke which renders them as sharp as spikes."

They marched in silence until ordered to lie down on the war-torn field, where they were to await the signal to advance. Not until six shells were fired in quick succession from the French batteries were they to leap up and charge for the redoubt. "Our watchword was 'Rochambeau,'" Martin remembered, "a good watchword, for being pronounced 'Ro-sham-bow,' it sounded, when pronounced quick, like 'rush-on-boys.'"

The Americans lying on the dirt that night were motivated by something more than the usual patriotism. They were angry. At the beginning of the siege, one of their favorite officers, Colonel Alexander Scammell from New Hampshire, had been captured while inspecting the newly abandoned redoubts of the British outer works, only to be brutally shot in the back by one of Tarleton's cavalrymen. Scammell had since died of his wounds—just one of the many outrages committed by the British. Upon their arrival in Virginia, allied soldiers had discovered the body of a young pregnant woman who had been stabbed to death in her bed. "The barbarians had opened both of her breasts," a French officer recounted, "and written above the bed canopy, 'Thou shalt never give birth to a rebel.' In another room was just as horrible a sight, five cut-off heads, arranged on a cupboard in place of plaster-cast figures, which lay broken to pieces on the floor."

As the British army made its slow, destructive way across Virginia, Cornwallis had ordered his men to poison the inhabitants' wells with the corpses of the many escaped slaves who had died of smallpox. As a result, drinkable water was almost impossible to find, and illness was rampant in both the French and American camps. But for many of the Americans, the consummate outrage had been committed not by Cornwallis and Tarleton, but by Benedict Arnold.

A little more than a month before, the already reviled traitor had dared to return to Connecticut and lead an expedition against the port of New London, just thirteen miles from his birthplace in Norwich. Not only had he burned much of the town, but his redcoats had led a bloody assault on Fort Griswold on the opposite shore of the river, where dozens of American militiamen had been butchered as they attempted to surrender. Entire Connecticut families had been virtually wiped out. According to a former neighbor of Arnold's, "No instance of conduct in the enemy since the war has raised so general a resentment as that at New London."

Almost exactly a year before, news of Arnold's treason had forced the citizens of the United States to realize that the Revolutionary War was theirs to lose; three months later it had been Arnold's appearance in Virginia that had moved Washington to send Lafayette, as well as the French naval squadron under Destouches, to the Chesapeake—a movement of ships and soldiers that had anticipated what was now about to unfold. Perhaps inevitably, given his seeming ubiquity throughout this pivotal year, Arnold was once again the great motivator as the soldiers under the French marquis's overall command prepared to storm redoubt number 10. According to Lafayette, "We had promised ourselves to avenge the New London affair."

At about eight p.m., the heavens above Yorktown brightened with the nearly simultaneous burst of six shells. "The words 'Up, up!' were then reiterated through the detachment," Martin remembered. "We immediately moved silently on toward the redoubt. . . . Just as we arrived at the abatis, the enemy discovered us and directly opened a sharp fire." They had reached the area where two days of shelling had created a series of holes "sufficient," according to Martin, "to bury an ox in." Unfortunately, the intense darkness of the night made these chasms impossible to see. Suddenly the men in front of Martin dropped out of sight. "I thought the British were killing us off at a great rate," he remembered. Soon Martin was tumbling into the same hole that had just swallowed his compatriots, and he "found out the mystery of the huge slaughter."

The plan had been for the Sappers and Miners to first clear away the abatis before Hamilton and his men charged into the redoubt. But, as Stephen Olney remembered, "This seemed tedious work in the dark within three rods [about fifty feet] of the enemy." Rather than wait, the soldiers of the First Rhode Island decided to scramble over and through the maze of sharpened tree branches. Leading the way was Alexander Hamilton, who used the back of one of his men to vault himself onto the parapet.

Right there with Hamilton was Olney, who instead of a musket carried an espontoon, a long pole with a sharp blade at the end. As soon as he appeared at the edge of the redoubt, six or eight enemy soldiers lunged at him with their bayonets. "I parried as well as I could," he remembered, "but they broke off the blade [of my espontoon], and their bayonets slid down the handle . . . and scaled my fingers; one bayonet pierced my thigh; another stabbed me in the abdomen, just above the hipbone. One fellow fired at me, and I thought the ball took effect in my arm." By then, two of Olney's men had loaded their muskets and begun firing on the enemy, some of whom surrendered, some of whom did their best to escape. "In the heat of the action," Martin remembered, "I saw a British soldier jump over the walls of the fort next the river and go down the bank, which was almost perpendicular and twenty or thirty feet high. When he came to the beach he made off for the town, and if he did not make good use of his legs I never saw a man that did."

Hamilton made sure that none of his men stooped to the level of Arnold's soldiers at Fort Griswold. "Incapable of imitating examples of barbarity and forgetting recent provocations," he wrote in his report to Lafayette, "the soldiery spared every man who ceased to resist."

When they had been planning this assault earlier in the day, Lafayette's French counterpart Baron de Vioménil had dared to propose that given the danger of the operation, perhaps it was best if more-experienced French troops attacked both redoubts. Lafayette had, of course, been outraged by the suggestion that the men he commanded were in any way inferior to the French. Now, as he stood atop the freshly taken redoubt, he sent his aide on a mission to inform the baron that "he was in his redoubt and to ask . . . where he was." As it turned out, the French soldiers, following the usual protocol, were still waiting for their sappers to clear away the abatis when Lafayette's aide arrived with his general's impertinent message. "Tell the marquis I am not in mine," de Vioménil angrily responded, "but will be in five minutes."

The French were true to their leader's word and soon took the redoubt. Watching the night's action from a nearby battery with his artillery chief Henry Knox at his side, Washington was heard to say, "The work is done, and well done," before he mounted his horse and returned to headquarters.

According to the Hessian jaeger captain Johann Ewald, the taking of the two redoubts came as a distressing surprise to Cornwallis's officers. "Now people make long faces and say, 'Who would have thought of this stroke.'" Earlier that day, Cornwallis had decided that, despite having promised the former slaves their freedom, the dwindling supply of provisions required that he jettison them from his fortress. "On the same day of the enemy assault," Ewald recorded, "we drove back to the enemy all of our black friends. . . . We had used them to good advantage and set them free, and now, with fear and trembling, they had to face the reward of their cruel masters." By this act of betrayal, Cornwallis proved that he had no more concern for the African Americans in his camp than he had for the horses, whose bodies still littered the Yorktown shore.

That night Ewald went out on what he called "a sneak patrol." Just beyond the fortifications of Yorktown he discovered "a great number of these unfortunates. In their hunger, these unhappy people would have soon devoured what [food] I had. And since they lay between two fires, they had to be driven on by force." Caught in the no-man's-land between the British and the allies (who would undoubtedly return them to slavery), the African Americans had nowhere left to go.

THE TWO NEWLY ACQUIRED redoubts were quickly incorporated into the allies' second parallel, allowing a whole new array of cannons, howitzers, and mortars to begin firing just three hundred yards from the already battered British line. The French were recognized as the greatest artillerists in the world: not only was the quality of their weaponry first-rate, but their officers and men were superbly trained. The Americans, on the other hand, had to rely on an inferior hodgepodge of artillery pieces. Nonetheless, thanks to the Herculean efforts of thirty-one-year-old Henry Knox, they managed to inflict more than their share of damage on the British defenses. "The [American] artillery was always very well served," General Chastellux wrote; "the general incessantly directed it and often himself pointing the mortars; seldom did he leave the batteries. The English marveled at the exact fire and terrible execution of the French artillery; and we marveled no less at the extraordinary progress of the

American artillery." Chastellux praised Knox as being of a "buoyant disposition, ingenious and true; it is impossible to know him without esteeming and loving him." But even the normally cheerful Knox had his limits.

Knox was standing in redoubt number 10 with Alexander Hamilton. Washington had recently instituted an order requiring the men in the trenches to shout out a warning when they saw an enemy shell headed in their direction. Hamilton, the excitable romantic, felt the order was "unsoldierly." Knox, the more even-tempered pragmatist, thought it made sense. Suddenly two British shells, their fuses fizzing furiously, landed in the redoubt as the soldiers around them shouted, "A shell!" Despite their differing views of Washington's order, both officers saw fit to run as quickly as possible for cover, with Hamilton making sure to put the much larger Knox between him and the explosives. Not taking kindly to being used as what he called "a breastwork," Knox grabbed Hamilton and threw him toward the shell. "All this was done rapidly," a man named Aeneas Monson, who witnessed the struggle, recounted, "for in two minutes the shells burst and threw their deadly missiles in all directions. It was now safe and soldierlike to standout." Brushing the dirt from his uniform, Knox turned to his companion and smiled. "Now, what do you think, Mr. Hamilton, about crying 'shell'?"

In contrast to his young subordinates, Washington had long since established a reputation for almost unbelievable equanimity in the face of enemy fire. "He was incapable of fear," Thomas Jefferson later wrote, "meeting personal danger with the calmest unconcern." At one point during the siege, a cannonball landed so close to Washington and the chaplain who happened to be standing next to him that their hats were covered with sand and dirt. "Being much agitated," the chaplain took off his hat and said, "See here, General." Evidently amused by his companion's alarm, Washington advised the chaplain to take the hat back home with him to New Hampshire and "show it to your wife and children."

. . .

In the early morning hours of October 16, soon after the loss of redoubts 9 and 10 but before the French could start firing from two unfinished batteries in the center of the second parallel, Cornwallis ordered one of his colonels to lead four hundred soldiers on a desperate mission. They were to cross behind the enemy lines and "spike" the French cannons by jamming pieces of metal into the vents. By silencing the French artillery before the guns began to fire, the sortie might buy the British army at least a few more days.

At four a.m., the soldiers surprised the French pickets and seized the redoubts only to discover that the nails they'd been given were too large for the job, requiring that they resort to sticking their bayonet points into the vents and breaking them off. For the most part, though, the maneuver was brilliantly executed, and "there was rejoicing," Ewald reported, as the officers assured themselves that "this stroke will save us."

At ten o'clock, Ewald was standing near the water when the two new enemy batteries began to fire. All of the risk and derring-do had been for naught because the French had been able to extract the broken bayonet blades with apparent ease. "Within an hour they battered our works so badly in the flank and rear," Ewald wrote, "that all our batteries were silenced within a few hours."

With the rescue fleet from New York nowhere in sight, Cornwallis decided there was only one thing left to do. He must attempt an escape. Thanks to de Grasse's continuing refusal to send any warships up the York, the way was still clear to cross the river. "As soon as night fell," Ewald recounted, "a number of boats were brought to the shore in which a part of the best men who were still healthy were to be passed over to Gloucester." Leaving only a small part of his army to keep the enemy occupied for as long as possible from the redoubts of Yorktown, Cornwallis and the majority of his force would cross the river, surprise the small allied army at Gloucester, then fight their way back to New York. It was a desperate ploy, to be sure, but by reducing the number of soldiers at Yorktown, it might prevent the inevitable surrender from being as catastrophic as it would otherwise have been if it included the entire British army. "The whole thing seemed to me like a delusion which misleads people for a moment," Ewald remembered. Nonetheless, Cornwallis was about to give it a try.

ADMIRAL THOMAS GRAVES and the British fleet had returned to New York on September 19. It was quickly determined "to attempt by the united efforts of army and navy to relieve Lord Cornwallis in the Chesapeake." In the days ahead, dockworkers labored from sunrise until "near ten at night" to ready Graves's damaged ships for a rematch with the French.

On September 25, Admiral Digby arrived from England. His three men-of-war brought the total number of ships of the line to twenty-five, but the real news was that one of Digby's officers included the sixteen-year-old midshipman Prince William Henry, son of King George III. The British navy and army were in a state of crisis, but that did not prevent its officers and men, as well as the loyalists of New York, from being dazzled by the presence of the prince, the first member of the royal family to visit America. "The graceful appearance and manner of the Prince," the normally levelheaded Frederick Mackenzie recorded in his diary, "with his liveliness and affability gives universal satisfaction." After spending the morning of September 27 waving to the crowd assembled outside his window, the prince and Sir Henry Clinton "walked through a part of the town . . . with crowds after him."

It made for a strangely festive atmosphere just at the moment when their country's fate hung so perilously in the balance. To no one's surprise, the repair of Graves's ships took longer than expected. Instead of departing in early October, as originally hoped, the fleet, along with five thousand soldiers under the command of Clinton himself, might not sail south again until the middle of the month.

Part of the problem was that Graves, who, the loyalist William

Smith reported, "considers himself as ruined already," was highly skeptical about the possibility of rescuing Cornwallis. At a meeting on October 8, he dared to ask "whether it was practicable to relieve Lord Cornwallis in the Chesapeake?" Samuel Hood was outraged. "This astonished me exceedingly," he wrote, "as it seemed plainly to indicate a design of having difficulties started against attempting what the generals and admirals had *most unanimously* agreed to."

Clinton, who rightly blamed Cornwallis for creating this mess in the first place, insisted that it was now all up to the British navy. "He had nothing to do with the difficulties which it was [the admiral's] business to foresee and provide for," he told William Smith. Despite the darkness of the present moment, Clinton still clung to the fantasy that should the rescue attempt succeed, he would get "the credit of restoring the tranquility of the empire."

Should the rescue attempt fail, however, a far greater disaster potentially awaited them. In addition to losing Cornwallis's army of seven thousand men, they might lose most of the British fleet in North America and the Caribbean, not to mention Clinton's five thousand soldiers, turning a momentous defeat into an outright catastrophe capable of toppling the British Empire. One of Graves's captains went so far as to say that "the loss of two line of battle ships in effecting the relief of [Cornwallis's] army is of much more consequence than the loss of [that army]." They were caught in a collective nightmare of dread and indecision, powerless to act just when events seemed to demand that something—*anything*—be done.

Adding to the air of unreality was Cornwallis's seeming nonchalance. Back on September 20, when his lordship announced that the French fleet had landed three thousand soldiers in Jamestown, he claimed, according to the crew of the express boat that returned with the message, to be "not apprehensive." As late as October 8, an express arrived with the report that when Cornwallis received Clinton's assurances "of reinforcement," he had sent along the verbal message "But don't hurry too fast." As a result, Smith wrote, there was "much joy at headquarters."

. . .

Captain Johann Ewald would never forget the night that Cornwallis decided to transport his men across the York River to Gloucester. "It was as dark as a sack and one could neither see nor hear anything because of the awful downpour and heavy gale. Moreover, there was a most severe thunderstorm, but the violent flashes of lightning benefited us, since we could at least see around us for an instant."

The weather had seemed fine when they departed at ten p.m. in a fleet of sixteen large rowing vessels. But then it started to blow and rain, capsizing several of the boats and driving others down the river. By two in the morning, Cornwallis was forced to abandon what Ewald called with considerable irony "the whole praiseworthy plan." By daybreak, the wind had begun to die; by nine in the morning, all the troops were back in Yorktown.

Unaware that the enemy lines had been virtually empty of soldiers during the night, the allied forces spent the morning blasting away at the British fortifications. "The whole peninsula trembles under the incessant thunderings of our infernal machines," James Thacher recorded in his diary. "We have leveled some of their works in ruins and silenced their guns; they have almost ceased firing. We are so near as to have a distinct view of the dreadful havoc and destruction. . . . But the scene is drawing to a close."

That morning, October 17, 1781, Cornwallis met with his principal officers. They agreed that in a few more hours, their fortifications "would be in such a state as to render it desperate. . . . We at that time could not fire a single gun. . . . Our numbers had been diminished by the enemy's fire, but particularly by sickness, and the strength and spirits of those in the works were much exhausted by the fatigue of constant watching and unremitting duty." Cornwallis decided it would be "wanton and inhuman to the last degree to sacrifice the lives of this small body of gallant soldiers who had ever behaved with so much fidelity and courage, by exposing them to an assault, which from the numbers and precautions of the enemy could not fail to succeed."

At ten in the morning, a British drummer boy appeared on the fortifications surrounding Yorktown. No one could hear him, but he was beating the signal for a parley. Beside him stood an officer with a white handkerchief in his hand. Once the French and American guns had stopped firing, an unearthly quiet enveloped the smoking wreck of Yorktown. Lord Cornwallis, they soon learned, had "proposed to capitulate."

It was exactly four years to the day since General John Burgoyne's surrender at Saratoga. The American wilderness was what had overwhelmed Burgoyne, who underestimated the challenge of maintaining a supply line from upstate New York to Canada. Cornwallis had had his own nearly disastrous flirtation with the interior of the North American continent during his pursuit of Nathanael Greene across North Carolina. Finally, however, the British general had been defeated, not by the land or even another army, but by the sea. Never fully appreciating his dependence on the British navy, he had wandered the edges of the Tidewater in careless disregard of the potential dangers lurking beyond the horizon. In coastal America, the navy held ultimate sway.

Without Cornwallis's head-scratching insistence on remaining, in Washington's words, "passive beyond our expectation," the Chesapeake strategy originally promulgated by Rochambeau would have been an anticlimactic failure. As Alexander Hamilton had written back on August 22, "It is ten to one that our views will be disappointed by Lord Cornwallis retiring to South Carolina by land." Instead, Cornwallis had remained on his lonely point between the James and York rivers as first a vast fleet of French ships and then an equally large enemy army assembled around him. He later claimed that Clinton's assurances of rescue had given him no other choice but to wait it out. But that required him to ignore irrefutable evidence of the impossibility of a British fleet penetrating the French-occupied waters of the Chesapeake. Instead of providing Clinton with a realistic assessment of the situation from the start, Cornwallis had jauntily advised his commander in chief not to "hurry too fast." In the end, only Washington—and perhaps Spanish envoy Francisco Saavedra, who had urged de Grasse to take as many ships as possible north from the Caribbean—understood just how crucial it was for an army to have the navy at its back. As Washington wrote to Lafayette in the weeks after Yorktown, "It follows then as certain as that night succeeds the day, that without a decisive naval force we can do nothing definitive, and with it, everything honorable and glorious."

On the day after the British surrender, Henry Knox received a letter from his good friend Nathanael Greene. After fighting yet another bloody but indecisive battle at South Carolina's Eutaw Springs, Greene and his small band of soldiers continued to work their way toward the ultimate prize, British-occupied Charleston. He was, of course, very glad to hear of the promising developments in Virginia. However, he was too honest not to admit to having mixed feelings about the glorious victory that was about to come Washington's way. Only after suffering an exhausting winter chasing Greene's army across North Carolina, capped by the Battle of Guilford Courthouse, had Cornwallis decided to head to the Tidewater. "We have been beating the bush," Greene wrote, "and the General has come to catch the bird. . . . The General is a most fortunate man, and may success and laurels attend him. We have fought frequently and bled freely, and little glory comes our share."

Four years before at Saratoga, American commander Horatio Gates had agreed to the outrageously lenient terms of surrender insisted on by John Burgoyne. Washington quickly made it evident that this time negotiations were to proceed on *his* terms. Knowing Cornwallis wanted to prolong discussions for as long as possible in hopes the British fleet would finally make an appearance,

Washington insisted that his lordship provide him with "proposals in writing" in no less than two hours. When the proposals failed to appear at the appointed time, the allied artillery resumed firing. That resulted in the almost immediate appearance at the parapet of Cornwallis's second in command, General Charles O'Hara, with his superior's response. Washington found several of Cornwallis's proposals "inadmissible," but had seen enough, he recorded in his diary, "to believe that there would be no great difficulty in fixing terms. Accordingly, hostilities were suspended for the night."

"The night was remarkably clear," Lieutenant Colonel St. George Tucker remembered, "and the sky decorated with ten thousand stars." Instead of the fiery tails of explosive shells, the American, French, British, and German soldiers were treated to another kind of pyrotechnics. "[N]umberless meteors gleaming through the atmosphere afforded a pleasing resemblance to the bombs which had exhibited a noble firework the night before," Tucker continued, "but happily divested of all their horror. At dawn of day the British gave us a serenade with the bagpipe . . . and were answered by the French with the band of the regiment of Deux Ponts." When the sun rose at 5:59 a.m., both the allied and British works were crowded with soldiers as the two armies stared at each other in the soft light of morning.

No one knew what the ultimate repercussions of Cornwallis's surrender would be, and yet everyone realized that something of tremendous importance had already occurred. After six and a half years of fighting, a war that had started with a skirmish on a village green in Lexington, Massachusetts, had come down to this: two armies gazing at each other across the burned and torn-up remains of Yorktown.

Later that morning Cornwallis received Washington's summation of the terms he would accept. His lordship had proposed that "the British [troops] shall be sent to Britain and the Germans to Germany under engagement not to serve against France, America, or their allies," and that his army receive "the customary honors." Washington would have none of it. The year before, at the fall of Charleston, the American army under Benjamin Lincoln had been denied those honors, despite putting up a brave six-week defense. Cornwallis's army would suffer the same indignity, and needless to say, the troops would remain prisoners of war in America.

"Your Lordship will be pleased to signify your determination either to accept or reject the proposals now offered," Washington wrote, "or a renewal of hostilities may take place." Cornwallis promptly agreed to Washington's terms as long as the British sloop of war *Bonetta* was "left entirely at my disposal from the hour that the capitulation is signed." In addition to carrying Cornwallis's dispatches (but not Cornwallis himself) back to Clinton, the vessel would provide the loyalists and deserters in Yorktown with a way to escape to New York.

Two commissioners were appointed on each side (with the allies represented by John Laurens and Lafayette's brother-in-law the Vicomte de Noailles), and formal negotiations began that morning. Cornwallis was resigned to the fact that his soldiers must remain prisoners in America, but he had a much harder time with being denied the terms of an honorable surrender. As the British commissioners pointed out, it had been Clinton, not Cornwallis, who had been in command at Charleston. But as Laurens countered, "it is not the individual that is here considered. It is the nation."

The haggling among the commissioners was "so procrastinated" that by the time they retired for the night, no formal treaty had been drafted. Refusing to allow the negotiations to continue any longer, Washington told Laurens and Noailles to write up "the rough draft of the articles," and he would send them to Cornwallis in the morning with the understanding "that I expected to have them signed at 11 am and that the garrison would march out at 2 pm." And so, before noon on October 19, the "Articles of Capitulation" were signed, according to a note made at the bottom of the document, "in the trenches before Yorktown."

Under the terms of the capitulation, approximately seven thousand British and German soldiers had been subtracted from the ranks of the king's forces in North America. That in itself did not represent a deathblow to the British war effort. The question was what the symbolic value of the surrender would be back in England. Even if the king should prove unyielding, would his ministry and, most important, would Parliament begin to believe that the time had come to acknowledge the independence of the former colonies?

ON THAT VERY SAME DAY, October 19, the British fleet finally departed from Sandy Hook. Five days later, a small boat bearing three men who had escaped from Yorktown on the night of the capitulation managed to wave down one of the British frigates sailing in advance of the giant fleet. Lord Cornwallis, they reported, had surrendered.

Admiral Rodney later insisted that in Graves's place, he would have established a blockade at the Capes of Virginia so as to "block [the French fleet] up to eternity." But Graves was no Rodney, and after several aimless days cruising in sight of Cape Henry, the British fleet returned to New York. It was, Samuel Hood wrote to a friend in England, "a most heartbreaking business."

ON THE MORNING OF OCTOBER 19, a portion of the trenches and fortifications surrounding Yorktown were leveled so that the British could march out of their works onto the road leading to Williamsburg for the "grand exhibition." The Americans were lined up on the right side of the road; the French on the left. At the end of the half-mile-long gauntlet of soldiers, the Duc de Lauzun's hussars encircled the field where the British were to deposit their arms. In addition to the nineteen thousand allied soldiers were an equal number of spectators. Around two o'clock, the British, led not by Cornwallis, who claimed to be ill, but by General O'Hara, marched out of Yorktown to the slow beat of the drum, their twenty-two regimental flags ignominiously furled and stored in their cases, and the band playing what was later said to be the mournful tune "The World Turned Upside Down."

From the first, the British made no attempt to hide their contempt for the Americans. O'Hara knew perfectly well who was the commander in chief of the allied forces, but instead of presenting his sword to Washington, who sat astride his reddish-brown horse at the head of the American army, the British general turned to his left and asked for Rochambeau, who quickly directed him to Washington. Feigning embarrassment, O'Hara presented his sword to Washington, who directed him to give it to *his* second in command, Benjamin Lincoln.

Whether or not it happened just then, at some point during the ceremony, the horse on which sat Admiral de Barras (who was there in place of the genuinely indisposed de Grasse) arched its back and, according to Baron von Closen, "vent[ed] himself." This so flustered the French admiral (who was "anything but a good horseman") that he cried out, "Good heavens! I believe my horse is sinking!!"

The contrast between the two allied armies could not have been more pronounced. According to von Closen, the Americans were "eclipsed by our army in splendor of appearance and dress, for most of these unfortunate persons were clad in small jackets of white cloth, dirty and ragged, and a number of them were almost barefoot." Of course, the shabby appearance of the Americans only made the shame felt by the British all the more difficult to bear, and they showed, according to von Closen, "the greatest scorn for the Americans" by directing their eyes only to the French as they marched between the two lines of soldiers. Angered by "their studied disregard," Lafayette ordered his drum major to begin playing "Yankee Doodle," and "[t]he band's blare made them turn their eyes toward his side of the line."

The British were clearly not at their best. Some said they were drunk; others said they "behaved like boys who had been whipped at school." The German soldiers, on the other hand, who, in Martin's words, "did not greatly care whose hands they were in," remained calm and dignified throughout. It was in the field at the end of the two lines of soldiers that the pride of the British was, according to James Thacher, "put to the severest test. Here their mortification could not be concealed." Biting their lips and in some cases openly weeping, the soldiers hurled their weapons to the ground in a clear attempt to damage them. "This irregularity," Thacher wrote, "was checked by the authority of Lincoln." Once divested of their arms and their colors, the soldiers marched back to Yorktown, where they were to remain under guard until they could be removed to their places of imprisonment.

On the night of the British surrender, Washington hosted a dinner to which both French and British officers were invited. Already it had become obvious that despite being allies, the French and Americans did not necessarily *like* each other, which was perhaps not unsurprising given that only thirty years before, during the Seven Years' War, the two peoples had been mortal enemies. Johann Ewald claimed that if the armies of France and America had not been separated during the previous winter, "many a French grenadier's saber would have been plunged into American blood. . . . For one continually hears, *'Fripons, ces Américains!'* ['Knaves, these Americans!']. . . . And how many quarrels I have seen between officers and sentries of these nations . . . [which] certainly results from national enmity."

Much to Washington's distress, it also became evident during the dinner on October 19 that while the British despised the Americans, they did not feel the same toward the French. "The English and French got on famously with one another," Comte de Clermont-Crèvecoeur observed. "When the Americans expressed their displeasure on this subject, we replied that good upbringing and courtesy bind us together and that, since we had reason to believe that the Americans did not like us, they should not be surprised at our preference."

Anyone who has been left out of the conversation at a star-studded dinner party knows what the American officers were feeling. "Such a jealousy came over General Washington," Ewald remembered, "that he cast stern expressions toward the French generals over the too-friendly relations between the French and our officers. . . . [A] cool conduct began to prevail among the two diverse nations which, in good fortune, had formed only one." Making matters worse, Lord

Cornwallis, who had failed to attend Washington's dinner, chose to accept the invitation of General de Vioménil.

What the French officers failed to appreciate was that by serving the cause of the American Revolution, they had helped to undermine their own privileged position in France's ancien régime. They might look with disdain on the lowly Americans, but those uncultured commoners were the living embodiment of the forces that would, in just a decade's time, tear their own society apart. More than a few of the French officers who chose to ignore their American allies that evening were destined to lose their exquisitely coifed heads to the guillotine.

The day after the surrender, Baron von Closen accompanied General Rochambeau on a trip to Yorktown to visit Cornwallis. "I will never forget how frightful and disturbing was the appearance of the city . . . from the fortifications on the crest to the strand below. One could not take three steps without running into some great holes made by bombs, some splinters, some balls, some half-covered trenches, with scattered white or Negro arms or legs, some bits of uniforms. Most of the houses riddled by cannon fire, and almost no window panes in the houses."

They found his lordship in the wreck of a house that was serving as his residence. "His appearance gave the impression of nobility of soul," von Closen remembered, "magnanimity, and strength of character; his manner seemed to say, 'I have nothing with which to reproach myself, I have done my duty and I held out as long as possible.'"

Given the evidence of suffering and death surrounding him, it must have been a difficult pose to maintain. The British and German casualties (about 300 killed and twice that many wounded) had been relatively light given the amount of metal that had rained down on Yorktown. It was a different story, however, when it came to the 4500 slaves Cornwallis had welcomed into his camp.

Untold numbers had been killed by allied fire during the siege (according to the German soldier George Flohr, African Americans made up "the majority of the dead" in Yorktown) but there were hundreds, if not thousands, more who had died—or were about to die—of disease, starvation, and exposure. "During the siege," Joseph Plumb Martin remembered, "we saw in the woods herds of Negroes which Lord Cornwallis (after he had inveigled them from their proprietors) in love and pity to them, had turned adrift with no other recompense for their confidence in his humanity than the smallpox for their bounty and starvation and death for their wages. They might be seen scattered about in every direction, dead and dying with pieces of ears of burnt Indian corn in the hands and mouths, even of those that were dead."

It is one of the great and deplorable ironies of our country's history that in the days after the victory that did more than any other to win the citizens of the United States their liberty and freedom, the slaveholders of Virginia descended on Yorktown to ensure that those African Americans who had not already died were denied *their* liberty and freedom. Some of the slaveholders had traveled from as far away as Richmond, but there was at least one who was already on the scene: His Excellency George Washington.

Washington had lost seventeen of his slaves to the British the previous spring. To facilitate the recapture of his and other African Americans, he had been sure to include a clause in the Articles of Capitulation that read: "It is understood that any property obviously belonging to the inhabitants of these states, in the possession of the garrison, shall be subject to be reclaimed." He had even designated what might be termed an official slave catcher, David Ross, to whom all officers and soldiers were to turn over their black servants for return to their proper masters. According to Daniel Trabue, who along with his brother ventured into Yorktown after the siege, "The Negroes looked condemned"—as, of course, they were.

One can only wonder what the hundreds of African American soldiers in Washington's army felt about this horrifying scene. As had been proven time and again throughout the war—from the Battle of Bunker Hill to the Siege of Yorktown—the black soldiers were more than deserving of the freedom their service had earned them. If two of the white officers who led the charge on redoubt number 10, Alexander Hamilton and John Laurens, had had their way during the winter of Valley Forge—when they hatched a plan by which enslaved African Americans in the south would gain their freedom by serving in the Continental army—the American force at Yorktown might have been mostly black. Washington had initially approved of Hamilton and Laurens's plan, writing that "blacks in the southern parts of the continent offer a resource to us that should not be neglected." Several years later, however, when Laurens brought his proposal before the South Carolina legislature, Washington changed his mind, claiming the plan would be "productive of much discontent in those who are held in servitude." As commander in chief of the Continental army, he knew he needed all the soldiers he could get. As a private citizen, however, he feared the plan might endanger his way of life, a life built on slavery. And as might be expected, without Washington's approval, Laurens's proposal went nowhere.

At least for now, Washington was unable to compromise his own financial interests for the greater good of not just the war effort but the future of his country. For as he and fellow slaveholder Thomas Jefferson came to recognize, slavery was the "moral depravity" that might one day tear America apart. "We have the wolf by the ear," Jefferson would write, "and we can neither hold him, nor safely let him go."

Years later, the British traveler Benjamin Henry Latrobe commented on the "many wagon loads of the bones of men, women, and children, stripped of the flesh by the vultures and hawks" that still littered the Virginia countryside. Yorktown was the site of a great victory, but it was also where the road to the Civil War began. As Washington confided to his cousin Lund, to whom he had written two years before about the possibility of selling off all his slaves at Mount Vernon, there might one day be a "punishment . . . for our want of public, and indeed private virtue."

NOTHING HAPPENED QUICKLY in the eighteenth century, especially with an ocean between America and Europe. It would be

months before Washington learned anything definitive about how
the news of Yorktown had been received in Europe, allowing the
British army plenty of time to deliver the blow that could render the
recent allied triumph meaningless. He had to assume the fighting was
going to continue through 1782, if not beyond.

The day after Cornwallis's surrender, Washington sent de Grasse
a proposal. Now was the time, he insisted, to turn their attention to
Charleston. He knew the admiral needed to get back to the Caribbean, but if he would give him just two more months, they could
"destroy the last hope" of the enemy.

For the next two weeks, de Grasse considered the proposal, finally
agreeing to the half measure of sailing Lafayette and a small army to
Wilmington, North Carolina, which from Washington's perspective
was better than nothing. In the end, however, de Grasse rejected even
that plan. Undeterred, Washington then asked him to think about a
spring campaign. Trying to be polite, the weary admiral once again
demurred. His "wretched health" made it impossible for him to look
that far ahead. No one, whether it was in the French, American, or
British military forces, had the stamina to keep up with the forty-
nine-year-old Washington, even after six years of war.

By November 5, he had finished attending to the countless details
associated with the aftermath of the siege. The prisoners, ordnance,
and stores had been distributed; reinforcements had been sent south to
assist Nathanael Greene; the rest of the Continental army was headed
back north to the Hudson River while Rochambeau and the French
remained in Virginia for the winter. That morning Washington set
out to rejoin his army. But first he needed to stop at the home of Martha's brother-in-law, Burwell Bassett, in nearby Eltham, Virginia,
where his twenty-six-year-old stepson Jacky Custis was recovering
from "camp fever" contracted while serving as his aide at Yorktown.

But as he soon discovered, Jacky's illness had taken a sudden and
tragic turn. Within minutes of his arrival, Washington later recounted
to Lafayette, "poor Mr. Custis breathe[d] his last; this unexpected
and affecting event threw Mrs. Washington and Mrs. Custis (who

were both present) into such deep distress" that he put off all immediate plans of rejoining the army.

Washington's life had been full of death—his father, his beloved half brother Lawrence, and so many others had died before their time, and now the lighthearted and largely ineffectual Jacky was gone. Four years later, Washington would write his former aide Jonathan Trumbull on his father's death. "I can offer nothing which your own reason has not already suggested on this occasion," he consoled in what might be the least comforting letter of condolence ever written. "[N]or shall I add more on this subject to you as it would only be a renewal of sorrow by recalling afresh to your remembrance things which had better be forgotten." This was a man who only looked ahead.

By November 13, he and Martha were at Mount Vernon. On the way, he had stopped to see his mother, who was not at home. "My dear George," she subsequently wrote, "I was truly uneasy by not being at home when you went through Fredericksburg. It was an unlucky thing for me. Now I am afraid I never shall have that pleasure again." That her son had just won the victory of his already distinguished military career went, of course, unmentioned.

And so, as the country around him celebrated the miraculous turn the war had taken, Washington spent the week in a house of mourning. "Mr. Custis' death has given much distress in this family," he wrote to his friend Benjamin Harrison. Already, however, his mind was turning back to the war. "My greatest fear," he wrote to Nathanael Greene, "is that Congress viewing this stroke in too important a point of light, may think our work too nearly closed, and will fall into a state of languor and relaxation; to prevent this error I shall employ every means in my power." On November 20, after only a week at Mount Vernon, Washington, Martha, and a few members of his staff started for Philadelphia.

CHAPTER 10

"The North River Captain"

SEVERAL WEEKS AFTER the British surrender at Yorktown, Henry Knox wrote to his friend Nathanael Greene. The two had witnessed George Washington's evolution from the rash, forty-three-year-old commander in chief who yearned to burn Boston to the ground in the winter of 1775–1776 to the careful yet cunning strategist capable of holding both an army and a country together through six years of war. His performance at Yorktown, however, had revealed facets of his character that not even Knox knew existed. "I cannot refrain adding one word more about our good General," he confided to Greene. "He improves in his understanding & abilities hourly . . . , they appear greater in proportion to the opportunities. He is more and more confident of his own judgment which by far exceeds those whose opinions he condescends to."

Despite being a confirmed landlubber himself, Knox chose to capture Washington's remarkable growth as a leader with a nautical reference. Recalling those days in New York when the commander in chief had demonstrated an unexpected talent for navigating a boat up and down the Hudson (also known as the North) River, Knox wrote: "[B]ut I will not now [go] into a panegyric on him. *You must know him* as the North River captain and know that it is only the exercise of his own judgment which was wanting to perfect his character."

It turned out to be a most prescient analysis. By that spring, Washington was back on the Hudson, this time in a house built of stone in Newburgh, New York. After several years of trying, French naval superiority had won him the victory that might persuade the enemy to negotiate an end to the war. However, given the communication lag between America and Europe, it might be months before he heard about possible treaty negotiations in Paris. For the foreseeable future, he must remain on the offensive, and for that to happen he needed the French navy. As he'd written to Lafayette before leaving Mount Vernon back in November, "No land force can act decisively unless accompanied by a maritime superiority." Now, more than ever, he needed the Comte de Grasse.

To a certain extent, the Battle of the Chesapeake had been won in spite of the French admiral. His decision to sail out of the bay in a chaotic frenzy had resulted in a line of battle that would have provided a more competent opponent than Thomas Graves with the opportunity to destroy the French vanguard before the rest of the fleet could have come to its defense. On April 12, 1782, near an archipelago of islands between Guadeloupe and Dominica called the Saintes, de Grasse's impulsiveness finally caught up with him. Even though a larger and faster British fleet was in pursuit of his own, he decided to rally to the defense of the *Zélé*, the French 74 that had just suffered its fourteenth collision in thirteen months by running into his own flagship. Admiral George Rodney, just back from medical treatment in England, did what Graves had refused to do off the Capes of Virginia: Instead of lining up his battleships in a careful row, he went in for the kill. After close to twelve hours of fighting, the British had captured five French ships, including the *Ville de Paris*, requiring that de Grasse suffer the humiliation of surrendering to the enemy.

The magnitude of de Grasse's defeat prompted Spain and France to abandon their plans to attack Jamaica, which would continue to

By arriving at Chesapeake Bay with twenty-eight ships of the line, the Comte de Grasse virtually ensured the capture of Cornwallis's army. However, his insistence on initiating operations against the British army left him ill prepared for the arrival of the fleet commanded by Thomas Graves. As Washington remarked, de Grasse's considerable talents were "marred by his own impetuosity."

Although history has named de Grasse the hero of the Battle of the Chesapeake, it was Louis-Antoine de Bougainville and the French vanguard that did most of the fighting. As even de Grasse admitted, "the honors of the day" belonged to Bougainville.

Admiral George Rodney, though a difficult, irascible leader, was one of Britain's greatest naval commanders. Health problems, however, prevented him from participating in the Battle of the Chesapeake.

With Rodney on his way to England for medical attention, command of the British fleet devolved to the less talented Thomas Graves.

Graves's second in command at the Battle of the Chesapeake was Samuel Hood. Although Hood was an officer of considerable ability, his constant carping ill served the British fleet at the Battle of the Chesapeake.

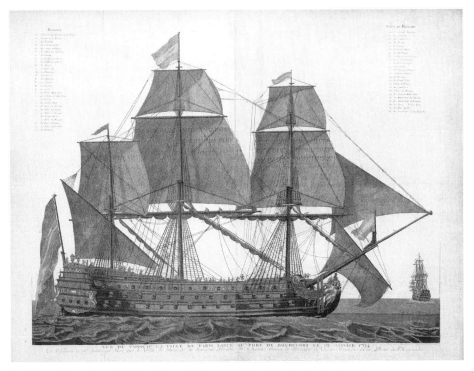

De Grasse's flagship, the *Ville de Paris,* the largest ship of the line in the French navy.

A 1962 painting of the Battle of the Chesapeake by V. Zveg.

If there was an American counterpart to Spanish envoy Francisco Saavedra, who operated as the allied fixer in the Caribbean, it was Superintendent of Finance Robert Morris. Not only did Morris extend his considerable personal credit to help fund the Yorktown campaign, he worked tirelessly to consolidate the supply operations of both the American and the French armies.

Just twenty-four years old, with an army less than half the size of the enemy's, the Marquis de Lafayette did his best to prevent Cornwallis from escaping from his isolated outpost between the James and York rivers at Yorktown.

To Lafayette's regret, Washington chose the New Englander Benjamin Lincoln, who had commanded the American army during the fall of Charleston, to serve as his second in command at Yorktown.

Artillery chief Henry Knox performed brilliantly at Yorktown. According to French general Chastellux, "It is impossible to know him without esteeming and loving him."

Despite being just twenty years old at Yorktown, Sergeant Joseph Plumb Martin had already fought in most of the major battles of the war. Here he is, almost seventy years later, with his wife, Lucy. Martin's journal of his war experiences, published in 1830, is one of the best first-person accounts of the conflict. He died in 1850 at the age of eighty-nine in Stockton Springs, Maine.

A watercolor drawing from the diary of Jean Baptiste Antoine de Verger showing, from left to right, a black private in the Rhode Island light infantry company, a soldier in the Canadian regiment commanded by Moses Hazen, a Virginia rifleman, and a Continental army gunner.

Washington and his generals at Yorktown by Charles Willson Peale. Washington points toward the river with his riding whip, with Rochambeau to his left. Note the carcasses of the British horses on the river's shoreline.

A later depiction of Washington and his generals by Auguste Couder. Washington and Rochambeau are issuing orders in front of the tent.

A view of the Siege of Yorktown and the York River sketched by a British officer on Gloucester Point.

Benjamin Henry Latrobe's sketch of Secretary Thomas Nelson's house in Yorktown showing the extensive damage the structure suffered during the battle. According to a story told to Latrobe more than fifteen years later, the large hole between the window and the door on the left was made by an American artilleryman who, in answer to a bet, shot thirteen consecutive cannonballs through the opening.

Alexander Hamilton before the attack on redoubt number 10 at Yorktown, painted by Alonzo Chappel.

Accompanying Hamilton during the attack on redoubt 10 was his good friend and fellow former aide to Washington, John Laurens, who had spent the previous winter as an American emissary to France and would die the following year during a minor skirmish in South Carolina.

Although the fortification is too large and the attack is being conducted in daylight rather than at night, this 1840 painting by Eugène Lami captures the energy and violence of the storming of the British redoubt.

In John Trumbull's rendering of the surrender at Yorktown, Benjamin Lincoln, mounted on a white horse, accepts the sword of Cornwallis's stand-in, Charles O'Hara, as Washington and his officers watch on the right and Rochambeau and the French high command watch on the left.

A different view of the surrender by Louis-Nicolas van Blarenberghe, showing the long gauntlet of allied soldiers through which the British were forced to pass and the area to the left where they deposited their weapons.

Seven months after the Battle of the Chesapeake, Admiral de Grasse suffered a defeat so devastating that Washington feared the reversal had negated all that had been gained at Yorktown. Here de Grasse's flagship, the *Ville de Paris* (to the right), is pummeled by Samuel Hood's much smaller *Barfleur* at the Battle of the Saintes.

We will never know how involved Horatio Gates was in what came to be known as the Newburgh conspiracy. Washington, however, was convinced that "under a mask of . . . apparent cordiality," his longtime nemesis was doing everything he could to undermine his authority.

Guy Carleton, Henry Clinton's replacement as British commander in chief, oversaw the evacuation of New York in 1783. Despite Washington's objections, Carleton insisted that any former slaves who had spent a year or more with the British would be protected from recapture by American slave catchers.

John Trumbull's 1824 painting of George Washington resigning his commission to Congress on December 23, 1783. Trumbull has taken the liberty of placing Martha Washington and her grandchildren on the balcony on the upper right. They were actually at Mount Vernon in anticipation of Washington's arrival.

To his "vine and fig tree" at last: Benjamin Henry Latrobe's 1796 painting of George Washington and family enjoying the view of the Potomac from the piazza at Mount Vernon.

serve as Britain's primary base in the Caribbean. When Washington learned of what came to be known as the Battle of the Saintes, he feared the catastrophe might inspire the British to renew the war effort. "The disastrous event of the naval action in the West Indies may indeed, and probably will now give a total alteration to the complexion of the campaign," he wrote to Nathanael Greene. With their naval superiority restored, the British were free to resume hostilities in the south. "At present," Washington admitted to James McHenry, another former aide, "we are enveloped in darkness; and no man, I believe, can foretell all the consequences which will result from the naval action. . . . To say not worse of it, it is an unfortunate affair."

WORD OF CORNWALLIS'S DEFEAT at Yorktown reached London on Sunday, November 25, 1781. Prime Minister North received the news, according to Secretary of State Germain, "as he would have taken a ball in his breast. . . . For he opened his arms exclaiming wildly as he paced up and down the apartment, during a few minutes, 'Oh God! It is all over!' words which he repeated many times, under emotions of the deepest agitation and distress."

King George III, however, remained resolute, declaring that the defeat would not make "the smallest alteration in these principles of my conduct." But in the months ahead, even the king came to recognize that he had little choice in the matter. The English people had grown tired of war, and once the news of Rodney's victory at the Saintes reached London, it became possible for Britain to make peace with her former colonies in North America knowing that the Empire's position in the all-important Caribbean was secure.

By the summer of 1782, Sir Henry Clinton had been replaced by Sir Guy Carleton, the former military governor of Canada, making him the fourth British commander in chief Washington had faced since the beginning of hostilities in 1775. Unknown to Washington, who remained skeptical of Britain's interest in peace, Carleton was under orders to begin the process of extracting the royal army from

North America. Even after Carleton wrote to Washington on August 2, confirming that not only had "negotiations for a general peace . . . commenced at Paris," but also that King George had instructed his chief negotiator to propose "the independency of the Thirteen Provinces," the American commander in chief worried that the British were "only gaining time to become more formidable at sea; to form new alliances, if possible; or to disunite us."

He had ample reason for concern. If the pace of treaty negotiations did not increase soon, there might not be a country left to declare victory. It had only been the need for an army that had brought the country together in common cause. Now that the war seemed to be drawing to a close, the states were showing less and less interest in supporting what Alexander Hamilton, who soon joined Congress as a delegate from New York, called "Continental views." Recent efforts to fund the federal government through the collection of import duties, while initially embraced as a sensible solution to the problem, were doomed to failure when Rhode Island and Virginia refused to approve them. Instead of a union of states, America was in danger of becoming a fractious collection of little nations, each one demanding that its own interests prevail.

Already New York, Massachusetts, and New Hampshire were squabbling about the territory between them as the settlers living in those contested lands (which they called Vermont) threatened to align themselves with British Canada if Congress did not grant them statehood. Even if America secured its independence, that did not guarantee it would become a viable republic. As Maurice Morgann, General Carleton's secretary, predicted, a "federal union" based only on "verbal maxims of general liberty and brotherly love" would soon degenerate into "despotism and mutual rage." Even now, with hostilities between the British and American armies drawing to a close, a brutal civil war continued to rage throughout the middle and southern states as patriots and loyalists battled it out in a seemingly ceaseless cycle of murder and retribution.

That summer Washington made the mistake of inserting himself into a particularly nasty sequence of reprisals that had resulted in the hanging of a captured American army officer in Sandy Hook, New Jersey. If the British did not hand over the culprit responsible for the officer's death, Washington vowed to execute a randomly selected British prisoner in his place. When the lot fell to Charles Asgill, a young Yorktown prisoner with the same genial charm that had made British spy chief Major John André such a sympathetic character, Washington realized that his attempts to contain the chaos had only added to the moral confusion of the times.

He was ultimately saved from this largely self-created dilemma by the intervention of the French foreign minister, the Comte de Vergennes, whose letter on the behalf of Asgill's terrified mother moved Congress to order the British officer's release. Nonetheless, the incident gave Washington a renewed appreciation for how anger and vengeance could consume a country without a strong central government. "[F]rom the observations I have made in the course of this war," he wrote to his friend Benjamin Harrison, who was now governor of Virginia, "I am decided in my opinion that if the powers of Congress are not enlarged and made competent to all *general purposes,* that the blood which has been spilt, the expense that has been incurred and the distresses which have been felt will avail us nothing; and that the bond, already too weak, which holds us together, will soon be broken; when anarchy and confusion must prevail."

WASHINGTON HAD HOPED TO SPEND the winter of 1782–1783 at Mount Vernon. By the middle of October, he realized he must remain with the army in Newburgh. Never before, not even during the winter at Valley Forge, had there been "so great a spirit of discontent" among the officers of the Continental army. The American people, the officers had come to realize, did not want to pay them for having won their independence. "Hitherto the officers have stood between the lower order of the soldiery and the public," he wrote to Joseph Jones, a Virginia delegate to Congress, "and in more instances than one, at the hazard of their lives, have quelled very dangerous mutinies. But if their discontents should be suffered to rise equally high, I know not what the consequences may be." That winter he must "stick very close to the troops . . . and try, like a careful physician, to prevent if possible the disorders getting to an incurable height."

That fall, the Comte de Rochambeau and the French army paused briefly beside the Hudson on their way to Boston and eventual transportation to the Caribbean and France. Although Washington would be sorry to say goodbye to Major General Chastellux (who remained in the United States for another year), his farewell letter to Rochambeau was considerably more restrained. The two leaders had worked well enough together at Yorktown, but the road to getting there, during which Rochambeau had (in accordance to the dictates of his government) kept his American counterpart in the dark about the whereabouts of the French fleet, had left Washington embittered and resentful.

In the years to come, when questioned about the Yorktown campaign, Washington insisted that his early preference for New York instead of the Chesapeake had been a mere ruse designed to deceive the British, and that "it was never in contemplation to attack New York." Unfortunately, Washington's diary makes clear that this simply was not the case. As his biographer Ron Chernow explains, it was "awkward for him to admit that he had . . . opposed a campaign that served as the brilliant capstone of his military career. He wanted to portray himself as the visionary architect of the Yorktown victory, not as a general misguidedly concentrating upon New York while his French allies masterminded the decisive blow."

In Washington's defense, it was only hindsight that made the Chesapeake strategy look so brilliant. So many events outside of his and Rochambeau's control had to happen—from Admiral Rodney's decision to return to England for medical attention, to de Grasse's decision to sail to the Chesapeake with the entire French fleet, to Clinton's refusal to interfere in any way with the allied army's departure from White Plains, to Cornwallis's determination to remain at

Yorktown even after the arrival of a large French fleet—that it was impossible for either leader to know with any certainty in the summer of 1781 that the Chesapeake was where they might secure the victory that won the war. As we have seen, Washington had his reasons to initially prefer New York, especially since the appearance of the French fleet at Sandy Hook would have allowed for the transportation of the allied army by water—an opportunity lost by Rochambeau's scheming behind his back. No wonder Washington remained sensitive and defensive about his role in the Yorktown campaign in later years.

IN OCTOBER 1782, he learned of the tragic death of his former aide John Laurens "in a trifling skirmish in South Carolina." By then, Washington's infected gums and decaying teeth had become almost unendurable, information that became public knowledge when the British gleefully published an intercepted letter in the New York press. And then there was the matter of his eyes.

Like many men in their fifties, he was having increasing trouble making out the words on a written page. After trying on the spectacles of an assortment of friends and associates, he identified "the glass of such spectacles as suit my eyes" and sent the lenses to the noted astronomer and inventor David Rittenhouse in Philadelphia so that "he may know how to grind his crystals." After close to eight years of being what he called "on the stretch," Washington had visibly aged. In addition to his failing eyes and teeth, his once reddish hair was turning gray.

In February 1783, matters among the officers of the Continental army were reaching a crisis. With the weather miserably cold, the officers, when not attending dancing classes in the newly built common building known as "the Temple," had little to do but brood on what Washington called "the long and great sufferings of this army . . . unexampled in history" and wonder what Congress was going to do to set things right. A committee of three officers had been sent to

Philadelphia back in December. Since the states refused to grant Congress the right to collect the taxes required to pay the army, the officers had asked that, at the very least, the delegates determine what was owed each of them for future reimbursement. But even this request was encountering resistance.

By the end of the month Washington began to suspect that an effort was under way among the politicians in Philadelphia to create an alliance between the officers and the government's creditors that might pressure the states into granting Congress the financial powers needed to pay off its debts. Using the army to intimidate the states into funding the federal government was, of course, a very dangerous game. "[W]hen once all confidence between the civil and military authority is lost," Joseph Jones wrote to Washington on February 27, "by intemperate conduct or an assumption of improper power, especially by the military body, the Rubicon is passed and to retreat will be very difficult, from the fears and jealousies that will unavoidably subsist between the two bodies."

Washington wanted more than anything else to see Congress invested with the powers it needed to properly rule the country; he also recognized that the Continental army had been terribly mistreated. But he would never countenance using the military to force the hand of civil government. As proven by Caesar in Ancient Rome and Cromwell during the English Revolution, this was the first step on the road to dictatorship. Just the year before, a colonel in the Continental army had made the mistake of suggesting that Washington be named king of the United States. "[Y]ou could not have found a person to whom your schemes are more disagreeable," Washington had thundered back in response. "[B]anish these thoughts from your mind, and never communicate . . . a sentiment of the like nature." Instead of Caesar, he preferred the classical example of Cincinnatus, the Roman general who traded his sword for the quiet of his farm. As they all knew, Washington would never challenge the sovereignty of Congress.

To circumvent their commander in chief, some officers were currently trying to, according to Joseph Jones, "lessen your popularity in the army in hopes ultimately the weight of your opposition will prove no obstacle to their ambitious designs." Hamilton, whose contacts in the army were as good as anyone's, reported that Washington's "extreme reserve, mixed sometimes with a degree of asperity of temper, both of which were said to have increased of late, had contributed to the decline of his popularity."

This was not the first time Washington's authority had been challenged. During the winter at Valley Forge, after the loss of Philadelphia to the British, there were delegates in Congress and officers in the Continental army who had begun to talk about replacing him with Horatio Gates, the hero of Saratoga. What was happening now in Newburgh, however, was far more serious, since it threatened the legitimacy of the country's government. And as it so happened, Gates, whom Washington referred to as "the old leven," had rejoined the army in Newburgh. It will never be known for certain how extensively Gates was involved in the plan to undermine the commander in chief; for his part, Washington believed that "under a mask of the most perfect dissimulation and apparent cordiality," Gates was positioning himself (now that the hard work was done) to become the next leader of the Continental army.

On March 10, an inflammatory address, penned by a member of Gates's staff, began to circulate among the officers at Newburgh. The United States had proven to be, the anonymous author proclaimed, "a country that tramples upon your rights, disdains your cries and insults your distresses." Only now, while they were still army officers, did they have the power to get their way. They must "assume a bolder tone" and "suspect the man who would advise to more moderation and longer forbearance." In other words, they should not listen to Washington and remember "that in any political event, the army has its alternative." The address ended with the suggestion that they meet the next day and come up with a plan.

Washington's response was immediate. The following morning he issued general orders declaring "his disapprobation of such disorderly proceedings." Instead of meeting that day, they should gather four days later, at noon on Saturday, March 15. "After mature deliberation," they would be in a better position to do the right thing—both for themselves and for their country. Horatio Gates would preside over the meeting and report to him afterward. Washington was clearly creating the expectation that with Gates running the meeting, the officers would be free to do as they pleased. But, as it turned out, Washington had no intention of allowing them to convene a meeting without him.

The Temple was a simple rectangular building with a stage and a lectern at one end. Soon after Gates began the meeting at noon, Washington arrived at the door and asked to be given the opportunity to speak. The unexpected appearance of the commander in chief at such an emotionally freighted moment had a riveting effect. According to Captain Samuel Shaw, "Every eye was fixed upon the illustrious man."

He started with an apology, claiming that he had not originally planned to attend the meeting until a second anonymous address (which insisted that Washington's general orders of March 11 had, in effect, sanctioned whatever the officers decided to do) made it necessary that he "avail himself of the present opportunity." To do so with "the greater perspicuity," he had prepared a speech, which with "the indulgence of his brother officers, he would take the liberty of reading to them."

"By an anonymous summons," he began, "an attempt has been made to convene you together; how inconsistent with rules of propriety! How unmilitary! And how subversive of all order and discipline, let the good sense of the army decide." Instead of appealing to "the reason and judgment of the army," the author of the address had purposely sought to agitate their "feelings and passions." This was a topic that Washington, who had spent his adult life attempting to curb his own volcanic temper, knew something about. To do what was right, instead of what felt good in the moment, they must all seek "cool, deliberative thinking and that composure of mind which is so necessary to give dignity and stability to measures."

What bothered him the most about the anonymous address was that its author had advised them "to suspect the man who shall recommend moderate measures." This, of course, was a direct assault on both his integrity and his authority. "I spurn it," he asserted, "as every man who regards that liberty and reveres that justice for which we contend undoubtedly must; for if men are to be precluded from offering their sentiments on a matter . . . , reason is of no use to us, the freedom of speech may be taken away and dumb and silent we may be led, like sheep, to the slaughter." By allowing someone to manipulate their emotions, the officers were, in effect, forfeiting their liberty. In the end, Washington was making a passionate argument for the primacy of reason and the danger of demagoguery.

Ultimately, it was up to them. He did, however, want them to appreciate the extraordinary opportunity that circumstances had placed before them. By refusing the appeal of a writer who would "overturn the liberties of our country, and . . . open the flood gates of civil discord and deluge our rising empire in blood," the officers would "give one more distinguished proof of unexampled patriotism and patient virtue . . . and by the dignity of your conduct afford occasion for posterity to say, when speaking of the glorious example you have exhibited to mankind, 'had this day been wanting, the world had never seen the last state of perfection to which human nature is capable of attaining.'"

It was a magnificent rhetorical performance. But it was not enough. The officers gathered in this low, seventy-foot-long room remained sullen and unconvinced. Never before had Washington experienced the full, unmitigated displeasure of his officers. "On other occasions," Samuel Shaw remembered, "he [had] been supported by the exertions of an army and the countenance of his friends; but in this he stood single and alone. There was no saying where the passions of an army, which were not a little inflamed, might lead. . . . Under these circumstances he appeared, not at the head of his troops, but as it were in opposition to them; and for a dreadful moment the interests of the army and its general seemed to be in competition!"

Washington had one last communication he wanted to share with them: a letter from the Virginia delegate Joseph Jones that spoke to the support the officers had in Congress. He had read only a few sentences when he paused. He was evidently having trouble making out Jones's handwriting. "Gentlemen," he said, "you will permit me to put on my spectacles, for I have not only grown gray, but almost blind, in the service of my country." No one in the room had ever seen him wearing glasses—a sign of human frailty that overwhelmed them. "There was something so natural," Shaw recalled, "so unaffected, in this appeal, as rendered it superior to the most studied oratory; it forced its way to the heart, and you might see sensibility moisten every eye."

Once he had finished reading Jones's letter, he left the building as quickly as he had entered it. In what must have been a prearranged sequence of motions, several officers sympathetic to his cause moved that a committee be elected to draft resolutions for Washington to forward to Congress. Soon Henry Knox and two others had produced a statement pledging the officers' "unshaken confidence in the justice of Congress and their country" and requesting that Washington plead their case for them. The resolutions passed unanimously; even John Armstrong, the officer who had written the anonymous address, voted in support of the motion that branded his creation "infamous."

"I rejoice in the opportunities I have had," Samuel Shaw later wrote, "of seeing this great man in a variety of situations—calm and intrepid where the battle raged, patient and persevering under the pressure of misfortune, moderate and possessing himself in the full career of victory. Great as these qualifications deservedly render him, he never appeared to me more truly so, than at the assembly [at Newburgh]." Washington, the North River captain, had succeeded in putting down the mutiny that might have destroyed the United States. As Thomas Jefferson wrote the following year, "the moderation and virtue of a single character has probably prevented this revolution from being closed as most others have been by a subversion of that liberty it was intended to establish."

THE SOLDIERS CALLED IT "George Washington's watch chain": the huge links of iron that stretched across the Hudson at West Point to prevent British ships from sailing up the river. Every autumn since 1778 the chain was taken up, and every spring, once the ice had cleared, it was laid down again. In the spring of 1783 the soldiers stationed at West Point were placing bets on what was going to happen to the chain. "[F]or the putting down or the keeping up of the chain was," according to Sergeant Joseph Plumb Martin, "the criterion by which we were to judge of war or peace." There were still plenty of British soldiers stationed in New York and elsewhere, as well as prisoners of war and loyalists who would need to be evacuated, but before that could happen, peace must be declared. As it turned out, the chain (sections of which can still be seen on the grounds of West Point) was never again laid across the Hudson.

On April 19, which happened to be the anniversary of the skirmishes at Lexington and Concord, Washington's general orders announced the conclusion of the war. "Nothing now remains," the orders read, "but for the actors of this mighty scene to preserve a perfect, unvarying consistency of character through the very last act; to close the drama with applause; and to retire from the military theatre with the same approbation of angels and men which have crowned all their former virtuous actions." So that the soldiers could "drink perpetual peace, independence and happiness to the United States of America," Washington ordered that "an extra ration of liquor . . . be issued to *every* man."

But for Martin and his comrades in arms, the news was bittersweet. "We had lived together as a family of brothers for several years . . . ; had shared with each other the hardships, dangers, and sufferings incident to a soldier's life; had sympathized with each other in trouble and sickness. . . . And now we were to be . . . parted forever, as unconditionally separated as though the grave lay between. . . . Ah! It was a serious time."

Making it all the harder was the knowledge that they had nothing to show for their years of service to their country. "Starved, ragged, and meager," they were about to return to civilian life in far worse shape than when they had joined the army. "All that they could do," Martin wrote, "was to make a virtue of necessity and face the threatening evils with the same resolution and fortitude that they had for so long a time faced the enemy in the field." Finally on June 11, their captain handed out furloughs granting them permission to go home. "When the country had drained the last drop of service it could screw out of the poor soldiers," Martin remembered, "they were turned adrift like old worn-out horses."

A total of about 200,000 Americans had served in the war, but that did not mean the rest of the country of about 3 million would show them any gratitude or respect. Americans in 1783 were desperate to put the trauma of the Revolution behind them, and these broken and penniless soldiers were a daily reminder of what they preferred to forget. "What scornful looks and hard words have I experienced," Martin wrote forty-seven years later. "I hope I shall one day find land enough to lay my bones."

That spring Washington received a letter from Lafayette, who had long since returned to France. Now that peace was looking like a certainty, he had a "wild scheme" to propose: the two of them should buy a small plantation together and "try the experiment to free the Negroes and use them only as tenants. Such an example as yours might render it a general practice." Lafayette's time in Virginia had given him a firsthand knowledge of the horrifying realities of southern slavery. He still loved Washington like a father, but something needed to be done to ensure that the promise of the Declaration of Independence—"liberty and justice for all"—applied to all

Americans, no matter what their skin color. For as Lafayette later claimed, "I would never have drawn my sword in the cause of America, if I could have conceived that thereby I was founding a land of slavery."

Washington praised his friend for the "benevolence of your heart," while insisting that he would be "happy to join you in so laudable a work." That did not prevent him, however, from pursuing a policy that was diametrically opposed to the one proposed by Lafayette. The preliminary peace treaty between America and Britain included an article insisting on the return of any slaves who had sought refuge with the British. Just as had occurred at Yorktown, slave catchers had begun to descend on British-held New York. Unlike at Yorktown, however, the former slaves had an advocate in British general Carleton.

In May, Washington met with Sir Guy on the banks of the Hudson to discuss the specifics of the British evacuation. By this time, Washington had received inquiries from his slaveholding friends in Virginia about how best to reclaim their property, and he wanted to make sure Carleton was enforcing the relevant article in the treaty. According to Chief Justice William Smith, who was part of the British delegation, Washington "delivered himself without animation, with great slowness, and a low tone of voice." It was obviously an awkward moment for the American commander, especially when Carleton insisted that Britain's commitment to the loyalists must be kept "with all colors." Any former slave who had spent a year or more with the British was given a certificate that protected him or her from capture. Already, one Harry Washington, formerly of Mount Vernon, had sailed along with 132 emancipated blacks for Nova Scotia. When Washington learned that Carleton had already begun transporting loyalists and free African Americans to Canada, he blurted out, "Already embarked!" In the end, Washington was powerless to prevent Carleton from pursing his liberal interpretation of the peace accord, and in the months ahead, somewhere in the neighborhood of 4000 former slaves would secure their freedom by escaping from New York on British ships.

. . .

Being a planter from Virginia, Washington continued to view enslaved Africans as property; he had no such local prejudices when it came to what he called "the Union." As the commander in chief of the Continental army, he had kept his views on the matter private, but now, as he prepared to resign his commission to Congress and become, once again, a private citizen, he felt it time to make his views public because, he wrote in a Circular to the States, "it is yet to be decided whether the Revolution must ultimately be considered as a blessing or a curse."

From Washington's perspective, the fate of the country depended on a strong central government. "[W]hatever measures have a tendency to dissolve the Union," he asserted, "ought to be considered as hostile to the liberty and independence of America. . . . We . . . may find by our own unhappy experience that there is a natural and necessary progression, from the extreme of anarchy to the extreme of tyranny; and that arbitrary power is most easily established on the ruins of liberty abused." It was a brilliant summation of his thought up until that time, but it was not, for the most part, well received. "The murmur is free and general," the Virginian Edmund Randolph wrote that summer, "against what is called the unsolicited obtrusion of his advice."

Throughout the final years of the war, the states had operated, for the most part, independently. Accustomed to going their own way, the states—along with the American people—saw no immediate need for a strong central government, especially in the giddy euphoria surrounding the end of the conflict. Before constructive change could occur, conditions in America must get frighteningly worse. "Like young heirs come a little premature perhaps to a large inheritance," Washington wrote to his former neighbor George Fairfax, "it is more than probable they will riot for a while; but in this if it should happen, tho' it is a circumstance which is to be lamented . . . , [it] will work its own cure, as there is virtue at the bottom." They did not want to hear what he had to say at this point, but Washington still had faith in the American people.

THAT SPRING CONGRESS once again let him down. The expectation had been that the government would settle the officers' accounts while providing them with the token amount of three months' pay before they left the service. But even these trifling measures proved impossible. Inevitably the officers (like the enlisted men) felt betrayed—not only by their country but by their commander in chief, who had encouraged them to trust Congress. When Washington invited the officers to a farewell dinner, they spurned the invitation, "declaring they thought the present period more adapted to sorrow than mirth." It was "a parting scene," he wrote bitterly to the president of Congress, that "will not admit of description."

Soon after, the Congressional delegates received what more than a few Continental officers viewed as their deserved comeuppance. In June, some disgruntled soldiers stationed in Lancaster, Pennsylvania, marched on Philadelphia demanding their back pay. Washington was ultimately forced to send fifteen hundred soldiers to put down the mutiny, and Congress decided that for reasons of safety, it must relocate to Princeton, New Jersey. Caught between the hostility of his own officers and the desperate demands of a Congress reduced to an embarrassing caricature of its former self, Washington needed, more than anything else, a vacation. For a few weeks at least, the country would be left to its own, however inadequate, devices.

In July, he and New York governor George Clinton (who also happened to be a brigadier general in the Continental army) loaded some provisions and gear into a boat and headed up the Hudson for a two-week tour of the region Horatio Gates and Benedict Arnold had made famous. Not only did they explore the battlefields of Saratoga, as well as Lake George and the southern portion of Lake Champlain, they ventured up the Mohawk River to Fort Stanwix, which Arnold had saved from a British siege in the weeks before the victory at Saratoga.

Instead of the tangled legacies of the two men Washington may have despised more than any others on the planet, it was the wonder and potential of the American wilderness that seized his imagination. "I could not help taking a more contemplative and extensive view of the vast inland navigation of these United States," he wrote to Chastellux, "and could not but be struck with the immense diffusion and importance of it; and with the goodness of that Providence which has dealt her favors to us with so profuse a hand. . . . I shall not rest contented 'till I have explored the Western Country, and traversed those lands (or great part of them) which have given bounds to a new empire."

Washington might have looked forward to a triumphant tour of the capitals of Europe, where he would have been the object of unprecedented praise and adulation. Instead he yearned only to explore the wilderness of his adventurous youth. He dreamed, he wrote to Lafayette, of venturing up the St. Lawrence River to the Great Lakes, then down the Mississippi to New Orleans and Florida and finally home. "A great tour this, you will say. Probably it may take place nowhere but in imagination. . . . If it should be realized, there would be nothing wanting to make it perfectly agreeable but your company." And so, while Lafayette imagined joining him in the experiment that freed America of slavery, Washington fantasized about exploring the west. As he was well aware, many of the region's native inhabitants had been drawn into the bloody fighting that had raged throughout this distant portion of the country during the Revolution. So as to prevent future violence, he recommended to Congress that "a boundary line be drawn between them and us beyond which we will endeavor to restrain our people from hunting or settling." But as he no doubt suspected, no measure could easily constrain the insatiable lust of the American people for land.

With the end of his tour of duty fast approaching, Washington devoted considerable time to settling his accounts. Back in 1775, he had volunteered to serve without pay as long as Congress covered his expenses. He ultimately submitted a bill for £8422 (roughly $1.2 million in today's dollars). Washington was disappointed by how low the figure turned out to be, but unlike what had happened to his fellow officers, Congress agreed to pay the requested amount.

Even more important to Washington was the vast number of official papers chronicling his eight years as commander in chief. He might not want to be crowned king, but he did want to be remembered. Two years before, he had commissioned Richard Varick, who had been on Benedict Arnold's staff, to organize his war correspondence into what proved to be twenty-eight different volumes. By the fall of 1783, it was time to pack up the books and send them to Mount Vernon. "I am fully convinced," he wrote to Varick in appreciation, "that neither the present age nor posterity will consider the time and labor which have been employed in accomplishing it, unprofitably spent." And since Varick had completed the job before the end of the war, what became one of the essential building blocks of Washington's future legacy had been created at the public expense.

In late August, Congress requested that he come to Princeton for some final consultation as commander in chief. He and Martha took up residence in nearby Rocky Hill. Washington appears to have enjoyed this fall idyll in New Jersey, during which he had the opportunity to personally congratulate Nathanael Greene on his successes in the south. In one of the few recorded instances in which Washington is known to have told a joke, he responded to the president of Congress's claim that financial superintendent Robert Morris "had his hands full" with the quip, "I wish he had his pockets full."

By early November, Congress had received word that the final draft of the peace agreement between Britain and America had been signed. Washington decided it was time to issue his "Farewell Orders" to the army, even though more than two-thirds of its soldiers had already returned home. What they had accomplished, he insisted, was "little short of a standing miracle." What he took most pride in was how "men who came from different parts of the Continent, strongly disposed, by the habits of education, to despise and quarrel with each other, [had] instantly become but one patriotic band of brothers." The army was, in other words, what the United States might one day become under the leadership of a strong central government.

On November 4, just two days after issuing his farewell orders, Washington learned that without consulting him, Congress had adjourned more than a week ahead of schedule. What's more, he wrote to Alexander Hamilton, they had done so "without bringing the peace establishment or any of the many other pressing matters to a decision." Once again, he had to step into the void and bring the war to its ultimate conclusion.

NOT UNTIL NOVEMBER 25, 1783, did the British succeed in getting all the soldiers, loyalists, and freed ex-slaves loaded into the awaiting fleet of transports and naval vessels. A total of almost 33,000 people (not counting the soldiers and sailors) had left New York, making it what has been called "the largest movement of ships and people in the history of the British Empire." The United States had won its independence, but thousands of Americans had decided they must live elsewhere.

Washington entered the city on his gray horse Nelson with his traveling companion, Governor Clinton, at his side. They were followed by a long line of soldiers, politicians, and prominent citizens marching eight in a row. The British had expected New York to erupt in violence on the Rebels' return, but there was not a mob to be seen. "These Americans . . . are a curious original people," a British officer observed, *they know how to govern themselves, but nobody else can govern them.*"

Those who had not seen New York since the beginning of the war were appalled by the filth and disrepair. A fire had broken out soon after the British took the city in 1776, destroying close to a third of downtown, and nothing had been done to repair the damage. People still lived in tents and shacks in this fire-blackened portion of Manhattan. Many of the public buildings had been converted into prisons, holes hacked into the floors for the disposal of human waste. Worst of all were the prison ships anchored just across the East River in Brooklyn's Wallabout Bay, where an estimated 10,000 American prisoners had died in conditions of unimaginable squalor.

For the British, who never earned back the loyalty of the vast majority of their former colonists, New York represented the great lost opportunity of the war. If Sir Henry Clinton had reinstated civil government and encouraged the loyalists to begin rebuilding the city, he might have transformed Manhattan into a vibrant example of how the British Empire could restore peace, order, and English liberty throughout war-torn America. Instead he turned the city into a patriot killing ground. The New York historian Edwin Burrows has estimated that as many as 32,000 Americans had been imprisoned in and around New York. Of those, as many as 18,000 died. Since a total of about 35,800 Americans died in the War of Independence, this means that approximately half those deaths occurred in the environs of Manhattan. The New Englanders had Lexington and Concord, Bunker Hill, and the Siege of Boston. The southerners had a long list of brutal battles, including Camden, King's Mountain, and Guilford Courthouse. But no portion of the United States had witnessed more death than New York.

A greased flagpole made it more difficult than it might otherwise have been to replace the British flag with the stars and stripes, but soon the American standard was flying over the city for the first time. For the next eight days, Washington attended to both public and private matters, shopping for silverware and teapots for Mount Vernon and making sure that several key spies in patriot service, such as the printer James Rivington (who appears to have secured the copy of the royal navy's signal book that had been sent to Admiral de Grasse), were compensated for the considerable risks they had taken during the war.

Washington held out hope of returning to Mount Vernon by Christmas. But first he had to resign his commission to Congress, which had relocated to Annapolis. To keep to his schedule, he determined to leave New York on Thursday, December 4, after a final meeting with his officers at Fraunces Tavern on Pearl Street.

They convened at noon on the second floor. By that point, the malcontents had long since left for home. The forty or so officers in the room that afternoon were unwavering in their regard for the commander in chief. They'd all taken their seats by the time Washington entered the room, his face betraying an emotion that the young cavalry officer and spy chief Benjamin Tallmadge described as "too strong to be concealed."

The officers ate in what Tallmadge remembered as "almost breathless silence" until Washington filled his glass with wine and turned to face them. "With a heart full of love and gratitude," he said, "I now take leave of you. I most devoutly wish that your latter days may be as prosperous and happy as your former ones have been glorious and honorable." Once they had downed their glasses of wine, he continued. "I cannot come to each of you, but shall feel obliged if each of you will come and take me by the hand."

Henry Knox was the closest to Washington, and when he turned in his direction, the commander in chief took him by the hand, and with tears streaming down their faces, they embraced. "In the same affectionate manner," Tallmadge remembered, "every officer in the room marched up to, kissed, and parted with his General-in-Chief." Here, at long last, the true, almost frightening intensity of Washington's buried emotional life had been revealed. "It was indeed too affecting to be of long continuance," Tallmadge wrote, "for tears of deep sensibility filled every eye—and the heart seemed too full, that it was ready to burst from its wonted abode."

It was soon time for Washington to leave. A corps of light infantry escorted him to Whitehall, where a barge was tied to the dock. "We all followed in mournful silence to the wharf," Tallmadge recalled, "where a prodigious crowd had assembled." As soon as he had taken a seat and the twenty-two oarsmen began to row, Washington turned, waved his hat, and "bid us a silent adieu."

. . .

NOT UNTIL DECEMBER 23, by which time Congress had managed to assemble a quorum of just twenty legislators, did Washington stride into the statehouse in Annapolis. The galleries were packed with people; among the crowd, interestingly enough, was Horatio Gates. Another Washington antagonist, Thomas Mifflin, one of the leading members of the Conway Cabal, was now president of Congress. When Washington stood to make his speech, his right hand trembled so badly that he had to hold it with his left. "Having now finished the work assigned me," he read, "I retire from the great theatre of action; and bidding an affectionate farewell to this august body under whose orders I have so long acted, I here offer my commission and make my leave of all the employments of public life."

By the end of 1783, the United States was a façade of a country—a collection of squabbling states with the barest window dressing of a federal government. Washington might have looked at the assembly of mostly second- and third-rate politicians now in control of the country and convinced himself he must do something about it. But he had had enough. He wanted to go home. When told by the American-born painter Benjamin West that Washington planned to retire to his farm after the war, King George III said, "[I]f he does that, he will be the greatest man in the world."

Washington had long since learned that greatness was attained not by insisting on what was right for oneself but by doing what was right for others. As he had written to Admiral de Grasse, "[A] great mind knows how to make personal sacrifices to secure an important general good." He also understood that this required a leader to attend to the countless, largely unappreciated details that made something as complicated as an army (or a nation) work. "I have undergone more than most men are aware of," he wrote to Richard Henry Lee in 1777, "to harmonize so many discordant parts." Washington could be forbidding and remote, but there was also a surprising gentleness about him that instilled a remarkable sense of loyalty in just about everyone (with some notable exceptions) who had the privilege to serve under him. Perhaps Abigail Adams put it best: "He possesses a dignity that forbids familiarity, mixed with an easy affability that creates love and reverence."

Greatness, Washington realized, was ultimately determined by that sternest and cruelest of judges: posterity. By insisting that "it is our duty to make the best of our misfortunes and not to suffer passion to interfere with our interest and the public good," he was acting on what he had called in the summer of 1781 "the great scale." Now, two years later, it was time for him as military commander to step aside. For this republican experiment to succeed, the young country's next hesitant steps must be made without him.

It was an approximately fifty-mile ride from Annapolis to Mount Vernon. Over the course of the last eight years Washington had slept in 280 different houses, but this time he was headed home. Accompanying him were his enslaved manservant Billy Lee and his two aides, David Humphreys and Benjamin Walker. By the evening of the following day, Christmas Eve, they had Mount Vernon in sight.

Washington had spent the Revolution trying to convince an army and a nation that, despite all evidence to the contrary, the future was theirs. Now that the future had finally arrived, there was no place he'd rather be than here, at his beloved Mount Vernon, on a hill overlooking a river, almost two hundred miles from the open sea.

EPILOGUE

Aftermath

Enough. Launching my yawl no more for
fairyland, I stick to the piazza.
—Herman Melville,
"The Piazza" (1856)

Six years after the conclusion of the Revolutionary War, France was gripped by its own revolution with the storming of the Bastille on July 14, 1789. By then, George Washington had begun his first term as president, an office created by the Constitutional Convention in Philadelphia during the summer of 1787, less than a year after an insurrection of farmers in western Massachusetts, known as Shays's Rebellion, helped bring mounting concerns about the weakness of the country's federal government to a crisis point.

As president, Washington prevented the country from becoming embroiled in the mounting hostilities among Britain, France, and Spain while deftly handling a tax-related insurrection in western Pennsylvania known as the Whiskey Rebellion. Throughout the eight years of his presidency, the American electorate became increasingly polarized into two political factions: the Federalists—generally well-to-do merchants and landowners whose international sympathies lay with Britain and who subscribed to the financial policies promulgated by Secretary of the Treasury Alexander Hamilton—and the Democratic Republicans—primarily farmers and plantation owners who sided with Secretary of State Thomas Jefferson in his enthusiasm for the French Revolution and his distrust of Hamilton's efforts to create a strong federal bank, policies that would ultimately make the War of 1812 an inevitability during the administration of Jefferson's ideological soulmate James Madison.

What follows is an alphabetical listing of the major characters along with brief descriptions of what happened to them after the American Revolution.

BENEDICT ARNOLD: Arnold left for England in the fall of 1781 in the same ship as Lord Cornwallis. The two generals got along famously, and in several instances in the years to come Cornwallis interceded on behalf of Arnold's sons when it came to their education and military careers. Arnold's friendship with Cornwallis proved to be one of the few bright spots in his postwar life. Without any military prospects in England, he moved to New Brunswick, Canada, where he established himself as a merchant. Bad business deals and controversy dogged him at every turn, and he was burned in effigy by his Canadian neighbors prior to his return to England, where he fought a bloodless duel with Lord Lauderdale over a disparaging remark made by the nobleman in Parliament. After years of unsuccessfully petitioning the British government for the financial favors he felt were his due, he died in 1801 at the age of sixty.

In the early years of the war, Arnold had been one of the country's best generals, but it was as a traitor that he may have done the most for the cause of the United States. Not only did the news of his treason have a galvanizing effect on the American people, his subsequent appearance in Virginia as a British brigadier general initiated the movement of troops that climaxed ten months later with the victory at Yorktown. Whether revered or vilified, Arnold was the lightning rod of the American Revolution.

LOUIS-ANTOINE DE BOUGAINVILLE: After his brilliant performance at the Battle of the Chesapeake, Bougainville, along with several other French captains, was accused of failing to support Admiral de Grasse during the Battle of the Saintes. Although sentenced to a reprimand, Bougainville emerged from the controversy as one of

France's leading naval and scientific authorities. The French Revolution forced him into virtual hiding in Normandy, and after a brief stint in jail, he came to the attention of Napoleon, who appointed him to the French Senate. He died in 1811 at the age of eighty-one, recognized as one of the great global explorers of the eighteenth century and his key role in the naval battle that helped win the United States her independence almost forgotten.

SIR GUY CARLETON: Having overseen the evacuation of New York with both humanity and forcefulness, Carleton was awarded the title of Lord Dorchester after his return to England. In 1786, he was named, for the third time, governor-general of Canada, a post he held for a decade. For many Americans, Canada provided an increasingly enticing example of what the thirteen colonies might have looked like had they remained within the British Empire. In the years to come, twenty thousand "late loyalists" emigrated north, where, ironically (given what inspired the Revolution in the first place), the taxes were considerably lower. Carleton died in England in 1808 at the age of eighty-four, one of the few British generals to have survived the Revolutionary War with his reputation intact.

FRANÇOIS JEAN DE BEAUVIOR CHASTELLUX: Instead of departing from America with General Rochambeau and the rest of the French army, Chastellux stayed behind in Philadelphia, not returning to France until 1783. In addition to receiving honorary degrees from the College of William and Mary and the University of Pennsylvania, he penned a memoir of his time in America. Shortly after marrying the twenty-eight-year-old Marie Brigitte Plunkett, lady-in-waiting to the Duchesse d'Orléans, he died in Paris in 1788 at the age of fifty-four, a year before the outbreak of the Revolution that devastated the lives of so many of the aristocrats in the French army.

SIR HENRY CLINTON: Refusing to serve as the scapegoat for Britain's loss of her American colonies, Clinton launched a pamphlet war in which he enumerated the mistakes of his predecessors, Howe and Gage, but directed most of his ire against the highly popular Cornwallis. Although his pamphleteering won him few friends, Clinton made a comeback of sorts in his later years, being named governor of Gibraltar in 1794. Unfortunately, the onset of an illness prevented him from leaving England, where he died the following year at age sixty-five.

BARON VON CLOSEN: As one of the most trusted members of Rochambeau's staff, von Closen remained with the French general in Virginia throughout the winter after Yorktown, ultimately returning to France in 1783 after some unhappy months in the Caribbean and Venezuela. Von Closen remained loyal to the king during the early stages of the French Revolution, becoming a major general in 1792 before resigning his commission and returning to his native Germany, where he died in 1830 at the age of seventy-eight after a distinguished second career as a civil servant.

LORD CORNWALLIS: Instead of bearing responsibility for the disaster at Yorktown, Cornwallis was judged to be the victim of the combined incompetency of Henry Clinton and Thomas Graves, and he returned to London a hero. His popularity and political connections enabled him to rise above the pamphlet war with Clinton, and in 1786 he was appointed field marshal and governor-general of India, where he enjoyed all of the military success that had eluded him in America. He subsequently served with distinction in Ireland before returning to India, where he died in Ghazipur in the northeastern portion of the country in 1805 at the age of sixty-six.

JOHANN EWALD: One of the most capable light-infantry officers of the Revolutionary War, Ewald returned to his native Hesse-Kassel in 1784, where he published *Essay on Partisan Warfare* to much acclaim. Because he was the son of a shopkeeper, his opportunities for promotion were limited, and in 1788 he changed his allegiance to the Danish army, in which he served with distinction for a quarter of a century. He died in Kiel (then part of Denmark) in 1813, at the age of sixty-nine, a national hero in his adopted country.

BERNARDO DE GÁLVEZ: After his great victory at Pensacola (which ultimately led to Spain's regaining control of all of Florida), Gálvez was promoted to lieutenant general and named governor of Louisiana. He was also made a *conde* (the equivalent of a count), complete with a coat of arms featuring the phrase *"Yo solo"* ("I alone") in reference to his having braved the entrance of Pensacola Bay without the support of the Spanish navy. Soon after being named viceroy of New Spain in 1786, he died of a fever in Mexico City, at the age of forty.

HORATIO GATES: Within weeks of the demise of the Newburgh conspiracy in 1783, Gates returned to his plantation in Virginia to attend to his ailing wife Elizabeth, who died that June. In 1786, Gates married the wealthy spinster Mary Vallance, and the two eventually moved to an estate in Manhattan named Rose Hill, now part of the Murray Hill–Gramercy–Flatiron region of New York City. He died in 1806 and was buried in the yard of Trinity Church; he was seventy-eight.

GEORGE III: Despite losing the American colonies, the British king experienced something of a renaissance in the years after the war. Personally frugal and devoted to his wife, he was increasingly admired by his people—good feelings reinforced by years of unprecedented economic growth and Britain's ultimately successful war against Napoleon and France. Even as he succumbed to the madness associated with what seems to have been a blood disease, he remained a beloved symbol of the continuing resilience of the British Empire. He died in 1820 at the age of eighty-one.

GEORGE GERMAIN: Unlike his sovereign, Secretary of State Germain could not escape the stigma of having mismanaged the war that lost the American colonies. The king offered some compensation by making him Viscount Sackville of Bolebrook in Kent, but this did not prevent his peers in the House of Lords from dubbing him "the greatest criminal his country had ever known." He died in 1785 at the age of sixty-nine.

COMTE DE GRASSE: Although an inquiry officially cleared him of wrongdoing at the Battle of the Saintes, de Grasse's naval career was over. Barred from the court of the king, he retired to his estate, where in 1784 he received four British cannons captured at Yorktown as an expression of thanks from the American Congress. He died in 1788 at the age of sixty-five, just before the outbreak of the French Revolution, during which his Yorktown cannons were melted down to mint coins. His son and four daughters sought asylum in the United States, where they were granted citizenship and stipends from Congress. In 1978, the U.S. navy commissioned the destroyer USS *Comte de Grasse,* which served until June 1998. After a stint as a parts hulk in the navy yard in Philadelphia, the *Comte de Grasse* was towed 275 miles off the coast of North Carolina for a naval training exercise and ultimately sunk in 12,000 feet of water.

THOMAS GRAVES: Graves was never officially blamed for his performance at the Battle of the Chesapeake, although Samuel Hood and George Rodney were merciless in their condemnation. During his return voyage to Great Britain in 1782, Graves suffered the indignity of having to abandon his flagship in a storm (which also claimed de Grasse's former flagship, the *Ville de Paris*) and arrived home in a troop transport. In 1794, Graves was second in command to Admiral Richard Howe in the British victory over the French at the Battle of the Glorious First of June and was awarded the title of Baron Graves of Gravesend in the County of Londonderry. He died in 1802 at the age of seventy-six.

NATHANAEL GREENE: The southern states expressed their appreciation for Greene's efforts on their behalf by awarding him land in the Carolinas and Georgia, where he, his wife, Caty, and their children ultimately settled at a two-thousand-acre plantation near Savannah called Mulberry Grove. On a hot day in June 1786, Greene was stricken by sunstroke and died at the age of forty-three. According to Alexander Hamilton, Greene's premature death robbed the country of a "universal and pervading genius which qualified him not less for the Senate than for the field."

ALEXANDER HAMILTON: As Washington had recognized early in the war, Hamilton was one of the most brilliant men of his age. From *The Federalist Papers,* to the Constitutional Convention, to his role as secretary of the treasury, no one short of Washington, Jefferson, and possibly James Madison did more to create the form of government we have today. But as Washington also recognized, Hamilton's immense ambition and impulsiveness courted controversy, and he died on July 12, 1804, of injuries sustained in a duel with Vice President Aaron Burr. He was forty-nine.

SAMUEL HOOD: On his return to England after playing an important role in the British victory at the Saintes, Hood was praised by the king as "the most brilliant officer of the war." With the outbreak of the French Revolution, he was named commander of the British fleet in the Mediterranean, during which he served as a mentor to the young Horatio Nelson. Unable to contain his need to criticize, he was ultimately dismissed from command after writing an indiscreet letter to the First Lord of the Admiralty. He died at Bath in 1816 at the age of ninety-one.

THOMAS JEFFERSON: During the summer of 1781, as war raged in his native Virginia, Jefferson, who had just stepped down as governor of the state, went into seclusion and wrote *Notes on the State of Virginia*. Soon after the victory at Yorktown, Jefferson successfully defended himself against charges of neglect of duty during the invasion of Benedict Arnold. However, his performance as a wartime governor came back to haunt him throughout a political career that culminated in his becoming a two-term president of the United States. Even on his deathbed he was forced to confront the legacy of those years, when he spoke with the son of Henry Lee, whose account of the war included a condemnation of Jefferson's actions. Jefferson died six days later on July 4, 1826, at the age of eighty-three.

HENRY KNOX: Even before the war had ended, Knox spearheaded the creation of the Society of the Cincinnati, a hereditary association of American and foreign officers who had fought in the Revolution that still exists. At the time of its inception, however, the order was perceived by many (including Thomas Jefferson) as dangerously aristocratic. And, in truth, despite having fought to create a republic and having served as President Washington's first secretary of war, Knox, the former bookseller, yearned to live in the style of the British nobility. After securing (through legally dubious means) a huge tract of land in Maine once owned by his wife Lucy's loyalist family, he built a mansion in the town of Thomaston that dwarfed even Mount Vernon. Financially overextended and stricken by personal tragedy (he and Lucy outlived ten of their thirteen children while their only surviving son, Henry, proved a ne'er-do-well drunkard), Knox died in 1806 of an infection associated with a chicken bone that became lodged in his throat; he was fifty-six. Although esteemed for his role as artillery chief in the Continental army, Knox created a very different legacy in Maine, ultimately becoming the inspiration behind the grasping and unrelenting Colonel Pyncheon in Nathaniel Hawthorne's *The House of the Seven Gables*.

GILBERT DU MOTIER, MARQUIS DE LAFAYETTE: In the summer of 1784, the twenty-six-year-old Lafayette returned to America and spent ten days at Mount Vernon, reporting to his wife that "in retirement General Washington is even greater than he was during the Revolution. His simplicity is truly sublime." On his return to France, Lafayette became a leading military figure in the French

Revolution, where his reputation rose and finally fell as his country slid increasingly into violence and chaos. After several years in an Austrian prison, he retired to his wife's property outside Paris. In 1824, by which time Napoleon had fallen and the Bourbon monarchy had been restored, Lafayette returned to America for a more-than-year-long tour where he was feted everywhere he went. Back in France, he lived once again in relative obscurity before briefly stepping back into the limelight during the Revolution of 1830. He died in Paris in 1834; at the graveside, his son George Washington Lafayette scattered soil from Bunker Hill over his casket. He was seventy-six.

Duc de Lauzun: During the Siege of Yorktown, Lauzun's legion, stationed across the river in Gloucester, outdueled Banastre Tarleton's cavalry in a brief, ultimately indecisive skirmish. Since it was one of the few episodes during the siege that involved hand-to-hand combat, Rochambeau chose to award Lauzun, along with Guillaume de Deux-Ponts, who led the charge on redoubt number 9, the honor of delivering the news of Yorktown to France. Lauzun embraced the ideals of the French Revolution, only to be arrested and on December 30, 1793, executed by the guillotine during the so-called Reign of Terror. He was forty-six.

Henry Lee: After witnessing the surrender of the British at Yorktown, Lee pursued a political career, serving as governor of Virginia and returning briefly to the military at Washington's request to help put down the Whiskey Rebellion in 1794. On Washington's death in 1799, Lee, then serving in the U.S. Congress, delivered the famous eulogy describing the former general and president as "first in war, first in peace, first in the hearts of his countrymen." Financial problems plagued Lee all his life, and he wrote his account of the Revolutionary War, *Memories of the War in the Southern Department of the United States,* from debtor's prison. An ardent Federalist, he was badly beaten while protecting a political ally and friend during a riot in Baltimore in 1812. After five years in the Caribbean attempting to regain his health, Lee decided to return to America, making landfall at the island plantation in Georgia once owned by his commander in the south, Nathanael Greene. In failing health, Lee died under the care of Greene's daughter on March 25, 1818, age sixty-two. Despite Lee's ardent support of the Union, his youngest son, Robert, would become the commander of the Confederate forces during the Civil War.

BENJAMIN LINCOLN: Following his tenure as secretary of war (1781–1783), Lincoln led the Massachusetts militia in the suppression of Shays's Rebellion in 1787, the event that convinced political leaders throughout the country that the existing form of federal government needed an overhaul. The following year, Lincoln attended the Massachusetts state convention that ratified the United States Constitution, and in 1789, the newly elected president George Washington appointed him collector of the port of Boston, a lucrative sinecure that he held until 1809. He died in his native Hingham on May 9, 1810, age seventy-seven.

JOSEPH PLUMB MARTIN: In the years after the war, Martin, with nothing to show for his seven years of service, moved to what is today Stockton Springs, Maine, at the mouth of the Penobscot River, land over which Henry Knox eventually established ownership. When Knox's intermediaries demanded that he pay $170 (about $3200 today) for his hundred-acre farm, Martin was unable to come up with the money, and in December 1801 he wrote Knox a letter. "I throw myself and family wholly at the feet of your Honor's mercy," he pleaded, "earnestly hoping that your Honor will think of some way, in your wisdom, that may be beneficial to your Honor and save a poor family from distress." Knox, however, turned a deaf ear to Martin's appeal, and in 1818 the indigent veteran lost his farm. In 1830, by which time he was living on a military pension of $96 (about $2460 today) a year, Martin published his memoir, *A Narrative of Some of the Adventures, Dangers and Sufferings of a Revolutionary Soldier,* perhaps the most insightful and refreshingly acerbic firsthand account of the war that exists. He died on May 2, 1850, at the age of eighty-nine, and is buried at the Sandy Point Cemetery in Stockton Springs.

DANIEL MORGAN: Although lingering health problems prevented him from participating in the Siege of Yorktown, Morgan was able to oversee the housing of British prisoners near his home in Winchester, Virginia. According to local tradition, Morgan employed some of the Hessians under his supervision in building the stone mansion he called Saratoga in memory of the battle in which he played a vital part. Unlike so many of his military peers, Morgan proved to be a successful businessman and landowner. He came out of retirement in 1794 to play a key role in subduing the Whiskey Rebellion in western Pennsylvania, then served briefly in the House of Representatives, until poor health forced him to return to Winchester. When informed that he had less than a week to live, he reportedly told the physician, "Doctor, if I could be the man I was when I was 21 years of age, I would be willing to be stripped stark naked on the top of the Alleghany Mountains, to run for my life with the hounds of death at my heels." Morgan died on July 6, 1802, at age sixty-six. His victory at Cowpens on January 17, 1781, stands as one of the most brilliant of the war, confirming his status as the greatest leader of light infantry in the Continental army.

ROBERT MORRIS: Without Morris's personal financial support, Washington would have never been able to get the Continental army to Yorktown. When Washington became president, he offered Morris the post of secretary of the treasury, a position Morris chose to decline (and which ultimately went, at his recommendation, to Alexander Hamilton) in favor of serving in the U.S. Senate. Morris's vast financial empire collapsed in the Panic of 1797, and he was ultimately forced into debtor's prison. Not until Congress passed the Bankruptcy Act of 1800 was he able to secure his release, and he died in Philadelphia on May 8, 1806, at the age of seventy-two.

Charles O'Hara: Having served as Cornwallis's surrogate during the surrender ceremony at Yorktown, O'Hara declined his lordship's invitation to accompany him to India, ultimately serving as military governor at Gibraltar. In 1793, he led British forces in the unsuccessful defense of Fort Mulgrave in Toulon, where he was captured by the young Napoleon. After several years imprisoned in Luxembourg and Paris, O'Hara was exchanged for Rochambeau's son, and resumed his role as governor-general of Gibraltar, where his many affairs and passel of illegitimate children earned him the title Cock of the Rock. He died on February 21, 1802, at age sixty-one.

Jean-Baptiste Donatien de Vimeur, Comte de Rochambeau: On his return to France, Rochambeau was made governor of Picardy. He initially supported the Revolution and led the French army against the Austrians. After suffering several defeats and becoming disenchanted with the violent direction the Revolution had taken, he resigned from the army in 1792. In 1794, he was arrested and if not for the death of Robespierre, would have in all likelihood been guillotined. He withdrew to his home in Vendôme, and in 1804 was appointed to the Legion of Honor by Napoleon. On May 10, 1807, he died at Thoré, at age eighty-one.

George Rodney: Rodney returned to England a hero, only to have his conduct at St. Eustatius during the winter of 1781 destroy his life. In 1785, Britain's High Court of Appeals for Prizes determined that Rodney must repay the island merchants for the goods he'd seized, a verdict that left him financially ruined. By then his repeated infidelities had prompted his second wife to leave him, and he died on May 24, 1792, in his son's home, at the age of seventy-four. Erratic, self-centered, and overbearing, Rodney was nonetheless one of Britain's greatest admirals, and Americans owe their independence, in part, to his not having been in command of the British fleet at the Battle of the Chesapeake.

FRANCISCO SAAVEDRA DE SANGRONIS: When Spain decided not to invade Jamaica after de Grasse's defeat at the Battle of the Saintes, Saavedra was assigned to Venezuela, where he served until 1788, when he returned to Spain. In 1797, he was appointed minister of finance, where he helped create the Bank of Amortization before being named minister of state. A serious illness required him to retire soon after, but when France invaded Spain in 1808, he returned to public service. He died on November 25, 1819, at the age of seventy-three, the largely unheralded Spanish emissary who had provided the often impetuous Admiral de Grasse with the ships, money, and organizational principles needed to achieve victory both on the Chesapeake and at Yorktown.

FRIEDRICH VON STEUBEN: Although von Steuben's performance in Virginia in 1780–1781 was marred by controversy, he had been indispensable three years earlier at Valley Forge, when he instilled much needed discipline and order in the Continental army. After commanding a division at the Siege of Yorktown, he assisted in the demobilization of the American forces until his discharge in March 1784. Along with Henry Knox, he took a leading role in the creation of the Society of the Cincinnati. He became an American citizen, and on the verge of bankruptcy in the late 1780s, he appealed to Congress for financial assistance and was granted an annual pension of $2800 (about $55,430 today). He retired to a farm in Remsen, New York, where he died on November 28, 1794, at age sixty-four.

BANASTRE TARLETON: It's safe to say that no British officer (with the exception of Benedict Arnold) was as thoroughly despised by his American opponents as Tarleton. Fearing reprisals after Cornwallis's surrender, he requested and received protection from the French; at one point he suffered the indignity of having his horse taken from him by its Virginian owner. Once back in England, however, he received a hero's welcome. He became an intimate friend of the king's dissolute eldest son and heir to the throne and boasted frequently of his conquests, both in battle and in the bedroom. In addition to unfairly criticizing Cornwallis in his self-congratulatory memoir of the war, *A History of the Campaigns of 1780 and 1781,* Tarleton made a bitter enemy of the future Duke of Wellington. While many of his fellow officers served with great glory in the Napoleonic Wars, he languished in England. When his friend the Prince Regent became George IV, Tarleton was belatedly awarded the Order of the Bath. He died on January 16, 1833, at age seventy-eight.

GEORGE WASHINGTON: Although he made much of his desire to retire to his "vine and fig tree" at Mount Vernon, the ever restless Washington soon began to pursue his dream of connecting the east to the west via the Potomac River by building a series of canals and locks under the direction of the Potomac Company—what would be accomplished forty years later with the completion of the Erie Canal. His central role in the Revolutionary War made it inevitable that he be called to serve his country once again. In 1787, he presided over the Constitutional Convention, and in 1788, he was elected the country's first president. During the eight years of his presidency, he made sure to visit all thirteen states in an effort to create a greater sense of national solidarity. In the fall of 1796, he announced he would not be seeking a third term and was soon back at Mount Vernon for good.

Around that time, he was visited by the young architect Benjamin Henry Latrobe, who had recently arrived in America from England. "Washington has something uncommonly majestic and commanding in his walk, his address, his figure and his countenance," Latrobe recorded in his journal. "His face is characterized however more by intense and powerful thought, than by quick and fiery conception. There is a mildness about its expression; and an air of reserve in his manner lowers its tone still more. He is 64, but appears some years younger, and has sufficient apparent vigor to last many years yet." As it turned out, Washington had just three years left to live.

As Latrobe had sensed, Washington's genius had to do with

intensity and perseverance rather than the quick flashes of brilliance that characterized the jittery virtuosity of a Hamilton. No one had Washington's ability to sort through the distractions of life and recognize what really mattered, and no one had his capacity to learn under some of the most challenging conditions a leader has ever known. In the beginning of the war he had come to understand that the dangers of a disastrous defeat far outweighed the promise of an overwhelming victory and that it was in his country's best interests that he fight a primarily defensive war—a difficult, even agonizing decision given Washington's naturally aggressive temperament. With the entry of France into the war in 1778, he saw that naval superiority was the key to an allied victory. For the next three years he pursued that goal with a single-minded determination that ultimately led to victory at Yorktown, even if it required him to pay deference to the often maddening demands of the French. With the arrival of peace, he recognized that the future of the country depended on a strong central government; once a new constitution was in place, he dedicated the next eight years to inventing the office of the presidency. By the end of his life he'd realized that the greatest threat to the country's future came from slavery.

During the Revolutionary War he had paid lip service to efforts to eradicate the institution and had even flirted with the idea of ridding himself of his own slaves in 1779. In each instance, however, he had continued to behave like a Virginia slave owner, insisting on the retrieval of escaped slaves at Yorktown in 1781 and at New York in 1783, and taking extraordinary (though unsuccessful) measures during his final year as president to retrieve the enslaved man and woman who had fled from his household in Philadelphia. This did not prevent him from recognizing slavery's pernicious effects. "I can clearly foresee," Jefferson overheard him say, "that nothing but the rooting out of slavery can perpetuate the existence of our union." If slavery should ever come to divide the United States, he insisted, in an eerily clairvoyant anticipation of the Civil War, "he had made up his mind to remove and be of the Northern [portion]." Washington, it is clear, would have never gone the way of Robert E. Lee. But what could he do at this late stage of his life to make his position known? He could change his will.

In July 1799, he retired to his study and set to work. Of the 317 slaves at Mount Vernon, he owned only 124 outright. Forty were rented from a neighbor, and the rest, 153, were the property of the Custis estate and were to be inherited by Martha's grandson on her death. At the very least, Washington could free his own slaves, thus becoming the only slaveholding Founding Father to do so.

In December of that year, after a five-hour ride across his property in a freezing rain, he came down with a sore throat. Within a few days, his throat was so constricted that he could barely breathe. His old friend, the physician James Craik, was called for, but none of the traditional treatments, which included bleeding, did any good. "Doctor," Washington said at one point, "I die hard, but I am not afraid to go." He maintained a stoic calm until the very end and passed away on December 14, 1799, while taking his own pulse. He was sixty-seven.

ACKNOWLEDGMENTS

ALTHOUGH THE Reverend Eugene McDowell did not live to see the publication of this book, he contributed greatly to its research, providing me with his own heavily annotated copy of John Buchanan's indispensable *The Road to Guilford Courthouse* as well as the many pictures he and his wife, Cathy, took during a tour of the Revolutionary War battlefields of the Carolinas.

My thanks to Michael Hill for his research help, especially when it came to the vast amount of primary source material (much of it copied from the Archives Nationales Marine in Paris) at the Library of Congress; thanks also to Jeff Flannery at the LOC. Thanks to Carol Harris for her expert translation assistance. Larrie Ferreiro, author of *Brothers at Arms,* could not have been more generous with his expertise and extensive contacts in France. Christian McBurney, author of *Spies in Revolutionary Rhode Island,* was also most helpful. Without the Fifth Annual Conference on the American Revolution at Colonial Williamsburg in 2016 (led by Bruce and Lynne Venter and Ed Lengel), I might never have met Larrie, Christian, and a host of other Revolutionary War scholars. My special thanks to Mark Lender and James Kirby Martin, both regulars at the conference, for sharing two unpublished articles about Benedict Arnold. John Hattendorf at the Newport War College provided me with essential guidance at the beginning and end of the project. I owe Jean-Marie Kowalski of the

Ecole Navale in Brest a huge debt of gratitude for his willingness to speak with me during a 2016 research trip to France. A conversation with Michael Crawford and Dennis Conrad at the Naval History and Heritage Command at Washington, D.C., was equally enlightening; thanks also to Alexis Catsambis of the Command's Underwater Archaeology Branch for providing the great map of Destouches's and Arbuthnot's Race to the Chesapeake. My thanks to Ellen McCallister Clark, Library Director at Anderson House, the home of the Society of the Cincinnati in Washington, D.C., for her guidance in exploring the Society's collection. Carolyn Vega, Associate Curator at the Morgan Library and Museum, helped me decipher a critical passage in a manuscript letter by Henry Knox. Arthur Kelly shared with me his exquisite collection of historic maps and trove of articles about Benjamin Franklin's chart of the Gulf Stream. Special thanks to Curt Viebranz and Douglas Bradburn at George Washington's Mount Vernon and the Fred W. Smith National Library. Papers delivered by Olivier Chaline and Jean-Marie Kowalski at the 2015 SAR Annual Conference on the American Revolution held at George Washington's Mount Vernon were extremely helpful to me. Special thanks to the staffs at the National Park Service sites at King's Mountain, Guilford Courthouse, and Yorktown.

For reading and commenting on the manuscript, I am indebted to Admiral John Baldwin, Michael Crawford, Richard Duncan, Larrie Ferreiro, William Fowler, Peter Gow, John Hattendorf, Peter Henriques, Michael Hill, Bruce Miller, Jennifer McArdle Philbrick, Melissa Philbrick, Samuel Philbrick, Thomas Philbrick, and Admiral James Stavridis.

Jenny Pouech was a huge help when it came to securing permissions for the images in this book. Jeffrey Ward did his usual stellar job with the maps. Thanks to Nate Roberts, Greg Derr, and John Mynttinen at Poets Corner Press on Nantucket for all the copying help.

At Viking, I have had the privilege to work with the incomparable Wendy Wolf for twenty years and counting. Many thanks also to Brian Tart, Andrea Schulz, Bruce Giffords, Louise Braverman, Chris

Smith, Terezia Cicel, Kate Stark, and Marysarah Quinn. Thanks also to Kathryn Court and Patrick Nolan at Penguin. Thanks to Jason Ramirez for the jacket design.

My agent, Stuart Krichevsky, has provided me with essential guidance for more than twenty years. Here's to another decade together. Thanks also to his coworkers Laura Usselman, Aemilia Phillips, Hannah Schwartz, and to everyone at SKLA. Thanks to Rich Green at ICM Partners for all his support and enthusiasm. Many thanks to Meghan Walker of Tandem Literary for keeping me connected to my readers through my website and social media.

Finally, special thanks to my wife, Melissa, and to all our family members for their patience and support.

NOTES

ABBREVIATIONS

ACRA—The American Campaigns of Rochambeau's Army, vol. 1, edited by Howard C. Rice Jr. and Anne S. K. Brown

ANM—Archives Nationales Marine in Paris

DAW—Diary of the American War by Captain Johann Ewald, translated and edited by Joseph P. Tustin

DAR—Documents of the American Revolution, edited by K. G. Davies

GJG—General Joseph Graham and His Papers on North Carolina Revolutionary History, edited by William A. Graham

LAAR—Lafayette in the Age of the American Revolution, Selected Letters and Papers, edited by Stanley J. Idzerda

LOC—Library of Congress

MHS—Massachusetts Historical Society

NA, ADM—National Archives, Records of the Admiralty, in Greenwich, England

PGNG—The Papers of General Nathanael Greene, edited by Richard K. Showman and Dennis M. Conrad

WGW—The Writings of George Washington, edited by John C. Fitzpatrick

WMQ—William and Mary Quarterly

I have adjusted the spelling and punctuation of quotations to make them more accessible to a modern audience—something that has already been done by the editors of several collections cited below.

PREFACE ✦ The Land and the Sea

For an account of French admiral d'Estaing's unsuccessful operations in North America, see my *Valiant Ambition*, pp. 216–19, 251–53. As far as the pivotal nature of the Battle of the Chesapeake, Harold Larrabee in *Decision at the Chesapeake* describes it as "the one decisive engagement" of the Revolutionary War while also citing Emil Reich's claim that "it deserves the name of 'British naval Waterloo off Cape Henry,'" p. xiii. According to W. M. James in *The British Navy in Adversity*, "Yorktown has often been described as one of the 'decisive battles of the world,' but it was the naval skirmish off the Chesapeake that was decisive," p. 299. One of the few authors to give George Washington (subsequently referred to as GW) his due when it comes to his understanding of sea power is Dudley Knox in *The Naval Genius of George Washington:* "The cause of American Independence was indeed fortunate in having combined in Washington the rare qualities of a great general and a great naval strategist," p. 6.

CHAPTER 1 ✦ The Building Storm

The Marquis de Barbé-Marbois's Oct. 15, 1779, account of the sail from Fishkill to West Point with GW at the helm is in a note in *The Papers of George Washington*, 22:443. For information regarding GW's youth in the Tidewater, I have looked to Jack Warren's "The Childhood of George Washington" and Philip Levy's *Where the Cherry Tree Grew*. Levy describes Ferry Farm as being painted red so as to give it "the appearance of being built in more expensive brick when viewed from a distance," p. 46. David Humphreys's unfinished manuscript *Life of General Washington* is particularly interesting because it includes insertions on the part of Washington that either correct or expand upon Humphreys's account of his life. In one of those remarks, Washington wrote that his half brother Lawrence "received many distinguished marks of patronage and favor," p. 8. Levy writes in *Where the Cherry Tree Grew* of how Lawrence's proposal that his younger brother embark on a naval career placed him "at the center of a tug-of-war" between Lawrence and Mary Ball Washington, p. 64. The youthful GW's insistence that "he will be steady and thankfully follow" his brother's advice is in William Fairfax's Sept. 10, 1746, letter to Lawrence Washington in Moncure Conway's *Barons of the Potomac and the Rappahannock*, p. 238. Jack Warren in "The Childhood of George Washington" cites the cousin's claim that "he was ten times more afraid of Mary than he was of his own parents," p. 5799. While I agree with Warren's insistence that there "is no evidence that Washington was enthusiastic" about Lawrence's plan for him to enter the royal navy (p. 5808), I have less sympathy than he does for the position of Washington's mother. While Warren insists that there "is no justification for the romantic tradition that Mary intervened at the last moment" (p. 5808), GW passed over without comment Humphreys's claim that he had "his baggage prepared for embarkation but the plan was abandoned in consequence of the earnest solicitations of his mother," p. 8. Humphreys's description of Mary's "entreaties and tears," as well as his supposition that Washington might have become "an Admiral of distinction" if he'd followed Lawrence's advice is in his *Life of General Washington*, p. 102. According to Samuel Eliot Morison in "The Young Man George Washington," Mary "was a selfish and exacting mother, whom most of her children avoided as early as they could; to whom they did their duty, but rendered little love," p. 40, adding, "Yet for one thing Americans may well be grateful to Mary Ball: her selfishness lost George Washington an opportunity to become a midshipman in the Royal Navy," p. 41.

    William Fairfax reports that the young GW referred to Lawrence as his "best friend" in his Sept. 10, 1746, letter to Lawrence in Conway's *Barons of the Potomac*, p. 238. Levy cites GW's

1749 letter to Lawrence about his brother's cough, p. 75. *The Diaries of George Washington*, edited by Donald Jackson and Dorothy Twohig, vol. 1, contains a useful editorial note titled "Voyage to Barbados, 1751–52" that refers to GW's use of "nautical acronyms" in his diary, p. 26. According to W. H. Smyth's *Sailor's Word Book*, hull down "is said of a ship when at such a distance that, from the convexity of the globe, only her masts and sails are to be seen," p. 395. GW's Oct. 19, 1751, description of how the seas are "jostling in heaps" is in the *Diaries*, 1:58, as is the entry "strongly attacked with the smallpox," p. 82. Levy cites Lawrence's letter in which he says he will "hurry home to my grave," p. 75. Robert Dalzell and Lee Baldwin Dalzell in *George Washington's Mount Vernon* write insightfully about GW's renovation of Mount Vernon and how "[t]he placement of Washington's elegant new parlor and dining room on the other side of the ground floor reversed that orientation, which symbolically may have been the most important of all the changes he made," p. 52. According to James Flexner in *George Washington: The Forge of Experience*, GW "never showed any taste for the ocean, traveling, even at greater inconvenience, overland," p. 31. The Dalzells make the same point, claiming that GW was "more at home on a horse than he would ever be on water," while citing GW's 1760 reference to America as an "infant woody country," in *George Washington's Mount Vernon*, p. 53.

William Fowler in *Rebels Under Sail* estimates that that the cost of the Continental navy amounted to about 8 percent of all Congressional spending, p. 70. Jonathan Dull describes the efforts of the Continental navy as inflicting "no more than a few pinpricks against the British navy" in "Was the Continental Navy a Mistake?," pp. 168–69. For an alternative view, see Sam Willis's *The Struggle for Sea Power*, in which he argues that the mere existence of an American navy "could, in essence, export the revolution, and show the world that the rebellious colonies were acting as a sovereign state with major pretensions at being a world power," p. 92. See also William S. Dudley and Michael Palmer, "No Mistake About It: A Response to Jonathan R. Dull," *The American Neptune* 45 (1985), pp. 244–48. My thanks to Michael Crawford for bringing these two sources to my attention. On the other hand, this kind of international image building did little to fulfill GW's immediate needs during the Revolution. GW's Oct. 4, 1780, letter to James Duane in which he refers to "false hopes" is in *WGW*, 20:118, as is his Oct. 5 letter to John Cadwallader in which he writes of "accumulating distresses," p. 122. Larrie Ferreiro discusses the French government's program of *revanche* in the years after the Seven Years' War in *Brothers at Arms*, pp. 19–38. Jonathan Dull in *The French Navy and American Independence* writes insightfully about France's aims in joining the American Revolutionary War against Britain. According to Dull, French foreign minister Vergennes realized that "the solution to his problems lay in reconciliation with England. . . . Anglo-French cooperation could greatly limit the power of the other continental powers which had great armies but not the finances to engage in major wars. . . . A half-century before, the England and France of Walpole and Fleury had cooperated as equals; France had been secure, but now England was the England of Pitt: arrogant, aloof, contemptuous of France. To reduce England to a position of equality, France had to take from her a share of her strength, her monopoly of American trade and markets," pp. 10–11. Emmanuel de Fontainieu in *The* Hermione: *Lafayette's Warship and the American Revolution* provides a good summary of the jousting between the French and British navies from 1778 through 1780, pp. 129–57. Andrew O'Shaughnessy in *The Men Who Lost America* details how the British allocated their fleet between the Caribbean and North America, p. 224. GW writes of the "chasm" between him and the French fleet in the Caribbean in a Nov. 10, 1779, letter to his stepson John Parke Custis, in *WGW*, 17:90–91.

W. Reid describes the route of the *Phoenix* before she was hit by the hurricane in October 1780 in *An Attempt to Develop the Law of Storms*, p. 396. Maj. Gen. John Campbell, who was in command of British forces at Pensacola, writes of his preparations for an attack by the

Spanish in a Nov. 26, 1780, letter to Secretary of State Germain, in *DAR*, 18:232. I talk about the *Phoenix*'s mission up the Hudson River in July 1776 in *Valiant Ambition*, p. 10. The *Phoenix*'s role in the British counterfeit operation during the war is discussed in Karl Rhodes's "The Counterfeiting Weapon," p. 34, in which he quotes Benjamin Franklin about how it influenced the rapid depreciation of American currency. Reid in *An Attempt to Develop the Law of Storms* reprints Benjamin Archer's letter to his mother describing the wreck of the *Phoenix*, pp. 299–310. For a useful and illustrated account of how a square-rigged vessel jibed or wore under bare poles, see John Harland's *Seamanship in the Age of Sail*, p. 219. José Millas pinpoints the location of the wreck of the *Phoenix* on the southern coast of Cuba in *Hurricanes of the Caribbean*, p. 251; he quotes a letter written by Dr. Gilbert Blane that describes the devastation wreaked in Barbados by the next storm, in the "Great Hurricane of 1780," p. 254; and he hypothesizes that the velocity of the winds must have reached over 200 mph if, as Blane claimed, the bark was stripped from the trees, p. 255. Wayne Neely in *The Great Hurricane of 1780* describes the effects of the hurricane on St. Lucia and Martinique, as well as that of Solano's Hurricane, pp. 109–12. Reid quotes Admiral Rodney's Dec. 10, 1780, letter to his wife about his reaction to the devastation at Barbados in *An Attempt to Develop the Law of Storms*, p. 346.

William Willcox in "The British Road to Yorktown" writes of Cornwallis being "largely unaware of the cardinal fact that the army depended on the navy," and continues, "To turn him loose in the Carolinas was to invite disaster," p. 3. Lord Rawdon writes of the "fund of disaffection" the British had discovered in the Carolinas after the defeat of Gates at Camden in an Oct. 24, 1780, letter to Maj. Gen. Alexander Leslie in *DAR*, 18:189–90. Rawdon also writes of Cornwallis's hope that Ferguson's expedition in the direction of North Carolina would "awe that district into quiet," p. 190. Andrew O'Shaughnessy cites Ferguson's tactless proclamation to the citizens of North Carolina in *The Men Who Lost America*, p. 264. My description of the Battle of King's Mountain is based in part on a visit to the battlefield in the fall of 2015. O'Shaughnessy in *The Men Who Lost America* quotes Cornwallis's letter to Ferguson assuring him that "I now consider you perfectly safe," p. 265. Charles O'Hara writes of how "the most trifling check to our arms acts like electrical fire" in a Nov. 1, 1780, letter to the Duke of Grafton in "Letters of Charles O'Hara to the Duke of Grafton," pp. 159–60. Henry Clinton writes of how the loss at King's Mountain was "the first link in a chain of evils" that ultimately resulted in "the total loss of America" in *The American Rebellion*, p. 226. John Hattendorf in *Newport, the French Navy, and American Independence* writes about the difficulties the French had with the British blockade at Newport, pp. 70–71. Larrie Ferreiro in *Brothers at Arms* recounts how the three French frigates departed from Newport in the remnants of Solano's Hurricane on Oct. 28, 1780, p. 275.

CHAPTER 2 ✦ "AN ENEMY IN THE HEART OF THE COUNTRY"

For an account of GW's response to Benedict Arnold's betrayal and his words to Lafayette, see my *Valiant Ambition*, pp. 311–20. Lafayette writes of wishing the Battle of King's Mountain could have been "postponed" in a Nov. 10, 1780, letter to Nathanael Greene (subsequently referred to as NG) in *PGNG*, 6:476. Terry Golway in *Washington's General: Nathanael Greene and the Triumph of the American Revolution* cites NG's anguished description of his limp and being considered an "inferior point of light," p. 45. NG's Nov. 19, 1780, letter to GW, in which he speaks of the "almost insurmountable difficulties" of commanding the southern army is in *PGNG*, 6:488. GW's Dec. 13, 1780, response, in which he speaks of the "complicated distresses" of being in command, is in *WGW*, 20:469. According to the editors of *PGNG*, "It can hardly be a coincidence that NG, who had not done so before, began to cite the ideas of Frederick the Great of Prussia . . . soon after spending nearly a month with Baron Steuben, a disciple of Frederick's," *PGNG*, 6:535. As part of NG's program to learn as much as possible about North Carolina's rivers, he instructed General Edward Stevens on Dec. 1, 1780, to "explore carefully the river, the depth of water, the current and the rocks and every other obstruction that will impede the business of transportation. . . . [W]ater transportation is such an amazing saving of expense that small difficulties should not discourage the attempt," *PGNG*, 6:513. NG describes patriots and loyalists in North Carolina attacking each other with "relentless fury as beasts of prey" in a Dec. 28, 1780, letter to Samuel Huntington in *PGNG*, 7:9. He speaks of North Carolina's being "in the utmost danger of becoming a desert" in a Dec. 29, 1780, letter to Robert Howe in *PGNG*, 7:17. For an excellent discussion of NG's decision to divide his army (in which he cites the reference to its being "the most audacious and ingenious piece of military strategy of the war"), see Christopher Ward's *The War of the Revolution*, 2:750–51. NG writes of how his decision to divide his force "makes the most of my inferior force" in a letter written between Dec. 26, 1780, and Jan. 23, 1781, to an unidentified correspondent in *PGNG*, 6:588. NG's description of his "flying army" and "Camp of Repose" are in *PGNG*, 6:588.

For an account of how a meteor strike thirty-five million years ago helped create the contours of the Chesapeake Bay, see Bruce Linder's *Tidewater's Navy*, pp. 1–2, as well as Wiley Poag's *Chesapeake Invader: Discovering America's Giant Meteorite Crater*, pp. 3–126. Benedict Arnold describes the "hard gale" that battered his fleet as they sailed for the Chesapeake, as well as his raid on Richmond, in a Jan. 21, 1781, letter to Henry Clinton in *DAR*, 19:40–43. William Willcox in "The British Road to Yorktown" speaks of how Clinton hoped to apply a "tourniquet on the artery of American supplies" by establishing a naval post in the Chesapeake, p. 5. Johann Ewald describes Arnold as "a man of medium size, well built, with lively eyes and fine features" in *DAW*, p. 295. Clinton writes of why he was "induced to select Arnold for this service" in his *American Rebellion*, p. 236. Clinton instructs Arnold to attack Rebel magazines only if it can be done "without much risk" in a Dec. 14, 1780, letter in *DAR*, 18:256. William Tatham's June 13, 1805, letter to William Armistead Burwell, in which he describes Thomas Jefferson's speculation that the fleet seen at the mouth of the James was "nothing more than a foraging party," as well as his delayed decision to send out the entire militia, is in the *Papers of Thomas Jefferson*, 4:273, 258. Arnold enumerates what was destroyed in Richmond in a Jan. 21, 1781, letter to Clinton in *DAR*, 19:40. Michael Kranish in *Flight from Monticello* cites the testimony of Jefferson's slave Isaac in which he describes how a British officer came looking for Jefferson with a pair of "silver handcuffs," p. 193. Arnold accuses Jefferson, "the so-called governor," of being "inattentive to the preservation of private property" in his Jan. 21, 1781, letter to Clinton in *DAR*, 19:41. Isaac Arnold in *The Life of Benedict Arnold* writes of how the British bonfire created the intense "smell of tobacco in Richmond," p. 343. Michael Kranish in *Flight from Monticello* cites the claim that "even the hogs got drunk" in Richmond, p. 194. Johann Ewald's comparison of Arnold's expedition up the James to "those of the freebooters" is in *DAW*, p. 269. Lieutenant Colonel John G. Simcoe in *A Journal of the Queen's Rangers* recounts how Arnold's insistence that they march directly from Richmond back to Westover was based on his experience as an American general opposing the British raid on Danbury, p. 164. Clinton's claim that Arnold's "active and spirited conduct on this service . . . justly merited the high military character his past actions with the enemy had procured him" is in his *American Rebellion*, p. 236. The reference to Arnold's being "bold, daring and prompt in the execution of what he undertakes" is in *The Diary of Frederick Mackenzie*, 2:466. Johann Ewald writes of his detestation of Arnold for being a traitor in *DAW*, p. 296; he also recounts General Nelson's threat to "hang [Arnold] up by the heels according to the orders of Congress," p. 261. The American officer's answer to Arnold's asking what he thought the Americans would do with him if they caught him first appeared in the Aug. 1, 1781, issue of the *New Jersey Journal* and is in Frank Moore's *Diary of the American Revolution*, 2:461.

Clinton writes of how the American mutinies in New Jersey "were critically favorable to our operations in the Chesapeake as they prevented General Washington's immediately detaching troops to disturb General Arnold" in his *American Rebellion*, p. 243. Arnold's claim that the mutinies "will be attended with happy consequences" is in a Jan. 23, 1781, letter to Clinton in the Clinton Papers at the Clements Library and is cited by Clare Brandt in *The Man in the Mirror*, p. 245. In a Jan. 8, 1781, letter to GW, Anthony Wayne relates how the mutineers rejected the idea of "turning *Arnolds*" in *WGW*, 21:87. GW writes of "the alarming crisis" represented by the mutiny of the Pennsylvania Line in a Jan. 7, 1781, letter to Henry Knox in *WGW*, 21:68. In a Nov. 20, 1780, letter to John Sullivan, GW writes of the need for the Continental Congress to commit "more of the executive business to small boards or responsible characters" in *WGW*, 20:372. I write about this late-inning shift in the Continental Congress from a "dogmatic" to a "pragmatic" approach to winning the war in *Valiant Ambition*, pp. 322–23. GW writes of how John Laurens was being sent to France to provide "a military view" of the current state of the war effort in a Jan. 15, 1781, letter to Benjamin Franklin in *WGW*, 21:100. GW complains of the "accommodation . . . which will not only subvert the Pennsylvania line, but have a very pernicious influence on the whole army" in a Jan. 22, 1781, "Circular to the New England States and New York" in *WGW*, 21:130. GW's Jan. 25, 1781, order to Timothy Pickering for a "sleigh, pair of horses and driver" is in *WGW*, 21:142. James Thacher's description of the execution of the two New Jersey mutineers is in his *A Military Journal During the American Revolutionary War*, pp. 245–46. GW's Jan. 27, 1781, letter to "The Commissioners for Redressing the Grievances of the New Jersey Line," in which he tells of the mutineers' "[u]nconditional submission," is in *WGW*, 21:147.

John Tilley in *The British Navy and the American Revolution* provides an excellent description of the effects of the January gale on the British fleet at Gardiners Bay, pp. 211–13. Guillaume de Deux-Ponts describes how on Jan. 20, 1781, two ships of the line and a frigate sailed from Newport to meet the frigates *Surveillante* and *Hermione* and how the three ships returned the following day after "they experienced bad weather" in *My Campaigns in America*, p. 99. Frederick Mackenzie describes the January storm as the "severest that has been felt here for many years" in his *Diary*, 2:460. GW dubs Arnold the "arch traitor" in a March 21, 1781, letter to Benjamin Harrison in *WGW*, 21:342. GW details his plan to send the entire French fleet with a division of soldiers to attack Arnold in Portsmouth in a Feb. 15, 1781, letter to Rochambeau in *WGW*, 21:231–32. Lafayette writes that Admiral de Ternay "found no way to bypass [the British blockade] except by way of the next world" in a Jan. 30, 1781, letter to Prince de Poix in *LAAR*, 3:302. The British reference to the French fleet's "wretched system of discipline" is in William Green, *The Memoranda of William Green, Secretary to Vice-Admiral Marriot Arbuthnot, in the American Revolution*, p. 95. According to Louis-Alexandre Berthier, who was part of Rochambeau's army stationed in Newport, Admiral de Ternay "had kept the fleet virtually idle in the harbor, unprepared for action," in *ACRA*, p. 241. Lafayette writes of how GW is anxiously awaiting confirmation about the losses of the British fleet and "how much Destouches can take advantage of it" in a Feb. 7, 1781, letter to Luzerne in *LAAR*, 3:317. GW writes to Jefferson about the advantages of flat-bottomed troop transports that could be moved over the peninsulas of the Tidewater by wagon in a Nov. 8, 1780, letter in *WGW*, 20:326. Ironically, GW's first wartime experience with this type of craft, often referred to as a bateaux, was in the summer and fall of 1775, when he helped coordinate the design and building of flat-bottomed boats for Arnold's expedition through the wilderness of modern Maine to Quebec; see my *Valiant Ambition*, pp. 36–37. In a March 21, 1781, letter to NG, GW writes that "while there is an enemy in the heart of the country," he cannot realistically expect any supplies and reinforcements from Virginia, in *WGW*, 21:346.

Mathieu Dumas was the aide to Rochambeau who describes the time GW took the helm of the barge and proclaimed, "Courage my friends; I am going to conduct you, since it is my duty to hold the helm," in Gilbert Chinard, ed., *George Washington as the French Knew Him*, pp. 41–42. This was, by no means, the first time GW had experienced difficulties on an ice-choked river. At the age of twenty-one, while attempting to cross the Allegheny River in a crude raft, GW tumbled into the water and was forced to spend the night on an island. The next morning GW and his companion discovered that the river had frozen, allowing them to complete the crossing on foot. See GW's Dec. 23, 1753, account in *WGW*, 1:22–30. De Chastellux's glowing description of GW's physical appearance and charm is in his *Travels in North America in the Years 1780, 1781 and 1782*, 1:114. I cite Gouverneur Morris's description of GW's passions as "almost too mighty for man" in my *Bunker Hill*, p. 240. Alexander Hamilton describes his confrontation with GW in a Feb. 18, 1781, letter to his father-in-law, Philip Schuyler, in *The Papers of Alexander Hamilton*, 2:563–68. I cite Henry Knox's description of the British officer who was "awestruck as if he was before something supernatural" in *Valiant Ambition*, p. 30. Rochambeau's Aug. 27, 1780, letter to Lafayette, in which he accuses him of placing "private or personal ambition" ahead of the safety of the French army, is in *LAAR*, 3:155–56. The Feb. 19, 1781, letter to Rochambeau in which GW complains of having to "impatiently wait" for a response to his proposal to send the entire French fleet after Arnold is in *WGW*, 21:247. GW's Feb. 25, 1781, letter, in which he laments that the return of the *America* and the repair of the *Bedford* "puts it out of Monsieur Destouches's power to give us any further assistance," is in *WGW*, 21:289. F. R. Lassiter in "Arnold's Invasion of Virginia" quotes Richard Henry Lee's Jan. 26, 1781, letter to Theodorick Bland insisting that with one ship of the line and two frigates "the militia now in arms [around Portsmouth] are strong enough to smother these invaders in a moment," p. 188. Lassiter also details how Congress then pressured French minister Luzerne to contact Destouches in Newport about sending what would become the Tilly expedition to Portsmouth. Luzerne then used the promise of a French expedition to Virginia to pressure that state into dropping its claim to territories in modern-day Ohio, so that Maryland would agree to ratify the Articles of Confederation; see note in *LAAR*, 3:319. So it could be argued that if the Tilly expedition foiled Washington's original plan to take Arnold, it did at least make possible the passage of the Articles of Confederation. Louis-Alexandre Berthier, in *ACRA*, describes how Tilly decided to take prizes so as to "compensate for his inability to carry out his orders," p. 240. Rochambeau's Feb. 25, 1781, letter to GW, in which he announces that he and Destouches have decided to send the entire French fleet to the Chesapeake, is in *WGW*, 21:279. Lafayette's March 8, 1781, letter to Luzerne, in which he says he is "very glad we have finally found a means to set Monsieur de Rochambeau in motion," is in *LAAR*, 3:384.

CHAPTER 3 ♦ "DELAYS AND ACCIDENTS OF THE SEA"

Louis-Alexandre Berthier writes of "the energy with which the British repaired their ships, knowing as they did that the French squadron was preparing to sail" in *ACRA*, p. 241. Edwin Stone in *Our French Allies* claims that GW decided to ride to Newport "to hasten the departure of the naval expedition under Destouches," p. 362. Baron Ludwig von Closen describes GW's reaction to the loss of his horse in his *Revolutionary Journal*, p. 62. GW's Feb. 24, 1781, letter to Rochambeau, in which he writes of "the flattering distinction paid to the anniversary of my birthday," is in *WGW*, 21:286. Claude Manceron in *The Wind from America* cites GW's letter to Lafayette in which he complains of how "Destouches seems to make a difficulty, which I do not comprehend, about protecting the passage of your detachment down the bay," p. 346. The Duc de Lauzun in his *Memoirs* writes of how officers under Rochambeau had taken a vow not to serve under Lafayette, pp. 193–94; he also writes that Rochambeau's selection of Baron de Vioménil as a commanding officer for the troops being sent to Portsmouth "was peculiarly distasteful to [GW], and he did not conceal his annoyance," p. 197. Claude Blanchard in his *Journal* describes the delay-ridden departure of the French fleet from Newport harbor, p. 94. GW writes about the "unfortunate and to me unaccountable delay" of the French fleet from Newport in a March 23, 1781, letter to Philip Schuyler in *WGW*, 21:361. Destouches makes the claim that he would never have set out on March 8, "except for the presence in Newport of General Washington," in a June 12, 1781, letter in ANM B4 191, at LOC, adding, "What I so greatly feared occurred—the next day the wind turned contrary and gave the enemy time to be informed of our departure." Suggesting that hindsight had informed this claim is Destouches's earlier letter of May 30, 1781, in which he takes credit for delaying the fleet's leave-taking on March 8 "until night was coming on, to hide my departure from the enemy," in ANM B4 191, at LOC.

Arbuthnot describes the eastern end of Long Island as "an uninhabited land [with only] a few Indians" in a March 30, 1781, letter to Sandwich in John Sandwich, *Papers*, 4:167; Arbuthnot's Feb. 16, 1781, letter to Sandwich, in which he lists his many medical complaints, is cited in John Tilley's *The British Navy and the American Revolution*, p. 214; Tilley also cites Arbuthnot's letter in which vows to "put up a bold countenance," p. 213. Arbuthnot provides a detailed account of how he went about the repair of the *Bedford* in a March 20, 1781, letter to Philip Stephens in NA, ADM 1/486. For an account of the British spies who provided both Arbuthnot and Clinton with information about the French fleet's preparations to leave Newport, see Christian McBurney's *Spies in Revolutionary Rhode Island*, pp. 101–6. GW writes of the "delays and accidents of the sea" in a March 11, 1781, letter to Lafayette in *WGW*, 21:333. According to Sam Willis in *Fighting at Sea in the Eighteenth Century*, "a ship with a clean bottom would sail as much as 1.5 knots faster than a fouled one," p. 28. John Lacouture in "The Gulf Stream Charts of Benjamin Franklin and Timothy Folger" discusses Walter Haxton's description of what he called the Northeast Current, https://www.nha.org/library/hn/HN-v44n2-gulfstream.htm. De Louis Vorsey in "Pioneer Charting of the Gulf Stream: The Contributions of Benjamin Franklin and William Gerard De Brahm" cites Franklin's observation that English packet captains "were too wise to be counseled by simple American fishermen," p. 108. When it comes to the French edition of Franklin's chart, see Ellen Cohn's "Benjamin Franklin, George-Louis Le Rouge and the Franklin/Folger Chart of the Gulf Stream," pp. 124–42. According to Baron Ludwig von Closen, the French army officers aboard the French squadron "blamed M. Destouches for having been too far out to sea, instead of going directly towards the Chesapeake, as did Arbuthnot, who, by the course he followed along the coast took a short cut and gained an advantage over our fleet, which made a great turn and found bad weather and a contrary wind in approaching the Chesapeake from that side," in von Closen's *Revolutionary Journal*, pp. 74–75. My thanks to Jean-Marie Kowalski, Michael Crawford, and especially Larrie Ferreiro (who is at work on a forthcoming article about the race between Destouches and Arbuthnot to the Chesapeake) for providing logs from both the British and French fleets, as well as an analysis of their relative positions; my thanks to Alexis Catsambis of the Naval History and Heritage Command for creating two maps of the fleets' tracks to the Chesapeake, one of which demonstrates that the French entered the Gulf Stream toward the end of the voyage. Louis-Alexandre Berthier tells of how the French fleet became divided in the fog and how Destouches attempted to "rally his squadron" in *ACRA*, p. 242.

Destouches outlines his plan to "so entrench myself in the James River that I could not be chased out by any naval force" in a May 30, 1781, letter in ANM B4 191, at LOC. For the signals Arbuthnot used on March 16, 1781, see Julian Corbett's *Signals and Instructions*, pp. 236–58. In his discussion of the line of battle, Sam Willis in *Fighting at Sea in the Eighteenth Century* writes that "[t]o attain unity and cohesion was the holy grail of fleet performance," p. 67; Willis also discusses the evolution of the 74, p. 60. In *The Price of Admiralty*, John Keegan provocatively compares the line of battle to the development of trench warfare: "Eighteenth-century battles at sea, it is not going too far to say, resembled First World War battles on land. They were characterized by the same concern for prearrangement, the same 'flank to flank' rules of engagement, the same lack of 'hands on' control as soon as action was joined and the same failure to return a decisive result—though fortunately not by the same catastrophic cost in human life," p. 49. Keegan also compares a ship of the line to the tank of the twentieth century, "a machine which would combine the qualities of maneuver and firepower within itself," p. 47. Patrick O'Brian in *Men-of-War* provides the statistics about the number of oak trees that went into building a 74, p. 18. According to N. A. M. Rodger in *The Wooden World*, "French ships are traditionally said to have fired high, on the up roll, to disable the enemy's masts and rigging, while British ships fired low, on the down roll to batter the hull and kill the gunners. . . . To fire high was the logical choice of the commander who desired to disable a superior enemy and then escape. . . . To fire low was to aim to finish the action as quickly and decisively as possible," p. 56. Willis cites Captain John Jervis's comment, "Two fleets of equal force never can produce decisive events unless they are equally determined to fight it out," in *Fighting at Sea*, p. 133. According to Jean-Baptiste-Antoine de Verger in *ACRA*, Destouches "had not expected to find the enemy fleet in the Chesapeake [so] his mission could no longer be accomplished. He realized the impossibility of disembarking troops under fire, even from his warships, while opposed by a superior squadron," p. 127. Although many authors have written about the Battle of Cape Henry on March 16, 1781, most appear to have given scant attention to a ten-diagram account of the battle at the Service Historique de l'Armée, Etat-Major de l'Armée, Vincennes, which includes detailed captions that in some cases correspond almost word for word with Destouches's own descriptions of the battle in his May 30 and June 12, 1781, letters. John Harland in *Seamanship in the Age of Sail* describes the French command associated with tacking a square-rigged ship as a prayer "reflecting the uncertainty of the outcome attending tacking," p. 183. Destouches writes that the breaking of the maintopsail yards of the *Eveillé* and *Ardent* "made me lose hope of keeping upwind of the enemy" in his May 30, 1781, letter in ANM B4 191, at LOC. The reference to "drilling rain" is in the March 16, 1781, entry of the *Royal Oak*'s logbook in NA, ADM 51/815. Guillaume de Deux-Ponts writes of how the British "gained sensibly" on the rear of the French line and how as the faster of the British ships advanced ahead of the slower ships in their own line, Arbuthnot's line was divided into "two divisions," in *My Campaigns in America*, p. 105. In describing how both fleets prepared for battle, I have depended primarily on David Steel's *The Elements and Practice of Rigging, Seamanship, and Naval Tactics*, 4:135–36. Arbuthnot writes of how he hailed Phillips Cosby (captain of the *Robust*) as the fleet tacked to port in his March 30, 1781, letter to Sandwich in the *Sandwich Papers*, 4:168; in the same letter he claims that "[n]othing could bear a more pleasing prospect than my situation," p. 168.

Michael Palmer in *Command at Sea* writes of the Académie de Marine and the French numerary signaling system, pp. 123–26. Sam Willis in *Fighting at Sea* describes the workings of the French "Evolutionary Squadron," p. 66. Emmanuel de Fontainieu in *The Hermione* also discusses the importance of the squadron as well as the impact of the square-off between the *Belle Poule* and *Arethusa*, pp. 82, 129–30. Julian Corbett cites Kempenfelt's withering comparison between British and French tactical systems in *Signals and Instructions*, p. 3. Verger in *ACRA* makes the claim that Destouches had up until 1:00 p.m. on March 16, 1781, tried "neither to seek combat nor to avoid it" and that his aim subsequently became to preserve "the honor of the King's arms without endangering his fleet," p. 127. Destouches claims

Arbuthnot had not "foreseen" his reversal of course, "which threatened to batter the head of their line against two scythes," in a June 12, 1781, letter in ANM B4 191, at LOC. Arbuthnot describes Cosby's unexpected decision to attack the *Conquérant* before he could order him to shorten sail and "continue to press the enemy on the larboard tack" in his March 30, 1781, letter to Sandwich in the *Sandwich Papers*, 4:168. In a March 19, 1781, letter to Lieutenant Blackwell, Lieutenant Mears claims that "had our line been well closed before the action commenced (and which only lasted an hour) we should have given a very good account of them" in Frederick Mackenzie's *Diary*, 2:505. Destouches writes of how the "three vessels from their van were in a head-on position athwart mine" in a June 12, 1781, letter in ANM B4 191, at LOC. Arbuthnot tells of how he was forced to follow the three ships, in his van "under the fire of the enemy," as well as the damage inflicted on his ship in his March 30, 1781, letter to Sandwich in the *Sandwich Papers*, 4:168–69. John Tilley discusses how Arbuthnot's "defective vision" might have contributed to his failure to raise the blue and yellow signal flag indicating "engage the enemy as close as possible" in *The British Navy and the American Revolution*, p. 225. Berthier writes of how the ships in the rear of the British line were "in a quandary, whether to continue to windward or bear away," in *ACRA*, p. 243. Willis discusses the effects of roll on naval combat in *Fighting at Sea*, pp. 119–20. Claude Blanchard recounts how he took a pinch of snuff on the quarterdeck of the *Duc de Bourgogne* in the midst of the battle, as well as the losses suffered on the decks of the *Conquérant* in his *Journal*, pp. 96–98. The account of how a French soldier who'd just had his leg blown off exclaimed, "Thank heaven, I still have two arms and a leg to serve my King!" is in *ACRA*, p. xxvii. Blanchard describes the soldiers' deaths as "glorious, but useless" in his *Journal*, p. 137. Destouches recounts how he ordered his squadron to come up "successively upwind in each other's wake" in his June 12, 1781, letter in ANM B4 191, at LOC; he recounts how "[t]he *Neptune* placed itself in musket range" of the *Robust*'s poop in his May 30, 1781, letter. Charles O'Hara in an April 20, 1781, letter to the Duke of Grafton passes along the account of the battle he received from a captain who was in the action and who refers to the "very dishonorable humiliating day's disgrace," as well as how Arbuthnot "behaved as shamefully ill as the French behaved gallantly well," in "Letters to the Duke of Grafton," p. 178. Comte de Barras writes that Destouches's plan to attack Arnold "could no longer be successful, except insofar as he should succeed, against all probability, not only in beating, but even in totally destroying this stronger squadron," in a Sept. 30, 1781, letter in ANM B4 19, at LOC. Brian Tunstall in *Naval Warfare in the Age of Sail* claims that "Destouches had clearly won and with five British ships practically immobilized, he could have done as he pleased," p. 169.

The poem in Ewald's papers referring to "Honor is like an island" is in *DAW*, p. 298; his account of what occurred at Portsmouth in the tense days after the Battle of Cape Henry is also in *DAW*, pp. 288–91. In a March 26, 1781, letter, Lafayette writes that "I am sorry" the French fleet "did not pursue their advantage" in *LAAR*, 3:417. His March 27, 1781, letter to Thomas Jefferson, in which he speaks of his disappointment about the outcome and "that with a naval superiority our success would have been certain," is in *LAAR*, 3:418. Clermont-Crèvecoeur's insistence that Destouches "could not bring himself to renew the battle when prudence indicated a retreat" is in *ACRA*, p. 24. W. M. James cites de Barras's claim that Destouches's decision to sail to Newport was justified by a "principle in war" in *The British Navy in Adversity*, p. 274; James adds, "Strange thoughts and a strange 'principle of war.' England was fortunate in her enemy at a moment when superior forces were everywhere closing round her," p. 275. De Barras speaks of how Destouches opted to "retreat with honor after punishing the enemy's arrogance and establishing the reputation of French arms in the eyes of the people of America" in his Sept. 30, 1781, letter, in ANM B4 19, at LOC. Brian Tunstall describes the end result of the Battle of Cape Henry as "farcical" in *Naval Warfare*, p. 169.

CHAPTER 4 * BAYONETS AND ZEAL

GW's March 31, 1781, letter to Destouches in which he writes that "the winds and weather had more influence than valor or skill" is in *WGW,* 21:399. GW's intercepted March 28, 1781, letter to Lund Washington, in which he insists "the destruction of Arnold's corps would have been inevitable" if the French had only done as he requested in a timely fashion is in *WGW,* 21:386. Rochambeau writes of his disappointed reaction to GW's letter to Lund, which had appeared in the loyalist *Gazette,* in an April 26, 1781, letter in the Washington Papers at LOC. Lafayette writes of how the publication of GW's letter to Lund has caused him "pain on many political accounts" in an April 15, 1781, letter to GW in *LAAR,* 4:33–34. GW's April 30, 1781, attempt at an apology to Rochambeau, in which he writes "it would be disingenuous in me not to acknowledge that I believe the general import to be true," is in *WGW,* 22:16. Charles Ross writes of Jemima Tullikens's claim that "sorrow . . . [had] destroyed her life" in the introduction to Cornwallis's *Correspondence,* 1:14. Cornwallis's letters to his brother about how his wife's death had "destroyed all my hopes of happiness in this world" and how he "must shift the scene" and return to America and the army he loves are cited by Franklin and Mary Wickwire in *Cornwallis,* p. 115. See also Andrew O'Shaughnessy's *The Men Who Lost America,* which discusses Cornwallis's fidelity to the memory of his wife, p. 255.

Piers Mackesy in *The War for America* writes of how through the establishment of a functional British state in South Carolina the "advantages of British sovereignty would then become apparent," and quotes the memorandum in the Germain papers about how this could "bring about what will never be effected by mere force," p. 252; Mackesy also writes of "Germain's concept of a methodical and static consolidation," p. 344. O'Shaughnessy cites Cornwallis's admission that the Battle of Cowpens "has almost broke my heart," p. 267. In an April 20, 1781, letter, Charles O'Hara writes that "[a]ll was to be risked" in "the beating or driving of Greene's army out of the Carolinas" in "Letters to the Duke of Grafton," p. 173. According to William Willcox in *Portrait of a General,* after Cornwallis learned in late December that "his star was in the ascendant in England," he "now scorned to retreat, threw caution to the winds, and set off in pursuit of Greene. He did not give his reasons for this sudden offensive, but it may have been rooted less in military logic than in his new sense of what the government expected of him," pp. 370–71. In the mid-nineteenth century, Benson Lossing in *The Pictorial Field-book of the Revolution,* vol. 2, retraced portions of Cornwallis's and NG's marches through North Carolina and wrote, "No one can form an idea of the character of the roads in winter, at the South, where the red clay abounds, without passing over them. Until I had done so, I could not appreciate the difficulties experienced by the two armies in this race toward Virginia, particularly in the transportation of baggage wagons or artillery," 2:395 note. According to Joel Achenbach in *The Grand Idea,* "The more a road was traveled by horses and wagons, the more the surface became chewed up and rutted, and eventually the whole track would be lower than the surrounding terrain, ensuring that water would flow into it. The situation tended to get worse rather than better. Roads were not self-healing, and eventually the track through the woods would not really be a road at all, just a linear bog," pp. 59–61. In a March 17, 1781, letter to Germain, Cornwallis recounts how "I employed a halt of two days in collecting some flour and in destroying superfluous baggage and all my wagons. . . . I must in justice to this army say that there was the most general cheerful acquiescence," *DAR,* 20:86. O'Hara writes of Cornwallis's determination to follow NG "to the end of the world," in the April 20, 1781, letter to the Duke of Grafton, p. 174.

The editors of *PGNG* cite William Johnson's description of NG's leaving his camp at Cheraw to join Morgan as "the most imprudent action of his life" in *PGNG,* 7:209. Joseph Graham in *GJG* writes of NG's council of war on a log by the Catawba River and how a British officer "thought to be Lord Cornwallis" was seen "viewing us with spy-glasses," p. 19.

According to William Gordon in *The History of the Rise, Progress, and Establishment of the Independence of the United States of America*, "Morgan was for retreating over the mountains, a different route from what Greene proposed." Gordon, who received his information from NG himself, quotes Morgan as insisting "he would not be answerable for consequences if it was not followed," as well as NG's reply, "Neither will you, for I shall take the measure upon myself," 3:164. In a Feb. 1, 1781, letter to NG, Isaac Huger explains, "The river is so rapid that it is impossible for boats to stem it. . . . Col. Kosciuszko's boats are not with us," in *PGNG*, 7:17. Huger adds that he has requested that Kosciuszko "forward such boats as were finished and to put the rest in charge of Col. Wade and to order the artificers to join the army," suggesting that some of the flat-bottomed boats may have ultimately joined NG's army to the north. NG describes himself as being of the "Spanish disposition" in a Jan. 25, 1781, letter to Caty Greene in *PGNG*, 7:193. NG writes of his hopes of "ruining Lord Cornwallis if he persists in his mad scheme of pushing through the country," in a Jan. 30, 1781, letter to Isaac Huger in *PGNG*, 7:220. Joseph Graham recalls Davidson's comment that NG "appeared to know more about" the Catawba "than those who were raised on it" in *GJG*, p. 290.

Joseph Graham in *GJG* writes of how the British cannonade at Beatty's Ford could be heard for twenty-five miles and "came down the river like repeated peals of thunder," p. 295. He also describes how each British soldier equipped himself for the crossing at Cowan's Ford "with fixed bayonets, muskets empty, carried on the left shoulder at a slope . . . each man had a stick about the size of a hoop pole eight feet long, which he kept setting on the bottom below him, to support him against the rapidity of the current, which was generally waist-deep and in some places more," p. 291. British sergeant Roger Lamb writes in his *Journal* of "their knapsacks on their back, sixty or seventy rounds of powder and ball . . . tied at . . . their necks," p. 345; he also describes how Cornwallis "dashed first into the river," and how the horse "did not fall until he reached the shore," as well as how "O'Hara's horse rolled with him down the current," p. 345. Graham writes of the British dead being found "lodged in fish traps and in brush about the banks," in *GJG*, p. 299; he also describes how the regulars "had to pull up by the bushes" as they climbed the shore, as well as the circumstances of General Davidson's death, p. 294. John Buchanan in *The Road to Guilford Courthouse* quotes Nicholas Gosnell's colorful recollection of Cornwallis's arrival on the east bank of the Catawba and how the militiamen "made straight shirt tails" as they ran from the British, p. 348.

Graham in *GJG* describes the incident at Torrence's Tavern, pp. 296–98; he also describes the encounter between the militia and O'Hara's Guards on the banks of the Yadkin at Trading Ford, pp. 300–301. Daniel Morgan writes of being "violently attacked with the piles" in a Feb. 6, 1781, letter to NG in *PGNG*, 7:254. Buchanan in *The Road to Guilford Courthouse* cites NG's statement "There are few Morgans to be found," p. 351. Don Higginbotham in *Daniel Morgan* recounts how Morgan was whipped by a British officer during the Seven Years' War, pp. 4–5. Lawrence Babits in *A Devil of a Whipping* cites Thomas Young's account of how Morgan told his men "the old wagoner would crack his whip over Ben [Tarleton]," p. 55. On NG's council of war at Guilford Courthouse, see *PGNG*, 7:261–62. According to Henry Lee, Edward Carrington was so involved in scouting the Dan that he did not join NG's army until just two days before it arrived at Guilford Courthouse, in *Memoirs of the War in the Southern Department of the United States*, 2:298. According to Carrington "when the retreat was determined on, it was predicated on the certain knowledge that there was but one boat at Dix's Ferry . . . and that between there and Boyd's ferry inclusive, five more were to be found. . . . There were then no other boats in the river, other than the wide and shallow flats at the ferries, which it was impossible to carry against the current," in *PGNG*, 7:271. Lawrence Babits and Joshua Howard in *Long, Obstinate, and Bloody* describe Otho Williams's flying army as "both a decoy and a blocking force to delay and harass Cornwallis's army," p. 29. Henry Lee recounts the routine developed by Williams's flying army of three hours, sleep per man every night with a 3:00 a.m. wakeup to "secure breakfast" once they'd moved some distance from their night's campsite, in *Memoirs*, 2:279. Lee also describes how "[t]he demeanor of the hostile troops became so pacific" (p. 290), as well as the speed advantage enjoyed by the American cavalry; according to Lee, much of it also had to do with the superior riding ability of the Americans raised to the south of Pennsylvania: "The boys from seven years of age begin to mount horses, riding without saddle and often in the fields when sent for a horse, without bridles. . . . Thus they become so completely versed in the art of riding by the time they reach puberty as to equal the most expert horsemen anywhere," p. 324. Lee makes the claim "Only when a defile or a water course crossed our route did the enemy exhibit any indication to cut off our rear" in his *Memoirs*, 2:290.

William Davie in *The Revolutionary War Sketches* describes how he and NG would study the map each night at midnight to determine how to best provide the army with provisions, p. 41. The correspondence between NG and Otho Williams during Feb. 13–14, 1781, as they approached the Dan River is in *PGNG*, 7:285–87. Lee writes of how the "horses were turned into the stream, while the dragoons, with their arms and equipments, embarked in the boats," in his *Memoirs*, 2:292. John Buchanan in *The Road to Guilford Courthouse* writes of how Cornwallis pushed his army 40 miles in thirty-one hours while also pointing out that NG's army had covered that same distance in only twenty hours, p. 358; according to Buchanan, the closest British supply base to Cornwallis once he reached the edge of the Dan River was in Camden, South Carolina, about 250 miles to the south. Cornwallis complains of "our intelligence" being "exceedingly defective" and how the Americans had managed to collect more boats on the lower fords of the Dan "than had been represented to me as possible," in a March 17, 1781, letter to Germain in *DAR*, 20:88. Henry Lee describes NG's orders to himself and Pickens as being to "repress the meditated rising of the loyalists" in his *Memoirs*, 2:303. Cornwallis describes how he "erected the King's standard" and sent Tarleton to help bring in "a considerable body of friends" who lived between the Haw and Deep rivers in his March 17, 1781, letter to Germain in *DAR*, 20:88. Henry Lee tells how he passed Pyle's loyalists "with a smiling countenance" in his *Memoirs*, 2:311; he also recounts how the loyalists "rejoiced in meeting us," p. 308. While Lee claimed that Pickens's militia were responsible for starting the melee (by not sufficiently concealing themselves), Joseph Graham in *GJG* insists that the cavalry officer Captain Joseph Eggleston struck the first blow after a loyalist claimed he was "A friend of his Majesty," pp. 318–19; see also the account in *PGNG*, 7:359, which refers to the loyalists crying out, "To the king!" Buchanan in *The Road to Guilford Courthouse* cites the reference to Andrew Pickens being so guarded that "[h]e would first take the words out of his mouth . . . and examine them before he uttered them," p. 299. Pickens's enthusiastic claim that the Pyle's Massacre had "knocked up Toryism altogether in this part" is in his Feb. 26, 1781, letter to NG in *PGNG*, 7:358.

In his April 20, 1781, letter, O'Hara writes of how "the two armies were never above 20 miles asunder, they constantly avoiding a general action, and we as industriously seeking it," in "Letters to the Duke of Grafton," p. 177. Gordon tells of how NG "took a new position every night and kept it as a profound secret with himself where the next was to be so that Lord Cornwallis could not gain intelligence of his situation in time to avail himself of it," in *The History of the Rise, Progress, and Establishment of the Independence of the United States of America*, 3:172–73; Gordon also reports that each soldier in NG's army received a gill of rum on March 13, as well as that NG was "fearful lest Lord Cornwallis should not attack them in front, but change his position and fall upon their flanks," p. 173. Babits and Howard, in *Long, Obstinate, and Bloody*, cite Williams's description of "[t]he roar of musketry and cracking of the rifles," p. 125. Cornwallis writes of how "[t]he excessive thickness of the woods rendered our bayonets of little use," in his March 17, 1781, letter to Germain in *DAR*, 20:91. Lamb describes how he saved a disoriented Cornwallis from riding into the midst of the Virginia militiamen in his *Journal*, p. 362. Buchanan cites Nathaniel Slade's description of how the muzzle flashes of the British Guards and the First Maryland "seemed to meet," in *The Road to Guilford Courthouse*, p. 378. Henry Lee recounts the exchange between Cornwallis and O'Hara before Cornwallis ordered a cannon be fired on Washington's cavalry, even though it meant some British Guards would inevitably fall to friendly fire, in his *Memoirs*, 2:353. Although Babits and Howard, in *Long, Obstinate, and Bloody*, insist that the conversation never took place (p. 162), I, like, Buchanan in *The Road to Guilford Courthouse*, see no reason to doubt the gist of Lee's account, especially given the earlier demands Cornwallis had made on his men. As Buchanan writes, Cornwallis "did what he had to do. What he did was terrible but what choice had he?," p. 379. O'Hara recounts the terrible toll of the battle as well as the sufferings the British army endured during their "two days and nights" on the battlefield after the fighting in his April 20, 1781, letter to the Duke of Grafton, p. 177. Lamb in his *Journal* describes the "complicated scene of horror and distress" and how an estimated fifty men died of their wounds during the rainy night after the battle, p. 357. NG's March 18, 1781, letter to Joseph Reed, in which he refers to the battle as "long, obstinate, and bloody," is in *PGNG*, 7:450. In his *Correspondence*, Cornwallis writes of being "quite tired of marching about the country in quest of adventures" in an April 10, 1781, letter to William Phillips, p. 88. NG writes, "We fight, get beat, rise, and fight again," in an April 28, 1781, letter to Chevalier de la Luzerne in *PGNG*, 8:167–68. NG writes of his hopes for "universal joy through America" in a March 18, 1781, letter to Caty Greene in *PGNG*, 7:446–47. GW writes of how NG deserved "the honors of the field" in an April 18, 1781, letter in *WGW*, 21:471. He advises "not to look back unless it is to derive useful lessons from past errors" in a March 26, 1781, letter to John Armstrong in *WGW*, 21:378.

CHAPTER 5 ✦ THE END OF THE TETHER

In a Feb. 28, 1781, letter, GW advises Jacky Custis to "hear dispassionately and determine coolly" in *WGW*, 21:318; he continues: "To be disgusted at the decision of questions because they are not consonant to your own ideas, and to withdraw ourselves from public assemblies . . . upon suspicion that there is a party formed who are inimical to our cause . . . is wrong because these things may originate in a difference of opinion." GW's March 21, 1781, letter to Benjamin Harrison, in which he discusses the effort to establish a pension for his mother and the "want of duty on my part" that implies, is in *WGW*, 21:341. GW's April 30, 1781, letter to Lund Washington, in which he writes of the *Savage* incident and how "[i]t would have been a less painful circumstance to me to have heard that in consequence of your non-compliance with their request, they had burnt my house and laid the plantation in ruins," is in *WGW*, 22:14–15. On the *Savage* incident, see George Grieves's "Notes on Conversation with Lund Washington" in Chastellux's *Travels in North America*, 2:597. GW's April 5, 1781, letter to John Laurens, in which he speaks of the country having reached "the end of our tether," is in *WGW*, 21:437–39. GW's March 27, 1781, letter to Benjamin Harrison, in which he insists that "[t]he most powerful diversion that can be made in favor of the Southern states will be a respectable force in the neighborhood of New York," is in *WGW*, 21:381–83.

   In *Portrait of a General*, William Willcox cites Cornwallis's description of a retreat to Charleston as "disgraceful," p. 386; according to Willcox, Cornwallis's decision to march to Virginia "seems to have been the act of a man driven beyond the limits of clear thinking, for the arguments against it were as obvious and cogent then as they are today." In an April 10, 1781, letter to Clinton, Cornwallis writes of how "[t]he rivers of Virginia are advantageous to an invading army" in Benjamin Stevens, ed., *The Campaign in Virginia*, 1:399. The phrase "taking possession of places at one time and abandoning them at another" is in Germain's May 2, 1781, letter to Clinton in *DAR*, 20:133. Piers Mackesy in *The War for America* cites

Samuel Graves's comparison of the movements of the British army to "the passage of a ship through the sea whose track is soon lost," p. 252. Cornwallis writes of how after "the experiment I had made [in North Carolina] had failed," the only option he felt he had was to take the war to Virginia in a June 30, 1781, letter to Clinton in Clinton's *American Rebellion*, p. 535. Cornwallis makes the declaration that "[i]f we mean an offensive war in America, we must abandon New York and bring our whole force into Virginia" in an April 10, 1781, letter to Clinton in Stevens, *The Campaign in Virginia*, 1:399. With hindsight inevitably informing his memory, Clinton claimed he believed it was in his country's best interests "to assemble our whole force at New York and remain upon the defensive, as the commander in chief was then fully persuaded . . . that rebellion in America was at its last gasp; and a very few more months' escape from disaster on our side promised us every good effect of the most decisive victory, by insuring to Great Britain the future dependence of the revolted colonies on a firm and permanent basis" in his *The American Rebellion*, p. 293. Germain writes of being "very well pleased to find Lord Cornwallis's opinion entirely coincides with mine of the great importance of pushing the war on the side of Virginia with all the force that can be spared" in a June 6, 1781, letter to Clinton in *DAR*, 20:157. Cornwallis writes of how "the return of General Greene to North Carolina . . . put a junction with General Phillips out of my power" in an April 23, 1781, letter to Clinton in Stevens, *The Campaign in Virginia*, 1:425. In "The British Road to Yorktown," William Willcox writes of how Cornwallis's decision to bolt to Virginia was influenced by the knowledge that Clinton's dispatches were on their way from Charleston: "Rather than return to being a subordinate, Cornwallis would force his own design on his superiors. . . . Cornwallis was playing for vast stakes in a game which he did not fully understand," p. 14.

Lafayette refers to General Phillips's "having killed my father" in an April 17, 1781, letter to NG in *LAAR*, 4:40. Lafayette proclaims that "Phillips is my object" in a May 4, 1781, letter to GW in *LAAR*, 4:82–83. NG advises Lafayette "not to let the love of fame get the better of your prudence" in a May 1, 1781, letter in *LAAR*, 4:74. Lafayette writes of the likelihood of his tiny army's being "completely thrashed by the smallest of the two armies that do me the honor of visiting" in a May 9, 1781, letter to Luzerne in *LAAR*, 4:79. Rochambeau writes that "[m]y private letters informed me that if I had been in France the king would have appointed me Minister of War" in his *Memoirs*, p. 44. The Duc de Lauzun recounts Rochambeau's anger on learning "that men whom he had treated most kindly had by no means spared him in their letters" in his *Memoirs*, p. 199. Charles Lee Lewis in *Admiral De Grasse and American Independence* cites a letter written by the French minister of war, the Marquis de Segur, over the period of Feb. 25 to March 19, 1781, to Rochambeau in which he explains the French government's instructions concerning "the conduct of the war in America," which contains the caveat, "If through unseen events . . . Washington's army may disintegrate and cease to exist, the king wishes you then to disobey the orders and requisitions that the admiral might make for you to leave the coast, for in that case it will be prudent to conserve your means . . . to retire to the Antilles, if it is possible or to St.-Domingue [Haiti], depending on the season," p. 129. Chastellux writes of how Rochambeau "sees everything darkly" in his May 28, 1781, letter to Luzerne in Randolph Adams's *The Burned Letter of Chastellux*, p. 6. William Smith records Clinton's insistence that Rochambeau was "utterly against the American Alliance," in an Aug. 23, 1781, entry in his *Memoirs*, p. 434. Chastellux tells of Rochambeau having "taken an aversion to this whole country" in his May 28, 1781, letter to Luzerne in Adams's *Burned Letter*, p. 6. Chastellux's May 21, 1781, letter to GW, in which he reveals that the de Grasse fleet sailed from Brest in March and speaks of "the secrecy of your excellency, as one of [your] numerous virtues," is in *Founders Online*, National Archives, http://founders.archives.gov/documents/Washington/99-01-02-05733. On the Wethersfield Conference and GW's intercepted letters discussing the conference's outcome, see Lee Kennett's *The French Forces in America*, pp. 104–7. GW writes of the "insurmountable difficulty" of transporting the army to Virginia by land and the possibility that the allies might "extend our views to the southward" in a May 22, 1781, entry of his *Diary*, in which he recorded the results of the conference, p. 218.

Flora Fraser in *The Washingtons* cites the reference to the "plain Dutch house" that served as GW's headquarters in New Windsor, p. 241. GW writes of Martha's illness and her still being "weak and low," as well as his hope that his stepson can accompany her back to Virginia, in a May 31, 1781, letter to John Parke Custis in *WGW*, 22:142. Ron Chernow discusses GW's decision to return the medicinal gifts to Martha from a loyalist in *Washington*, p. 400, as does Fraser in *The Washingtons*, p. 244. GW writes of how "Our allies in this country expect, and depend upon being supported by us in the attempt we are about to make" in the May 24, 1781, document "Circular to New England States" in *WGW*, 22:110–11. It was no accident that just as had occurred the previous month with GW's letters about the failed Destouches expedition, his letters about the Wethersfield Conference were confiscated by the British; as James Flexner writes in *George Washington in the American Revolution*, GW "was anxious that the information should be leaked to the enemy. . . . He felt that the possibility of an actual attack on New York was very remote. The objective visibly achieved was to take pressure off the south by frightening Clinton. The captured letter served this end to perfection," p. 431. In addition to capturing Washington's letters, the British also apprehended several French letters, including one from Chastellux to Luzerne in which he complained of Rochambeau's "incredible ignorance." As Adams writes in *The Burned Letter of Chastellux*, pp. 6–8, Clinton made sure the letter got into the hands of Rochambeau, who recognized that Clinton's "intention had not been most assuredly to set my wits at ease" (*Memoirs*, p. 47), and after letting Chastellux know he had the letter in his possession, proceeded to burn it. According to Rochambeau in his *Memoirs*, moving the French fleet to Boston rather than keeping it in Newport "might have delayed for a whole month the junction of our fleet to that of de Grasse," p. 48. Lauzun claimed in his *Memoirs* that the delivery of Rochambeau's letter proposing that de Barras's fleet remain in Newport "put [Washington] in such a rage that he refused to answer it," p. 200. GW's June 4, 1781, letter to Rochambeau, in which he insists that "I must adhere to my *opinion* and to the plan which was fixed at Wethersfield as most eligible," is in *WGW*, 22:157.

George Mason writes of his fears that the French were purposely "spinning out the war" to his son George in a June 3, 1781, letter, available at http://consource.org/document /george-mason-to-george-mason-jr-1781-6-3/. GW's June 7, 1781, letter to Rochambeau about the newspaper story referring to de Grasse's activities in the Caribbean is in *WGW*, 22:170. Rochambeau's May 28, 1781, letter to de Grasse, in which he suggests, "The southwesterly winds and the state of distress in Virginia will probably make you prefer Chesapeake Bay," is in Lewis's *Admiral De Grasse*, p. 121. Rochambeau's June 12, 1781, letter to GW, in which he admits to having been in correspondence with de Grasse and having suggested that it would be "a great stroke to go to the Chesapeake Bay," is reprinted in a note in *WGW*, 22:206. GW's June 13, 1781, letter to Rochambeau, in which GW reminds the French general "that New York was looked upon by us as the only practicable object under present circumstances" and speaks of the benefits of "coming suddenly" to New York, is in *WGW*, 22:208. GW talks about how "it could not be foreknown where the enemy would be most susceptible of impression," as well as the importance of using naval superiority to "transport ourselves to any spot with the greatest celerity," in a July 31, 1788, letter to Noah Webster—see *Founders Online*, National Archives, last modified March 30, 2017, http://founders.archives.gov /documents/Washington/04-06-02-0376. Although GW's insistence "that it was never in contemplation to attack New York" was clearly a bit of after-the-fact revisionism on his part, the letter nonetheless provides valuable insights into the importance GW placed on transporting the allied army by water. GW's insistence that "I will not lament or repine at any act of Providence" is cited in my *Bunker Hill*, p. 287.

Louis Gottschalk in *Lafayette and the Close of the American Revolution* describes how American cannonballs passed through the house in which General Phillips lay dying, insisting that Lafayette "had not, in fact, known that Phillips was sick," p. 231. Lafayette writes, "We have everything to fear from [the British] cavalry," in a May 18, 1781, letter to NG in *LAAR*, 4:112. Tarleton writes of how favorable news about the war in South Carolina "eased" Cornwallis's anxiety and "gave him brilliant hopes of a glorious campaign" in Virginia in *A History of the Campaigns of 1780 and 1781*, p. 291. Michael Kranish in *Flight from Monticello* cites Cornwallis's claim that "[t]he boy cannot escape me," p. 264. Johann Ewald compares Cornwallis's army and its huge number of horses and escaped slaves to "a wandering Arabian or Tartar horde" in *DAW*, p. 305; he also discusses the terrible heat and "the torment of several billions of insects," p. 314, and how the British army has "made people miserable by our presence," p. 302. On Tarleton's raid on Charlottesville and his almost seizing Jefferson, see Kranish's *Flight from Monticello*, pp. 279–89. Lafayette complains that Baron von Steuben "is so *unpopular* that I do not know where to put him" in a June 16, 1781, letter to Luzerne in *LAAR*, 4:188. Ewald cites the confiscated letter by Lafayette in which he writes, "You can be entirely calm with regards to the rapid marches of Lord Cornwallis," in *DAW*, p. 302. Jefferson's May 28, 1781, letter to GW assuring him that his appearance in Virginia would "restore full confidence in salvation" is in his *Papers*, 6:33. Richard Henry Lee's June 12, 1781, letter to GW claiming he would "bring into immediate exertion the force and recourse of this state," as well as his June 12, 1781, letter to James Lovell of the Continental Congress, in which he proposes that GW be granted "dictatorial powers" (and which he included with his own letter to GW), is in his *Letters*, 2:237. GW hypothesizes that Cornwallis's activities in Virginia have been motivated by Britain's hope to "urge the plea of *uti possidetis* in the proposed mediation" in a June 8, 1781, letter to Jefferson in *WGW*, 22:189. John Ferling discusses the principle of *uti possidetis* and how the territory of the United States might have been divided up between the Americans and British in the event of a peace conference in "John Adams, Diplomat," pp. 241–42. GW writes of "acting on the great scale" in a June 7, 1781, letter to Joseph Jones in *WGW*, 22:179.

CHAPTER 6 ✦ "A RAY OF LIGHT"

For information on Admiral George Rodney I have relied on David Spinney's excellent biography *Rodney*. According to Spinney, as a result of Rodney's pursuit of the French fleet in the winter and spring of 1780, Admiral de Guichen "broke down under the strain," p. 336. Spinney cites Samuel Hood's claim concerning Rodney that "the lures of St. Eustatius were so bewitching as not to be withstood by flesh and blood," p. 363. According to Karl Tornquist in *The Naval Campaigns of Count de Grasse During the American Revolution*, de Grasse's "brutal character agreed with his grim appearance," p. 42. Spinney cites Hood's claim that during their encounter off Martinique, de Grasse had, "I thank God, nothing to boast of," p. 371. In a letter to French naval minister Castries about his encounter off Martinique with the fleet commanded by Hood, de Grasse complained "that it was only too true that the sailing of the English was superior to ours," cited in Charles Lee Lewis's *Admiral De Grasse and American Independence*, p. 110.

As Jonathan Dull writes in "Mahan, Sea Power, and the War for American Independence," "France was absolutely dependent on the 50 ships of the line Spain could contribute . . . which in turn left France no choice but to acquiesce in Spain's war aims and strategy. . . . [H]er assistance . . . could be obtained only through the promise of territorial acquisition," p. 62.

Francisco Saavedra de Sangronis writes of gaining "the goodwill of the general officers, not with artifices or intrigues . . . but with a frank and impartial policy" in his *Journal*, p. 109. Saavedra writes of how Bernardo de Gálvez "knew better than I the insufficiency of his resources" in his *Journal*, p. 116. In addition to Saavedra's *Journal*, my account of the Battle of Pensacola is based, in part, on Kathleen DuVal's *Independence Lost: Lives on the Edge of the American Revolution*, pp. 188–218. Saavedra writes of the "terrifying claps of thunder" accompanying a tornado on May 6, 1781, in his *Journal*, p. 167. He writes of how the British fortification exploded on May 8, 1781, "with a terrifying noise," p. 170. Gálvez's personal motto of *"Yo solo"* appears on the monument to him at Pensacola, Florida. Saavedra writes of how he was instructed to confer with de Grasse "about the operations that must be executed" in his *Journal*, p. 191.

In a letter cited by Spinney, Rodney refers to his "complaint" as "a stricture," which a doctor friend of his later claimed "must have killed me if I had stayed on a month longer in the West Indies," p. 383; Spinney also cites Hood's reference to "the unsteadiness of the commander in chief," p. 376. According to Barbara Tuchman in *The First Salute*, "The consequences of Rodney's failure to pursue [when he encountered the French fleet off Barbados] was that de Grasse was not halted and reached America according to plan," p. 231. On Rochambeau's march from Providence to White Plains, see Robert Selig's *The Washington-Rochambeau Revolutionary Route*, pp. 60–66. GW complains of how "[t]hings drag on like a cart without wheels" in a July 10, 1781, letter to Joseph Jones in *WGW*, 22:354. GW writes of not being "highly sanguine in my expectations" about the July 2 operation against the British fortifications along the north edge of Manhattan and of "the exceeding great advantage" that would be gained if the operation should be successful in a July 1, 1781, letter to Rochambeau in *WGW*, 22:307. French Ensor Chadwick, in his preface to *The Graves Papers*, writes of how after Graves's departure from New York on July 21, 1781, New York was "from a naval standpoint, wholly defenseless," p. lxi. GW writes of the futility of "urging a measure to which [de Barras's] own judgment was opposed" in the July 29, 1781, entry of his *Diaries*, 2:247 (he had begun keeping one that spring). Cornwallis's July 8, 1781, letter to Clinton, in which he questions "the utility of a defensive post in this country, which cannot have the smallest influence on the war in Carolina," is cited in Clinton's own *The American Rebellion*, p. 35. Clinton describes Portsmouth as a "sickly post," while urging the superiority of Yorktown as "a naval station for large ships as well as small," in a July 8, 1781, letter to Cornwallis cited in *The American Rebellion*, pp. 541–42. Lafayette refers to the "devil Cornwallis" in a July 9, 1781, letter to Vicomte de Noailles in *LAAR*, 4:241; he writes about the rumor that Cornwallis will be sailing for England and how he will "rejoice for it" in a July 20, 1781, letter to GW in *LAAR*, 4:255. Lafayette wonders whether the British are sailing for "some other quarter" than New York since they did not leave their moorings even though the wind was favorable for sailing out of the Chesapeake in a July 29, 1781, letter to Thomas Nelson in *LAAR*, 4:283. Lafayette wonders whether the British troops that just landed at Yorktown are a feint to draw him "very low down" the peninsula between the York and James rivers in an Aug. 4, 1781, letter to Anthony Wayne in *LAAR*, 4:294.

On the possibility that a copy of the royal navy's signal book was procured by the British spy James Rivington in New York and sent to Luzerne and ultimately de Grasse, see Richard Peters's letter to GW, in which he writes, "I some time ago procured a copy of the British signals for their fleet and gave to the Minister of France to transmit to Comte de Grasse," cited by Todd Andrlik in "James Rivington: King's Printer and Patriot Spy?," https://allthingsliberty.com/2014/03/james-rivington-kings-printer-patriot-spy/. Rochambeau's June 11, 1781, letter to de Grasse, in which he warns the admiral that "the Americans are at the end of their resources," is cited by Lewis in *Admiral De Grasse*, pp. 123–25. The concern that de Grasse's decision to sail to the Chesapeake "would not be reproached by all in case of failure" is from an anonymous officer's journal and is quoted in John Shea, ed., *The Operations of the French Fleet Under the Count de Grasse*, p. 150. Saavedra recounts how he and de Grasse discussed "the cordiality and good faith with which the Spaniards and the French must cooperate," as well as the hope that a British defeat in the Chesapeake would force "the English cabinet [to] lose the hope of subduing" the Americans, in his *Journal*, p. 200. Saavedra tells of de Grasse's concerns about finding "five or six" ships to protect Haiti and how Saavedra's proposal to use Spanish warships stationed in Havana "pleased the comte enormously" in his *Journal*, pp. 201–2. Saavedra describes how the bread ovens in French warships create a "foul-smelling smoke," as well as the sailors' love of wine and tafia, in his *Journal*, p. 190. Tornquist describes how the brick bulkhead in the *Intrepide* created "[a] fortune in this misfortune" by providing the crew with time to reposition the ship and throw some of the vessel's gunpowder into the harbor in *The Naval Campaigns of Count de Grasse*, p. 51. Chevalier de Goussencourt, in an account reprinted by Shea in *The Operations of the French Fleet*, describes how *"Sauve qui peut!"* was cried out before the *Intrepide* exploded, as well as how "the sun disappeared from us" because of the black smoke and how the waterfront "received her whole broadside" from the ship's cannons, p. 60. Tornquist describes how the ship's stern "sprang into the air" in *The Naval Campaigns of Count de Grasse*, p. 52. De Grasse's July 28, 1781, letter, in which he writes of how he has decided "to take everything on myself for the common cause," is in Lewis's *Admiral De Grasse*, pp. 138–39. In Shea's *Operations of the French Fleet*, Goussencourt describes Cap François as "the Paris of the isles," p. 57. For information about the horrific conditions of African slavery in eighteenth-century Haiti, I have relied on Madison Smartt Bell's *Toussaint Louverture*, pp. 6–16. Saavedra writes of how the refusal of the island's planters to lend de Grasse money threatened to leave the French fleet "idle in port," as well as how de Grasse eventually agreed to go through with what he deemed a "risky operation" and send Saavedra on a "swift frigate" to Havana, in his *Journal*, pp. 208–9.

Rodney's July 7 dispatch, in which he promises to "keep as good a look out as possible" on the movements of the French, "by which my own shall be regulated," is cited in Chadwick, *The Graves Papers*, p. 39. Chadwick traces the series of British miscommunications in July 1781, crowned by Rodney's failure to inform Hood of intelligence indicating that the Chesapeake was de Grasse's destination, in *The Graves Papers*, pp. 39–60. Spinney writes of Rodney's hope that his health would improve enough that he could rejoin the British fleet as it made its way up the coast of North America in *Rodney*, p. 378. GW's June 28, 1781, letter to Henry Knox, in which he writes of being "more and more dubious of our being able to carry into execution the operations we have in contemplation," is in *WGW* 22:272. GW writes to Lafayette that "it is more than probable that we shall also entirely change our plan of operations" in a July 30, 1781, letter in *WGW*, 22:433. GW writes of having "turned my views more seriously (than I had ever before done) to an operation to the southward" in his *Diaries*, 2:249. According to Lee Kennett in *The French Forces in America*, GW "most likely evaded the subject [of marching to the Chesapeake] for the same reason that Rochambeau wanted to open it. The French would want to make advance preparations . . . [that] could well be disastrous, since news of the preparations would soon reach Clinton. As usual, Washington placed great emphasis on secrecy and surprise," p. 129. On Allan McLane's secret mission to Haiti aboard the *Congress*, see Fred Cook's "Allan McLane: Unknown Hero of the Revolution," www.americanheritage.com/content/allan-mclane-unknown-hero-revolution. GW's Aug. 2, 1781, letter to Robert Morris, in which he discusses the possibility of securing the vessels he needed in Philadelphia to transport his troops "at the moment they may be wanted," is in *WGW*, 22:450. Richard Borkow in *George Washington's Westchester Gamble* cites Richard Peters's account of how GW responded to the news that de Grasse was sailing to the Chesapeake and not Sandy Hook with "expressions of intemperate passion," as well as how he appeared at breakfast soon after "as composed as if nothing extraordinary had happened," p. 141. According to Borkow, "Washington's initial irritation was no doubt due to the summary cancellation of his plans and the sudden narrowing of his options. . . . [H]e had requested, even if the allies were to turn to a southern operation, that de Grasse's fleet arrive first in New York Harbor. The American army could then, he hoped, be transported to Virginia aboard de Grasse's ships and the dangers associated with a long march avoided," p. 141. GW's quartermaster, Timothy Pickering, also witnessed GW's anger over the news about de Grasse and recorded this remarkable cry of anguish from his commander in chief: "I wish to the Lord the French would not raise our expectation [of] a cooperation, or fulfill them!" in Octavius Pickering and Charles Upham's *The Life of Timothy Pickering*, 2:55.

My account of Cuba and the Old Bahama Channel is based largely on the 2015 *Sailing Directions of the Caribbean Sea*, published by the National Geospatial-Intelligence Agency, 1:45–65. In *Admiral De Grasse*, Lewis writes of how the Old Bahama Channel provided de Grasse with "a safer rendezvous" point with the *Aigrette* while making it less likely "the British would learn of the probable destination of the fleet," p. 140. Goussencourt, in Shea's *Operations of the French Fleet*, writes of the "unsupportable contrariety of winds" and how the *Northumberland* was almost lost on a reef while in the narrowest portion of the Old Bahama Channel, pp. 62–63; an anonymous officer, whose journal is also in Shea, refers to "the old channel, the famous dreaded channel, where no French fleet had ever passed," p. 152. Saavedra writes of how "[a]midst all this difficulty a decision urgently had to be made" when he heard that a recent convoy to Spain had taken most of the public money off the island in his *Journal*, p. 211. In "Las Damas de la Havana, El Precursor, and Francisco de Saavedra," James Lewis explains the reasons that Saavedra was able to raise the money so quickly in Havana and dispels the myth of "*las damas de la Havana*," while listing those who contributed the 500,000 pesos, pp. 96–98. The reference to this money providing the basis "upon which the edifice of American independence was raised" is in the notes to Saavedra's *Journal*, p. 213. Lafayette's Aug. 6, 1781, letter to GW, in which he explains the reasons for the "fluctuation in my intelligences" about Cornwallis's activities in the Chesapeake and speculates about the "happy turn" American fortunes would take with the appearance of the French fleet, is in *LAAR*, 4:300. Edmund Morgan in *The Genius of George Washington* cites GW's 1777 letter to Thomas Nelson about the dangers of positioning an army on the "narrow neck of land" at Yorktown, p. 8. GW writes of the epiphany he experienced when he learned that Cornwallis had taken up a position at Yorktown ("as clear to my view as a ray of light") in a July 31, 1788, letter to Noah Webster, available at *Founders Online*, National Archives, last modified March 30, 2017, http://founders.archives.gov/documents/Washington /04-06-02-0376.

CHAPTER 7 * "THE SPUR OF SPEED"

Major Samuel Shaw's angry July 12, 1780, letter, in which he claims "'Tis really abominable, that we should send to France *for* soldiers, when there are so many sons of America idle," is in John Lamb, *Memoir of the Life and Times of General John Lamb*, p. 243. For an excellent account of how an eighteenth-century siege was conducted, see the chapter "Siege Warfare" in James Falkner's *Marshall Vauban and the Defense of Louis XIV's France*, pp. 21–45. On how d'Estaing's 1778 decision to abandon the attack on Newport and sail to Boston instead forced American forces under General Sullivan (with some help from NG) to retreat across Rhode Island's Aquidneck Island, see my *Valiant Ambition*, pp. 218–19. GW's Aug. 15, 1781, letter to de Barras, in which he encourages the French admiral to abandon his plans to sail for Newfoundland and "form the junction, and as soon as possible, with Admiral de Grasse in

Chesapeake Bay," is in *WGW*, 22:500. Douglas Southall Freeman writes of Hamilton's sending in his commission and GW's use of Tilghman to assure Hamilton that he would receive the field position he desired in *George Washington*, 5:310. I cite GW's description of the New England militiamen he inherited at Boston as "an exceeding dirty and nasty people" in *Bunker Hill*, pp. 241–42. Baron von Closen observes, "Three quarters of the Rhode Island regiment consists of negroes, and that regiment is the most neatly dressed, the best under arms, and the most precise in its maneuvers," in his *Revolutionary Journal*, p. 92; von Closen also makes the remark about how "incredible" it is an army of "men of every age, even of children of fifteen, of whites and blacks, almost naked, unpaid, and rather poorly fed" can "withstand fire so steadfastly," adding, "I admire the American troops tremendously," p. 92. In *The Genius of George Washington*, Edmund Morgan quotes GW's advice to be "not too familiar, lest you subject yourself to a want of that respect, which is necessary to support a proper command," while making the observation "The remoteness that still surrounds him was a necessary adjunct of the power he was called upon to exercise," p. 7. Von Closen writes of "[t]he calm and calculated measure" of GW in his *Revolutionary Journal*, p. 92.

Charles Rappleye writes insightfully of Morris's efforts to assist GW's Yorktown campaign; according to Rappleye, "the loose coalition of moderates who became the Nationalist faction . . . emerged as the most capable and most adroit administrators the struggle would produce," in *Robert Morris*, p. 228. Robert Selig in *March to Victory* cites James Hendricks's Aug. 21, 1781, letter, in which he predicts the French army's use of specie "will effectively prevent the [American] commissioners from procuring any [provisions]," pp. 32–33; Selig also writes of how Robert Morris and Timothy Pickering divided up the commissary duties with Morris "in charge of finding supplies [and] Pickering and his staff focused on selecting roads and campsites," p. 30; and how Pickering "after being informed of Washington's decision to march to Virginia, had only four days to accomplish myriad supporting tasks," p. 30. In an Aug. 19, 1781, entry in his *Revolutionary Journal*, von Closen writes of how the French commissary had been "sent to make some purchases of flour and some forages along the right bank of the North River under the pretext of having some ovens built for the army at Chatham. That there would be many demonstrations there, and that the necessary bricks would even be collected along the Raritan," p. 104. James Thacher in his *Military Journal* writes of how GW "makes the great plans and designs under an impenetrable veil of secrecy" and how "[o]ur situation reminds me of some theatrical exhibition," pp. 261–62. GW writes of how "[t]he success of our enterprise depends upon the celerity of our movements" in an Aug. 24, 1781, letter to Benjamin Lincoln in *WGW*, 23:43. GW writes of how the entire French army halted "for the purpose of bringing up our rear as because we had heard not of the arrival of de Grasse and [I] was unwilling to discover our real object to the enemy" in an Aug. 29, 1781, entry in his *Diaries*, 2:257. In an Aug. 27, 1781, letter to Col. Samuel Miles, GW writes of how he "delayed having these preparations made until this moment, because I wished to deceive the enemy with regard to our real object as long as possible," in *WGW*, 23:54–55. GW's Aug. 28, 1781, letter to Lt. William Colfax, in which he complains of Colfax's unavailability and requests that "[w]hen business or inclination (especially on a march) calls you from your command I should be glad to know it," is in *WGW*, 23:62. In a Sept. 6, 1781, letter to Timothy Pickering, GW writes that it is of the "utmost importance . . . that gent. who are acting at the head of departments should at this present period be with the troops," adding he should "join them with all possible dispatch," in *WGW*, 23:92.

Samuel Hood's letter to Henry Clinton, written at sea on Aug. 25, 1781, which includes a listing of his "line of battle" and the confident statement "And I trust you will think it equal fully to defeat any designs of the enemy, let de Grasse bring or send what ships he may in aid of those under Barras," is quoted in French Ensor Chadwick, ed., *The Graves Papers*,

p. 141. In an Aug. 30, 1781, letter to Philip Stephens, Hood writes, "I put to sea on Aug. 10 at dawn of day, not caring to wait for the St. Lucia ships, lest the enemy should get to America before me," quoted in Chadwick's *The Graves Papers*, pp. 57–58; in the same letter, he recounts "finding no enemy had appeared either in the Chesapeake or Delaware," p. 58. Months later, in a May 4, 1782, letter to Philip Stephens in *The Graves Papers*, Graves insisted that Hood "never saw the Capes of the Chesapeake, nor any other land until he made the Neversink [coastal highlands near Sandy Hook]," p. 161. In "New Light on the Battle Off the Virginia Capes: Graves vs. Hood," Michael Crawford, using coordinates from the logs of Hood's fleet, convincingly makes the case that Graves was correct, http://www.tandfonline .com/eprint/YTYCdX47G7KDpdGAiQhy/full. William Smith writes that "Sir Henry is all mystery, seems to approve but changes and resolves nothing," in an Aug. 1, 1781, entry in his *Memoirs*, p. 429. Andrew O'Shaughnessy in *The Men Who Lost America* discusses the well-paid and exceedingly comfortable life Clinton had constructed for himself in New York, p. 238. Smith writes of the sycophants in Clinton's military family along with the despairing judgment, "Poor Sir Henry! His want of parts renders him insensible of his dangers," in an Aug. 15, 1781, entry in his *Memoirs*, p. 430. Clinton makes the claim that "I was in no capacity to interrupt [GW's] march to the southward whenever he pleased to make it" and that he "could not entertain the most distant suspicion that [GW] really intended to march his army to the Chesapeake" because he "had every reason to be certain of our having a naval superiority" in *The American Rebellion*, pp. 327–28.

In an Aug. 30, 1781, letter to Philip Stephens, Graves writes, "Whether the French intend a junction, or whether they have left the coast, is only to be guessed at," in Chadwick's *The Graves Papers*, p. 53. Hood describes his meeting with Clinton and Graves and how "I humbly submitted the necessity which struck me very forcibly of such of Graves's squadron as were ready coming without the bar immediately," in an Aug. 30, 1781, letter to Philip Stephens, in *The Graves Papers*, p. 58. Smith recounts how Clinton and Graves were "not fond of" Hood's proposal to sail for the Chesapeake immediately, as well as Hood's declaration "that the French are gone to Havana and will be coming here," and that the British fleet "will be superior to the united force of French and Spaniards after their detachment for the trade home" in an Aug. 29, 1781, entry in his *Memoirs*, p. 435. On the incident leading to Graves's court-martial in 1757, see John Tilley's *The British Navy and the American Revolution*, p. 127.

GW's Sept. 2, 1781, letter to Lafayette, in which he expresses his fear that "by occupying the Chesapeake," the British fleet will "frustrate all our flattering prospects in that quarter," is in *WGW*, 23:77. GW's Sept. 4, 1781, letter to NG, in which he admits that "the present time is as interesting and anxious a moment as I have ever experienced," is in *WGW*, 23:85. James Thacher writes of how "[o]ur destination can no longer be a secret" in his *Military Journal*, p. 262. GW enclosed the list of wood flats, schooners, and sloops capable of carrying 4150 men with his Aug. 31, 1781, letter to Benjamin Lincoln in *WGW*, 23:71; he advises Lincoln that "[s]ome delicacy must be used" in making sure the American soldiers left room for the French in an Aug. 28, 1781, letter to Lincoln, p. 60. Rochambeau tells of how the Delaware River was low enough that his army was able to cross it at a fording place "near Trenton" in his *Memoirs*, p. 62. Rappleye describes how GW and Rochambeau and their staffs took over Morris's house on Front Street in Philadelphia, "Mattresses were strewn on the floor, and for the next week the house served as temporary headquarters for the allied high command," in *Robert Morris*, p. 260. GW's Sept. 2, 1781, instructions to Lt. Col. Jean Baptiste Gouvion, in which he is ordered to assess the condition of the roads to the south and "excite the inhabitants," is in *WGW*, 23:79. GW writes of his "strongest fears" concerning his army not receiving enough provisions in a country "otherwise well provided" is in a Sept. 3, 1781, circular sent to the states of New Jersey, Delaware, and Maryland in *WGW*, 23:81–82. Rappleye writes of the "hybrid currency" Morris created, which came to be called Morris notes, or "Bobs" for short, in *Robert Morris*, pp. 258–59. In an Aug. 9, 1781, entry in his *Diary*, Frederick Mackenzie recounts a report by a British spy claiming the Americans are "very ill supplied with provisions. . . . At the same time the French troops were furnished with one and half pounds of bread per day, and numbers of them came into the Continental camp and offered to sell their loaves, which weight 3 pound for half a dollar in cash, as no other money is circulating. This has given great offense to the Continental soldiers and militia, who abuse the French and say that they who have never done any service to the country are well paid, fed and clothed, while themselves, who have been fighting for the country, are almost destitute of everything. The French soldiers are frequently knocked down, and their loaves taken from them. The French will not suffer the Rebel soldiers to come into their encampment," 2:583–84.

Thacher describes how the American soldiers marched "in slow and solemn step" through Philadelphia while kicking up "a dust like a smothering snow storm" in his *Military Journal*, pp. 263–64. Lee Kennett in *The French Forces in America* recounts how the French soldiers paused outside of Philadelphia to powder their hair and put on their white gaiters, p. 135, while Thacher notes that rather than the fife and drum of the Americans, the French employed "a complete band of music" in his *Military Journal*, p. 264. Baron von Closen writes of the sensation created by "the gilded contingent" of the French army in Philadelphia in his *Revolutionary Journal*, p. 120. Jean-Baptiste-Antoine de Verger describes how President Thomas McKean asked Rochambeau "if it would be proper for him to salute the field officers" in *ACRA*, p. 134.

GW's Sept. 2, 1781, letter to Lafayette, in which he confesses to being "distressed beyond expression" and requests that he send any news of de Grasse *"on the Spur of Speed,"* is in *WGW*, 23:77. Clinton's Sept. 2, 1781, letter to Cornwallis, in which he reveals that GW "is moving an army to the southward with an appearance of haste," is in Benjamin Franklin Stevens, ed., *The Campaign in Virginia*, 2:149. Mackenzie writes of how Clinton has allowed GW "to advance a good way into Jersey, without molestation or obstruction; while the army in Virginia . . . is now entirely unprepared for being attacked by a fleet and an army," in an Aug. 29, 1781, entry in his *Journal*, p. 606. GW writes of "everything in a tolerable train" in Philadelphia in a Sept. 5, 1781, entry in his *Diaries*, 2:258. Von Closen describes how Mauduit du Plessis served as their tour guide as Rochambeau and his officers sailed down the Delaware River during their tour of the fortifications at Fort Mifflin, Red Bank, and Billingsport in his *Revolutionary Journal*, pp. 121–23. Guillaume de Deux-Ponts writes of how GW is "of a natural coldness and of a serious and noble approach" in *ACRA*, p. 126. Douglas Southall Freeman recounts how GW received the packet of expresses from Mordecai Gist about three miles past Chester, Pennsylvania, in *George Washington*, 5:321. In describing GW's astonishing demonstration of joy on the Chester waterfront, Baron von Closen writes, "One must experience such circumstances to appreciate the effect that such gratifying news can have," in his *Revolutionary Journal*, p. 123. James Thacher describes how the city of Philadelphia reacted to the news of de Grasse and how "[s]ome merry fellows mounted on scaffolds and stages" in his *Military Journal*, p. 265. The Duc de Lauzun makes the claim that "I have never seen a man more overcome with great and sincere joy" in his *Memoirs*, p. 204. Guillaume de Deux-Ponts recounts how GW "put aside his character as arbiter of North America and contented himself for the moment with that of a citizen, happy at the good fortune of his country," in *ACRA*, p. 126. Baron von Closen writes of how GW and Rochambeau "embraced *warmly* on the shore" in *Revolutionary Journal*, p. 123; von Closen also insists that "one must not count his chickens before they are hatched," p. 123.

Cornwallis's Sept. 1, 1781, note to Clinton, *"An enemy's fleet within the Capes, between 30 and 40 ships of war, mostly large,"* is in Stevens's *The Campaign in Virginia*, 2:147. Clinton's Sept. 6, 1781, letter to Cornwallis, in which he writes, "I can have no doubt that Washington is moving with at least 6000 French and rebel troops against you," is also in Stevens, pp. 152–53. Frederick Mackenzie makes the prediction that "an action must ensue" between de Grasse and Graves in a Sept. 3, 1781, entry in his *Diary*, p. 612. William Smith predicts, "A week will decide perhaps the ruin or salvation of the British Empire," in a Sept. 4, 1781, entry in his *Memoirs*, p. 438. Robert Selig in *March to Victory* lists the number of vessels assembled at Head of Elk, and details how many men from both armies traveled by water and by land, p. 40. Jonathan Trumbull writes of how "[t]he country through which we have passed [was] greatly pleased with the prospect of our expedition" in a Sept. 7, 1781, entry in "Minutes of Occurrences Respecting the Siege and Capture of Yorktown," p. 333. GW writes of how "no circumstance could possibly have happened more opportunely" in his announcement of de Grasse's arrival in the Chesapeake to the American troops in the general orders of Sept. 6, 1781, in *WGW*, 23:93–94. Selig in *March to Victory* cites Robert Morris's worried observation that the American soldiers showed "great symptoms of discontent . . . on their passing through this city," p. 39. GW's Sept. 6, 1781, letter to Robert Morris, pleading that the money to pay the Continental soldiers be delivered "on the Wings of speed" is in *WGW*, 23:89. Charles Rappleye in *Robert Morris* details the complex negotiations between Morris and Rochambeau that resulted in the loan of the specie and how the American paymaster dramatically knocked off the heads of the casks of borrowed coins, pp. 261–62. John Hudson's claim that the money he received at Head of Elk was the "only pay that I ever drew for my service during the war" is in Selig's *March to Victory*, p. 40.

Jonathan Trumbull describes the "[g]reat joy" in Baltimore on GW's arrival in a Sept. 8, 1781, entry in "Minutes," p. 333. I have relied on Robert and Lee Dalzell's *George Washington's Mount Vernon* for my description of the two major renovations of GW's house, pp. 47–49, 67–69, 90–93. The Dalzells write of "Lund's understandable doubts about the wisdom of spending so much time, energy, and money rebuilding a house that might at any minute be destroyed," p. 103. In *Valiant Ambition* I cite GW's Sept. 30, 1776, letter to Lund Washington, in which he writes of being in "an unhappy, divided state," while detailing changes to the new room on the north end of the house, pp. 19–20. The Dalzells chronicle the progress of Mount Vernon's renovations through the war years in *George Washington's Mount Vernon*, pp. 107–11. GW's March 28, 1781, letter to Lund, in which he asks him a long list of questions about the house and then adds, "An account of these things would be satisfactory to me . . . as I have these kind of improvements very much at heart," is in *WGW*, 21:386. GW writes of "a spirit of exertion" he was pleased to observe in Maryland in a Sept. 11, 1781, letter to Governor Thomas Sim Lee in *WGW*, 23:112. GW writes of having "reached my own seat at Mount Vernon (distant 120 miles from Head of Elk) where I staid till the 12" in his *Diaries*, 2:260. The Dalzells cite an Aug. 19, 1776, letter to Lund, in which GW details the kinds of trees to be planted "without any order or regularity (but pretty thick, as they can at any time be thin'd)" on the north and south ends of the house, in *George Washington's Mount Vernon*, p. 108. The October entry in a 2018 calendar published by the Mount Vernon Ladies' Association in cooperation with George Washington's Mount Vernon states that "[t]he most prominent feature on the 3rd floor [of Mount Vernon] is the large oval or 'oxeye' window," which has recently undergone restoration by the organization's preservation carpenter. The Dalzells state that GW's "first rebuilding of Mount Vernon was not particularly original," while detailing how he decided "to stray . . . from the path of architectural correctness" by adding features (the cupola and the piazza) in the second renovation that were in GW's description "things not quite orthodox," in *George Washington's Mount Vernon*, pp. 90–93; they also cite Bryan Fairfax's 1778 letter to GW in which he writes, "I like the house because it is uncommon," p. 5.

GW's Sept. 9, 1781, letter to Peter Waggoner ordering the local Virginia militia to improve the roads is in *WGW*, 23:109. Selig writes that a supply train of 1500 horses, 800 oxen, and 220 wagons headed to Virginia from Maryland in *March to Victory,* p. 41. The Dalzells write that "[t]he new roof leaked, and badly" and describe the unfinished north room as "an empty shell" in *George Washington's Mount Vernon,* p. 113. Jonathan Trumbull describes Mount Vernon as "[a]n elegant seat and situation, great appearance of opulence and real exhibitions of hospitality and princely entertainment," in a Sept. 11, 1781, entry in "Minutes," p. 333. GW's Sept. 10, 1781, letter to Lafayette, in which he asks him to "keep Lord Cornwallis safe, without provisions or forage until we arrive," is in *WGW,* 23:110. Trumbull describes GW being "[m]uch agitated" after receiving the message that "[t]he French were gone out from the bay in pursuit of the English" in his Sept. 13, 1781, entry in his "Minutes," p. 333.

CHAPTER 8 • *"Ligne de Vitesse"*

According to Olivier Chaline, de Grasse's fleet was pushed so far to the northeast by the Gulf Stream during its passage from Cuba that it actually overshot the Chesapeake. Chaline has also determined that at one point de Grasse's fleet was so close to Hood's (which had left the Caribbean after the French) that the two fleets may have even sighted vessels from each other's squadrons in "Season, Winds and Sea: The Improbable Route of de Grasse to the Chesapeake," https://vimeo.com/174351130. In a Sept. 4, 1781, letter to GW, Louis Lebègue Duportail writes, "When 27 of line are in Chesapeake, when great American and French forces are joined, we must take Lord Cornwallis or be all dishonored," in Washington and de Grasse, *Correspondence of General Washington and Comte de Grasse, 1781, August 1–November 4* (subsequently referred to as *Correspondence*), p. 13. Charles Lee Lewis cites the Comte d'Orvilliers's 1772 assessment of de Grasse as "the best skilled captain in the squadron," as well as how "[h]is frequent collisions with other ships . . . seems to demand something more perfect in his estimate of a situation at a glance," in *Admiral De Grasse and American Independence,* p. 49. GW writes of how de Grasse's character was "marred by his own impetuosity" in an April 28, 1788, letter to Rochambeau in the Washington Papers, https://founders .archives.gov/documents/Washington/04-06-02-0212; see also www.revolutionary-war-and -beyond.com/george-washington-letter-to-the-marquis-de-lafayette-april-28-1788.html. The reference to de Grasse's "[f]eeling the full cost of time" appears in "Summary of the Campaign Through the End of October 1781" (which may have been authored by de Grasse himself) in ANM B4 184, at LOC. In a Sept. 2, 1781, letter to GW, Duportail, who had just spoken in detail with de Grasse, refers to the fact that Cornwallis's works at Yorktown "shall be forced with difficulty" in *Correspondence,* p. 13. One of the more undermanned ships in de Grasse's fleet was the 80-gun *Auguste,* captained by Louis-Antoine de Bougainville, which was missing 200 of her approximately 700-man crew, according to Jean-Marie Kowalski in "The Battle of the Chesapeake from the Quarterdeck," p. 4. De Grasse describes the officers and sailors who transported Saint-Simon's troops up the James River as "the best drilled part of the crew" in the account attributed to him in John Shea, ed., *The Operations of the French Fleet Under the Count de Grasse,* p. 155. In a Sept. 4, 1781, letter to GW, de Grasse writes, "I am doing the impossible to hasten [the arrival] of your troops, by sending to meet you six or seven men-of-war, chosen from amongst those of my fleet which draw the least water, in order to take on board the greatest number possible. These ships will be followed by frigates, and generally by every ship fit to mount the river," in *Correspondence,* pp. 18–19. Lafayette was mindful of de Grasse's overly impetuous nature; in a Sept. 1, 1781, letter to GW, he writes, "My little influence will be employed in preaching patience as our affairs cannot be spoiled unless we do spoil them ourselves," in *LAAR,* 4:382.

According to J. A. Sullivan, "Certainly Graves was not considered by the Admiralty to be fit to be in chief command of a fleet," in "Graves and Hood," p. 175. Sam Willis in

Fighting at Sea in the Eighteenth Century points out that Graves was "fresh from the Channel Fleet, where he had been well schooled in the tolerant command methods of Howe and Kempenfelt," while Hood "had been schooled in unquestioning obedience to the exact wording of signals by the intolerant Rodney," p. 101. In *Rodney,* David Spinney cites the letter in which Rodney reminds a subordinate that "the painful task of thinking belongs to me," p. 330. Sullivan in "Graves and Hood" writes that Hood "expected de Grasse to take twelve sail of the line to America, 'about the number they had coppered,'" because he was "confident that de Grasse could not abandon a convoy and the whole of the West Indies and Jamaica stations," p. 183. In a Sept. 14, 1781, letter to Philip Stephens, Graves writes, "We soon discovered a number of great ships at anchor, which seemed to be extended across the entrance of the Chesapeake, from Cape Henry to the Middle Ground," in French Ensor Chadwick, ed., *The Graves Papers,* p. 62. In a Sept. 16, 1781, letter to George Jackson, Hood tells how by 11:00 a.m. on Sept. 5, the French fleet was visible "with their topsail yards hoisted aloft as a signal for getting under sail," in Chadwick, *The Graves Papers,* p. 87.

My description of the activities of the French fleet during the Battle of the Chesapeake are based on the logs of the *Marseilles, Auguste, Zélé, Saint Esprit, Pluton,* and *Citoyen,* as well as accounts by de Grasse and other participants in the battle. All English translations of French logs were performed for the author by Carol Harris. Ensign Fabry of the *Auguste* describes how on Sept. 5 the frigate *Aigrette,* "which was anchored very near the coast outside Cape Henry, apparently having dragged its anchor due to the strength of the tide, made signals to request assistance," in ANM B4 235, at LOC. In a French log from ANM B4 184 reprinted in Chadwick, *The Graves Papers,* the log keeper writes, "Ten o'clock the *Marseilles* signaled six sails in the West; next, it signaled twenty-five," p. 212. According to the log keeper of the *Citoyen* in ANM B4 238, reprinted in Chadwick, *The Graves Papers,* "The ships that were anchored the farthest out in the bay signaled twenty-five sails to the east," p. 228. According to Colin Pengelly in *Sir Samuel Hood and the Battle of the Chesapeake,* "It is hard to understand why de Grasse was so unprepared for the appearance of a British fleet on the coast. Given the fifty-fifty chance that the next fleet he saw would be hostile, a prudent commander would have moored in a more defensible manner and had his frigates more widely spread to give adequate warning," p. 134. Jean-Marie Kowalski in "The Battle of the Chesapeake from the Quarterdeck" writes that "the French ships cannot raise their second anchor because this operation could not be completed without a light craft," p. 4. Kowalski stated that de Grasse's order for a *"ligne de vitesse"* marked only the second time in the history of the French navy that a battle had begun under these circumstances, in an interview with the author on Oct. 4, 2016, in Brest. Chevalier Balthazar de Gras-Préville, captain of the *Zélé,* records in his log that de Grasse made the "[s]ignal to form a battle line regardless of assigned positions [*ligne de vitesse, ligne de bataille formés sans égard aux postes précédement assignés au vaisseaux qui doivent la composer*]," in ANM B4 259, at LOC. Chevalier de Thy's account of sailing his 74 *Citoyen* out of the Chesapeake on Sept. 5 is in ANM B4 238, at LOC, and reprinted in Chadwick, *The Graves Papers,* pp. 227–31. Ensign Fabry describes how the *Caton* inserted itself between the *César* and the *Destin,* and how "[t]he latter only saved its bowsprit by backing all sails," in ANM B4 235, at LOC.

Karl Tornquist tells of de Grasse's "brutal" character, and how "with the sharpest reproaches made known the dissatisfaction he felt with the behavior of some of the captains," in *The Naval Campaigns of Count de Grasse During the American Revolution,* p. 108. Chevalier de Goussencourt in Shea's *The Operations of the French Fleet* describes the state in which the French fleet left the Chesapeake on Sept. 5: "The fleet formed in a very bad order; for, to tell the truth, there were only four vessels in line, the *Pluto,* the *Bourgogne,* the *Marseilles,* and the *Diadème.* The *Reflechi* and the *Caton* came next, half a league to the lee of the first; and the rest of the fleet a league more to the lee of the latter, the *Ville de Paris* in the center;

the English were in the best possible order, bowsprit to stern, bearing down on us, and consequently to our windward," p. 69. Hood's Sept. 6, 1781, memorandum, in which he details how the French vanguard would have been "demolished . . . a full hour and [a] half . . . before any of the [French] rear could have come up" if Graves had immediately attacked is in Chadwick, *The Graves Papers*, p. 90. De Gras-Préville, captain of the *Zélé*, writes of how "[t]he English army bore away before the wind a bit to make us suspect its intention was to cross these ships' course" in his log in ANM B4 259, at LOC. According to Kowalski, "As the British were still approaching very fast and heading southwest, some French officers come to think that the British intended to cut the line," p. 5. In his *Diary*, Frederick Mackenzie quotes an account of the battle clearly penned by Graves (or someone under his direction): "The French van had extended themselves considerably too much from their own center and seemed to present the favorable moment for an attack," 2:644. Willis in *Fighting at Sea* writes of how "the West Indies squadron worked with a signal book altered by Rodney, while the North American squadron used those altered and issued by Arbuthnot in 1779–80, to which Graves had supplemented a list of 49 signals in 1781. With only five days elapsing between the fleets joining for the first time and the engagement, there was insufficient time to achieve a shared doctrine in either detail or application," p. 101. See also Sullivan's "Graves and Hood," which goes into detail about signal confusion during the battle, pp. 185–87.

Graves's Sept. 14, 1781, letter to Philip Stephens, in which he writes of how he adjusted his line so as to "bring his Majesty's fleet nearly parallel to the line of approach of the enemy," is in Chadwick's *The Graves Papers*, p. 62. In *Sir Samuel Hood and the Battle of the Chesapeake*, Pengelly points out that by ordering his fleet to jibe in unison, Graves "reversed the order so that Drake's division was in the leading position and Hood's in the rear. Drake's was the weakest part of the British fleet, yet when the action came it would be exposed to the brunt of the French fire," p. 136. The log keeper of the *London* recorded that Graves signaled for the fleet to be "brought to" so as to "let the center of the enemy's ships come abreast of us," as well as the timing of the admiral's decision to engage the French: "The enemy's ships advancing very slow, and evening approaching, the Admiral, judging this to be the moment of attack, made the signal for the ships to bear down and engage their opponents; filled the main-topsail and bore down to the enemy," reprinted in William Graves's *Two Letters Respecting the Conduct of Rear-Admiral Graves in North America*, p. 8. When it comes to the confusion created by Graves's signals during the battle, Sullivan writes, "The evidence of the logs of the vital ships in the signaling system, i.e. the repeating flagships and frigates, all go against Graves, and sufficient evidence being available as to the confusion of signals, it has to be accepted that Graves's Admirals and Captains had to fight their battle on what they thought was being signaled and divined," in "Graves and Hood," pp. 187–88.

With the exception of Kowalski and Pengelly, commentators have tended to ignore the effect that the more than 30-degree shift in wind had on the dynamics of this two-hour battle, which contributed to the isolation of the two vans and made it difficult for the ships in the rearguards to enter the battle. According to Pengelly, the wind shift "took away from the British some of the advantage they had enjoyed in the windward position," while placing de Grasse's "van further to windward of the center, leaving it unsupported," p. 146. One of the best contemporary accounts of the effect the wind shift had on the battle is in "Summary of the Campaign Through the End of October 1781": "Battle was joined very briskly, but the winds which headed by 3 points [33 degrees] at the moment the action commenced, prevented it from becoming generalized for the reason that both [fleets] found themselves on a bow and quarter line and that the English rear-guard and part of their center, which at this point were no longer within range of our line, sailed close-hauled to remain in the wake of their van which found itself too closely squeezed by ours to be able to bear down more itself," in ANM B4 184, at LOC. Even without the wind shift, the length of the British line would have, as Sullivan points out in "Graves and Hood," made it doubtful "whether Hood starting the battle a mile or so behind the center division, which itself never engaged close, could ever have obtained the glorious victory which was expected of him," p. 191. De Gras-Préville, captain of the *Zélé*, records in his log how "[f]rom the center the [rest of the] two navies looked on," in ANM B4 259, at LOC.

Aboard the *Auguste*, Fabry records in his log, "The *Auguste* was one of the first to get under sail, and immediately set all sails to reach the head of the line, abandoning a kedge anchor and a hawser," in ANM B4 235, at LOC. Mary Kimbrough, in *Louis-Antoine de Bougainville*, cites Diderot's description of Bougainville's being "ballasted to starboard by a treatise on differential and integral calculus and to port by a voyage around the world," p. 27; she also discusses the division within the French navy according to "Reds" and "Blues," explaining that in the case of the latter, "some were nobles who had begun their careers in the army and then transferred to the navy, men who had never been marine guards. . . . Others were merchant marine officers, often pressed into royal service during wartime, and still others were non-nobles, like Bougainville, who had transferred from other military branches. . . . These 'intrus,' or intruders, were the object of scorn by the reds, often because of their 'humble birth,'" pp. 50–51. See also Michael Duffy's "Types of Naval Leadership in the Eighteenth Century," in which he cites a contemporary reference to how in the French navy "they all hate each other," p. 52. Francisco Saavedra tells how each French ship of the line "is a battlefield" in his *Journal*, p. 189. Tornquist in *The Naval Campaigns of Count de Grasse* recounts how de Grasse and Bougainville were on "unfriendly terms" after the engagement off Martinique on April 29, 1781, p. 62. According to Captain de Thy of the *Citoyen*, the "oblique positions" of the ships in the British van meant that the French "could fight them with advantage," in a log reprinted in Chadwick's *The Graves Papers*, p. 231. Fabry on the *Auguste* writes of "the enemy's van having sailed . . . to a very small half-cannon-range . . . [before] the firing [became] fiercely engaged." Fabry also writes that the first five ships in the French van were "the *Pluton*, the *Bourgogne*, the *Marseilles*, the *Auguste*, and the *St. Esprit*," in ANM B4 235, at LOC. In a Sept. 16, 1781, letter to George Jackson, Hood writes that the *Shrewsbury* was "totally disabled very early from keeping her station by having her fore and main topsail yards shot away, which left her second (the *Intrepid*) exposed to two ships of superior force," in Chadwick, *The Graves Papers*, p. 90. Goussencourt, in Shea's *The Operations of the French Fleet*, writes that soon after the beginning of the fighting the British "poured their first broadside into the *Reflechi*, killing the captain," p. 70. Captain de Thy of the *Citoyen* writes, "All that could be seen was fire and smoke on either side," in Chadwick, *The Graves Papers*, p. 232.

Goussencourt writes of how the *Princessa* "set fire to [the *Diadème*] at every shot, the wadding entering her side," in Shea's *The Operations of the French Fleet*, p. 71; Goussencourt also describes the difficulties the French van experienced in attempting to comply with de Grasse's order to bear off more than 20 degrees in the midst of the battle: "Then DG signaled to the vessels at the head of the line, to bear away two points, which was impracticable, as they were fighting within gun-shot distance, and would have got a very severe handling, had they presented the stern. The four ships in the van found themselves, consequently, entirely cut off from the rest of the fleet and constantly engaged with seven or eight vessels at close quarters," pp. 70–71. Fabry on the *Auguste* writes of how by 5:00 p.m., the enemy had come "within the infinitesimally small range of langridge shot," in ANM B4 235, at LOC. Kimbrough in *Louis-Antoine de Bougainville* cites Bougainville's claim, "We fought so closely that the Comte de Grasse told me publicly at our first interview [afterward]: 'That is what I call fighting; I thought you had boarded!,'" p. 184. In *The Naval Campaigns of Count de Grasse*, Tornquist recounts how the bowline was shot off the foretopsail of the *Auguste* and how it was ultimately repaired, pp. 62–63. According to William Falconer's *A New Universal Dictionary of the Marine*, a bowline is "a rope fastened near the middle of the leech, or perpendicular edge of the square sails, by three or four subordinate parts, called bridles. It is only used when . . . the sails must be all braced sideways, or close-hauled to the wind: In this situation, the bowlines are employed to keep the weather, or windward, edges of the principal sails tight forward and steady, without which they would be always shivering, and rendered incapable of service," p. 54. According to John Harland's *Seamanship in the Age of Sail*, in the event of the bowline's parting, "[i]f the weather permits, a man may be lowered from the yardarm to repair the damage. If not the sail must be got in and the work done on the yard," p. 298. Goussencourt in Shea's *Operations of the French Fleet* recounts how the *Auguste* "was too far to leeward and in no condition to relieve the *Diadème*, which could scarcely hold out," and how the *Saint Esprit* came to the *Diadème*'s aid by unleashing "a terrible fire" on the *Albion*, pp. 71–72. Captain Framond's account of the *Caton*'s heroics is in his Oct. 25, 1781, letter in ANM B4 184, at LOC. Goussencourt, who appears to have been aboard the *Saint Esprit*, writes, "For our part we were so tired that though within gunshot, the vans no longer fired," in Shea's *Operations of the French Fleet*, p. 72.

According to Captain de Thy on the *Citoyen*, "by crowding sail, we closed our line to the extent possible," in Chadwick's *The Graves Papers*, p. 232. According to Graves, "The van of the enemy bore away to enable their center to support them . . . ; the action did not entirely cease until a little after sunset. . . . [T]he center of the enemy continued to bear up as it advanced and at that moment seemed to have little more in view than to shelter their own van as it went away before the wind," in a Sept. 14, 1781, letter to Philip Stephens, in *The Graves Papers*, p. 62; in that same letter, Graves describes the damage to his own fleet while admitting that the French "had not the appearance of near so much damage as we had sustained," p. 63. Kimbrough in *Louis-Antoine de Bougainville* cites Bougainville's claim that "the admiral publicly declared to Generals Washington and Rochambeau that the honors of the day were due to me as commander of the vanguard," p. 185. Tornquist writes of the "unfriendly terms" that had previously existed between de Grasse and Bougainville and how after the Battle of the Chesapeake, they "became attached to one another," in *The Naval Campaigns of Count de Grasse*, p. 62.

Harold Larrabee in *Decision at the Chesapeake* cites de Grasse's Sept. 7, 1781, letter to Bougainville, in which he writes of his hope that "we shall meet them at closer range tomorrow morning," pp. 215–16, as well as Bougainville's Sept. 9, 1781, journal entry, in which he writes of his fear "that the British might try to get to the Chesapeake under a press of sail," p. 218. In a Sept. 16, 1781, letter to George Jackson, Samuel Hood writes of "a most glorious opening" that Graves declined to take advantage of at the Battle of the Chesapeake in Chadwick, *The Graves Papers*, p. 87. The day after the battle, Graves wrote a memorandum about the use of signals that was, in the words of Sullivan, "intended as a rebuke to Hood" for not engaging the enemy earlier; Sullivan cites the note written by Lieutenant Graves of the *London* (a relative of the admiral) on a page of the memorandum insisting that "a most glorious victory was lost" by Hood's having "kept his wind," in "Graves and Hood," pp. 189–90. In *Decision at the Chesapeake*, Larrabee cites the interchange among Graves, Hood, and Drake that appeared in the London *Political and Military Journal* in 1782, p. 213. For the correspondence between Graves and Captain Finch of the *Terrible*, see Chadwick, *The Graves Papers*, pp. 108–9. The description of "the explosion of the *Terrible*" is recorded in the logbook of the *Royal Oak* in NA, ADM 51/815. The proceedings of Graves's Sept. 13, 1781, council of war, in which it was decided to "proceed with all dispatch to New York," is in Chadwick, *The Graves Papers*, p. 84; interestingly, Graves assumed he'd fought the combined fleets of de Grasse and de Barras at the Battle of the Chesapeake and learned that de Barras had reached the bay after the battle only once the British fleet had returned to New York.

Richard Ketchum in *Victory at Yorktown* cites St. George Tucker's description of Lafayette hugging GW "with as much ardor as ever an absent lover kissed his mistress on his return," p. 186. In a Sept. 25, 1781, letter to de Grasse, GW writes of how the Battle of the Chesapeake offers "the happiest presages of the most complete success" in *Correspondence*, p. 31. De Grasse complains of being "annoyed" at the slow progress of GW's army to the Chesapeake in a Sept. 16, 1781, letter to GW in *Correspondence*, p. 34. Jonathan Trumbull writes of "the fine little ship *Queen Charlotte*" in his "Minutes," p. 333. According to James Flexner, in *George Washington in the American Revolution*, GW "had always consistently avoided water travel. This visit to de Grasse comprised the first considerable trip over the open water he had made since he had accompanied, when in his teens, his dying brother to the tropical Indies," p. 450. In "George Washington: Waterman-Fisherman," Donald Leach writes that in 1770 a carpenter "sheathed the bottom of Washington's schooner with copper to protect the hull from teredo or shipworms," p. 17. Leach also discusses the importance of shad fishing to the economy of Mount Vernon, pp. 5–8; see also John McPhee's *The Founding Fish*, pp. 163–65. According to Edmund Morgan in *The Genius of George Washington*, GW "realized early in the war that without local naval superiority to stand off the British warships, he could not capture a British army at any point on the coast. Washington understood this better than his more experienced French helpers. The Comte de Grasse . . . seems to have missed the whole point of the Yorktown strategy, complaining to Washington that he would prefer to cruise off New York where he might encounter the main British fleet, rather than be an idle spectator in the Chesapeake," p. 9. According to Dudley Knox in *The Naval Genius of George Washington*, GW's "naval judgment on several occasions during the intricate operations within the Chesapeake was wisely deferred to by de Grasse and proved to be eminently sound," p. 127. Trumbull describes the French fleet as "a grand sight" in his "Minutes," p. 333. Flexner cites the legend that de Grasse hugged GW while exclaiming, *"Mon cher petit general!,"* in *George Washington in the American Revolution*, p. 449. De Grasse's promise to lend GW 2000 men for a coup de main is in *Correspondence*, p. 40. Trumbull describes the visit to the *Ville de Paris*, which he dubs "the world in miniature," in his "Minutes," p. 334. On Jean Audubon, father of John James Audubon and captain of the *Queen Charlotte*, see Richard Rhodes's *John James Audubon: The Making of an American*, pp. 4–5. Joseph Plumb Martin describes his travels to Williamsburg in *Ordinary Courage: The Revolutionary War Adventures of Joseph Plumb Martin* (subsequently referred to as *Journal*), pp. 140–44. James Thacher refers to the French fleet as "the most noble and majestic spectacle I ever witnessed" in his *Military Journal*, p. 269. Martin describes that same sight as "a swamp of dry pine trees" in his *Journal*, where he also writes about paying "our old acquaintance, the British, at Yorktown, a visit," p. 144.

In a Sept. 16–17, 1781, letter to Clinton, Cornwallis writes, "If I had no hopes of relief, I would rather risk an action than defend my half-finished works," in Benjamin Franklin Stevens, ed., *The Campaign in Virginia*, 2:157; after learning that de Barras's fleet had joined de Grasse's, he wrote, "If you cannot relieve me very soon, you must be prepared to hear the worst," p. 158. Captain Thomas Symonds's Sept. 8, 1781, letter to Graves, in which he details the ways in which he has helped Cornwallis invest Yorktown, including anchoring the *Guadaloupe* across a creek "to enfilade a gulley," is in Chadwick, *The Graves Papers*, pp. 103–4. Tornquist describes how the British fireships were "a beautiful and at the same time devastating sight," in *The Naval Campaigns of Count de Grasse*, pp. 65–66. In a Sept. 22, 1781, letter to GW, de Grasse hypothesizes that Cornwallis intended to use the fireships to win "temporary possession of the river" so that the British army could escape "the right bank of the James"; in that same letter, he writes, "It is time to begin to close in on the enemy, and to give him a taste of our combined strength," in *Correspondence*, p. 42. In a Sept. 23, 1781, letter to Thomas McKean, GW writes, "The intelligence [your letter] contains is so important, that

I immediately transmitted it to de Grasse whose superiority, even supposing Digby should have arrived with ten ships, will be considerable," in *WGW*, 23:129. Baron von Closen describes how de Grasse and the other French naval officers were "alarmed and disquieted" by the rumor of Digby's bringing another ten ships of the line to New York, in his *Journal*, p. 133. De Grasse tells GW that he must leave the Chesapeake and take up "a less disadvantageous position" outside the Capes in a Sept. 23, 1781, letter in *Correspondence*, pp. 45–46. GW's Sept. 24, 1781, letter in which he speaks of "the painful anxiety" de Grasse's decision has caused him, as well as de Grasse's Sept. 25, 1781, announcement "that the plans I had suggested for getting under way while the most brilliant and glorious did not appear to fulfill the aims we had in view," and GW's Sept. 27, 1781, reply "that a great mind knows how to make personal sacrifices," are all in *Correspondence*, pp. 48–54. Flexner in *George Washington in the American Revolution* cites Rochambeau's 1788 letter to GW in which he writes of de Grasse, "By the vivacity of his head, he did take always violent parts," p. 449. Trumbull writes of the "most wonderful and very observable coincidence of favorable circumstances" in his "Minutes," p. 334. GW writes of "[t]he line being formed" in his *Diaries*, 2:262.

CHAPTER 9 ✦ YORKTOWN

In an Oct. 1, 1781, letter to de Grasse, GW enumerates the many reasons for "stationing two or three ships above the enemy's posts on York River; for want of this only means completing the investment of their works—the British remain masters of the navigation for 25 miles distance above them, and have by their armed vessels, intercepted supplies of the greatest value on their way to our camp. . . . We are even necessitated for the protection of Williamsburg and the magazines in our rear to leave a post of 700–800 men in that quarter. . . . We are besides reduced to the impossibility of concerting measures with the corps of [allied] troops at Gloucester—being obliged in order to communicate with them to make a circuit of near 90 miles . . . but what is still more decisive consideration is that Lord Cornwallis has by the York River an outlet left for his retreat," *Correspondence*, pp. 62–63. In an Oct. 2, 1781, letter to GW, de Grasse claims that if French ships were to be sent up the York River, they "will be invested every night by fire rafts," while insisting that "what your excellency proposes [is] not so much an impossibility but . . . a thing unfavorable to the French [navy] without resulting in the least benefit. It seems to me that batteries placed on the brink of the river would prevent [Cornwallis's] escape. I am speaking perhaps as a blind man discoursing on colors, but you will pardon it to me as I have no knowledge of the locality," *Correspondence*, pp. 68–69. GW complains of "determining upon a plan of attack and approach . . . without the assistance of the shipping" in a Sept. 29, 1781, entry in his *Diaries*, 2:262. In an Oct. 22, 1781, letter to Henry Clinton, Cornwallis explains why he had decided to abandon his outer works: "upon observing that the enemy were taking measures, which could not fail of turning my left flank in a short time . . . , I withdrew within the works on the night of the 29th," in Benjamin Franklin Stevens, ed., *The Campaign in Virginia*, 2:209. Tarleton writes of how "great time would have been gained by holding and disputing the ground inch by inch" in his *A History of the Campaigns of 1780 and 1781*, pp. 374–75. Jonathan Trumbull writes of how the allied forces "find ourselves very unexpectedly upon very advantageous ground" in his "Minutes of Occurrences Respecting the Siege and Capture of Yorktown," p. 335. Baron von Closen in his *Revolutionary Journal* talks of how "[t]he profound knowledge of Rochambeau (who was engaged in his 15th siege) guided in a large measure the successive works of the besieging army," p. 156. For an excellent account of the mechanics of a siege, as well as how it unfolded at Yorktown, see John W. Wright's "Notes on the Siege of Yorktown in 1781 with Special Reference to the Conduct of a Siege in the Eighteenth Century," pp. 229–50.

Joseph Plumb Martin describes how he and the other Sappers and Miners laid out the first parallel, as well as their interchange with GW, and how the next night, within 600 yards of the British, they dug the trench "under their noses," in his *Journal*, pp. 146–47. Daniel Trabue's remarks on the spectacle of soldiers "working with spades making a ditch" are in "Journal of Colonel Daniel Trabue," p. 111. Martin recounts how the British "began to fire where they ought to have done sooner" in his *Journal*, pp. 147–48. Napoleon's dictum that "the artillery . . . takes a stronghold, the infantry simply assists," is in Wright's "Notes on the Siege of Yorktown," p. 233. Jerome Greene in *The Guns of Independence* writes of how "a traditional ceremony marked the formal opening of the trenches" and how Alexander Hamilton added his own audacious twist by ordering his men to perform the manual of arms in sight of the enemy; Greene also cites James Duncan's claim that Hamilton "wantonly exposed the lives of his men," pp. 167–68. Trabue tells of how the men in the trenches "could hear the ball go by" in his *Journal*, p. 112. Martin writes of being on the "tiptoe of expectation and impatience" in anticipation of the opening up of the batteries on the first parallel in his *Journal*, p. 148. Greene writes of the devastating effect of GW's first shot, an 18-pounder cannonball that killed Cornwallis's commissary general, in *The Guns of Independence*, p. 191. In "Yorktown During the Revolution," Edward Riley cites the chaplain M. l'Abbé Robin's description of the "parabolic path [of] the slow and destructive bomb," p. 276; Riley also cites Johann Doehla's accounts of the explosions of several allied bombs in the shallows of the York River and how he held "a piece of an exploded bomb in my hands which weighed more than thirty pounds and was over three inches thick," as well as how the inhabitants of Yorktown "dug in among the sand cliffs," pp. 274, 275. Johann Ewald describes how the bodies of the dead horses floated back to the beach off Yorktown "in heaps" in *DAW*, p. 336. St. George Tucker writes of how "[a]n immense number of Negroes have died in the most miserable manner" in "St. George Tucker's Journal of the Siege of Yorktown," p. 387.

John O. Sands in *Yorktown's Captive Fleet* lists the sixty-nine vessels known to have been part of the British fleet both scuttled and anchored between Yorktown and Gloucester, pp. 181–220. Frederick Mackenzie describes the express boat bound from New York to Yorktown in a Sept. 27, 1781, entry of his *Diary*: "An armed boat went off this night with letters in cypher . . . to Lord Cornwallis. This boat rows 14 oars, and carries 16 men, with 4 swivels. . . . [S]he is built like a whaleboat, is quite open and is rigged with two lateen sails. She has already been three times between Chesapeake and New York; twice since the French fleet has been in the bay. During her last passage to this place, she was obliged to anchor for 62 hours in open sea during a gale of wind that blew on shore," 2:650. Cornwallis tells of how "[w]e have lost about seventy men and many of our works are considerably damaged" in an Oct. 11, 1781, letter to Clinton in Stevens, *The Campaign in Virginia*, 2:175–77. St. George Tucker tells of how Cornwallis "has built a kind of grotto . . . where he lives underground" in his "Journal," p. 387. In an Oct. 11, 1781, entry in his "Minutes," Jonathan Trumbull writes of how "[t]he *Charon* being placed in such situation as greatly to annoy our troops in the battery above the town, produced that resentment which [was] the cause of her unhappy fate," p. 336. John Wright in "Notes on the Siege" describes the process by which "hotshot" was fired, p. 243. Bartholomew James tells of how the *Charon* was "in flames from the hold to the mastheads" in his *Journal*, p. 121. James Thacher describes his "fine view of this conflagration" in his *Military Journal*, p. 274. James's account of the "dreadful slaughter" and his emotions while watching "one of the finest ships in the navy of her rate totally destroyed" are in his *Journal*, pp. 121–22. James also writes of "the distressing cries of the wounded, and the lamentable sufferings of the inhabitants" and the "perfect undaunted resolution" of the British soldiers in his *Journal*, pp. 122–23. Lafayette speaks of how "[t]he troops of both nations chafe at the slowness of the approach" in an Oct. 12, 1781, letter to Luzerne in *LAAR*, 4:416.

Jerome Greene cites Rochambeau's statement to an aide that "[w]e shall see tomorrow whether the pear is ripe" in *The Guns of Independence*, p. 224.

Ron Chernow recounts how Hamilton determined to go directly to GW to complain about Lafayette's selection of de Gimat to lead the attack on redoubt number 10, and how he returned to his tent shouting "We have it!" in *Alexander Hamilton*, pp. 162–63. Greene recounts how GW "turned down Lafayette's repeated requests that he be named second in command" in *The Guns of Independence*, p. 128. Edmund Morgan cites GW's advice to his plantation manager at Mount Vernon to keep "all men . . . at a proper distance" in *The Genius of George Washington*, p. 7. Catherine Williams cites Stephen Olney's description of the attack on redoubt number 10, beginning with his account of GW's "harangue," in *Biography of Revolutionary Heroes*, pp. 267–78. Martin describes how the branches of the abatis were cut with a "slashing stroke," as well as how the watchword "Rochambeau" sounded like "rush-on-boys," in his *Journal*, p. 149. Greene cites the various accounts of the mortal wounding of Alexander Scammell, as well as an account of how Cornwallis had "thrown into the wells heads of steers, dead horses, and even the bodies of dead negroes," in *The Guns of Independence*, pp. 117–19, 110. Karl Tornquist writes of the brutal killing of a pregnant woman in *The Naval Campaigns of Count de Grasse*, p. 57. My account of Benedict Arnold's raid on New London is largely dependent on Eric Lehman's *Homegrown Terror: Benedict Arnold and the Burning of New London*, in which he cites Arnold's neighbor Jedidiah Huntington's insistence that "[n]o instance of conduct in the enemy since the war has raised so general a resentment," pp. 136–74. In an Oct. 16, 1781, letter to Luzerne, Lafayette writes, "We had promised ourselves to avenge the New London affair," in *LAAR*, 4:421. Martin recounts the challenges of negotiating shell holes big enough to "bury an ox in," as well as how the British soldier escaped the redoubt by leaping over the cliff to the beach, in his *Journal*, p. 150. Hamilton tells of how the American soldiers "spared every man who ceased to resist," in an Oct. 15, 1781, letter to Lafayette in *LAAR*, 4:420. The exchange of letters between Lafayette and Baron de Vioménil during the attacks on redoubts numbers 9 and 10 is recounted in Thacher's *Military Journal*, p. 276. Greene in *The Guns of Independence* cites the account of GW's telling Henry Knox, "The work is done, and well done," p. 253.

Johann Ewald in *DAW* recounts the British response to the taking of the redoubts, as well as the expulsion of the African Americans from Yorktown, pp. 335–36. Samuel Adams Drake cites Chastellux's praise of Henry Knox in *Life and Correspondence of Henry Knox*, pp. 72–73. Greene cites Aeneas Monson's account of Hamilton and Knox's wrestling match in redoubt number 10 in *The Guns of Independence*, p. 273. Joel Achenbach cites Thomas Jefferson's claim that GW was "incapable of fear" in *The Grand Idea*, p. 17. Thacher tells of GW's advice to the sand-covered chaplain in his *Military Journal*, p. 271. Ewald writes of how the British sortie against the two unfinished allied redoubts failed because the soldiers had brought "along wheel nails to serve for spiking, which were too large, instead of the proper steel spikes," as well as of how devastated the British were when the spiked guns began to fire the morning after the sortie, in *DAW*, p. 336. Ewald also tells of Cornwallis's decision to cross the York River and lead his men on a desperate breakout at Gloucester and how "[t]he whole thing seemed to me like a delusion which misleads people for a moment," pp. 336–38.

In an Oct. 14, 1781, letter to George Jackson, Samuel Hood writes of how "it was agreed to attempt by the united efforts of army and navy to relieve Lord Cornwallis in the Chesapeake" in Chadwick's *The Graves Papers*, p. 116. In a Sept. 27, 1781, entry in his *Diary*, Frederick Mackenzie writes, "The graceful appearance and manner of the Prince, with his liveliness and affability gives universal satisfaction," 2:648. William Smith describes how the prince spent "the morning at the window" before he walked about the town with Clinton "with crowds after him" in his *Memoirs*, p. 447; Smith also writes of how Graves "considers himself as ruined already," p. 449. In the Oct. 14, 1781, letter to Jackson, Hood recounts how Graves put forward the question "whether it was practicable to relieve Lord Cornwallis in the Chesapeake?," as well as his outraged response, in Chadwick, *The Graves Papers*, pp. 117–18. William Smith recounts his meeting with Henry Clinton during which the British commander insisted that he had "nothing to do with the difficulties" Graves was then encountering in repairing his fleet while also relaying his hope that if Cornwallis should be saved Clinton would get "the credit of restoring the tranquility of the empire," in *Memoirs*, pp. 451–52. Mackenzie reports the British captain's claim that "the loss of two line of battle ships in effecting the relief of [Cornwallis's] army is of much more consequence than the loss of [that army]" in an Oct. 16 entry in his *Diary*, 2:664. In a Sept. 20, 1781, entry in his *Memoirs*, William Smith records, "the boat from Lord Cornwallis that arrived Sept. 17 left him 11th. Our army in health. . . . The French fleet there. Had landed 3000 at Jamestown to join Lafayette. The Earl not apprehensive. Wish for the enemy," p. 445. On Oct. 8, Smith records, "Much joy at headquarters by a boat from Lord Cornwallis with letters of 24th. He had offered battle for two days to Washington and the French beyond his works, but they declined. . . . The dispatches assuring him of reinforcement arrived. The answer came: 'But don't hurry too fast,'" p. 456.

Johann Ewald writes of how it was as "dark as a sack" on the stormy night Cornwallis attempted to cross the river to Gloucester and how he was ultimately forced to abandon "the whole praiseworthy plan" in *DAW*, pp. 337–38. Thacher describes how "[t]he whole peninsula trembles under the incessant thunderings of our infernal machines" in his *Military Journal*, p. 277. In an Oct. 20, 1781, letter to Clinton, Cornwallis writes of how "I thought it would have been wanton and inhuman to the last degree to sacrifice the lives of this small body of gallant soldiers who had ever behaved with so much fidelity and courage. . . . I therefore proposed to capitulate" in Stevens, *The Campaign in Virginia*, 2:213. In an Oct. 11, 1781, letter to de Grasse, GW writes of how Cornwallis has been "passive beyond our expectation," in *Correspondence*, p. 82. In an Aug. 22, 1781, letter to his wife, Elizabeth, Alexander Hamilton writes, "It is ten to one that our views will be disappointed by Lord Cornwallis retiring to South Carolina by land," in his *Papers*, 2:667. In an Oct. 20, 1781, letter to Clinton, Cornwallis makes the claim that "nothing but the hopes of relief would have induced me to attempt its defense for I would either have endeavored to escape to New York by rapid marches from the Gloucester side immediately on the arrival of General Washington's troops at Williamsburg, or I would notwithstanding the disparity of numbers have attacked them in the open field, where it might have been just possible that fortune would have favored the gallantry of the handful of troops under my command; but being assured by your Excellency's letters that every possible means would be tried by the navy and army to relieve us, I could not think myself at liberty to venture upon either of those desperate attempts," in Stevens, *The Campaign in Virginia*, 2:207–8. GW insists that "without a decisive naval force we can do nothing definitive" in a Nov. 15, 1781, letter to Lafayette in *WGW*, 23:341. My thanks to Admiral John Baldwin for bringing this quote to my attention. In a Sept. 29, 1781, letter to Henry Knox, NG writes, "We have been beating the bush and the General has come to catch the bird," in *PGNG*, 9:411. In an Oct. 17, 1781, letter to Cornwallis, GW writes, "I wish, previous to the meeting of commissioners that your lordship's proposals in writing, may be sent to the American lines, for which purpose a suspension of hostilities, during two hours, from the delivery of this letter, will be granted," in *Correspondence*, p. 95. According to Ewald, "The English officer had scarcely reached the barrier when the fire of the besiegers was redoubled, whereupon a parley was sounded for a second time. General O'Hara was sent . . . to conclude as favorable a capitulation as could be made," *DAW*, p. 339. GW writes "tho' some of [Cornwallis's proposals] were inadmissible," he was led "to believe that there would be no great difficulty in fixing terms," in his *Diaries*, 2:269.

St. George Tucker writes of the "remarkably clear" night and the bagpipe serenade the next morning in his "Journal," p. 391. In a letter written at 4:30 p.m. on Oct. 17, 1781, Cornwallis informs GW that "the basis of my proposals will be that the garrisons of York and Gloucester shall be prisoners of war with the customary honors and for the convenience of the individuals whom I have the honor to command, that the British shall be sent to Britain and the Germans to Germany under engagement not to serve against France, America, or their allies," in *Correspondence*, p. 96. In a letter written to Cornwallis on Oct. 18, 1781, GW proposes much more severe terms, then demands that "Your Lordship will be pleased to signify your determination either to accept or reject the proposals now offered, in the course of two hours from the delivery of this letter, that commissioners may be appointed to digest the articles of capitulation or a renewal of hostilities may take place," in Stevens, *The Campaign in Virginia*, 2:194. Cornwallis responded that same day: "I agree to open a treaty of capitulation. . . . I shall in particular desire that the *Bonetta* sloop of war may be left entirely at my disposal from the hour that the capitulation is signed to receive an aide de camp to carry my dispatches to Clinton," in Stevens, *The Campaign in Virginia*, 2:195. John Laurens's insistence that "it is not the individual that is here considered. It is the nation" appears in George Scheer and Hugh Rankin, eds., *Rebels and Redcoats*, p. 569. In his *Diaries*, GW complains that the treaty negotiations are "so procrastinated" that the American commissioners "could do no more than make the rough draft of the articles," which moved him to insist that they be "copied" and sent to Cornwallis with the message "that I expected to have them signed at 11 am and that the garrison would march out at 2 pm," 2:269. Richard Ketchum cites the note that the Articles of Capitulation had been signed "in the trenches before Yorktown" in *Victory at Yorktown* p. 244.

In an Oct. 31, 1781, entry in his *Diary*, Frederick Mackenzie writes that "our fleet heard of the surrender of Yorktown on the 24th, by three men who escaped from thence the night of the capitulation," 2:683. Rodney's claim that if he had been in Graves's place, he would "block them up to eternity" is in an Oct. 19, 1781, letter to George Jackson in Chadwick, *The Graves Papers*, p. 135. In an Oct. 29, 1781, letter to George Jackson, Samuel Hood describes Cornwallis's surrender as "a most heartbreaking business" in *Letters Written by Sir Samuel Hood*, p. 39. Joseph Plumb Martin describes the surrender ceremony as the "grand exhibition" in his *Journal*, p. 152. Jerome Greene discusses the evidence that the British played "The World Turned Upside Down" in *The Guns of Independence*, p. 296. Baron von Closen recounts how when Admiral de Barras's "horse stretched to vent himself, he cried, 'Good heavens! I believe my horse is sinking!!,'" in his *Revolutionary Journal*, p. 156; von Closen also writes of how the American soldiers were "eclipsed by our army in splendor of appearance and dress," as well as how the British showed "the greatest scorn for the Americans," p. 154. Louis Gottschalk tells of how Lafayette "ordered his drum major to strike up 'Yankee Doodle.' The band's blare made them turn their eyes toward his side of the line" in *Lafayette and the Close of the American Revolution*, p. 326. In his *Journal*, William Feltman claimed that the "British prisoners all appeared to be much in liquor," p. 22. Greene cites the story from the *New Jersey Gazette* in which the author compares the British officers to "boys who had been whipped at school" in *The Guns of Independence*, p. 299.Martin writes that the German soldiers "did not greatly care" about having to surrender to the allied forces in his *Journal*, p. 153. James Thacher tells of how the British soldiers' "mortification could not be concealed" once it came time to ground their arms, in his *Military Journal*, p. 280.

Johann Ewald comments on the "national enmity" between the French and American soldiers, in *DAW*, pp. 339–40. Clermont-Crèvecoeur writes of how "good upbringing and courtesy" bound together the French and British officers, in *ACRA*, p. 64. Ewald describes GW's "jealousy" and how "cool conduct began to prevail among the two diverse nations which, in good fortune, had formed only one" in *DAW*, p. 342. Von Closen writes of accompanying Rochambeau on a visit to Yorktown to see Cornwallis in his *Revolutionary Journal*, p. 155. George Flohr's claim that African Americans made up the "majority of the dead" in Yorktown is in Robert Selig's "German Soldier in America: Journal of George Flohr," p. 584. Joseph Plumb Martin writes of how African Americans were "scattered about in every direction, dead and dying with pieces of ears of burnt Indian corn in the hands and mouths," in his *Journal*, p. 153. Verger in *ACRA* cites article 4 of the Articles of Capitulation: "any property obviously belonging to the inhabitants of these states . . . shall be subject to be reclaimed," p. 145. Daniel Trabue's claim that after the British surrender the African Americans "looked condemned" is in his *Journal*, p. 116. Henry Wiencek in *An Imperfect God* writes insightfully of GW's shifting opinion concerning John Laurens and Alexander Hamilton's plan for recruiting enslaved African Americans from the south for the Continental army, citing GW's initial claim that "blacks in the southern parts of the continent offer a resource to us that should not be neglected," as well as his ultimately self-serving judgment that the proposal would be "productive of much discontent in those who are held in servitude," pp. 223, 227. Michael Kranish cites Thomas Jefferson's reference to slavery as a "moral depravity," as well as his claim "We have the wolf by the ear, and we can neither hold him, nor safely let him go," in *Flight from Monticello*, p. 300. Alan Taylor cites Henry Latrobe's description of "many wagon loads of the bones of men, women, and children" littering the riverbanks of Virginia in *The Internal Enemy*, pp. 27–28. Wiencek cites GW's 1779 letter to Lund about the sale of his own slaves, in which he writes of a possible "punishment . . . for our want of public, and indeed private virtue," in *An Imperfect God*, p. 229.

In an Oct. 20, 1781, letter to de Grasse, GW urges the French admiral to assist him in attacking Charleston so as to "destroy the last hope" of the British in North America in *Correspondence*, p. 119. In an Oct. 29, 1781, letter to GW, de Grasse attributes his inability to commit to a spring plan to his "wretched health" in *Correspondence*, p. 151. A note in GW's *Diaries* attributes Jacky Custis's death to "camp fever," 2:273. In a Nov. 15, 1781, letter to Lafayette, GW recounts how he arrived at Martha's brother-in-law's house just in time "to see poor Mr. Custis breathe his last" in *WGW*, 23:340. In an Oct. 1, 1785, letter to Jonathan Trumbull, GW writes, "I can offer nothing which your own reason has not already suggested on this occasion," in *WGW*, 28:285. James Flexner cites the letter from GW's mother in which she recounts how she felt "truly uneasy by not being at home when you went through Fredericksburg" in *George Washington in the American Revolution*, p. 471. GW writes of how "Mr. Custis' death has given much distress in this family" in a Nov. 18, 1781, letter to Benjamin Harrison in *WGW*, 23:352. In a Nov. 16, 1781, letter to NG, GW admits, "My greatest fear is that Congress viewing this stroke in too important a point of light, may think our work too nearly closed," in *WGW*, 23:347.

Chapter 10 ✦ "The North River Captain"

Henry Knox's Nov. 1, 1781, letter to NG, in which he refers to GW as "the North River captain," appears in *PGNG*, 9:507; the original is in the collection of the Morgan Library in New York City; my thanks to Carolyn Vega at the Morgan for her help in confirming the wording of the letter. GW writes, "No land force can act decisively unless accompanied by a maritime superiority," in a Nov. 15, 1781, letter to Lafayette in *WGW*, 23:341. In a July 9, 1782, letter to NG, GW writes of how de Grasse's defeat at the Saintes "probably will now give a total alteration to the complexion of the campaign" in *WGW*, 24:409. In a July 18, 1782, letter to James McHenry, GW writes of how they "are enveloped in darkness" in the wake of the disastrous loss in *WGW*, 24:432. Germain's description of Lord North receiving the news of Yorktown like "he would have taken a ball in his breast" is in Henry Johnston's *The Yorktown*

Campaign and the Surrender of Cornwallis, p. 180, as is King George's claim that the defeat at Yorktown would not make "the smallest alteration" in British policy toward the Americans, p. 181. General Carleton and Admiral Digby's Aug. 2, 1782, letter to GW, in which they inform him that "negotiations for a general peace" have begun in Paris and that the king is prepared to recognize the independence of the United States, appears in *WGW*, 24:472. GW's Aug. 6, 1782, letter to NG, in which he expresses his fears that the British are "only gaining time to become more formidable at sea; to form new alliances, if possible; or to disunite us," is in *WGW*, 24:471. Alexander Hamilton speaks of "Continental views" in a March 17, 1783, letter to GW, in Hamilton's *Papers*, 3:292. William Fowler cites Maurice Morgann's prediction that any "federal union" based on "verbal maxims of general liberty and brotherly love" would degenerate into "despotism and mutual rage" in *American Crisis*, p. 80. For the sources related to GW's involvement in the Asgill affair, see David Humphreys's *The Conduct of General Washington Respecting the Confinement of Captain Asgill*, pp. 1–35. GW's March 4, 1783, letter to Benjamin Harrison, in which he makes the prediction that without a stronger federal government "anarchy and confusion must prevail," is in *WGW*, 26:184–85. GW writes of the "spirit of discontent" among the officers of the Continental army in an Oct. 2, 1782, letter to Benjamin Lincoln in *WGW*, 25:228. In a Dec. 14, 1782, letter to Joseph Jones, GW writes that once the officers refuse to protect the public from the discontents of the common soldiers, "I know not what the consequences may be," in *WGW*, 25:431. GW compares himself to "a careful physician" in an Oct. 17, 1782, letter to James McHenry in *WGW*, 25:269–70.

James Flexner writes of how in contrast to GW's affectionate letters to Chastellux, his letter of farewell to Rochambeau was "formal and stilted" in *George Washington in the American Revolution*, pp. 497–98. GW's claim that "it was never in contemplation to attack New York" is in his July 31, 1788, letter to Noah Webster in *Founders Online*, National Archives, last modified March 30, 2017, http://founders.archives.gov/documents/Washington /04-06-02-0376. Ron Chernow writes of GW's need "to portray himself as the visionary architect of the Yorktown victory, not as a general misguidedly concentrating upon New York while his French allies masterminded the decisive blow," in *Washington*, p. 404. GW informs Lafayette of the "trifling skirmish" in South Carolina that had taken the life of John Laurens in an Oct. 20, 1782, letter in *WGW*, 25:281. In a Jan. 10, 1783, letter to Tench Tilghman, GW writes that "I have sent Mr. Rittenhouse the glass of such spectacles as suit my eyes, that he may know how to grind his crystals," in *WGW*, 26:27. David Cobb recounts how "the General took his station in the desk or pulpit, which you may recollect, was in the Temple," in a letter reprinted in the notes of *WGW*, 26:222. GW writes of how the sufferings of the Continental army are "unexampled in history" in an Oct. 17, 1782, letter to James McHenry in *WGW*, 25:269. Hamilton admits to GW that he and others have been involved in a scheme to "form a mass of influence" that would pressure the states into increasing the powers of the federal government in a March 17, 1783, letter in his *Papers*, 3:293. Joseph Jones's Feb. 27, 1783, letter to GW, in which he writes of the dangers of what might occur once "all confidence between the civil and military authority is lost," as well as the efforts to "lessen your popularity in the army in hopes ultimately the weight of your opposition will prove no obstacle to their ambitious designs," is in *WGW*, 25:432. GW's outraged response to the proposal that he be named king of the United States is in his May 22, 1782, letter to Col. Lewis Nicola in *WGW*, 24:272. Hamilton's account of how GW's popularity has declined because of his "extreme reserve, mixed sometimes with a degree of asperity of temper" is in "Notes of Debates in Cont. Congress, Feb. 20, 1783," reprinted in *WGW*, 26:188. GW describes Horatio Gates as "the old leven" who operates "under a mask of the most perfect dissimulation and apparent cordiality" in a March 4, 1783, letter to Hamilton in *WGW*, 26:186. For the full text of the Newburgh address, written by John Armstrong, see http://teachingamericanhistory

.org/library/document/the-newburgh-address/. GW's March 11, 1783, orders, in which he states that "his duty as well as the reputation and true interest of the army requires his disapprobation of such disorderly proceedings," is in *WGW*, 26:208. Samuel Shaw's account of GW's appearance in the Temple on March 15, 1783, is in his *Journals*, pp. 103–4. GW's remarks before his officers that day are in *WGW*, 26:222–27. Col. David Cobb's letter, in which he quotes GW as saying "Gentlemen, you will permit me to put on my spectacles, for I have not only grown gray, but almost blind, in the service of my country," is cited in *WGW*, 26:222. William Fowler describes what happened among the officers after GW exited the Temple and cites the resolutions drafted by Henry Knox's committee, in which the officers express their "unshaken confidence in the justice of Congress," in *American Crisis*, pp. 186–88. Thomas Jefferson writes of how "the moderation and virtue of a single character has probably prevented this revolution from being closed as most others have been by a subversion of that liberty it was intended to establish" in an April 16, 1784, letter to GW in Jefferson's *Papers*, 7:106–7.

Joseph Plumb Martin writes about GW's "watch chain" at West Point and how it became "the criterion by which we were to judge of war or peace" in his *Journal*, pp. 170–71. GW's April 18, 1783, orders announcing the peace are in *WGW*, 26:334–37. Martin writes of how the announcement of peace heralded "a serious time" in his *Journal*, pp. 172–75. Lafayette's Feb. 5, 1783, letter to GW detailing his "wild scheme" by which slavery might be eradicated in the south, as well as GW's April 5, 1783, reply, in which he says he would be "happy to join you in so laudable a work," are in *WGW*, 26:300. Henry Wiencek cites Lafayette's insistence that "I would never have drawn my sword in the cause of America, if I could have conceived that thereby I was founding a land of slavery" in *An Imperfect God*, p. 261. William Smith describes the conversation between GW and Carleton in a May 6, 1783, entry in his *Memoirs*, p. 586. Maya Jasanoff writes of GW's slave Harry Washington's sailing from New York to Nova Scotia with 132 emancipated blacks in *Liberty's Exiles*, p. 90. GW writes of his "wish to see the Union of these states established upon liberal and permanent principles," in a March 31, 1783, letter to Alexander Hamilton in *WGW*, 26:277. GW's June 8, 1783, Circular to the States, in which he writes of the likelihood "that there is a natural and necessary progression, from the extreme of anarchy to the extreme of tyranny," is in *WGW*, 26:483–90. Edmund Randolph's June 28, 1783, letter to James Madison, in which he writes of the "unsolicited obtrusion" of GW's advice, is in *WGW*, 26:491. GW compares the American people to "young heirs come a little premature perhaps to a large inheritance" in a July 10, 1783, letter to George Fairfax in *WGW*, 27:58. William Fowler cites the letter of an officer named Walter Stewart, in which he describes how the officers rejected GW's invitation to a final dinner, "declaring they thought the present period more adapted to sorrow than mirth," in *American Crisis*, p. 210. GW writes of how his "parting scene" with his officers "will not admit of description" in a June 7, 1783, letter to the president of Congress in *WGW*, 26:478. GW writes of how his trip to the wilds of New York inspired within him "a more contemplative and extensive view of the vast inland navigation of these United States" in an Oct. 12, 1783, letter to Chastellux in *WGW*, 27:189–90. GW outlines his plans for a possible tour of the western wilderness in an Oct. 12, 1783, letter to Lafayette, in which he says "there would be nothing wanting to make it perfectly agreeable but your company," in *WGW*, 27:187. GW's proposal that "a boundary line" be placed between the Native Americans and American settlers in the west is in a Sept. 7, 1783, letter to James Duane in *WGW*, 27:134.

Ron Chernow discusses GW's submitting a bill for his expenses to Congress in *Washington*, p. 445. In a Jan. 1, 1784, letter to Richard Varick, GW thanks him for assembling his volumes of correspondence while making the claim that "I am fully convinced that neither the present age nor posterity will consider the time and labor which have been employed in accomplishing it, unprofitably spent," in *WGW*, 27:289–90. Joseph Manca cites GW's joke in "George Washington's Use of Humor During the Revolutionary War," https://allthings liberty.com/2015/02/george-washingtons-use-of-humor-during-the-revolutionary-war/. GW's Nov. 2, 1783, "Farewell Orders to the Armies of the United States" are in *WGW*, 27:223–25. GW's Nov. 6, 1783, letter to Alexander Hamilton, in which he complains of how Congress adjourned "without bringing the peace establishment or any of the many other pressing matters to a decision," is in *WGW*, 27:232. Sam Willis describes the exodus of loyalists and free blacks from the United States at the end of the Revolutionary War as "the largest movement of ships and people in the history of the British Empire" in *The Struggle for Sea Power*, p. 471. In *Liberty's Exiles*, Maya Jasanoff cites the British officer's observation that American people "*know how to govern themselves, but nobody else can govern them,*" p. 6. Edwin Burrows cites the statistics about deaths during the American Revolution in *Forgotten Patriots*, pp. 200–204; see also Holger Hoock's *Scars of Independence: America's Violent Birth*, pp. 215–24. On the likelihood that James Rivington served as a British spy, see Todd Andrlik's "James Rivington: King's Printer and Patriot Spy?," https://allthingsliberty.com/2014/03/james-rivington-kings-printer-patriot-spy/. Benjamin Tallmadge's account of GW's farewell to his officers at Fraunces Tavern is in his *Memoir*, pp. 63–64. GW's Dec. 23, 1783, "Address to Congress on Resigning his Commission" is in *WGW*, 27:285. Gordon Wood cites King George's prediction that if GW retired to private life "he will be the greatest man in the world" in "The Greatness of George Washington," p. 197. For GW's Sept. 27, 1781, letter to de Grasse about how "a great mind knows how to make personal sacrifices," see *Correspondence*, pp. 48–54. For his Oct. 17, 1777, letter to Richard Henry Lee about his efforts "to harmonize so many discordant parts," see *WGW*, 9:389. For Abigail Adams's July 12, 1789, letter to Mary Smith Cranch, in which she writes of GW's ability to inspire "love and reverence," see *Found Families: Digital Editions of the Papers of the Winthrops and the Adamses*, ed. C. James Taylor (Boston: Massachusetts Hist. Soc., 2018), www.masshist.org/apdez/. For GW's Aug. 28, 1778, letter to William Heath claiming "[I]t is our duty to make the best of our misfortunes and not suffer passion to interfere with our interest and the public good," see *WGW*, 12:365. For GW's June 7, 1781, letter to Joseph Jones, in which he speaks of working on "the great scale," see *WGW*, 22:179. My thanks to the historian Peter Henriques for bringing GW's comments about the importance of serving "the general good," as well as Abigail Adams's remarks about GW, to my attention.

Epilogue · Aftermath

On Benedict Arnold, see Clare Brandt's *The Man in the Mirror*, pp. 254–79. On Louis-Antoine de Bougainville, see Mary Kimbrough's *Louis-Antoine de Bougainville*, pp. 190–216. On Sir Guy Carleton, see Maya Jasanoff's *Liberty's Exiles*, pp. 198–209. On François Jean de Beauvoir Chastellux, see Howard Rice's introduction to Chastellux's *Travels in North America in the Years 1780, 1781 and 1782*, pp. 17–25. On Sir Henry Clinton, see William Willcox's *Portrait of a General*, pp. 445–91. On Baron von Closen, see the introduction by Evelyn Acomb in von Closen's *Revolutionary Journal*, pp. xxvii–xxxvi. On Lord Cornwallis, see Andrew O'Shaughnessy's *The Men Who Lost America*, pp. 282–85. On Johann Ewald, see Joseph Tustin's introduction in Ewald's *DAW*, pp. xxvii–xxxi. On Bernardo de Gálvez, see Thomas Fleming's "Bernardo de Galvez: The Forgotten Revolutionary Conquistador Who Saved Louisiana," www.americanheritage.com/content/bernardo-de-g%C3%A1lvez. On Horatio Gates, see Paul David Nelson, *General Horatio Gates*, pp. 276–97. On George III and George Germain, see O'Shaughnessy's *The Men Who Lost America*, pp. 43–46, 200–203. On Comte de Grasse, see Charles Lee Lewis's *Admiral De Grasse and American Independence*, pp. 288–312. On Thomas Graves, see the *Dictionary of Canadian Biography*, www.biographi

.ca/en/bio.php?id_nbr=2431. On NG, see Gerald Carbone's *Nathanael Greene,* pp. 221–35, and Terry Golway's *Washington's General,* in which appears Alexander Hamilton's claim that NG's "universal and pervading genius . . . qualified him not less for the Senate than for the field," p. 314. On Alexander Hamilton, see Ron Chernow's *Alexander Hamilton,* pp. 187–731.

On Samuel Hood, see Colin Pengelly's *Sir Samuel Hood and the Battle of the Chesapeake,* pp. 194–226. On Thomas Jefferson, see Michael Kranish's *Flight from Monticello: Thomas Jefferson at War,* pp. 290–331. On Henry Knox, see Mark Puls's *Henry Knox,* pp. 183–257, and Alan Taylor's *Liberty Men and Great Proprietors,* pp. 37–47, 244–45. On Lafayette, see Laura Auricchio's *The Marquis,* pp. 92–307, and James Gaines's *For Liberty and Glory,* pp. 192–450. On Duc de Lauzun, see the Appendix by C. K. Scott Moncrieff in Lauzun's *Memoirs,* pp. 223–25. On Henry Lee, see Charles Royster's *Light-Horse Harry Lee and the Legacy of the American Revolution,* pp. 57–252; Lee's funeral oration describing GW as "first in war, first in peace, first in the hearts of his countrymen" is cited at web.archive.org/web/20120228192657 /http://gwpapers.virginia.edu/project/exhibit/mourning/response.html. On Benjamin Lincoln, see David Mattern's *Benjamin Lincoln and the American Revolution,* pp. 150–218. On Joseph Plumb Martin, see the introduction by James Kirby Martin in Martin's *Journal,* pp. xiii–xv, and Taylor's *Liberty Men and Great Proprietors,* pp. 244–49. On Daniel Morgan, see John Buchanan's *The Road to Guilford Courthouse,* which includes the words he reputedly told the doctor on his deathbed, pp. 399–401. On Robert Morris, see Charles Rappleye's *Robert Morris,* pp. 358–530. The description of Charles O'Hara as the "Cock of the Rock" appears in *Revolutionary War Almanac* by John Fredriksen, p. 550. On Rochambeau, see Arnold Whitridge's *Rochambeau,* pp. 233–321. On George Rodney, see David Spinney's *Rodney,* pp. 413–30. On Francisco Saavedra de Sangronis, see Granville Hough's "Spanish Heroes of the American Revolution: Francisco Saavedra de Sangronis," http://www .somosprimos.com/hough/hough.htm#SAAVEDRA. On Friedrich von Steuben, see Paul Lockhart's *The Drillmaster of Valley Forge,* pp. 285–302. On Banastre Tarleton, see Robert Bass's *The Green Dragoon,* pp. 185–454. GW writes of his "anxious desire to quit the walks of public life, and under the shadow of my own vine, and my own fig tree," in an Oct. 11, 1783, letter to Chastellux in *WGW,* 27:189. See also Benjamin Latrobe's account of his 1796 visit to Mount Vernon in his *Virginia Journals,* 1:172, as well as Henry Wiencek's *An Imperfect God,* which cites GW's prediction "that nothing but the rooting out of slavery can perpetuate the existence of our union," p. 362, and Ron Chernow's *Washington,* which recounts the circumstances under which GW wrote his will and his conversation with Dr. Craik on his deathbed, pp. 799–804, 807–9.

BIBLIOGRAPHY

Achenbach, Joel. *The Grand Idea: George Washington's Potomac and the Race to the West.* New York: Simon and Schuster, 2002.

Adams, Randolph G. *The Burned Letter of Chastellux.* New York: Franco-American Pamphlet Series, Number 7, 1935.

———. "A View of Cornwallis's Surrender at Yorktown." *The American Historical Review* 37, no. 1 (October 1, 1931), pp. 25–49.

Allen, Gardner. *A Naval History of the American Revolution.* Vol. 2. 1913. Reprint, Williamstown, Mass.: Corner House, 1970.

Andrlik, Todd. "James Rivington: King's Printer and Patriot Spy?" *The Journal of the American Revolution,* March 3, 2014. https://allthingsliberty.com/2014/03/james-rivington-kings-printer-patriot-spy/.

———. *Reporting the Revolutionary War.* Naperville, Ill.: Sourcebooks, 2012.

Anon. "Arnold's Invasion." *WMQ* 6, no. 2 (1926), pp. 131–32.

Anthony, Walter C. *Washington's Headquarters, Newburgh, New York: A History of Its Construction and Its Various Occupants.* Newburgh, N.Y.: Newburgh Historical Society, 1928.

Archer, Lieutenant. "Account of the Loss of His Majesty's Ship Phoenix." In *The Mariner's Chronicle,* vol. 2, by Archibald Duncan, pp. 280–99. London: James Cundee, 1804.

Archibald, Edward H. *The Wooden Fighting Ship in the Royal Navy, A.D. 897–1860.* London: Blandford, 1968.

Armstrong, John. "The Newburgh Address," March 1783. http://teachingamericanhistory.org/library/document/the-newburgh-address/.

Arnold, Isaac. *The Life of Benedict Arnold: His Patriotism and His Treason.* Chicago: A. C. McClurg, 1905.

Auricchio, Laura. *The Marquis: Lafayette Reconsidered.* New York: Knopf, 2014.

Babits, Lawrence. *A Devil of a Whipping: The Battle of Cowpens.* Chapel Hill: University of North Carolina Press, 2001.

———, and Joshua Howard. *Long, Obstinate, and Bloody: The Battle of Guilford Courthouse.* Chapel Hill: University of North Carolina Press, 2013.

Baker, William. *Itinerary of General Washington from June 15, 1775, to December 23, 1783.* Philadelphia: J. B. Lippincott, 1892.

Balch, Thomas. *The French in America During the War of Independence of the United States, 1777–1783.* Translated by T. W. Balch. 2 vols. Boston: Gregg Press, 1972.

Bancroft, George. *History of the Formation of the Constitution of the United States of America.* Vol. 1. New York: D. Appleton, 1882.

Barbé-Marbois, François, Marquis de. *Our Revolutionary Forefathers: Letters of Barbé-Marbois, 1779–1785.* Edited and translated by Eugene Parker Chase. New York: Duffield, 1929.

Bass, Robert D. *Gamecock: The Life and Campaigns of General Thomas Sumter.* New York: Holt, 1961.

———. *The Green Dragoon: The Lives of Banastre Tarleton and Mary Robinson.* Orangeburg, S.C.: Sandlapper, 1973.

Baudry, Lieutenant Ambroise. *The Naval Battle: Studies of Tactical Factors.* London: Hughes Rees, 1914.

Baugh, D. A. "Sir Samuel Hood: Superior Subordinate." In *George Washington's Generals and Opponents,* edited by George Athan Billias, pp. 291–326. New York: Da Capo, 1994.

———. "Why Did Britain Lose Command of the Sea During the War for America?" In *The British Navy and the Use of Naval Power in the Eighteenth Century,* edited by J. Black and P. Woodfine, pp. 149–70. Atlantic Highlands, N.J.: Humanities Press International, 1988.

Baurmeister, Carl Leopold. *Confidential Letters and Journals, 1776–1784, of Adjutant General Major Baurmeister of the Hessian Forces.* Edited by Bernard A. Uhlendorf. New Brunswick, N.J.: Rutgers University Press, 1957.

Beakes, John. *Otho Williams in the American Revolution.* Mount Pleasant, S.C.: Nautical and Aviation Publishing, 2015.

Bell, Madison Smartt. *Toussaint Louverture.* New York: Vintage, 2007.

Bennett, G. M. "The Fleet Flagship: A Problem of Naval Command." *Journal of the Royal United Services Institute* 81 (1936), pp. 601–11.

Berlin, Ira. *The Long Emancipation: The Demise of Slavery in the United States.* Cambridge, Mass.: Harvard University Press, 2015.

Billias, George Athan, ed. *George Washington's Generals and Opponents: Their Exploits and Leadership.* New York: Da Capo, 1994.

Black, J., and P. Woodfine, eds. *The British Navy and the Use of Naval Power in the Eighteenth Century.* Atlantic Highlands, N.J.: Humanities Press International, 1988.

Blanchard, Claude. *The Journal of Claude Blanchard, Commissary of the French Auxiliary Army Sent to the United States During the American Revolution, 1780–1783.* Edited by Thomas Balch. Translated by William Duane. Albany, N.Y.: J. Munsell, 1876.

Bobrick, Benson. *Angel in the Whirlwind.* New York: Penguin, 1997.

Bolton, Charles K. *The Private Soldier Under Washington.* London: Kessinger, 2006.

Bonsal, Stephen. *When the French Were Here.* Garden City, N.Y.: Doubleday, 1945.

Borkow, Richard. *George Washington's Westchester Gamble: The Encampment on the Hudson and the Trapping of Cornwallis.* Charleston, S.C.: History Press, 2011.

Boudriot, Jean. "The French Fleet During the American War of Independence." *Nautical Research Journal* 25, no. 1 (1975), pp. 79–86.

Bougainville, Louis-Antoine de. *The French Royal Navy: Events During the Naval Wars Since 1740.* Montreal: Lawrence Lande Foundation for Canadian Historical Research, 1990.

Bourg, Baron Cromot du. "Diary of a French Officer, 1781." *Magazine of American History* 7 (1881), pp. 283–95.

Bowler, Arthur A. *Logistics and Failure of the British Army in America.* Princeton, N.J.: Princeton University Press, 1975.

Boyd, Thomas A. *Mad Anthony Wayne.* New York: Scribner, 1929.

Boynton, Edward, ed. *General Orders of George Washington Issued at Newburgh on the Hudson, 1782–83.* Harrison, N.Y.: Harbor Hill, 1973.

Brady, Patricia. *Martha Washington: An American Life*. New York: Viking, 2005.

Braisted, Todd W. "The Black Pioneers and Others: The Military Role of Black Loyalists in the American War of Independence." In *Moving On: Black Loyalists in the Afro-Atlantic World*, edited by John W. Pulis, pp. 3–37. New York: Garland, 1999.

Brandt, Clare. *The Man in the Mirror: A Life of Benedict Arnold*. New York: Random House, 1994.

Breen, Kenneth. "Divided Command: The West Indies and North America, 1780–1781." In *The British Navy and the Use of Naval Power in the Eighteenth Century*, edited by J. Black and P. Woodfine, pp. 191–206. Atlantic Highlands, N.J.: Humanities Press International, 1988.

———. "George Bridges, Lord Rodney, 1718?–1792." In *Precursors of Nelson: British Admirals of the Eighteenth Century*, edited by P. LeFevre and R. Harding, pp. 225–48. London: Chatham, 2000.

———. "Graves and Hood at the Chesapeake." *Mariner's Mirror* 66 (1980), pp. 53–65.

———. "Sir George Rodney and St. Eustatius in the American War: A Commercial and Naval Distraction, 1775–81." *Mariner's Mirror* 84 (1998), pp. 193–203.

Brookhiser, Richard. *Founding Father: Rediscovering George Washington*. New York: Free Press, 1997.

———. *Gentleman Revolutionary: Gouverneur Morris, the Rake Who Wrote the Constitution*. New York: Free Press, 2003.

Brooks, Noah. *Henry Knox*. New York: Putnam, 1900.

Brown, Wallace. *The Good Americans: The Loyalists in the American Revolution*. New York: William Morrow, 1969.

———. *The King's Friends: The Composition and Motives of the American Loyalist Claimants*. Providence: Brown University Press, 1965.

Brumwell, Stephen. *George Washington: Gentleman Warrior*. New York, London: Quercus, 2012.

———. *Redcoats: The British Soldier and War in the Americas, 1755–1763*. Cambridge, Mass.: Harvard University Press, 2002.

Buchanan, John. *The Road to Guilford Courthouse: The American Revolution in the Carolinas*. New York: John Wiley and Sons, 1997.

Buel, Richard, Jr. *In Irons: Britain's Naval Supremacy and the American Revolutionary Economy*. New Haven: Yale University Press, 1998.

Burnett, Edmund C. *The Continental Congress*. New York: Norton, 1964.

Burrows, Edwin G. *Forgotten Patriots: The Untold Story of American Prisoners During the Revolutionary War*. New York: Basic Books, 2008.

Calhoon, Robert M. *The Loyalists in Revolutionary America, 1760–1781*. New York: Harcourt Brace, 1973.

Callahan, North. *Henry Knox: General Washington's General*. New York: Rinehart, 1958.

Calloway, Colin. *The American Revolution in Indian Country: Crisis and Diversity in Native American Communities*. New York: Cambridge University Press, 1995.

Carbone, Gerald M. *Nathanael Greene: A Biography of the American Revolution*. New York: Palgrave Macmillan, 2009.

Carp, E. Wayne. *To Starve the Army at Pleasure: Continental Army Administration and American Political Culture, 1775–1783*. Chapel Hill: University of North Carolina Press, 1984.

Chadwick, French Ensor, ed. *The Graves Papers and Other Documents Relating to the Naval Operations of the Yorktown Campaign*. New York: Naval History Society, 1916.

Chaline, Olivier. "Admiral Louis Guillouet, Comte d'Orvilliers (1710–92): A Style of Command in the Age of the American War." In *Naval Leadership in the Atlantic World*, edited by R. Harding and A. Guimerá, pp. 73–84. London: University of Westminster Press, 2017. https://doi.org/10.16997/book2.g.

———. "Season, Winds and Sea: The Improbable Route of de Grasse to the Chesapeake." Paper delivered at the 2015 SAR Annual Conference on the American Revolution at George Washington's Mount Vernon, June 12–14, 2015.

Champagne, Roger. *Alexander McDougall and the American Revolution*. Schenectady, N.Y.: Union College Press, 1975.

Chastellux, Marquis de. *Travels in North America in the Years 1780, 1781 and 1782*. Translated by Howard Rice Jr. 2 vols. Chapel Hill: University of North Carolina Press, 1963.

Chavez, T. E. *Spain and the Independence of the United States*. Albuquerque: University of New Mexico Press, 2002.

Chernow, Ron. *Alexander Hamilton*. New York: Penguin Press, 2005.

———. *Washington*. New York: Penguin Press, 2010.

Chinard, Gilbert, ed. *George Washington as the French Knew Him*. Princeton, N.J.: Princeton University Press, 1940.

Christie, Ian R. *The End of North's Ministry, 1780–1782*. London: Macmillan, 1958.

Clary, David A. *Adopted Son: Washington, Lafayette, and the Friendship That Saved the Revolution*. New York: Bantam Dell, 2007.

Clerk, John. *An Essay on Naval Tactics*. 1790. Reprint, East Sussex, Eng.: Naval and Military Press, 2008.

Clinton, Henry. *The American Rebellion: Sir Henry Clinton's Narrative of His Campaigns, 1775–1782*. Edited by William B. Willcox. New Haven: Yale University Press, 1954.

Closen, Ludwig, Baron von. *Revolutionary Journal, 1780–1783*. Translated by Evelyn M. Acomb. Chapel Hill: University of North Carolina Press, 1958.

Clowes, William Laird. *The Royal Navy: A History from the Earliest Times to the Present*. Vol. 3. London: S. Low, Marston, and Co., 1898.

Cock, Randolph. "'The Finest Invention in the World': The Royal Navy's Early Trials of Copper Sheathing, 1708–1770." *Mariner's Mirror* 87 (2001), pp. 446–59.

Coggins, Jack. *Ships and Seamen of the American Revolution*. Harrisburg, Pa.: Promontory Press, 1969.

Cohn, Ellen R. "Benjamin Franklin, George-Louis Le Rouge and the Franklin/Folger Chart of the Gulf Stream." *Imago Mundi: The International Journal for the History of Cartography* 52 (2000), pp. 124–42.

Colles, Christopher. *A Survey of the Roads of the United States of America*. Edited by Walter Ristow. Cambridge, Mass.: Harvard University Press, 1961.

Commager, Henry Steele, and Richard B. Morris, eds. *The Spirit of 'Seventy-Six: The Story of the American Revolution as Told by Its Participants*. Edison, N.J.: Castle, 2002.

Conway, Moncure Daniel. *Barons of the Potomac and the Rappahannock*. New York: The Grolier Club, 1892.

Conway, Stephen. "British Army Officers and the American War for Independence." *WMQ* 41 (1984), pp. 265–76.

———. "'The Great Mischief Complain'd Of': Reflections on the Misconduct of British Soldiers in the Revolutionary War." *WMQ*, 3rd ser., 47 (1961), pp. 370–90.

———. "To Subdue America: British Army Officers and the Conduct of the Revolutionary War." *WMQ* 43 (1986), pp. 381–407.

Cook, Fred J. "Allan McLane: Unknown Hero of the Revolution." *American Heritage* 7, no. 6 (October 1956). www.americanheritage.com/content/allan-mclane-unknown-hero-revolution.

Corbett, Sir Julian. *Signals and Instructions, 1776–94*. 1905. Reprint, Greenwich, Eng.: Conway Maritime, 1971.

Cornwallis, Charles. *Correspondence of Charles, First Marquis Cornwallis.* Edited by Charles Ross. Vol. 1. London: John Murray, 1859.

Crary, Catherine S. "The Tory and the Spy: The Double Life of James Rivington." *WMQ* 16 (1959), pp. 61–72.

Crawford, Michael, ed. *The Autobiography of a Yankee Mariner: Christopher Prince and the American Revolution.* Washington, D.C.: Brassey's, 2002.

———. "New Light on the Battle Off the Virginia Capes: Graves vs. Hood." *Mariner's Mirror* 103, no. 3 (2017). www.tandfonline.com/eprint/YTYCdX47G7KDpdGAiQhy /full.

Creswell, John. *British Admirals of the Eighteenth Century: Tactics in Battle.* London: George Allen and Unwin, 1972.

Custis, George W. P. *Recollections and Private Memories of Washington.* Washington, D.C.: William Moore, 1859.

Daigler, Kenneth A. *Spies, Patriots, and Traitors: American Intelligence in the Revolutionary War.* Washington, D.C.: Georgetown University Press, 2014.

Dalzell, Robert, and Lee Baldwin Dalzell. *George Washington's Mount Vernon: At Home in Revolutionary America.* New York: Oxford University Press, 1998.

Dann, John C., ed. *The Revolution Remembered.* Chicago: University of Chicago Press, 1980.

Darnton, Robert. *George Washington's False Teeth: An Unconventional Guide to the Eighteenth Century.* New York: Norton, 2003.

Daughan, George C. *If by Sea: The Forging of the American Navy—From the Revolution to the War of 1812.* New York: Basic Books, 2008.

———. *Revolution on the Hudson: New York City, the Hudson River, and the War of Independence.* New York: Norton, 2016.

Davie, William. *The Revolutionary War Sketches of William R. Davie.* Edited by Blackwell P. Robinson. Raleigh: North Carolina Dept. of Cultural Resources, Division of Archives and History, 1976.

Davies, K. G., ed. *Documents of the American Revolution.* Vols. 18, 19 and 20, *Transcripts, 1781.* Dublin: Irish University Press, 1979.

Davis, Burke. *The Campaign That Won America: The Story of Yorktown.* 1970. Reprint, Fort Washington, Pa.: Eastern Acorn Press, 1997.

———. *The Cowpens–Guilford Courthouse Campaign.* Philadelphia: University of Pennsylvania Press, 2002.

Davis, Robert P. *"Where a Man Can Go": Major General William Phillips, British Royal Artillery, 1731–1781.* Westport, Conn.: Greenwood Press, 1999.

Dearborn, Henry. *Revolutionary War Journals of Henry Dearborn, 1775–1783.* Edited by Lloyd A. Brown and Howard H. Peckham. New York: Da Capo, 1971.

De Deux-Ponts, Count Guillaume. *My Campaigns in America: A Journal Kept by Count William De Deux-Ponts, 1780–81.* Edited by Samuel Abbott Green. Boston: Wiggin and Lunt, 1868.

De Lapeyrière, René-Calixte de Labat. "Journal." Edited by Gilbert Bodinier. In *La Glorieuse Campagne du Comte de Grasse, 1781–1782,* pp. 7–36. Paris: SPM, 2010.

Dempsey, Janet. *Washington's Last Cantonment.* Monroe, N.Y.: Library Research Associations, 1990.

Denny, Ebenezer. *Military Journal of Major Ebenezer Denny, October 18, 1781.* Philadelphia: J. B. Lippincott, 1859.

De Vaudreuil, Louis-Philippe. "Notes de Campagne du Comte Rigand de Vaudreuil 1781–1783." *Neptunia,* 1956, 1957, 1958–1959. U.S. Naval Academy Nimitz Library.

Dickinson, H. T., ed. *Britain and the American Revolution.* London: Longman, 1998.

Drake, Samuel Adams. *Life and Correspondence of Henry Knox.* Cambridge, Mass.: Wilson and Son, 1873.

Draper, Lyman C. *King's Mountain and Its Heroes: History of the Battle of King's Mountain, Oct. 7, 1780.* Cincinnati: Peter Thomson, 1881.

Duffy, Christopher. *Siege Warfare.* Vol. 2, *The Fortress in the Age of Vauban and Frederick the Great, 1680–1787.* London: Routledge, 1985.

Duffy, Michael. *Soldiers, Sugar and Seapower: The British Expeditions to the West Indies and the War Against Revolutionary France.* Oxford: Oxford University Press, 1987.

———. "Types of Naval Leadership in the Eighteenth Century." In *Naval Leadership in the Atlantic World,* edited by R. Harding and A. Guimerá, pp. 49–57. London: University of Westminster Press, 2017. https://doi.org/10.16997/book2.e.

Dull, Jonathan. *The Age of the Ship of the Line: The British and French Navies, 1650–1815.* Lincoln: University of Nebraska Press, 2009.

———. *American Naval History, 1607–1865: Overcoming the Colonial Legacy.* Lincoln: University of Nebraska Press, 2009.

———. *A Diplomatic History of the American Revolution.* New Haven: Yale University Press, 1985.

———. "France and the American Revolution Seen as Tragedy." In *Diplomacy and Revolution: The Franco-American Alliance of 1778,* edited by R. Hoffman and P. J. Albert, pp. 73–106. Charlottesville: University Press of Virginia, 1981.

———. *The French Navy and American Independence: A Study of Arms and Diplomacy, 1774–1787.* Princeton, N.J.: Princeton University Press, 1975.

———. "Mahan, Sea Power, and the War for American Independence." *International History Review* 10, no. 1 (1988), pp. 59–67.

———. *The Miracle of Independence: Twenty Ways Things Could Have Turned Out Differently.* Lincoln: University of Nebraska Press, 2015.

———. "Was the Continental Navy a Mistake?" *American Neptune* 44 (1984), pp. 167–70.

DuVal, Kathleen. *Independence Lost: Lives on the Edge of the American Revolution.* New York: Random House, 2016.

Edgar, Walter. *Partisans and Redcoats: The Southern Conflict That Turned the Tide of the American Revolution.* New York: William Morrow, 2003.

Eller, E. M. "Washington's Maritime Strategy and the Campaign That Assured Independence." In *Chesapeake Bay in the American Revolution,* edited by E. M. Eller, pp. 475–524. Centreville, Md.: Tidewater, 1981.

———, ed. *Chesapeake Bay in the American Revolution.* Centreville, Md: Tidewater, 1981.

Ellis, Joseph J. *American Sphinx: The Character of Thomas Jefferson.* New York: Vintage, 1998.

———. *His Excellency George Washington.* New York: Vintage, 2005.

Eulogies and Orations on the Life and Death of George Washington. Boston: Manning and Loring, 1800.

Ewald, Captain Johann. *Diary of the American War: A Hessian Journal.* Translated and edited by Joseph P. Tustin. New Haven: Yale University Press, 1979.

Fabian, Monroe H. *Joseph Wright: American Artist, 1756–1793.* Washington, D.C.: National Portrait Gallery, 1985.

Falconer, William. *A New Universal Dictionary of the Marine.* Edited by William Burney. 1815. Reprint, New York: Cambridge University Press, 2011.

Falkner, James. *Marshal Vauban and the Defense of Louis XIV's France.* Barnsley, Eng.: Pen and Sword Military, 2011.

Fallaw, R., and M. W. Stoer. "The Old Dominion Under Fire: The Chesapeake Invasions, 1779–1781." In *Chesapeake Bay in the American Revolution*, edited by E. M. Eller, pp. 432–74. Centreville, Md.: Tidewater, 1981.

Feltman, William. *The Journal of Lieut. William Feltman of the First Pennsylvania Regiment, 1781–1782*. Philadelphia: Historical Society of Pennsylvania, 1853.

Ferguson, E. James. *The American Revolution: A General History, 1763–1790*. Homewood, Ill.: Dorsey, 1974.

———. *The Power of the Purse: A History of American Public Finance, 1775–1790*. Chapel Hill: University of North Carolina Press, 1961.

Ferguson, Patrick. "An Officer Out of His Time: Correspondence of Major Patrick Ferguson, 1779–1780." Edited by Hugh F. Rankin. In *Sources of American Independence: Selected Manuscripts from the Collections of the William L. Clements Library*, edited by Howard H. Peckham, vol. 2, pp. 287–360. Chicago: University of Chicago Press, 1978.

Ferling, John. *The Ascent of George Washington: The Hidden Political Genius of an American Icon*. New York: Bloomsbury, 2009.

———. *First of Men: A Life of George Washington*. New York: Oxford University Press, 2010.

———. "John Adams, Diplomat." *WMQ*, 3d ser., 51, no. 2 (April 1994), pp. 227–52.

Ferreiro, Larrie D. *Brothers at Arms: American Independence and the Men of France and Spain Who Saved It*. New York: Knopf, 2016.

———. *Ships and Science: The Birth of Naval Architecture in the Scientific Revolution, 1600–1800*. Cambridge, Mass.: MIT Press, 2007.

Fleming, Thomas. "Bernardo de Galvez: The Forgotten Revolutionary Conquistador Who Saved Louisiana." *American Heritage* 33, no. 3 (April–May 1982). www.americanheritage.com/content/bernardo-de-g%C3%A1lvez.

———. *The Perils of Peace: America's Struggle for Survival After Yorktown*. New York: Smithsonian Books/Collins, 2007.

Flexner, James Thomas. *George Washington: The Forge of Experience*. Boston: Little, Brown, 1965.

———. *George Washington in the American Revolution, 1775–1783*. Boston: Little, Brown, 1967.

Flood, Charles Bracelen. *Rise, and Fight Again: Perilous Times Along the Road to Independence*. New York: Dodd, Mead, 1976.

Fontainieu, Emmanuel de. *The* Hermione: *Lafayette's Warship and the American Revolution*. Translated by Mary Podevin and Anna Fitzgerald. Paris: De Monza Editions, 2015.

Ford, W. C. "Henry Knox—Bookseller." *MHS Proceedings* 6 (1927–1928), pp. 227–303.

———, ed., et al. *Journals of the Continental Congress, 1774–1789*. 34 vols. Washington, D.C.: Government Printing Office, 1904–1937. http://lcweb2.loc.gov/ammem/amlaw/lwjc.html.

Fowler, William. *American Crisis: George Washington and the Dangerous Two Years After Yorktown, 1781–1783*. New York: Walker Books, 2013.

———. *Rebels Under Sail: The American Navy During the Revolution*. New York: Scribner, 1976.

Francisco, Peter. "Letter of Peter Francisco to the General Assembly," November 11, 1820. *WMQ* 13, no. 4 (April 1905), pp. 217–19.

Franklin, Benjamin. *The Papers of Benjamin Franklin*, edited by Leonard W. Larrabee. Vol. 35, edited by Barbara B. Oberg. New Haven: Yale University Press, 1959–2017.

Fraser, Flora. *The Washingtons: George and Martha "Joined in Friendship, Crowned in Love."* New York: Knopf, 2015.

Fredriksen, John. *Revolutionary War Almanac*. New York: Facts on File, 2006.

Freeman, Douglas Southall. *George Washington*. 6 vols. New York: Scribner, 1948–1957.

Frey, Sylvia. *The British Soldiers in America: A Social History of Military Life in the Revolutionary Period*. Austin: University of Texas Press, 1981.

———. *Water from the Rock: Black Resistance in a Revolutionary Age*. Princeton, N.J.: Princeton University Press, 1991.

Gaines, James R. *For Liberty and Glory: Washington, Lafayette, and Their Revolutions*. New York: Norton, 2007.

Gardiner, Leslie. *The British Admiralty*. London: William Blackwood and Sons, 1968.

Geake, Robert. *From Slaves to Soldiers: The Story of the First Rhode Island Regiment*. Yardley, Pa.: Westholme, 2016.

Gilbert, Benjamin. *Winding Down: The Revolutionary Letters of Lieutenant Benjamin Gilbert of Massachusetts, 1780–1783*. Edited by John Shy. Ann Arbor: University of Michigan Press, 1989.

Giroud, Vincent. *The Road to Yorktown*. New Haven: Yale University Library, 1992.

Glickstein, Don. *After Yorktown: The Final Struggle for American Independence*. Yardley, Pa.: Westholme, 2015.

Goldenberg, J. A., and M. W. Stoer. "The Virginia State Navy." In *Chesapeake Bay in the American Revolution*, edited by E. M. Eller, pp. 170–203. Centreville, Md.: Tidewater, 1981.

Golway, Terry. *Washington's General: Nathanael Greene and the Triumph of the American Revolution*. New York: Henry Holt, 2005.

Gordon, William. *The History of the Rise, Progress, and Establishment of the Independence of the United States of America*. Vol. 3. New York: Samuel Campbell, 1801.

Gottschalk, Louis R. *Lafayette and the Close of the American Revolution*. Chicago: University of Chicago Press, 1942.

———, ed. *Letters of Lafayette to Washington*. N.p.: printed by Helen Fahnestock Hubbard, 1944.

Graham, Gerald S. *The Royal Navy in the War of American Independence*. London: HMSO, 1976.

Graham, James. *The Life of General Daniel Morgan of the Virginia Line of the Army of the United States*. New York: Derby and Jackson, 1856.

Graham, William A., ed. *General Joseph Graham and His Papers on North Carolina Revolutionary History*. Raleigh, N.C.: Edwards and Broughton, 1904.

Grainger, John D. *The Battle of Yorktown, 1781: A Reassessment*. Woodbridge, Eng.: Boydell, 2005.

Graves, William. *Two Letters Respecting the Conduct of Rear-Admiral Graves in North America*. 1783. Reprint, Morrisania, N.Y.: Bradstreet and Sons, 1864.

Gray, Robert. "Colonel Robert Gray's Observations on the War in Carolina." *The South Carolina Historical and Genealogical Magazine* 11, no. 3 (July 1910), pp. 1–159.

Green, William. *The Memoranda of William Green, Secretary to Vice-Admiral Marriot Arbuthnot, in the American Revolution*. Edited by Henry S. Fraser. Providence: Rhode Island Historical Society, 1924.

Greene, Jerome. *The Guns of Independence: The Siege of Yorktown*. New York: Savas Beatie, 2005.

Greene, Nathanael. *The Papers of General Nathanael Greene*. Edited by Richard K. Showman and Dennis M. Conrad. Vols. 6–9. Chapel Hill: University of North Carolina Press, 1991–1997.

Greenwood, W. Bart. *The American Revolution: An Atlas of 18th-Century Maps and Charts*. Washington, D.C.: Government Printing Office, 1972.

Gregorie, Anne King. *Thomas Sumter*. Columbia, S.C.: R. L. Bryan, 1931.

Haggard, Richard. "The Nicola Affair: Lewis Nicola, George Washington, and American Military Discontent During the Revolutionary War." *Proceedings of the American Philosophical Society* 146, no. 2 (June 2002), pp. 139–69.

Hagist, Don. *British Soldiers, American War: Voices of the American Revolution*. Yardley, Pa.: Westholme, 2012.

Hall, Wilbur C. "Sergeant Champe's Adventure." *WMQ* 18, no. 3 (July 1938), pp. 322–42.

Hamilton, Alexander. *The Papers of Alexander Hamilton*. Edited by Harold C. Syrett. Vols. 2–3. New York: Columbia University Press, 1961–1962.

Hannay, David. *Rodney*. Boston: Gregg, 1972.

Harland, John. *Seamanship in the Age of Sail*. Annapolis, Md.: Naval Institute Press, 2000.

Harris, Robert. "French Finances and the American War, 1777–1783." *Journal of Modern History* 48, no. 2 (June 1976), pp. 233–58.

Hatch, Charles E., Jr. *The Battle of Guilford Courthouse*. Washington, D.C.: Office of History and Historic Architecture, Eastern Service Center, 1971.

Hattendorf, J. B. "The Idea of 'A Fleet in Being' in Historical Perspective." *Naval War College Review* 67, no. 1 (2014), pp. 43–60.

———. *Newport, the French Navy, and American Independence*. Newport, R.I.: Redwood, 2005.

———. *Talking About Naval History: A Collection of Essays*. Newport, R.I.: Naval War College Press, 2011.

Headley, J. T. *Washington and His Generals*. Vol. 1. 1813. Reprint, Yorklyn, Del.: Academy of Honor Press, 1998.

Henriques, Peter. "Major Lawrence Washington Versus the Reverend Charles Green: A Case Study of the Squire and the Parson." *Virginia Magazine of History and Biography* 100, no. 2 (April 1992), pp. 233–64.

———. *Realistic Visionary: A Portrait of George Washington*. Charlottesville: University of Virginia Press, 2008.

Henry, Robert. *Narrative of the Battle of Cowan's Ford, Feb. 1, 1781*. And *Narrative of the Battle of King's Mountain by Captain David Vance*. Greensboro, N.C.: D. Schenck, 1891.

Hibbert, Christopher. *George III: A Personal History*. New York: Basic Books, 2000.

———. *Redcoats and Rebels: The American Revolution Through British Eyes*. New York: Norton, 2002.

Higginbotham, Don. *Daniel Morgan, Revolutionary Rifleman*. Chapel Hill: University of North Carolina Press, 1961.

———. "The Early American Way of War: Reconnaissance and Appraisal. *WMQ*, 3d ser., 44 (April 1987), pp. 230–73.

———. *George Washington: Uniting a Nation*. Lanham, Md.: Rowman and Littlefield, 2004.

———. *The War of American Independence: Military Attitudes, Policies, and Practice, 1763–1789*. Boston: Northeastern University Press, 1983.

———. *Washington and the American Military Tradition*. Athens: University of Georgia Press, 2004.

———, ed. *Reconsiderations on the Revolutionary War: Selected Essays*. Westport, Conn.: Greenwood Press, 1978.

Hill, William. *Colonel William Hill's Memoirs of the Revolution*. Edited by A. S. Salley Jr. Columbia: Historical Commission of South Carolina, 1921.

Hodges, Graham Russell. *Root and Branch: African Americans in New York and East Jersey, 1613–1863*. Chapel Hill: University of North Carolina Press, 1999.

Hoffman, R., and P. J. Albert, eds. *Diplomacy and Revolution: The Franco-American Alliance of 1778*. Charlottesville: University Press of Virginia, 1981.

———. *Peace and the Peacemakers: The Treaty of 1783*. Charlottesville: University Press of Virginia, 1986.

Hoffman, R., Thad W. Tate, and P. J. Albert, eds. *An Uncivil War: The Southern Backcountry During the American Revolution*. Charlottesville: University Press of Virginia, 1985.

Hoock, Holger. *Scars of Independence: America's Violent Birth*. New York: Crown, 2017.

Hood, Sir Samuel. *Letters Written by Sir Samuel Hood in 1781–2–3.* Edited by David Hannay. London: Naval Records Society, 1895.

Howard, Hugh. *The Painter's Chair: George Washington and the Making of American Art.* New York: Bloomsbury, 2009.

Humphreys, David. *The Conduct of General Washington Respecting the Confinement of Captain Asgill.* New York, 1859 (reprinted from the *New Haven Gazette*, 1786).

——. *Life of General Washington.* Edited by Rosemarie Zagarri. Athens: University of Georgia Press, 1991.

Idzerda, Stanley. "Indispensable Allies: The French at Yorktown." *Wilson Quarterly* 5, no. 4 (Oct. 1, 1981), pp. 166–77.

Irvin, Benjamin H. *Clothed in Robes of Sovereignty: The Continental Congress and the People Out of Doors.* New York: Oxford University Press, 2014.

James, Bartholomew. *Journal of Rear-Admiral Bartholomew James, 1752–1828.* Edited by John Knox Laughton and James Young Falkland Sullivan. London: Navy Records Society, 1896.

James, W. M. *The British Navy in Adversity: A Study of the War of American Independence.* New York: Longmans, Green, 1926.

Jameson, J. F. "St. Eustatius in the American Revolution." *American Historical Review* 8, no. 4 (1903), pp. 683–708.

Jasanoff, Maya. *Liberty's Exiles: American Loyalists in the Revolutionary World.* New York: Knopf, 2011.

Jefferson, Thomas. *The Papers of Thomas Jefferson.* Vols. 4, 5, 6, and 7. Edited by Julian Boyd. Princeton, N.J.: Princeton University Press, 1950–1952.

Johnston, Henry P. *The Yorktown Campaign and the Surrender of Cornwallis, 1781.* New York: Harper and Brothers, 1881.

Journal of the Proceedings of His Majesty's Ship the London. National Archives, Public Records Office, Kew, Eng., Admiralty Records, ADM 51/552.

Keegan, John. *Fields of Battle: The Wars for North America.* New York: Vintage, 1997.

——. *The Price of Admiralty: The Evolution of Naval Warfare from Trafalgar to Midway.* New York: Penguin, 1988.

Kelly, Alfred, et al. *Leadership in the American Revolution.* Washington, D.C.: Library of Congress, 1974.

Kennedy, Paul M. *The Rise and Fall of British Naval Mastery.* London: Penguin, 2017.

Kennett, Lee. *The French Forces in America, 1780–1783.* Westport, Conn.: Greenwood Press, 1977.

Kerallain, Rene de. *Bougainville à l'armée du comte de Grasse, 1781–1782.* Paris: Maisonneuve Freres, 1928.

Ketchum, Richard. *Victory at Yorktown: The Campaign That Won the Revolution.* New York: Henry Holt, 2004.

Kimbrough, Mary. *Louis-Antoine de Bougainville, 1729–1811: A Study in French Naval History and Politics.* Lewiston, N.Y.: Edwin Mellen, 1990.

King, Rufus. *The Life and Correspondence of Rufus King.* Edited by Charles R. King. New York: Putnam, 1894.

Kirkwood, Robert. *The Journal and Order Book of Captain Robert Kirkwood of the Delaware Regiment of the Continental Line.* Edited by Rev. Joseph Brown Turner. 1910. Reprint, Port Washington, N.Y.: Kennikat, 1970.

Kirsche, James. *Gouverneur Morris: Author, Statesman, and Man of the World.* New York: St. Martin's, 2005.

Kite, Elizabeth. *Brigadier-General Louis Duportail, Commandant of Engineers in the Continental Army, 1777–1783.* Baltimore: Johns Hopkins Press, 1933.

Kitman, Marvin. *George Washington's Expense Account*. New York: Grove Press, 2001.

Knight, R. J. B. "The Introduction of Copper Sheathing into the Royal Navy, 1779–86." *Mariner's Mirror* 59 (1973), pp. 299–309.

———. "New England Forests and British Seapower: Albion Revised." *American Neptune* 46 (1986), pp. 221–29.

———. "The Royal Navy's Recovery After the Early Phase of the American Revolutionary War." In *The Aftermath of Defeat: Societies, Armed Forces and the Challenge of Recovery*, edited by G. J. Andreopoulos and H. E. Selesky, pp. 10–25, 160–62. New Haven: Yale University Press, 1994.

Knox, Dudley W. *The Naval Genius of George Washington*. Boston: Houghton Mifflin, 1932.

Kohn, Richard. "The Inside History of the Newburgh Conspiracy: America and the Coup d'Etat." *WMQ*, 3rd ser., 27 (April 1970), pp. 187–220.

Kowalski, Jean-Marie. "The Battle of the Chesapeake from the Quarterdeck." Paper delivered at the 2015 SAR Annual Conference on the American Revolution at George Washington's Mount Vernon, June 12–14, 2015.

Kranish, Michael. *Flight from Monticello: Thomas Jefferson at War*. Oxford: Oxford University Press, 2010.

———. "Jefferson on the Run." *American History* 45, no. 2 (2010), pp. 26–33.

Kwasny, Mark V. *Washington's Partisan War, 1775–1783*. Kent, Ohio: Kent State University Press, 1996.

Lafayette, Marquis de. *Lafayette in the Age of the American Revolution: Selected Letters and Papers, 1776–1790*. Vols. 3 and 4. Edited by Stanley J. Idzerda. Ithaca, N.Y.: Cornell University Press, 1980–1981.

———. *Memoirs, Correspondence, and Manuscripts of General Lafayette, Published by His Family*. New York: Saunders and Otley, 1837.

Lamb, John. *Memoir of the Life and Times of General John Lamb, an Officer of the Revolution*. Edited by Isaac Q. Leake. Albany, N.Y.: J. Munsell, 1857.

Lamb, Roger. *An Original and Authentic Journal of Occurrences During the Late American War*. Dublin: Wilkinson and Courtney, 1809.

Lambert, Robert Stansbury. *South Carolina Loyalists in the American Revolution*. Columbia: University of South Carolina Press, 1987.

Landers, Colonel H. L. *The Virginia Campaign and the Blockade and Siege of Yorktown, 1781*. Washington, D.C.: Government Printing Office, 1931.

Larrabee, Harold A. *Decision at the Chesapeake*. New York: Clarkson Potter, 1964.

———. "A Neglected French Collaborator in the Victory of Yorktown, Claude-Anne, Marquis de Saint-Simon (1740–1819)." *Journal de la Société des Americanistes* 24, no. 2 (1932), pp. 245–57.

Lassiter, F. R. "Arnold's Invasion of Virginia." *Sewanee Review* 9, no. 1 (1901), pp. 78–93, and no. 2, pp. 185–202.

Latrobe, Benjamin Henry. *The Virginia Journals of Benjamin Henry Latrobe, 1795–1798*. Edited by Edward C. Carter II. 2 vols. New Haven: Yale University Press, 1977.

Lauzun, Duc de. *Memoirs of Duc de Lauzun*. Translated by C. K. Scott Moncrieff. New York: Brentano's, 1928.

Leach, Donald B. "George Washington: Waterman-Fisherman, 1760–1799." *Yearbook of the Historical Society of Fairfax County* 28 (2001–2002), pp. 1–28.

Lee, Henry. *Memoirs of the War in the Southern Department of the United States*. 2 vols. Philadelphia: Bradford and Innskeep, 1812.

Lee, Richard Henry. *The Letters of Richard Henry Lee, 1779–1794*. Vol. 2. New York: Macmillan, 1914.

Lehman, Eric. *Homegrown Terror: Benedict Arnold and the Burning of New London*. Middletown, Conn.: Wesleyan University Press, 2014.

Lender, Mark Edward, and James Kirby Martin. "A Traitor's Epiphany: Benedict Arnold in Virginia and His Quest for Reconciliation." *Virginia Magazine of History and Biography* 125, no. 4, pp. 315–57.

Lengel, Edward G. *General George Washington: A Military Life*. New York: Random House, 2007.

———. *This Glorious Struggle: George Washington's Revolutionary War Letters*. New York: HarperCollins, 2008.

Levy, Philip. *Where the Cherry Tree Grew: The Story of Ferry Farm, George Washington's Boyhood Home*. New York: St. Martin's, 2013.

Lewis, Charles Lee. *Admiral De Grasse and American Independence*. Annapolis, Md.: United States Naval Institute, 1945.

Lewis, James H. "Las Damas de la Havana, El Precursor, and Francisco de Saavedra: A Note on the Spanish Participation in the Battle of Yorktown." *The Americas* 37 (July 1980), pp. 83–99.

Leyburn, James G. *The Scotch-Irish*. Chapel Hill: University of North Carolina Press, 1962.

Linder, B. *Tidewater's Navy*. Annapolis, Md.: Naval Institute Press, 2005.

Lockhart, Paul. *The Drillmaster of Valley Forge: The Baron de Steuben and the Making of the American Army*. New York: HarperCollins, 2008.

Longmore, Paul. *The Invention of George Washington*. Charlottesville: University Press of Virginia, 1999.

Lopez, Claude-Anne. *Mon Cher Papa: Franklin and the Ladies of Paris*. New Haven: Yale University Press, 1966.

Lossing, Benson. *Life and Times of Philip Schuyler*. New York: Sheldon, 1873.

———. *The Pictorial Field-book of the Revolution*. 2 vols. New York: Harper and Brothers, 1855.

Lowenthal, Larry. *Hell on the East River: British Prison Ships in the American Revolution*. Fleischmanns, N.Y.: Purple Mountain, 2009.

Lumpkin, Henry. *From Savannah to Yorktown: The American Revolution in the South*. New York: Paragon House, 1987.

Luvaas, Jay, ed. and trans. *Frederick the Great on the Art of War*. New York: Free Press, 1966.

Maass, John Richard, and Charles B. Baxley. *Horatio Gates and the Battle of Camden: "That Unhappy Affair," August 16, 1780*. Camden, S.C.: Kershaw County Historical Society, 2001.

Macintyre, Captain Donald, R.N. *Admiral Rodney*. New York: Norton, 1962.

Mackenzie, Frederick. *The Diary of Frederick Mackenzie*. Vol. 2. Cambridge, Mass.: Harvard University Press, 1930.

Mackesy, Piers. *The War for America, 1775–1783*. Lincoln: University of Nebraska Press, 1993.

Mahan, A. T. *The Influence of Sea Power upon History, 1660–1783*. Boston: Little, Brown, 1918.

———. *The Major Operations of the Navies in the War of American Independence*. 1913. Reprint, Gloucestershire, Eng.: Nonsuch, 2006.

Manca, Joseph. *George Washington's Eye: Landscape, Architecture and Design at Mount Vernon*. Baltimore: Johns Hopkins University Press, 2012.

———. "George Washington's Use of Humor During the Revolutionary War." *Journal of the American Revolution*, Feb. 5, 2015. https://allthingsliberty.com/2015/02/george-washingtons-use-of-humor-during-the-revolutionary-war/.

Manceron, Claude. *The French Revolution*. Vol. 2, *The Wind from America*. New York: Knopf, 1978.

Martin, James Kirby. *Benedict Arnold: Revolutionary Hero, An American Warrior Reconsidered*. New York: New York University Press, 1997.

Martin, Joseph Plumb. *Ordinary Courage: The Revolutionary War Adventures of Joseph Plumb Martin.* Edited by James Kirby Martin. Oxford: Wiley-Blackwell, 2013.

Masefield, John. *Sea Life in Nelson's Time.* London: Methuen, 1905.

Massey, Gregory. *John Laurens and the American Revolution.* Columbia: University of South Carolina Press, 2000.

Mattern, David B. *Benjamin Lincoln and the American Revolution.* Columbia: University of South Carolina Press, 1995.

Mayer, Holly. *Belonging to the Army: Camp Followers and Community During the American Revolution.* Columbia: University of South Carolina Press, 1999.

McAfee, Michael L. "Artillery of the American Revolution, 1775–1783." Washington, D.C.: American Defense Preparedness Association, 1974.

McBurney, Christian M. *Spies in Revolutionary Rhode Island.* Charleston, S.C.: History Press, 2014.

McDougall, Walter A. *Freedom Just Around the Corner: A New American History, 1585–1828.* New York: Perennial, 2004.

McJunkin, Joseph. "Memoir of Joseph McJunkin of Union." *The Magnolia, or Southern Appalachian* 2 (January 1843), pp. 30–40.

McLean, David. *Timothy Pickering and the Age of the American Revolution.* New York: Arno, 1982.

McNeill, William H. *The Pursuit of Power.* Chicago: University of Chicago Press, 1982.

McPhee, John. *The Founding Fish.* New York: Farrar, Straus and Giroux, 2003.

Middlekauff, Robert. *The Glorious Cause: The American Revolution, 1763–1789.* New York: Oxford University Press, 2005.

——. "Why Men Fought in the American Revolution." *Huntington Library Quarterly* 43 (Spring 1980), pp. 143–44, 148.

Middleton, Arthur Pierce. *Tobacco Coast.* Baltimore: Johns Hopkins University Press, 1953.

Millas, José. *Hurricanes of the Caribbean and Adjacent Regions, 1492–1800.* Cambridge, Mass.: Academy of the Arts and Sciences of the Americas, 1968.

Miller, D. L., et al. "Tree-Ring Isotope Records of Tropical Cyclone Activity." *Proceedings of the National Academy of Sciences of the United States of America* 103, no. 39 (2006), pp. 14294–97.

Miller, Nathan. *Sea of Glory: The Continental Navy Fights for Independence, 1775–1783.* New York: David McKay, 1974.

Miller, Richard. *In Words and Deeds: Battle Speeches in History.* Hanover, N.H.: University Press of New England, 2008.

Mintz, Max M. *Gouverneur Morris and the American Revolution.* Norman: University of Oklahoma Press, 1970.

Mitchell, Broadus. *Alexander Hamilton: Youth to Maturity, 1755–1788.* New York: Macmillan, 1962.

——. *The Price of Independence: A Realistic View of the American Revolution.* New York: Oxford University Press, 1974.

Moore, Frank. *Diary of the American Revolution.* Vols. 1 and 2. New York: Scribner, 1859.

——. *Songs and Ballads of the American Revolution.* New York: D. Appleton, 1855.

Moore, Warren. *Weapons of the American Revolution and Accoutrements.* New York: Promontory, 1967.

Morgan, Edmund S. *The Birth of the Republic, 1763–1789.* 3rd ed. Chicago: University of Chicago Press, 1992.

——. *The Genius of George Washington.* New York: Norton, 1980.

——. *Inventing the People: The Rise of Popular Sovereignty in England and America.* New York: Norton, 1988.

Morison, Samuel Eliot. "The Young Man George Washington." In *George Washington: A Profile,* edited by James Morton Smith, pp. 38–58. New York: Hill and Wang, 1969.

Morris, Richard B. *The Peacemakers: The Great Powers and American Independence.* New York: Harper and Row, 1965.

Morrissey, Brendan. *Yorktown, 1781: The World Turned Upside Down.* Long Island City, N.Y.: Osprey, 1997.

Mostert, Noel. *The Line upon a Wind: The Great War at Sea, 1793–1815.* New York: Norton, 2008.

Moultrie, William. *Memoirs of the American Revolution So Far as It Relates to the States of North and South Carolina, and Georgia.* 1802. Reprint, New York: Arno, 1968.

Muhlenberg, Henry. *Life of Major-General Peter Muhlenberg of the Revolutionary Army.* Philadelphia: Sherman, 1849.

Mulcahy, M. *Hurricanes and Society in the British Greater Caribbean, 1624–1783.* Baltimore: Johns Hopkins University Press, 2006.

Muller, John. *The Attack and Defense of Fortified Places, 1757.* Edited by David Manthey. Woodbridge, Va.: Invisible College, 2004.

Murdoch, David H., ed. *Rebellion in America: A Contemporary British Viewpoint, 1769–1783.* Santa Barbara, Calif.: Clio, 1979.

Murphy, Daniel. *William Washington: American Light Dragoon.* Yardley, Pa.: Westholme, 2014.

Myers, Minor, Jr. *Liberty Without Anarchy: A History of the Society of the Cincinnati.* Charlottesville: University of Virginia Press, 2004.

Nagy, John. *Invisible Ink: Spycraft of the American Revolution.* Yardley, Pa.: Westholme, 2011.

———. *Mutinies in the Ranks: Mutinies of the American Revolution.* Yardley, Pa.: Westholme, 2007.

Nash, Gary. *The Unknown American Revolution.* New York: Penguin, 2006.

"The Naval Engagement of De Grasse and Graves Off the Capes of the Chesapeake." *The Magazine of American History* 7 (1881), pp. 367–70.

Nebanzahl, Kenneth, and Don Higginbotham. *Atlas of the American Revolution.* Chicago: Rand McNally, 1974.

Neely, Wayne. *The Great Hurricane of 1780: The Story of the Greatest and Deadliest Hurricane of the Caribbean and the Americas.* Bloomington, Ind.: iUniverse, 2012.

Neimeyer, Charles Patrick. *America Goes to War: A Social History of the Continental Army.* New York: New York University Press, 1996.

Nelson, Eric. *The Royalist Revolution.* Cambridge, Mass.: Harvard University Press, 2014.

Nelson, James. *George Washington's Great Gamble and the Sea Battle That Won the American Revolution.* New York: McGraw-Hill, 2010.

Nelson, Paul David. *Anthony Wayne: Solider of the Early Republic.* Bloomington: Indiana University Press, 1985.

———. *Francis Rawdon-Hastings, Marquess of Hastings: Soldier, Peer of the Realm, Governor-General of India.* Cranbury, N.J.: Fairleigh Dickinson University Press, 2005.

———. *General Guy Carleton, Lord Dorchester: Soldier-Statesman of Early British Canada.* Madison, N.J.: Fairleigh Dickinson University Press, 2000.

———. *General Horatio Gates.* Baton Rouge: Louisiana State University Press, 1976.

———. "Horatio Gates at Newburgh, 1783: A Misunderstood Role." *WMQ,* 3rd ser., 29 (January 1972), pp. 143–58.

Nelson, William. *The American Tory.* New York: Oxford University Press, 1961.

Nester, William. *The Frontier War for American Independence.* Mechanicsburg, Pa.: Stackpole, 2004.

Newsome, A. R., ed. "A British Orderly Book, 1780–1781." *The North Carolina Historical Review* 9, no. 3 (July 1932), pp. 273–98, and 9, no. 4 (October 1932), pp. 366–92.

Norton, Mary Beth. *The British-Americans: The Loyalist Exiles in England, 1774–1789.* Boston: Little, Brown, 1972.

———. "Eighteenth Century American Women in Peace and War: The Case of the Loyalists." *WMQ*, 3rd ser., 33 (1976), pp. 386–409.

———. *Liberty's Daughters: The Revolutionary Experience of American Women, 1750–1800.* Ithaca, N.Y.: Cornell University Press, 1996.

O'Brian, Patrick. *Men-of-War: Life in Nelson's Navy.* New York: Norton, 1995.

O'Donnell, Patrick. *Washington's Immortals.* New York: Atlantic Monthly, 2016.

O'Donnell, William. *The Chevalier De La Luzerne: French Minister to the United States, 1779–1794.* Bruges: Bibliothèque de l'Université, 1938.

O'Hara, Charles. "Letters of Charles O'Hara to the Duke of Grafton." *The South Carolina Historical Magazine* 65, no. 3 (July 1964), pp. 158–80.

O'Shaughnessy, Andrew. *An Empire Divided: The American Revolution and the British Caribbean.* Philadelphia: University of Pennsylvania Press, 2000.

———. "'If Others Will Not Be Active, I Must Drive': George III and the American Revolution." *Early American Studies* 2, no. 1 (Spring 2004), pp. 1–47.

———. *The Men Who Lost America: British Leadership, the American Revolution, and the Fate of the Empire.* New Haven: Yale University Press, 2013.

Padfield, Peter. *Guns at Sea: A History of Naval Gunnery.* New York: St. Martin's, 1974.

———. *Maritime Supremacy and the Opening of the Western Mind: Naval Campaigns That Shaped the Modern World.* New York: Overlook, 2000.

Palmer, Dave. *Washington's Military Genius.* Washington, D.C.: Regency, 2012.

Palmer, John. *General von Steuben.* New Haven: Yale University Press, 1937.

Palmer, Michael A. *Command at Sea: Naval Command and Control Since the Sixteenth Century.* Cambridge, Mass.: Harvard University Press, 2005.

Pancake, John. *This Destructive War.* Tuscaloosa: University of Alabama Press, 1985.

Parker, Matthew. *The Sugar Barons: Family, Corruption, Empire, and War in the West Indies.* New York: Walker, 2011.

Pearson, Michael. *Those Damned Rebels: The American Revolution as Seen Through British Eyes.* New York: Putnam, 1972.

Peckham, Howard H. *The Toll of Independence.* Chicago: University of Chicago Press, 1974.

Pengelly, Colin. *Sir Samuel Hood and the Battle of the Chesapeake.* Gainesville: University Press of Florida, 2009.

Pennypacker, George. *George Washington's Spies on Long Island and in New York.* Brooklyn, N.Y.: Long Island Historical Society, 1939.

Philbrick, Nathaniel. *Bunker Hill: A City, a Siege, a Revolution.* New York: Viking, 2013.

———. *Valiant Ambition: George Washington, Benedict Arnold, and the Fate of the American Resolution.* New York: Viking, 2016.

Philbrick, Thomas. "The American Revolution as a Literary Event." In *Columbia Literary History of the United States*, edited by Emory Elliott, pp. 139–55. New York: Columbia University Press, 1988.

Phillips, Leon. *The Fantastic Breed: Americans in King George's War.* Garden City, N.Y.: Doubleday, 1968.

Pickering, Octavius, and Charles Upham. *The Life of Timothy Pickering.* 2 vols. Boston: Little, Brown, 1873.

Pielke, Roger A., Sr. *Hurricanes: Their Nature and Impact on Society.* New York: Wiley, 1998.

Poag, Wiley. *Chesapeake Invader: Discovering American's Giant Meteorite Crater.* Princeton, N.J.: Princeton University Press, 1999.

Polishook, Irwin. *Rhode Island and the Union, 1774–1795.* Evanston, Ill.: Northwestern University Press, 1969.

Pope, Dudley. *Life in Nelson's Navy.* Annapolis, Md.: Naval Institute Press, 1981.

Porter, Joseph W. "Memoir of General Henry Knox." *Bangor Historical Magazine* (February–March 1890), pp. 1–16.

Powars, David S. "The Effects of the Chesapeake Bay Impact Crater on the Geologic Framework and the Correlation of Hydrogeologic Units of Southwestern Virginia, South of the James River." Reston, Va.: U.S. Geological Survey, 2000.

Pula, James S. *Thaddeus Ko'sciuszko: The Purest Son of Liberty.* New York: Hippocrene, 1999.

Puls, Mark. *Henry Knox: Visionary General of the American Revolution.* New York: Palgrave Macmillan, 2008.

Rakove, Jack. *The Beginnings of National Politics: An Interpretive History of the Continental Congress.* New York: Knopf, 1979.

———. *Revolutionaries: A New History of the Invention of America.* Boston: Houghton Mifflin, 2010.

Rankin, Hugh F. "Charles Lord Cornwallis: Study in Frustration." In *George Washington's Generals and Opponents,* edited by George Athan Billias, pp. 193–232. New York: Da Capo, 1994.

———. *Francis Marion: The Swamp Fox.* New York: Crowell, 1973.

———. *The North Carolina Continentals.* Chapel Hill: University of North Carolina Press, 1971.

Raphael, Ray. *Founders: The People Who Brought You a Nation.* New York: New Press, 2009.

Rappaport, Edward, and Jose Fernandez-Partagas. "The Deadliest Atlantic Tropical Cyclones, 1492–1994." NOAA Technical Memorandum, NWS NHC-47, January 1995.

Rappleye, Charles. *Robert Morris: Financier of the American Revolution.* New York: Simon and Schuster, 2010.

Reid, W. *An Attempt to Develop the Law of Storms.* London: John Weale, 1838.

Resch, John, and Walter Sargent, eds. *War and Society in the American Revolution: Mobilization and Home Fronts.* DeKalb: Northern Illinois University Press, 2007.

Reynolds, Paul R. *Guy Carleton.* New York: William Morrow, 1980.

Reynolds, William R., Jr. *Andrew Pickens: South Carolina Patriot in the Revolutionary War.* Jefferson, N.C.: McFarland, 2012.

Rhodes, Karl. "The Counterfeiting Weapon." *Economic History* (Winter 2012), pp. 34–37.

Rhodes, Richard. *John James Audubon: The Making of an American.* New York: Knopf, 2004.

Rice, Howard C., Jr., and Anne S. K. Brown, eds. *The American Campaigns of Rochambeau's Army, 1780, 1781, 1782, 1783.* 2 vols. Princeton, N.J.: Princeton University Press, 1972.

Richard, Carl J. *The Founders and the Classics: Greece, Rome, and the American Enlightenment.* Cambridge, Mass.: Harvard University Press, 1994.

Riker, James. *Evacuation Day 1783.* New York: printed for the author, 1883.

Riley, Edward M. "Yorktown During the Revolution. Part II. The Siege of Yorktown, 1781." *Virginia Magazine of History and Biography* 57, no. 3 (July 1949), pp. 274–85.

Robertson, James. *The Twilight of British Rule in Revolutionary America: The New York Letter Book of General James Robertson.* Edited by Milton Klein and Ronald W. Howard. Cooperstown: New York State Historical Association, 1983.

Robinson, William. *Jack Nastyface: Memoirs of an English Seaman.* Edited by Oliver Warner. Annapolis, Md.: Naval Institute Press, 1973.

Robison, S. S., and M. L. Robison. *A History of Naval Tactics from 1530–1930: The Evolution of Tactical Maxims.* Annapolis, Md.: Naval Institute Press, 1942.

Rochambeau, Marshal Count de. *Memoirs of the Marshal Count de Rochambeau Relative to the War of Independence of the United States.* Translated by M. W. E. Wright. 1893. Reprint, New York: Arno, 1971.

Rodger, N. A. M. "Image and Reality in Eighteenth Century Naval Tactics." *Mariner's Mirror* 89 (2003), pp. 280–96.

———. *The Insatiable Earl: A Life of John Montagu, 4th Earl of Sandwich, 1718–92.* New York: Norton, 1993.

———. "Weather, Geography and Naval Power in the Age of Sail." *Journal of Strategic Studies* 22 (1999), pp. 179–200.

———. *The Wooden World: An Anatomy of the Georgian Navy.* New York: Norton, 1986.

Rodney, George, Lord. *Letter-Books and Order-Books of George, Lord Rodney, Admiral of the White Squadron, 1780–1782.* New York: Naval History Society, 1932.

Rose, Alex. *Washington's Spies: The Story of America's First Spy Ring.* New York: Bantam, 2007.

Royal Oak's Journal. National Archives, Public Records Office, Kew, Eng., Admiralty Records, ADM 51/815.

Royster, Charles. *Light-Horse Harry Lee and the Legacy of the American Revolution.* New York: Knopf, 1981.

———. *A Revolutionary People at War: The Continental Army and American Character, 1775–1783.* Chapel Hill: University of North Carolina Press, 1979.

Saavedra, Francisco. *Journal of Don Francisco Saavedra de Sangronis During the Commission Which He Had in His Charge from 25 June 1780 Until the 20th of the Same Month of 1783.* Edited by F. M. Padron. Gainesville: University of Florida Press, 1989.

Sabine, Lorenzo. *The Loyalists of the American Revolution.* Springfield, Mass.: Walden, 1957.

Sands, John O. *Yorktown's Captive Fleet.* Newport News, Va.: Mariners' Museum, 1983.

Sandwich, John. *The Private Papers of John, Earl of Sandwich, First Lord of the Admiralty, 1771–1782.* Vol. 4. Edited by G. R. Barnes and J. H. Owen. London: Naval Records Society, 1936.

Schama, Simon. *Rough Crossings: Britain, the Slaves, and the American Revolution.* New York: Ecco, 2006.

Schecter, Barnet. *The Battle for New York: The City at the Heart of the America Revolution.* New York: Walker, 2002.

———. *George Washington's America: A Biography Through His Maps.* New York: Walker, 2010.

Scheer, George F., and Hugh F. Rankin, eds. *Rebels and Redcoats.* New York: Da Capo, 1957.

Schenck, David. *North Carolina, 1780–81: Being a History of the Invasion of the Carolinas by the British Army Under Lord Cornwallis in 1780–81.* Raleigh, N.C.: Edwards and Broughton, 1889.

Schenkman, A. J. *Washington's Headquarters at Newburgh.* Charleston, S.C.: History Press, 2009.

Schiff, Stacy. *A Great Improvisation: Franklin, France, and the Birth of America.* New York: Henry Holt, 2006.

Schulz, Emily L., and Laura B. Simon. *George Washington and His Generals.* Mount Vernon, Va.: Mount Vernon Ladies' Association, 2009.

Scott, H. M. "The Importance of Bourbon Naval Reconstruction to the Strategy of Choiseul After the Seven Years' War." *The International History Review* 1, no. 1 (January 1979), pp. 17–35.

Scott, Samuel F. *From Yorktown to Valmy: The Transformation of the French Army in an Age of Revolution.* Niwot: University Press of Colorado, 2003.

Selby, J. E. *The Revolution in Virginia, 1775–1783*. Charlottesville: University of Virginia Press, 2007.

Selig, Robert A. "German Soldier in America: Journal of George Flohr." *WMQ* 50, no. 3 (July 1993), pp. 575–90.

———. *March to Victory: Washington, Rochambeau and Yorktown, 1781.* Washington, D.C.: Army Center of Military History, 2007.

———. "Private Flohr's Private Life." *American Heritage* (October 1994), pp. 94–95.

———. *The Washington-Rochambeau Revolutionary Route in the State of Delaware, 1781–1783.* Dover: State of Delaware, 2003.

Shaw, Samuel. *Journals of Samuel Shaw.* Edited by Josiah Quincy. Boston: Wm. Crosby and H. P. Nichols, 1847.

Shea, John Dawson Gilmary, ed. *The Operations of the French Fleet Under the Count de Grasse in 1781–2 as Described in Two Contemporaneous Journals.* New York: The Bradford Club, 1864.

Shelby, Isaac. "King's Mountain Letters of Colonel Isaac Shelby." Edited by J. G. de Roulhac Hamilton. *The Journal of Southern History* 4, no. 3 (August 1938), pp. 367–77.

Shomette, Donald. *Shipwrecks, Sea-Raiders, and Maritime Disasters Along the Delmarva Coast, 1632–2004.* Baltimore: Johns Hopkins University Press, 2007.

A Short Account of the Naval Actions of the Last War; In Order to Prove That the French Nation Never Gave Such Slender Proofs of Maritime Greatness as During That Period; With Observations on the Discipline, and Hints for the Improvement, of the British Navy. By an Officer. London: n.p., 1788.

Shreve, L. G. *Tench Tilghman: The Life and Times of Washington's Aide-de-Camp.* Centreville, Md.: Tidewater, 1982.

Shy, John. *A People Numerous and Armed: Reflections on the Military Struggle for American Independence.* New York: Oxford University Press, 1976.

Silverman, Kenneth. *A Cultural History of the American Revolution.* New York: Crowell, 1976.

Simcoe, Lieutenant Colonel John G. *A Journal of the Queen's Rangers.* 1844. Reprint, New York: Arno, 1968.

Simpson, Alan, and Mary Simpson. "A New Look at How Rochambeau Quartered His Army in Newport (1780–81)." *Newport History* 72, no. 249, article 7. http//digitalcommons .salve.edu/newporthistory/vol72/iss249/7.

Sinclair, John. *Thoughts on the Naval Strength of the British Empire.* London: T. Cadell, 1782.

Skeen, C. Edward. "The Newburgh Conspiracy Reconsidered, with a Rebuttal by Richard H. Kohn." *WMQ*, 3rd ser., 31 (April 1974), pp. 273–98.

Smith, James Morton, ed. *George Washington: A Profile.* New York: Hill and Wang, 1969.

Smith, Paul H. "The American Loyalists: Notes on Their Organization and Numerical Strength." *WMQ* 25 (1968), pp. 258–77.

———. *Loyalists and Redcoats: A Study in British Revolutionary Policy.* New York: Norton, 1964.

———. "Sir Guy Carleton: Peace Negotiations and the Evacuation of New York." *Canadian Historical Review* 50, no. 3 (1969), pp. 245–64.

Smith, William. *Historical Memoirs of William Smith, 1778–1783.* Edited by W. H. Sabine. New York: The New York Times and Arno Press, 1971.

Smyth, W. H. *Sailor's Word Book: A Dictionary of Nautical Terms.* 1867. Reprint, London: Conway Classics, 1996.

Spinney, David. *Rodney.* London: George Allen and Unwin, 1969.

———. "Rodney and the Saintes: A Reassessment." *Mariner's Mirror* 68 (1982), pp. 377–89.

Spring, Matthew. *With Zeal and with Bayonets Only: The British Army on Campaign in North America, 1775–1783.* Norman: University of Oklahoma Press, 2010.

Stauber, Leland. *The American Revolution: A Grand Mistake.* Amherst, N.Y.: Prometheus, 2009.

Steel, David. *The Elements and Practice of Rigging, Seamanship, and Naval Tactics.* Vol. 4. 1807. Reprint, New York: Cambridge University Press, 2011.

Stegeman, John F., and Janet A. Stegeman. *Caty: A Biography of Catharine Littlefield Greene.* Athens: University of Georgia Press, 1977.

Stephenson, Michael. *Patriot Battles: How the War of Independence Was Fought.* New York: Perennial, 2005.

Stevens, Benjamin Franklin, ed. *The Campaign in Virginia, 1781: An Exact Reprint of Six Rare Pamphlets on the Clinton-Cornwallis Controversy.* 2 vols. London: by the author, 1882.

Stevens, John Austin. *The Expedition of Lafayette Against Arnold.* Baltimore: Maryland Historical Society, 1878.

Stewart, R. A. *The History of Virginia's Navy of the Revolution.* Richmond, Va.: Mitchell and Hotchkiss, 1934.

Stinchcombe, William C. *The American Revolution and the French Alliance.* Syracuse, N.Y.: Syracuse University Press, 1969.

Stokes, I. N. Phelps. *The Iconography of Manhattan Island, 1498–1909.* 6 vols. Union, N.J.: Lawbook Exchange, 1998.

Stone, Edwin. *Our French Allies.* Providence, R.I.: Providence Press Co., 1884.

Sullivan, J. A. "Graves and Hood." *Mariner's Mirror* 49 (1983), pp. 175–94.

Swisher, James K. *The Revolutionary War in the Southern Back Country.* Gretna, La.: Pelican, 2008.

Syrett, David. *The Royal Navy in European Waters During the American Revolutionary War.* Columbia: University of South Carolina Press, 1998.

———. *Shipping and the American War, 1775–83: A Study of British Transport Organization.* London: Athlone, 1970.

Tallmadge, Benjamin. *Memoir of Colonel Benjamin Tallmadge.* New York: Thomas Holman, 1858.

Tarleton, Banastre. *A History of the Campaigns of 1780 and 1781 in the Southern Provinces of North America.* London: Cadell, 1787.

Taylor, Alan. *The Divided Ground: Indians, Settlers, and the Northern Borderland of the American Revolution.* New York: Vintage, 2007.

———. *The Internal Enemy: Slavery and War in Virginia.* New York: Norton, 2014.

———. *Liberty Men and Great Proprietors: The Revolutionary Settlement on the Maine Frontier, 1760–1820.* Chapel Hill: University of North Carolina Press, 1990.

Thacher, James, M.D. *A Military Journal During the American Revolutionary War, from 1775–1783.* Boston: Cotton and Barnard, 1823.

Thane, Elswyth. *The Fighting Quaker: Nathanael Greene.* New York: Hawthorn, 1972.

Thayer, Theodore. *Nathanael Greene, Strategist of the American Revolution.* New York: Twayne, 1960.

Tiffany, Osmond. *A Sketch of the Life and Services of Gen. Otho Holland Williams.* Baltimore: J. Murphy, 1851.

Tilghman, Tench. *Memoir of Col. Tench Tilghman.* Albany, N.Y.: J. Munsell, 1876.

Tilley, John A. *The British Navy and the American Revolution.* Columbia: University of South Carolina Press, 1987.

Tornquist, Karl Gustaf. *The Naval Campaigns of Count de Grasse During the American Revolution, 1781–1783.* Translated by Amandus Johnson. Philadelphia: Swedish Colonial Society, 1942.

Trabue, Daniel. "Journal of Colonel Daniel Trabue." In *Colonial Men and Times,* edited by Lillie DuPuy Van Culin Harper, pp. 3–156. Philadelphia: Ines and Sons, 1916.

Tracy, Nicholas. *Navies, Deterrence and American Independence: Britain and Seapower in the 1760s and 1770s*. Vancouver: University of British Columbia Press, 1988.

Treacy, M. F. *Prelude to Yorktown: The Southern Campaign of Nathanael Greene, 1780–1781*. Chapel Hill: University of North Carolina Press, 1963.

Tritten, J. J., and L. Donolo, eds. *A Doctrine Reader: The Navies of the United States, Great Britain, France, Italy and Spain*. Newport, R.I.: Naval War College, 1995.

Trumbull, John. *The Autobiography of Colonel John Trumbull*. Edited by Theodore Sizer. New Haven: Yale University Press, 1953.

Trumbull, Jonathan. "Minutes of Occurrences Respecting the Siege and Capture of Yorktown." *MHS Proceedings* 14 (1875–1876), pp. 331–38.

Tuchman, Barbara W. *The First Salute: A View of the American Revolution*. New York: Ballantine, 1988.

Tucker, Glenn. *Mad Anthony Wayne and the New Nation*. Harrisburg, Pa.: Stackpole, 1973.

Tucker, St. George. "St. George Tucker's Journal of the Siege of Yorktown, 1781." Edited by Edward M. Riley. *WMQ*, 3rd ser., 5 (July 1958), pp. 375–95.

Tunstall, Brian. *Naval Warfare in the Age of Sail: The Evolution of Fighting Tactics, 1650–1815*. Edison, N.J.: Wellfleet, 2001.

Twomey, Tom, ed. *Origins of the Past: History of Montauk and Gardiner's Island*. Bridgehampton, N.Y.: East End, 2013.

Upton, L. F. S. *The Loyal Whig: William Smith of New York and Quebec*. Toronto: University of Toronto Press, 1969.

Urban, Mark. *Fusiliers: The Saga of a British Redcoat Regiment in the American Revolution*. New York: Walker, 2007.

Valliant, Joseph N., Jr. "Revolution's Fate Sealed at Sea." *Military History* 12, no. 4 (August 1995), pp. 46–53.

Van Buskirk, Judith. *Generous Enemies: Patriots and Loyalists in Revolutionary New York*. Philadelphia: University of Pennsylvania Press, 2002.

Van Doren, Carl. *Mutiny in January*. New York: Viking, 1943.

Villiers, Patrick. "Chesapeake: La France au secours de l'Amérique." *Magazine de l'Histoire*, no. 38 (October 1981), pp. 91–93.

———. "Stratégie navale: Introduction au journal tenu pendant la guerre d'Amérique par René-Calixte de Lapeyrière." In *La Glorieuse Campagne du Comte de Grasse, 1781–1782*, pp. 43–62. Paris: SPM, 2010.

Volo, James M. *Blue Water Patriots: The American Revolution Afloat*. Lanham, Md.: Rowman and Littlefield, 2006.

Vorsey, De Louis. "Pioneer Charting of the Gulf Stream: The Contributions of Benjamin Franklin and William Gerard De Brahm." *Imago Mundi: The International Journal for the History of Cartography*, 2nd ser., 28, no. 2 (1976), pp. 105–20.

Wade, Herbert T., and Robert A. Lively, eds. *This Glorious Cause*. Princeton, N.J.: Princeton University Press, 1958.

Waite, Anthony. *Washington's Headquarters, the Hasbrouck House*. Albany: New York State Historic Trust, 1971.

Walker, Anthony. *So Few the Brave: Rhode Island Continentals, 1775–1783*. Newport, R.I.: Seafield, 1981.

Walker, Paul K., ed. *Engineers of Independence: A Documentary History of the Army Engineers in the American Revolution, 1775–1783*. Washington, D.C.: Government Printing Office, 1982.

Ward, Christopher. *The War of the Revolution*. Edited by John Richard Alden. 2 vols. New York: Macmillan, 1952.

Ward, Harry. *George Washington's Enforcers: Policing the Continental Army*. Carbondale: Southern Illinois University Press, 2006.

Warren, Jack. "The Childhood of George Washington." *The Northern Neck of Virginia Historical Magazine* 49, no. 1 (1999), pp. 5785–5809.

Washington, George. *The Diaries of George Washington, 1748–1799.* Vol. 2. Edited by John C. Fitzpatrick. Boston: Houghton Mifflin, 1925.

———. *The Diaries of George Washington, 1748–1765.* Vol. 1. Edited by Donald Jackson and Dorothy Twohig. Charlottesville: University Press of Virginia, 1976.

———. *George Washington's Newburgh Address.* Boston: MHS, 1966.

———. *The Papers of George Washington.* Vol. 22. Edited by Benjamin L. Huggins. Charlottesville: University of Virginia Press, 2013.

———. *The Papers of George Washington.* LOC. http//memory.loc.gov/amen/gwhtml/gwseries.

———. *The Writings of George Washington.* Vols. 1, 9, 12, 17, and 20–28. Edited by John C. Fitzpatrick. Washington, D.C.: Government Printing Office, 1937–1938.

———, and Comte de Grasse. *Correspondence of General Washington and Comte de Grasse, 1781, August 1–November 4.* Washington, D.C.: Government Printing Office, 1931.

Watson, Elkanah. *Men and Times of the Revolution.* Edited by Winslow C. Watson. New York: Dana, 1856.

Weigley, Russell F. *The Partisan War: The South Carolina Campaign of 1780–1782.* Columbia: University of South Carolina Press, 1970.

Weintraub, Stanley. *General Washington's Christmas Farewell: A Mount Vernon Homecoming, 1783.* New York: Free Press, 2003.

———. *Iron Tears: America's Battle for Freedom, Britain's Quagmire; 1775–1783.* New York: Free Press, 2005.

Wharton, James. "Washington's Fisheries at Mount Vernon." *The Commonwealth* (August 1952), pp. 11–13, 44.

White, Thomas. *Naval Researches; Or a Candid Inquiry into the Conduct of Admirals Byron, Graves, Hood and Rodney, in the Action off Grenada, Chesapeake, St. Christophers, and of the Ninth and Twelfth of April, 1782.* 1830. Reprint, Boston: Greg, 1972.

Whiteley, Emily Stone. *Washington and His Aides de Camp.* New York: Macmillan, 1936.

Whitridge, Arnold. *Rochambeau: America's Neglected Founding Father.* New York: Macmillan, 1965.

Wickwire, Franklin, and Mary Wickwire. *Cornwallis: The American Adventure.* Boston: Houghton Mifflin, 1970.

Wiencek, Henry. *An Imperfect God: George Washington, Slaves and the Creation of America.* New York: Farrar, Straus and Giroux, 2003.

Willcox, William. "Arbuthnot, Gambier, and Graves: 'Old Women' of the Navy." In *George Washington's Generals and Opponents,* edited by George Athan Billias, pp. 260–90. New York: Da Capo, 1994.

———. "The British Road to Yorktown." *American Historical Review* 52 (1947), pp. 1–35.

———. *Portrait of a General: Sir Henry Clinton in the War of Independence.* New York: Knopf, 1964.

———. "Rhode Island in British Strategy, 1780–1781." *Journal of Modern History* 17, no. 4 (December 1945), pp. 304–31.

Williams, Catherine. *Biography of Revolutionary Heroes; Containing the Life of . . . Captain Stephen Olney.* New York: Wiley and Putnam, 1839.

Williamson, Joseph. "Biographical Sketch of Joseph P. Martin, of Prospect, Maine, a Revolutionary Solider." *New England Historical and Genealogical Register* 30 (1876), pp. 330–31.

Willis, Sam. "The Capability of Sailing Warships, Part I: Windward Performance." *Northern Mariner* 13, no. 4 (2004), pp. 29–39.

———. "The Capability of Sailing Warships, Part II: Maneuverability." *Northern Mariner* 14, no. 3 (2005), pp. 57–68.

———. *Fighting at Sea in the Eighteenth Century: The Art of Sailing Warfare.* Woodbridge, Eng.: Boydell, 2008.

———. "Fleet Performance and Capability in the Eighteenth Century Royal Navy." *War in History* 11 (2004), pp. 373–92.

———. "The High Life: Topmen in the Age of Sail." *Mariner's Mirror* 90 (2004), pp. 152–66.

———. *The Struggle for Sea Power: A Naval History of the American Revolution.* New York: Norton, 2016.

Wood, Gordon S. *The American Revolution.* New York: Modern Library, 2002.

———. *The Creation of the American Republic, 1776–1787.* Chapel Hill: University of North Carolina Press, 1969.

———. "The Greatness of George Washington." *Virginia Quarterly Review* 68 (Spring 1992), pp. 189–207.

———. *The Radicalism of the American Revolution.* New York: Vintage, 1991.

Woodmason, Charles. *The Carolina Back Country on the Eve of the Revolution: The Journal and Other Writings of Charles Woodmason, Anglican Itinerant.* Edited by Richard J. Hooker. Chapel Hill: University of North Carolina Press, 1953.

Wright, John W. "Notes on the Siege of Yorktown in 1781 with Special Reference to the Conduct of a Siege in the Eighteenth Century." *WMQ* 12, no. 4 (October 1932), pp. 229–50.

Wright, Robert K. *The Continental Army.* Washington, D.C.: Center of Military History, 1989.

Young, Thomas. "Memoir of Thomas Young, a Revolutionary Patriot of South Carolina." *Orion 3* (October 1843), pp. 84–88, and (November 1843), pp. 100–105.

ILLUSTRATION CREDITS

Page 9 (bottom): Coiffure à la Belle Poule, courtesy of the Bibliothèque nationale de France.

Page 10 (top): Position of British fleet in Gardiners Bay, Feb. 16, 1781, sent by Rochambeau to George Washington, from the Washington Papers. Courtesy of the Library of Congress.

Page 10 (bottom): Admiral Mariot Arbuthnot by Charles Howard Hodges, © National Maritime Museum, Greenwich, London.

Page 11 (top): Diagrams of the Battle of Cape Henry. Collection of Service historique de la Défense.

Page 11 (bottom): Battle of Cape Henry, © DEA/M. SEEMULLER/De Agostini Picture Library/Getty Images.

Page 12 (top): View of the city, harbor, and roadstead of Newport, Rhode Island, circa 1781/ Historical Society of Pennsylvania.

Page 12 (bottom): Charles Cornwallis, 1st Marquess Cornwallis, 1798, by Thomas Gainsborough, © National Portrait Gallery, London.

Page 13: Jemima, Countess Cornwallis, 1771. Portrait after Reynolds, © The Trustees of the British Museum.

Page 14 (top): General Charles O'Hara, © Paul Fearn/Alamy Stock Photo.

Page 14 (bottom): Henry Lee (1756–1818) by Charles Willson Peale, from life, c. 1782. Courtesy of Independence National Historical Park.

Page 15: Bernardo de Gálvez, courtesy of the Library of Congress.

Page 16: Don Francisco Saavedra, © Photographic Archive Museo Nacional del Prado.

INSERT TWO, FOLLOWING PAGE 240

Page 1 (top): Admiral François-Joseph-Paul Count de Grasse (1722–1788) by Mathilde M. Leisenring (1870–1949) after Jean-Baptiste Mauzaisse (1784–1844). Gift of Archibald Barklie, 1934. Courtesy of U.S. Naval Academy Museum.

Page 1 (bottom): Count Louis-Antoine de Bougainville (1729–1811), French navigator. Miniature. © Jacques Boyer/Roger-Viollet/The Image Works.

Page 2: Admiral Rodney at the Battle of the Saintes by Thomas Gainsborough.

Page 3: Thomas Graves, 1st Baron Graves, by Francesco Bartolozzi, after 1794, © National Portrait Gallery, London.

Page 4: Admiral Samuel Hood by James Northcote, © National Maritime Museum, Greenwich, London, Caird Collection.

Page 5 (top): The *Ville de Paris* launched in Port Rochefort, 1764, courtesy of the Bibliothèque nationale de France.

Page 5 (bottom): Battle of the Virginia Capes, 5 September 1781, by V. Zveg. Courtesy of the U.S. Navy Art Collection, Washington, D.C. U.S. Naval History and Heritage Command Photograph.

Page 6: Robert Morris by Carl Peter Teigen. Copy after Charles Willson Peale. Harvard University Portrait Collection, purchased by the Harvard Graduate School of Business Administration for Morris Hall, 1927, H372. Photo: Imaging Department, © President and Fellows of Harvard College.

Page 7 (top): Marie Joseph Paul Yves Roch Gilbert Motier, Marquis de Lafayette (1757–1834), by Charles Willson Peale, after Charles Willson Peale, 1779–1780. Courtesy of Independence National Historical Park.

Page 7 (bottom): Benjamin Lincoln (1733–1810) by Charles Willson Peale, from life, c. 1781–1783. Courtesy of Independence National Historical Park.

Page 8: Henry Knox (1750–1806) by Charles Willson Peale, from life, c. 1784. Courtesy of Independence National Historical Park.

Page 9 (top): Joseph Plumb Martin, courtesy of the Stockton Springs Historical Society.

Page 9 (bottom): Verger's drawing of American soldiers at Yorktown, 1781, courtesy of Anne S. K. Brown Military Collection, Brown University Library.

Page 10 (top): George Washington and His Generals at Yorktown, circa 1781, by Charles Willson Peale, Museum Department. Courtesy of the Maryland Historical Society, 1845.3.1.

Page 10 (bottom): Siege of Yorktown, 17th October 1781, by Louis Charles Auguste Couder, 1836, © Château de Versailles, France/Bridgeman Images.

Page 11 (top): Siege at Yorktown, watercolor by an unknown artist, Lt. Col. John Graves Simcoe Papers/Special Collections, John D. Rockefeller Jr. Library, The Colonial Williamsburg Foundation.

Page 11 (bottom): Nelson House and Fortifications, Yorktown, Virginia, by Benjamin Henry Latrobe, *Latrobe Sketchbook,* Museum Department. Courtesy of the Maryland Historical Society, 1960.108.1.4.11.

Page 12 (top): Alexander Hamilton by Alonzo Chappel, © The Museum of the City of New York/Art Resource, NY.

Page 12 (bottom): John Laurens, 1780, watercolor on ivory by Charles Willson Peale, courtesy of the National Portrait Gallery, Smithsonian Institution.

Page 13 (top): The Storming of Redoubt #10, 1840, by Eugène Lami. Courtesy of the Library of Virginia.

Page 13 (bottom): British Surrender at Yorktown by John Trumbull, courtesy of the Architect of the Capitol.

Page 14 (top): The Surrender of Yorktown, 19th October 1781, by Louis-Nicolas van Blarenberghe, 1784, © Château de Versailles, France/Bridgeman Images.

Page 14 (bottom): The Battle of the Saints, 12 April 1782: Surrender of the "Ville de Paris," © National Maritime Museum, Greenwich, London, Caird Collection.

Page 15 (top): Horatio Gates, circa 1782, by James Peale, courtesy of the National Portrait Gallery.

Page 15 (bottom): General Sir Guy Carleton/Library and Archives Canada, Acc. No. 1997-8-1.

Page 16 (top): General George Washington Resigning His Commission by John Trumbull, courtesy of the Architect of the Capitol.

Page 16 (bottom): View of Mount Vernon with the Washington Family on the Piazza, 1796, by Benjamin Latrobe. Watercolor, ink, graphite, paper. Purchased with funds provided in part by an anonymous donor, 2013 [W-5307]. Courtesy of Mount Vernon Ladies' Association.

Endpapers: *Carte de la partie de la Virginie ou l'armée combinée de France & des États-Unis de l'Amérique a fait prisonnière l'Armée anglaise commandée par Lord Cornwallis le 19 octobre, avec le plan de l'attaque d'York-town & de Glocester,* by Esnauts and Rapilly. Courtesy of the Library of Congress, Maps Division.

INDEX

Page numbers in *italics* refer to maps and charts. Pages after 285 refer to the notes.

lack of resolve in, 115–16
naval superiority achieved by, 37, 179, 182, 196–98, 204–5, 240
naval superiority sought by, 106, 112, 115, 139–40, 154
in Newport, 20–21, 37–40, 46, 114, 116, 117–18, 137, 154–55
in plan to capture Arnold, 44–46
priorities differing from Washington's, 48–50, 112–13, 135, 137
and Race to Chesapeake, 52, 53, 54–55, 69, 218
ships of the line, 154, 183, 198, 199
signaling system of, 187
time-wasting activities of, 48–50, 73
as troop transport, 114, 115, 119–20, 137, 153
see also ships, French
French Revolution, 234, 265, 267, 268, 270, 271, 272–73
and Reign of Terror, 273, 276

Gage, Thomas, 156, 268
Gálvez, Bernardo de, 17, 18, 132, 133–34, 140, 141, 269
Gates, Horatio, 23, 261
at Camden, 19
and Newburgh conspiracy, 247, 248, 269
proposal to replace Washington with, 124, 247
at Saratoga, 228, 247, 255
after the war, 269
George III, king of England, 18, 109, 224, 231, 241, 261, 269
George IV, king of England, 278
Germain, George, 19, 76–77, 78, 79, 93, 107, 109, 241, 269–70
Germantown, British victory in, 108, 171
Gist, Mordecai, 171
Glorious First of June, Battle of, 270
Gloucester:
British attempt to escape to, 223–24, 226
British cavalry in, 273
British fortifications in, 138, 204
Gosnell, Nicholas, 84
Gouvion, Jean Baptiste, 165
Graham, Joseph, 83, 84, 85, 87, 95

Grandière, Charles-Marie de la, 61
Gras-Préville, Balthazar de, 187, 188
Grasse, François-Joseph-Paul, Comte de, 139–41, 147–51, 158
arrival at Chesapeake, 171–72, 174, 179–82, 183, 196–98, 228, 244
in Battle of Chesapeake, see Chesapeake, Battle of
and Battle of Saintes, 240–41, 266, 270, 277
en route to Caribbean, 130–31
en route to Chesapeake, 133, 148–49, 151, 152, 153, 154, 159–60, 161, 164, 180, 228
funding sought by, 139–40, 143–44, 150–51
in Haiti, 134–35, 139–41, 142–44, 151
impetuosity of, 181, 194, 201–3
in Martinique, 118, 130, 131, 134
oblivious to importance of naval superiority, 204–5, 223
and Old Bahama Channel, 144, 149–50, 151
relations with his officers, 132
reputation of, 185, 191
and Rochambeau, 112–13, 114, 118–20, 137, 139, 147, 174, 203
and Saavedra, 133, 135, 140–41, 144, 150–51, 174, 189, 228
secret orders from French ministry to, 112–13, 114, 146
Tobago taken by, 134
and troop transport, 119–20, 130, 148
after the war, 270
and Washington, 118, 147, 148, 196–98, 201–3, 204–5, 237, 240, 261
Washington uninformed about actions of, 113, 114, 118–19, 147, 170
in Yorktown area, 201, 204, 227, 228, 232
Graves, Samuel, 108
Graves, Thomas:
Arbuthnot replaced by, 137
and Battle of Cape Henry, 56, 163–64
in Battle of Chesapeake, 187–88, 190, 192, 194, 195–96, 240, 270; see also Chesapeake, Battle of
and Cornwallis's surrender, 231
Digby as replacement for, 155
en route to Chesapeake, 180, 182–83